ADRIATIC

SEA

R16

Chieti
Orsogna
Popoli
Casoli
Ortona
Pescina
zano
R17
C.di
Vasto
Sangro
R86
Arce
Isernia
Termoli
Tiri
CASSINO
Venafro
Vinchiatura
Campo
-basso
Fortore
GARGANO
PENINSULA

Foggia
R17
R16
Ausonia
R7
R6
R90
Ofanto
Barletta

Volturno
Caserta
BENEVENTO
Canosa
Capua
Melfi
Bari

NAPLES
AVELLINO
ALTAMURA
GAETA
Vesuvius
Teora
POTENZA
BRINDISI
Scafati
SALERNO
Battapaglia
R94
Taranto
CAPRI
Sorrento
Auletta
GULF OF
Sele
SALERNO
Paestum
GULF OF
R18
Vallo
Sapri
TARANTO

SEA
R19
CASTRO-
VILLARI
Scalea
R18
R19
R106

CALABRIA

CROTONE

CATANZARO

GULF OF
GIOIA
Gioia
LIPARI IS.
C.Milazzo
Bagnara
Orlando
Messina
Brolo
REGGIO
S.Fratello
Scaletta
ermini
R113
Tortorice
Barcellona
R114
nersee
Stefano
Randazzo
pedolce
R120
Troina
Bronte
Taormina
Petralia
Nicosia
eonforte
Mt.
Agira
Adrano
Etna
Acireale
RGENTO R121
Simeto
Paterno
R112
ENNA
Dittaino
Catania
R115
Calta-
girone
Lentini
Licata
Augusta
Gela
SYRACUSE
Vizzini R124
Vittoria
Ragusa
Avola
R115
Pachino

IONIAN

D1442886

~ARTHUR BANKS~

THE BATTLE FOR ITALY

W. G. F. Jackson

THE BATTLE FOR
ITALY

WITHDRAWN
UTSA Libraries

HARPER & ROW, PUBLISHERS
NEW YORK AND EVANSTON

First published 1967

© W. G. F. Jackson 1967

Made and printed in Great Britain for
Harper & Row, Publishers, Incorporated
Library of Congress catalogue card number: 67–21952

FOREWORD

---

by Field-Marshal The Earl Alexander of Tunis

I am very glad that General Jackson has written this comprehensive account of the operations in Sicily and Italy in which I commanded the Allied Army Group and, in the later stages, became Supreme Commander. Although I may not be able to subscribe to all the opinions and judgments expressed in General Jackson's book I do most thoroughly commend it as a balanced and lucid account of the Italian Campaign.

I am particularly pleased to have the opportunity to express my appreciation of the close and friendly relationship which existed, and still exists, between myself and my American Commanders, as well as all the other National Commanders I had under my command. They were all unselfish men whose co-operation and loyal support enabled me to accomplish so successfully the Directive given to me by the Combined Chiefs of Staff. It was a directive which called for selflessness. It was our task to draw upon ourselves the greatest number of German divisions so as to ensure Allied success in Normandy and upon the Russian front. This we did in spite of numerical inferiority and conditions of weather and terrain which so favoured the defence. We kept the Germans on the defensive for the whole of the long winter of 1943–44, and, at the critical moment when General Eisenhower's Armies crossed the Channel, we routed Kesselring's Tenth and Fourteenth Armies, taking Rome and forcing Hitler to send four more divisions into Italy to join the twenty-three already retreating before us. Thereafter, in spite of the transfer of many of my most experienced troops to North-West Europe, we continued to pin down increasing numbers of German divisions—all first-class fighting men, who did their duty and fought bravely and honourably on the battlefields of Italy. In the end we forced the German Armies in Italy to capitulate before those on the Western Front.

The limelight of world publicity swung away from the Allied Armies in Italy when Rome fell and interest has remained focused quite naturally on the Eastern and Western Fronts. I hope General Jackson's *Battle for Italy* will rekindle interest in that hard-fought campaign which did so much to ensure success on the main fronts. The Allied warriors of the Italian Campaign must not be forgotten.

Alexander of Tunis

CONTENTS

CONTENTS

THE ILLUSTRATIONS

THE ILLUSTRATIONS

The Author and Publishers wish to thank the following for permission to
reproduce the illustrations: Imperial War Museum, for figs 1, 4-8, 10, 11, 13-
18, 21 and 23-32; Keystone Press Agency Ltd, for figs 2 and 3; Suddeutscher
Verlag, Munich, for figs 9 and 12; Verlag Ullstein, Berlin, for figs 19, 20 and
22 and for the jacket illustrations.

THE MAPS

Note: For a full explanation of the abbreviations used in the sketch maps see Appendix A (page 323)

On the sketch maps the following conventions are used:

Allied Divisions

German Divisions

Italian Divisions

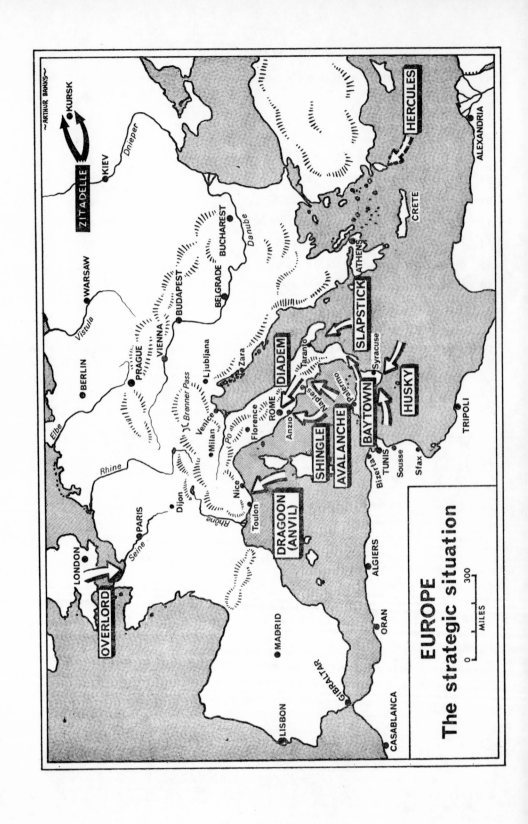

EUROPE
The strategic situation

Preface

Where will the Battle for Italy find its place in the history of war? The struggle for Monte Cassino caught the imagination of the world and will be written about for years to come. The hard-fought landings on Sicily, at Salerno and at Anzio will be remembered as the fore-runners and proving grounds for the invasion of Normandy. The tenacious defence of the Gustav and Gothic Lines will stand as a memorial to the fighting qualities of the German soldier. But what of the Italian Campaign itself? Scant attention has been paid to it so far. Even the British and American official historians have left this part of their work until last. And yet there are good reasons for believing that the Battle for Italy may become one of the most studied facets of Hitler's war.

The first reason for this sweeping prediction is that the Italian Campaign was the bone of contention between rival schools of strategic thought in both the Allied and Axis High Commands. On the Allied side it formed the focus of the divergent streams of British and American strategic thinking. Long experience had taught the British to value an indirect and pragmatic strategy when opposing Continental powers. They knew that they could not oppose the Axis directly on land and realized that they must depend on sea and air power to attack the periphery of Europe until their careful manipulation of alliances, their subversion of the Axis satellites, and the effects of their blockade and bombing of Germany enabled them to deliver the *coup de grace*—principally with American help. Their strategy had to be flexible enough to allow them to profit by the fortunes and misfortunes of war, enabling them to make best use of their limited resources to exploit success when it came and to stem failure before it could turn to disaster. Moreover, their great losses in the First World War had given them a deep-seated loathing of a direct Continental strategy with its use of massed armies leading inevitably to the horrors of attrition. Operations in the Mediterranean seemed to offer golden opportunities for their traditional strategy. Italy would become the Italian 'ulcer' draining away Hitler's strength as Napoleon's had been sapped by Wellington's campaign in Spain nearly 150 years before. If the Axis began to falter, the Allied armies in the Mediterranean would be poised ready to throw open Germany's back door and should be able to forestall the Russians in Central Europe. There should be no need to repeat the unimaginative Western Front strategy of the First World War. No major landings would be needed in France until Germany showed signs of collapse.

The background of American strategic thinking was very different. They were far nearer in military experience and inclination to the Germans and the French than to the British in their assessment of the relative importance of the principles of war. They prized the careful selection and the ruthless maintenance of the strategic aim, the concentration of maximum effort at the decisive point, and the strict limitation of diversionary operations. The principle of flexibility in strategic planning—a key feature in British thinking—came low in their list of priorities. The events of the First World War had confirmed them in their dislike of the indirect strategy preferred by the British. The Kaiser's Germany had been defeated by direct assault; Churchill's Gallipoli campaign had been a failure; the Salonika Expedition had led to nothing decisive; and Allenby's victories over the Turks in Palestine, although brilliant in British eyes, had been little more than another manifestation of British Imperialism. Just as the British wished to avoid a repetition of Ypres, the Somme and Paschendaele, so the Americans wanted to stop any waste of resources on diversionary operations. The British, however, had been fighting for two years and could rightly claim some experience in making war against the Axis. Their arguments might have won the day had it not been for political and economic factors within the United States which offset this British advantage. Politically, the Americans wished to have as little as possible to do with old-fashioned European power politics and British colonialism. They wished to end the war in Europe quickly so that they could turn against Japan, and they were determined to avoid being sucked into the political whirlpools of eastern and central Europe. Economically, their problem was how to mobilize their great resources. They had no need to outmanoeuvre their opponents; they had the strength to crush the Axis almost single-handed once American mobilization was complete. For this they needed a simple, direct and relatively inflexible strategy into which to gear their complex economy. Thus for military, political and economic reasons President Roosevelt and American Chiefs of Staff consistently favoured a massive direct assault upon the heart of Germany by the shortest route through North-West Europe; while Churchill and the British Chiefs of Staff, with equal consistency and sincerity, advocated setting southern Europe ablaze as the best way to bring Germany to her knees with a minimum loss of life.

In the Axis High Command there was a similar divergence of view on Mediterranean strategy. There was the natural division of opinion between the Italian and German High Commands, but this did not affect Axis policy in a decisive way because the Germans ignored their allies whenever it was in their interests to do so. The main differences lay in the advice offered to Hitler by his senior military officers and in his intuitive interpretation of that advice. The crucial question was whether Sicily and Italy should be defended at all, and, if so, how far south the Germans should attempt to stop the Allied advance through the Mediterranean. The traditional school of German strategists advocated concentrating Germany's resources against Russia to ensure her defeat before the Anglo-American threat could become a reality. They believed that, if need be, Germany should abandon southern Europe and should base the defence of her southern frontiers on the great sweep of the northern Apennines on the south side of the Po Valley or even on the Alps. The rival school of thought appreciated the significance of air warfare and argued that victory in the Steppes of Russia would avail Germany little if the Fatherland was under Anglo-American air bombardment from bases close to her southern frontiers as well as from the United Kingdom. In their view it was essential to keep the Allied air forces as far south as possible—preferably beyond the island ring stretching from Sardinia in the west through Sicily and Crete to the Aegean Islands in the east. Hitler's economic advisers supported this view because they needed the raw materials and industrial potential of Italy and the rest of southern Europe. Hitler himself tended towards this view initially out of loyalty to his old ally, Mussolini, and later because he could not bring himself to surrender occupied territory. His personal inclinations were, however, counter-balanced by the appalling German losses at Stalingrad and in Tunisia, which pointed to the need to economize in the use of German manpower and gave the traditionalist school their strongest argument. As the Allies debated how many ships, army divisions and air squadrons should be allotted to their commanders in the Mediterranean, similar discussions were taking place in Hitler's headquarters between the advocates and opponents of a forward strategy in the Mediterranean. The Battle for Italy is the story of the interplay and coincidences of these strategic controversies and their effect upon the soldiers, sailors and airmen whose task it was to implement the decisions of the rival high commands.

The second reason for studying the Battle for Italy is its place in the evolution of warfare. In many respects the Italian theatre served as the laboratory for testing the new techniques of the Air Age. First, there were the lessons of amphibious warfare. There had been no major amphibious operations since Gallipoli, which had taken place at the end of the 'horse-drawn' era. The Sicily, Salerno and Anzio landings, together with the many smaller amphibious operations which took place in the Mediterranean, enabled the Allies to perfect this form of warfare under modern conditions. So many myths and legends have grown up around the use and misuse of sea power that it is important for maritime nations like Britain and America to understand the true strengths and weaknesses of this mode of warfare. A study of the Normandy landings alone is dangerous unless the evolutionary processes and experiences gained in the Mediterranean are analysed as well. Secondly, there were the tactical lessons of the Italian campaign. Both sides were more equally matched than they were in Normandy. Neither achieved a marked numerical superiority and the great Allied material preponderance was offset by the defensive potential of the Italian countryside. The Germans no longer enjoyed the superiority in training, battle experience and equipment as they had done earlier in the war, but, although they had been thrown on the defensive by the disaster at Stalingrad and their losses in Tunisia, they were far from defeated and their morale remained almost unimpaired until the last week of the campaign. The British and American divisions for their part had found their feet in North Africa, but, thanks to the American policy of limiting the resources in the Mediterranean, they never enjoyed the overwhelming support to which Eisenhower's armies grew accustomed. The tactical lessons learnt in the hard school of the Italian theatre probably have greater validity than those learned in the comparative military luxury of North-West Europe where the contest was too one-sided. And finally, and perhaps most important of all, it was in the Italian theatre that the great experiments were carried out to test the validity of the airmen's claim to be able to win the land battle for the soldiers. There was first the successful reduction of the fortress island of Pantelleria by air action. Then there was the disruption of German counter-attacks on the Allied beachheads at Salerno and Anzio by air bombardment. These successes, however, were soon brought into perspective by the Allied air forces' failures at Cassino and in their inability to disrupt German supply lines throughout the Italian campaign in spite of the Peninsula offering ideal conditions for air-interdiction. The lessons learnt in the use of air power in Italy perhaps did more than anything else to convince Allied commanders that success in war depends on the use of all three fighting services in close co-operation. The newest Service, although frightening in its great potential for mass destruction, could not win wars alone. The German paratroopers at Cassino played their full part in exploding the air myth.

The story of the Battle for Italy falls into five distinct phases. In the First Phase the Allies approached the 'soft under-belly' of Europe full of doubts and fears. In the Second Phase they went to the opposite extreme. Urged on by the fleeting chance of driving Italy out of the war, they threw caution to the wind and tried to exploit Mussolini's downfall by landing at Salerno. The Italians' failure to help the Allies and the swift German reaction soon closed the breach in Hitler's 'Fortress Europe'. The Third Phase was one of disillusion. The Americans insisted on the withdrawal of troops for the invasion of Normandy, while the British decided to press on, in spite of winter, to capture Rome. The Allied commanders in the Mediterranean were doomed to disappointment by defeats at Cassino and at Anzio, but they had the good sense to halt operations in time to prepare a major offensive when fine weather returned in the spring. The Fourth Phase covers the brilliantly executed spring offensive of 1944 which was capped by the fall of Rome but marred by American insistence on further withdrawal of troops, this time for the attack on southern France. The Fifth Phase covers the second winter of despair and frustration, in which more withdrawals were made to strengthen Eisenhower's armies on the German frontier, and then the final triumph of the Allied armies in Italy when they forced the German Army Group 'C', which had opposed them for so long, to capitulate before the German forces in the other theatres of war laid down their arms. The theme of the story from the British point of view is one of lost opportunity due to American singleness of purpose; and from the American point of view it is the struggle to prevent British predilection for a Mediterranean strategy from weakening the main Allied effort in North-West Europe. Both sides can argue that the events of the Italian Campaign proved the rightness of their case, and so the issue remains to this day tantalizingly unresolved.

In the account of the Battle of Italy which follows the strategic decisions taken by both sides will be linked with their tactical consequences. To bring the narrative within the scope of a single volume the lowest operational formation whose actions can be described is the division. It is not possible to do justice to all the many fine actions fought by brigades and regiments or by individual units. It is easy to forget as the story unfolds what sums of human endeavour are generalized by such simple phrases as '4 Indian Division attacked but failed to take Point 593' or '36 (US) Division established a small bridgehead over the Rapido'. A division contains some 15,000 men and a corps perhaps as many as 75,000, but on the sketch maps they are shown as single arrows straddling some obscure topographical feature. To the men who fought in Sicily and Italy —there were about a million in uniform on both sides—the campaign has left searing memories. 'Sunny Italy' of the tourist brochure mocked them and is remembered as a land of soaking rain, glutinous mud and biting cold with only a few short months of glorious summer weather which were marred in their turn by billowing, all-penetrating, white dust. There was always one more mountain for the Allies to attack and for the Germans to defend, and one more river to be crossed and to be held. The Germans remember the incessant Allied air attacks and the depressing effect of rarely seeing a German aircraft overhead. They remember the frantic efforts to complete all unit moves and re-supply missions before dawn and the return of the Allied fighter-bombers. And perhaps their most vivid memory is of the remorseless artillery fire which preceded all Allied operations whether large or small. Time and again German prisoners complained that shelling in Italy was worse than anything they had experienced on the Russian front. The Allied soldiers remember the skill and dogged determination of their German opponents in defence and withdrawal: their cleverly sited reverse-slope positions which could not be reached effectively by Allied artillery; the close mutual support of their strong points; their methodical destruction of every bridge and culvert as they withdrew; their uncanny sixth sense which told them where to lay mines to catch the unwary Allied soldier; and the coolness of their lone tank or self-propelled gun crews left behind to cover demolitions, often delaying whole Allied regiments until dusk made it too dangerous for them to stay any longer. And both sides remember the drudgery of carrying ammunition and supplies forward up steep mountain tracks, frequently under fire and in pouring rain, and the return journey bringing down casualties from almost inaccessible positions. Such things can only be suggested here. For the feel of the battle, readers should turn to the vivid descriptions contained in first-hand accounts like Fred Majdalany's first book on Cassino, *The Monastery*, or the New Zealand Brigadier Kippenburger's *Infantry Brigadier*. Both were written shortly after the campaign when memories were fresh and before time had started the creation of new legends.

In the Appendices to this book there is a brief description of Allied and German divisional organizations for those who are not familiar with them, and there are the orders of battle of divisions for professional readers. As this is a complete story, with strategic and tactical events closely intertwined, a chronology of events has been provided as the last appendix.

January–August 1943

THE APPROACH TO
THE SOFT UNDER-BELLY
OF THE AXIS

'The paramount task before us is . . . to strike at the soft under-belly of the Axis in effective strength and in the shortest time.'
Extract from Churchill's note surveying prospects in the Mediterranean dated 12 November 1942

I

The Strategic Setting

'I remained obdurate, and, with the Combined Chiefs of Staff
solid behind me, insisted on Sicily.'
Churchill's Report on the Casablanca Conference

When Churchill, Roosevelt and their Combined Chiefs of Staff met at
Casablanca for the 'Symbol' conference in January 1943, the tide of Allied
fortunes had begun to turn. No one could tell at that time whether the
change was permanent or not. On the credit side, the Battle of El Alamein
had been won; Rommel had been forced back to Tripoli; the Anglo-
American landings in French North Africa had been successful; and on
the Russian Front, the German Sixth Army under von Paulus was
surrounded at Stalingrad. On the debit side, Rommel's Afrika Corps was
still in being and might yet spring some ugly surprise on the British
Eighth Army as it had done so often before; the British First Army had
failed to take Tunis and was bogged down in the North African mud
around Medjez-el-bab; von Paulus might survive long enough to reverse
the tables on the Russians when the spring came; and in the Atlantic the
decisive phase in the U–Boat war still lay too far in the future to give
the Allies much comfort as yet. As the Allied High Command met in the
Anfa Hotel outside Casablanca they were in no mood to take risks. No
one knew whether El Alamein and Stalingrad represented the Battle of
the Marne of the Second World War; and, if this was so, whether Nazi
Germany on the defensive would be any easier to beat than the Kaiser's
Reich.

The first question to be resolved by the conference was what to do if
and when the Axis forces had been driven out of North Africa. General
Marshall, the American Army Chief of Staff, stated and argued the
American proposals. In his view the soundest Allied strategy would be
an all-out bomber offensive against Germany, followed by an invasion of

northern France using the United Kingdom as a base. Operations in the Mediterranean should be used for diversionary purposes only. A direct attack across the Channel would take the shortest route from the United States to the heart of Germany and was unimpeded by the mountainous country and poor communications which obstructed the Mediterranean approaches. A cross-Channel operation would threaten the German homeland and would be the quickest and most effective way of relieving the German pressure on the Russians. Moreover, it would furnish a clear long-term objective for United States industrial and manpower mobilization. And, above all, it would lead to decisive action quicker than any other strategy. 'Every diversion or side issue from the main plot', said Marshall, 'acts as a suction pump.' The Allies could become involved in interminable operations in the Mediterranean and so delay, possibly fatally, the concentration of troops, ships and aircraft in the United Kingdom for the main effort. Proposals for further operations in the Mediterranean should be weighed against their probable effect on the cross-Channel operation and upon the critical shipping situation. He did not add (because Roosevelt would not allow him to do so) that, if the British wished to pursue their Mediterranean strategy, the United States would turn her efforts westwards, giving priority to the war against Japan in the Pacific theatre.

Sir Alan Brooke, Chief of the Imperial General Staff, replying for the British Chiefs of Staff, doubted whether Germany could be weakened sufficiently to allow a successful cross-Channel assault in 1943. If the Allies stood idly by until conditions were right, Russia would receive no diversionary support during the coming summer and large numbers of battle-experienced troops would be left unengaged in the Mediterranean. The Allies could count on re-entering Europe in force in 1944; until then they should try to make Germany disperse her forces as widely as possible. The best ways of doing this were to threaten Germany everywhere in the Mediterranean; to try to knock Italy out of the war; and to persuade Turkey to come in. Meanwhile the cross-Channel build-up should continue in the United Kingdom so that the Allies would be ready to seize the opportunity of invading North-West Europe as soon as conditions were right.

The naval and air chiefs in both staff teams saw advantages in a Mediterranean strategy for 1943. The sailors wished to save shipping on the long haul round the Cape of Good Hope by reopening the Mediterranean to through convoys. The airmen foresaw the benefits of establishing strategic bombers on Italian airfields. Air attacks mounted from the south as well as the west would force the Germans to disperse their fighter defences; and the targets in southern Germany and the Balkans—particularly the

Roumanian oilfields—would be brought within effective bombing range.

At the highest political level, Churchill was the principal advocate for continuing operations in the Mediterranean until conditions became favourable for a cross-Channel assault. Like Alan Brooke, he wished to feint at Sicily, Sardinia, Corsica, the Dodecanese and the coasts of Italy and Greece. He was not yet sure in which direction the main Mediterranean thrust should be made, but he was attracted by the possibility of eliminating Italy. The Balkans offered certain attractions: a successful attack there would rob Germany of essential raw materials; it would open the back door to the German Armies fighting in southern Russia; and it might encourage Turkey to join the Allies. Critics, however, would suggest that Churchill's leaning towards an invasion of the Balkans was also influenced by his desire to justify, in retrospect, his Gallipoli policy.

Roosevelt's views decided the argument. He held to a middle course for much of the debate, but in the end inclined towards the Mediterranean school. He wanted to keep US troops in action and, like Churchill, was attracted by the chance of driving Italy out of the war. The opinion thus swung against Marshall who conceded defeat on the grounds that shipping would be saved, Allied troops would be kept in action and the weakest Axis partner would be threatened. He made it quite clear, however, that he viewed with continued concern the danger of these diversionary operations in the Mediterranean drawing away strength from the main effort across the Channel.

The next question to be resolved was where to strike in the Mediterranean. The division of opinion this time was not between the British and American Chiefs of Staff, but within the British team. The British and American Chiefs of Staff believed that, if the aim was to eliminate Italy, then Sicily should be the next target. It was part of Italy and its loss would undermine Italian morale; Allied air power would be brought close to the Italian mainland; and the forcible removal of Axis aircraft from Sicily would clear the most dangerous section of the sea route to Suez. The British Joint Planners, supported by Lord Mountbatten, the British Chief of Combined Operations, were not so sanguine about attacking a target which might result in a very violent German reaction before the Allies were ready to meet them on equal terms. Dieppe had shown how hazardous amphibious operations could be. The planners recommended attacking Sardinia and Corsica first because the Germans could not reinforce their garrisons as easily as in Sicily and the operations would be more limited in scope. They hoped to clinch their case with the contention that an attack on Sardinia and Corsica could be mounted three months earlier than the larger operation which would be needed to conquer Sicily. Churchill refused to take counsel of his planners' fears and, having checked their calculations himself, he persuaded the conference to agree to an attack on Sicily during the most favourable period of the July moon. The strategic objectives of the operation, which was codenamed 'Husky', were:

(i) to make the Mediterranean line of communication more secure;
(ii) to divert German pressure from the Russian front;
(iii) to intensify pressure on Italy.

General Eisenhower was to remain Supreme Commander in the Mediterranean with General Sir Harold Alexander as his principal deputy, charged with the detailed planning and execution of ground operations, while Admiral Sir Andrew Cunningham and Air-Marshal Sir Arthur Tedder were to be the naval and air commanders. Appreciating that all these officers were already involved in the current operations in the Mediterranean, the Combined Chiefs of Staff authorized a special Husky planning Staff to be set up under Major-General Charles Gairdner at Eisenhower's headquarters in Algiers. This staff became known as H.Q. Force 141, taking its name from the number of the room in the Hotel St George in which it first met at the end of January 1943.

> 'There you have the two opposite ends of the scale. Rommel has become the greatest pessimist and Kesselring a complete optimist.'
>
> *Hitler, at midday conference 12 December 42*

Although there was argument and honest disagreement at Casablanca, the Allies had a common aim and an excellent organization in the Combined Chiefs of Staff to formulate and execute their agreed strategy. The Axis powers lacked both. The 'Pact of Steel', signed by Hitler and Mussolini in 1939, allied two unequal and alien peoples. The only common ground between them was similarity between their dictators' ideologies and a common antagonism towards the *status quo* powers. Mussolini envisaged two parallel wars, each dictator commanding in his own sphere of influence. As long as they were both winning, the little co-ordination that was needed could be carried out through normal diplomatic channels with an occasional high-level meeting. When the tide of success turned against the Axis, this mode of operation soon became inadequate; but, by then, the inequality of the partnership and the divergence of motives had become too great to allow the creation of anything like the Combined Chiefs of Staff. Economically, Italy had become a province of the Third Reich. Militarily, her forces were unable to face the Allies without German equipment and a stiffening of German troops. And yet, Mussolini's pride would not allow him to accept subordinate status. All operations in his Mediterranean sphere of influence were theoretically controlled by the Italian Supreme Command, the Commando Supremo; and all German units in the theatre were under Italian operational command. In practice, the Germans took advantage of the difficulty in closely defining the boundary between operational and administrative command. They made full use of their liaison and administrative staffs with the Italian Army to establish their own secret operational command network. Thus, not only was there no Combined Chiefs of Staff machinery on the Axis side, there were two chains of command; an overt channel from the Commando Supremo down to Italian formation commanders and thence to the German units, and a covert but much more powerful link from the German Supreme Command, the Ober Kommando Der Wehrmacht (OKW), to the German liaison officers and unit commanders in the field. Divergence of motive, inequality of resources and of fighting efficiency, and lack of an integrated chain of command led, as the Axis fortunes waned, first to mutual suspicion, then to disloyalty and double-dealing, and finally to open treachery.

By the end of 1942 Mussolini had begun to realize that he had chosen the wrong side. In his view there was only one sensible course for the Axis to take; make peace with Russia and turn the combined strength of Italy and Germany southwards against the Anglo-Americans in the Mediterranean. Mussolini made a number of attempts to persuade Hitler to consider this course of action but without success. He discussed his ideas with Göring in December 1942; he sent Ciano to Hitler's headquarters in East Prussia with the same ideas a few weeks later; he wrote personally on two occasions in March; and he made a personal representation at a conference with Hitler at Klesheim in April. Hitler would not listen. He was determined to stabilize the Eastern Front, if possible upon the Don which he envisaged as the future frontier of Europe with the Bolshevik East, before turning to face the Anglo-Americans. He accepted that he must now adopt a strategic defensive, but he believed Tunis could be held long enough to keep the Allies at bay until he had settled with the Russians. Mussolini was by now a sick man and could no longer stand up to his powerful partner; nor could be bring himself to break with Hitler, although he realized that the logical alternative to peace with Russia was negotiations with the Allies. Others in Italy, however, were working towards this alternative.

There were three principal factions in Italy trying, like Mussolini, to find a way out of the war: the dissident Fascists under Ciano and Grandi; the underground anti-Fascist parties; and a group of high-ranking military officers within the Commando Supremo who knew the true military

23

position and who wished to spare their country further useless sacrifice. The story of the intrigues, plots and counter-plots of these three groups is not part of the story of the Battle for Italy. Suffice it to say here that the more influential groups all wished to achieve their ends by a return to constitutional government under the Monarchy and all appreciated that a *coup d'état* against Mussolini would avail them little unless they could break the German alliance without incurring German vengeance. One way of doing this was to throw themselves on the mercy of the Allies, but, as yet, the Allies were too far away to protect them from the Germans and unfortunately they had shown singularly little sympathy for Italy in her predicament when they announced the 'unconditional surrender' formula after the Casablanca conference.

As so often happens with lost causes, events accelerated Italy's downward course. As the Italian desire for political and military independence grew, so each month brought a new strengthening of German domination. Field-Marshal Kesselring had been appointed German C-in-C in November 1941. In those early days he had only been responsible for command of the Second German Air Force, for liaison with the Commando Supremo, and for the administration of all German troops in the central Mediterranean and North Africa. He was, in effect, the housekeeper for Rommel and Mussolini's personal adviser on German military affairs. His colleagues in Rome were von Mackensen, the German ambassador, and General von Rintelen, the German military attaché. All three were men who worked well with the Italians and were determined to serve Italy to the best of their ability because they believed that this was the best way to help Germany win the war. By the beginning of 1943, Kesselring's powers had been increased gradually to those of a unified C-in-C of all German forces—land, sea and air—in the Mediterranean. His headquarters was at Frascati, just south of Rome, where he was in close touch with Mussolini and the Commando Supremo. The Italian Chief of Staff had been General Cavallero, who had co-operated wholeheartedly with the Germans and had, in consequence, earned the dislike of men like Ciano who were bent on undermining the German position. Mussolini's first attempt to exert his independence when he realized the war was lost took the form of sacking Cavallero and replacing him in February 1943 with General Ambrosio, who had anti-German tendencies and wished to reduce German influence in Italy. This change of appointment proved a forlorn gesture. Italy had either to make peace or accept further German help to continue the war; further German help meant further German domination and greater difficulty in breaking the German alliance when a suitable opportunity occurred.

When Ambrosio took over there was no agreed Axis view of the

Allied threat. The Commando Supremo thought Sardinia and Corsica the most likely targets after Tunis. The islands could be taken by converging attacks from Gibraltar and French North African ports, and could serve as a base for operations against southern France or Italy. Ambrosio appreciated the Allied train of thought with remarkable accuracy. He was inclined to believe that Sicily would be the next target as he felt that the Allies would give priority to clearing the Suez route. The capture of Sicily would drive Axis aircraft away from the narrow Sicilian Channel and would split the Italian fleet in two—half in the Gulf of Genoa and half in the Adriatic ports. Mussolini, always prone to wishful thinking, was sure that the Allies would attack France or Greece and not Italy. Hitler and OKW, fearing the worst from the German point of view, expected the next blow to fall in the Balkans. An Allied attack here would endanger Germany's sources of raw materials, particularly oil from Roumania; it would encourage the Balkan people in their revolt against German occupation; it would weaken the allegiance of Hitler's satellites who were already looking for ways of changing sides; and it might bring Turkey into the war. OKW's intelligence reports confirmed Hitler's fears. German agents detected the move of the New Zealand Division back to Egypt from Tunisia and the start of amphibious training in the Gulf of Suez. The famous intelligence plant on 'the man who never was'* reinforced German opinion that the eastern Mediterranean was the most likely area for future Allied operations. Kesselring was the only senior German commander to appreciate the threat correctly. As an airman, he realized that the Allies would need fighter cover over any major assault landing. Sicily was the only target which would be within range of Allied shore-based fighters when Tunis fell.

The Italians had a large number of men under arms but they were poorly equipped compared with the Germans or the Allies, and their morale was shaky. The Fleet, stationed at La Spezia, Taranto and Pola, was too weak to intercept an Allied invasion force and had only enough fuel oil for one fleet action. The Air Force was doing its best with its obsolescent aircraft but it was virtually ignored by the German Luftwaffe. The Army had suffered heavy losses in men and equipment in Russia and North Africa, and most of its best troops were still on foreign soil. There were 217,000 Italians in Russia; 579,000 in the Balkans, Greece and the Greek Islands; 200,000 in southern France and Corsica; and 147,000 about to march into captivity in Tunisia. Some 800,000 remained to garrison Italy, Sicily and Sardinia, but many of these were low-grade troops

* A body dressed as a Royal Marine officer with an official letter in its pockets suggesting an attack on Greece was dropped by submarine off the Portuguese coast. The contents of the letter were relayed to OKW by a German agent in Portugal.

belonging to static garrisons. All responsible Italian officers realized that Italy needed help badly, but they wished to avoid increasing German strength within the Italian sphere of influence in the Mediterranean. Ambrosio was prepared to ask the Germans for equipment but not for units, foreseeing that a large influx of German troops would restrict Italy's freedom of political manoeuvre. Mussolini supported this unrealistic policy because his personal prestige was at stake. He was still determined to maintain a semblance of independence and expected his new Chief of Staff to do so as well. Whether the Germans, and particularly Hitler, would accept such double-dealing was very doubtful. The Commando Supremo was sufficiently realistic to appreciate that the chances were slender.

Ambrosio's first steps to strengthen Italy's defences were designed to avoid asking for German help. He withdrew the Italian formations from Russia where their collapse, together with that of the other satellite contingents along the Don, had led to von Paulus' encirclement. He stopped the 4th (Livorno) Division moving from Sicily to Tunisia, and he tried without success to persuade OKW to release Italian units from southern France and the Balkans. This policy of avoiding seeking German help was not to last for very long. Tunis fell on 7 May forcing both OKW and the Commando Supremo to review their policies.

OKW's first reaction to the fall of Tunis was to follow their original appreciation of the Allied threat by strengthening their forces in the eastern Mediterranean. In six weeks their Balkan garrison rose from seven to 13 divisions. They next considered abandoning Italy south of the northern Apennines between Pisa and Rimini. This course had obvious political and military disadvantages: the break up of the Axis; probable defection of some of Germany's other satellites; loss of Italian industrial potential; loss of Italian garrisons in France and the Balkans which would have to be replaced by German divisions; loss of southern Italian airfields from which the Reich could be bombed, and so on. The list of disadvantages was long and formidable but the two key objections were psychological: Hitler was not prepared to let down his old friend Mussolini as long as the Duce would stand up and fight; and, secondly, Hitler could not bring himself to abandon territory without a struggle however much his generals pressed him to do so on military grounds. The latter was not yet such an obsession with him as it became in the later phases of the war, but it was already swaying his strategic thinking.

Hitler did not decide immediately what should be done. His ultimate decision to hold everywhere in the Mediterranean was brought about by the interaction of events and the competing influences of the two opposing schools of thought amongst his advisers. These can be called for simplicity the Rommel and Kesselring schools, although they were not looked upon as such by the Germans or Italians at the time. Rommel was an orthodox military strategist who disliked the Italians and distrusted them as much as they distrusted him. His advice to Hitler was always: abandon the Italians, withdraw to the strongest and militarily the soundest position to defend the southern approaches to the Reich, namely the Pisa-Rimini line, and concentrate Germany's strength on stabilizing the Russian Front. Kesselring, on the other hand, believed that the Italians would fight well for their homelands provided they were given enough willing German support to make success seem possible. There was no point in antagonizing the Italians when in return for relatively little German effort they could be kept as useful partners in Germany's herculean task of wearing out, if not defeating, the Russians and Anglo-Americans. If Italy left the Axis, Germany would have to hold her southern approaches alone. The Italians might not be much good but they would be more use on Germany's side than against her.

At first the Kesselring school won the advantage. On 4 May, Kesselring was authorized to offer Mussolini one German division for the defence of Italy. Two days later Hitler personally offered him three: one from Germany, one formed by the reconstitution of the Hermann Göring Division, only part of which had been lost in Tunisia, and a third from other units which had been on their way to Tunis but had not left Italy before it fell. Ambrosio was reluctant to accept these offers of help but on 10 May agreed to do so and asked for one division to be stationed in Sicily, one in Sardinia and the third in southern Italy. He stipulated that they must come under Italian operational command. Shortly after this Hitler offered two more divisions, making five in all. Mussolini was inclined to accept but Ambrosio asked him to reconsider the matter and on 12 May Mussolini turned the offer down.

This refusal by Mussolini opened the door to the Rommel school. Hitler had been suspicious of Italian motives since Mussolini had tentatively suggested peace with Russia earlier in the year. The sacking of Cavallero was another straw in the wind. An OKW report on the Italian situation presented to Hitler on 19 May painted a gloomy picture of Italian capabilities and their lack of determination. In a discussion which took place in the Führer's headquarters on this paper, Hitler gained further evidence of possible Italian treachery. He instructed OKW to prepare a contingency plan, codenamed 'Alarich', in case of Italian defection. Rommel was to command the operation from an Army Group Headquarters at Munich. Northern Italy was to be occupied initially by a force of six or seven divisions from the Eastern Front which would eventually be built up to some 13–14 divisions brought in from France and elsewhere.

Kesselring was to be responsible for the withdrawal of all German troops in southern Italy and Sicily back into Rommel's firm base in the north.

This was the first of a series of troughs in Italo-German relations which were to grow deeper each time until the Axis finally fell apart. There was no Allied follow-up immediately after the fall of Tunis as many Italians and Germans had expected, and so nerves became less tense and Kesselring managed to regain the initiative. Moreover, this lack of Allied action in the Mediterranean allowed Hitler's thoughts to swing back to the Eastern Front. When Stalingrad fell in February, he managed to seal off the Russian penetration by switching no less than 19 divisions from France to Russia. The German mobilization staffs had made good progress in re-raising in France the divisions lost when von Paulus surrendered his Sixth Army to the Russians. If the precedent of 1942 were to be followed, these reformed divisions would move back to the Eastern Front in time to renew the German offensive at the end of the spring thaw. When Tunis fell, it looked as if many of the new Stalingrad divisions would have to be moved south to protect Germany's southern frontiers, but when no immediate Allied follow-up occurred Hitler decided to prepare a limited offensive on the Eastern Front to eliminate the dangerous Russian salient around Kursk, while, at the same time, forestalling any offensive the Russians might be preparing. The Kursk operation was codenamed 'Zitadelle'. Troops earmarked for Alarich began to move eastwards and Rommel was appointed to command the German troops in Greece which Hitler still believed was the Allies next target.

Kesselring visited Sicily in late May and was disgusted with the Italian ineptitude in preparing the island's defences. On his return he obtained a firm agreement from Ambrosio for the employment of four German divisions. The German units stranded in Sicily when Tunis fell had been grouped into an *ad hoc* formation known as the Division Sizilien. This was to be reinforced and reconstituted as the 15 Panzer Grenadier Division, thus keeping alive the name of the famous Afrika Corps 15 Panzer Division which had been lost in Tunisia. A similar process was to take place in Sardinia, resulting in the resurrection of 90 Panzer Grenadier Division named after the equally famous 90 Light Division. The third division was the reconstituted Hermann Göring Division stationed near Naples. And the fourth was to be 16 Panzer Division (a reformed Stalingrad Division) which would be sent to Italy as soon as it had been reconstituted in France. To train and administer these divisions, Ambrosio surprisingly agreed to accept in Italy General Hube's XIV Panzer Corps Headquarters.

In parallel with these army reinforcements, Kesselring arranged with Hitler for strong Luftwaffe reinforcements to be flown to the Mediterranean, largely from the Eastern Front. Field Marshal von Richthofen, one of Germany's most experienced and successful tactical air force commanders, was transferred from Russia to take over the German Second Air Force in the Mediterranean and with him came a staff of equally experienced Luftwaffe officers from his Fourth German Air Force in southern Russia. The strength of the Luftwaffe rose from 820 to 1,280 aircraft in the six weeks following the fall of Tunis but, as the table below shows, this increase was spread over the whole Mediterranean theatre with an emphasis on the eastern section.

ON FORWARD AIRFIELDS*

	At the fall of Tunis	Beginning of July	
Sardinia	80	175	
Sicily	415	290	
Greece and Crete	125	305	
Totals on forward airfields	620	770	

IN CENTRAL RESERVE

	At the fall of Tunis	Beginning of July	
Southern France and Northern Italy	—	165	of which 260 were long-range bombers
Central and Southern Italy	200	345	
Total central reserve	200	510	
Grand totals	820	1,280	

Thus, while planning for the invasion of Sicily was going ahead on the southern shores of the Mediterranean, the Axis partners were taking faltering and indecisive steps to meet the next Allied move. OKW was concentrating on the eastern Mediterranean, leaving the Italians, with Kesselring's help, to look after the central area. There was no agreed strategy; German and Italian motives diverged; and, in the background, mutual suspicion was already weakening the Axis facade. The Anglo-Americans, by contrast, were agreed on their immediate strategic plans and now had to grapple with the tactical difficulties of an opposed amphibious operation—the first since the ill-fated Gallipoli landing of 1915.

* Figures from *Rise and Fall of the German Air Force* (Air Ministry Publication, 1948).

2

The Tactical Setting

'I had seen the fierce resistance that the Germans and Italians were showing in Tunisia and considered that it was essential to prepare to meet strong enemy reaction in Sicily.'

Montgomery, *El Alamein to the Sangro*

The Husky planners moved out of Eisenhower's headquarters early in February and set up their own establishment in the École Normale just outside Algiers. They found themselves in the unenviable position of being agents for absentee landlords. All the principal commanders for whom they would be drawing up plans were engaged in the Battle for Tunis. Alexander, Cunningham and Tedder were controlling the land, sea and air battles, and the two commanders (designate) for the British and American task forces for Husky were similarly engaged. General Montgomery, who, with his Eighth Army headquarters thinly disguised as Twelfth Army Headquarters, was to command the British task force, was still chasing Rommel; and General George Patton, the American task force commander, had been called forward from Morocco, where he had been Military Governor, to take over the command of II US Corps after its defeat in the battles around the Kasserine Pass in Tunisia. Thus none of the principal actors had time to study their future roles or give policy guidance to their agents—not a propitious start to planning the first major amphibious operation since Gallipoli and the first in the era of air forces and mechanized armies.

Absentee landlordism and great dispersion of key headquarters, from Cairo in the east to Oran in the west, were not the only difficulties faced by General Gairdner's staff. The Combined Chiefs of Staff had laid down the target date for Husky as the most favourable period in the July moon. They had assumed that operations would be over in North Africa by

1 May which would leave a little over two months to move the troops back to their assembly areas, to train them in amphibious warfare techniques, to stockpile the necessary logistic requirements and to assemble the ships and craft needed for the assault and follow-up. No one could in fact tell when the fighting in North Africa would stop; nor in what state the troops and their equipment would be when the end came. It was equally difficult to make valid assumptions on the Axis dispositions and intentions after what the Allies hoped would be a crushing defeat around Tunis. The Germans might decide to evacuate Tunisia before the Allies could close the Sicilian Channel to them. If this happened, Sicily might be held by a formidable German garrison, making an amphibious assault a very hazardous undertaking. On the other hand, they might cling on to a Tunisian bridgehead, as they had done recently in the Kuban in Russia, until it was too late to evacuate the bulk of their troops. The Sicilian garrison might then be predominantly Italian and a much easier nut to crack. As yet the planners had no evidence to suggest that Hitler would pursue his disastrous 'no withdrawal' policy. Lacking a firm operational picture, the Husky planners were forced to base their work during February and March upon the known limiting factors of geography, ranges of weapons and aircraft, availability of assault shipping and logistic requirements for a force of the size earmarked by the Chiefs of Staff. They could also use the experience gained at Dieppe and in the North African landings, but neither operation had much in common with Husky.

When the planners first met, they had before them work done by the British Joint Planners in London on three previous plans. The first was called 'Influx' and had been written in 1940 in the first waves of enthusiasm which swept through Whitehall after Wavell's desert victories. The second, 'Whipcord', was drafted in 1941 as a contingency plan in case, as the American Ambassador in Rome suggested, Italy appealed to the Allies for protection against the Germans. And the third was 'Husky', prepared as a feasibility study for the Casablanca conference and approved there by the Combined Chiefs of Staff as the outline for the 1943 invasion of Sicily.

The planners considered that there were three prerequisites for a successful amphibious operation: air superiority; naval superiority; and superiority in the speed with which the ground forces could be landed compared with the probable rate of Axis reinforcement. Naval superiority was already assured: the Italian Fleet had not been seen at sea since mid-1942. Air superiority and the speed of army build-up depended essentially on three things—airfields, ports and the effective range of shore-based fighters.

When planning started there were 19 airfields on the island; by the time the operation was launched these had grown to over 30. They were all grouped in three main complexes which for convenience will be named after the master airfield in each group. The key group was situated in the Catania plain around Gerbini. This Gerbini complex contained the main Luftwaffe headquarters, flying control and servicing organisations. The second complex was on the south-east coast stretching from Ponte Olivio to Comiso. This will be called the Ponte Olivio complex, although it extended a long way from this main airfield. The third was in the western tip of the island nearest to Tunisia; its key airfield was Castelvetrano. The

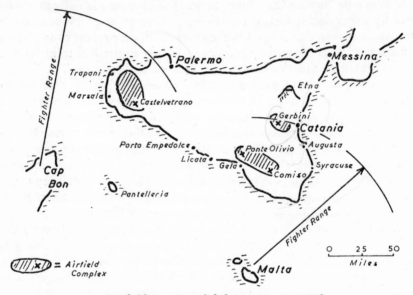

1   *Airfields, ports and fighter ranges in Sicily*

greater the number of airfields which could be captured early in the operation, the easier would be the Allied air forces' task in maintaining air superiority.

The Sicilian ports were few and very small. The planners estimated that the Allies would need a port capacity of 3,000 tons per day initially and this would have to be increased to 6,000 tons per day by the time that the whole invasion force and its supporting air forces were ashore. As yet, no one had any reliable experience of supplying a force over open beaches, and so it would be wrong to accuse the Husky planners of over-insurance when they insisted that ports with a sufficient capacity to support the force should be captured early in case bad weather cut down the flow of supplies across the beaches. The Sicilian ports, like the airfields, were in three groups: east-coast ports, western ports and south-coast ports. The best port on the island was Messina which, if grouped with the other east-coast ports of Catania, Augusta and Syracuse, could easily support the whole force. The second best port was Palermo which, if helped by Trapani and Marsala, could supply half the force. The third group was made up of three very small harbours—Licata, Gela and Porto Empedolce —which were hardly better than open beaches.*

Fighter cover for the operation could be provided from Malta and Cap Bon in Tunisia. Cover from Malta would just reach Catania at extreme range; and from Cap Bon, Palermo was also at extreme range. Messina, the best port, was out of reach for two reasons: it was out of fighter range; and it was within the heavily defended area of the Straits of Messina. Thus the planners were left with two groups of ports each of which could support only half the force: the eastern group, without Messina, and the western group. In each the largest port—Catania and Palermo—was at the extreme range and would have to be captured in a second phase of the operation after Allied fighters had been established ashore to provide air cover over it.

These limiting factors led the Joint Planners in London and the Husky planners to produce very similar concepts. Two separate task forces would be needed: an eastern task force should invade south-eastern Sicily, and a western task force should seize Palermo. Each task force would conduct its operation in two stages. The eastern force would first take Augusta, Syracuse, Gela and Licata, plus the Ponte Olivio group of airfields; and then, when the fighters had been established ashore, an assault would be launched against the port of Catania and the Gerbini airfield complex. In the west, the Castelvetrano airfield complex would be captured before the main assault force was landed near Palermo.

The planners estimated that by D+7 the three airfield complexes, enough ports to supply the forces without depending on beaches, and two good defensible beachheads would have been secured. They also estimated that 11 divisions, including two airborne divisions, would be

---

* The estimated capacities (in tons) of the ports were:

East Coast		Western Ports		South Coast	
East Coast		*Western Ports*		*South Coast*	
Messina	4,500	Palermo	2,500	Licata	600
Catania	1,800	Trapani	1,600	Gela	200
Augusta	600	Marsala	600	Porto	
Syracuse	1,000			Empedolce	600
Total	7,900	Total	4,700	Total	1,400
Without					
Messina	3,400				

ashore and that this would be an adequate force to withstand the inevitable Axis counter-attacks. It looked a simple and orderly plan which neatly solved the conflict between the air and logistic requirements. Unfortunately, when the absentee masters had time to study their agents' proposals they did not like what they saw. The air and logistic problems had been solved at the expense of the land battle. Unable to reach any firm conclusions about the state of the Axis and Allied troops after the fall of

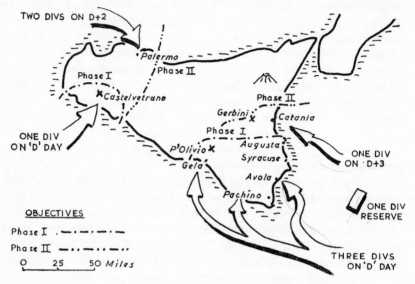

2   *The first plan for the invasion of Sicily*

Tunis, the planners had tended to ignore the tactical problems of the soldiers once they had been pitched ashore.

Between the middle of March and 12 May, when the Chiefs of Staff finally approved the Husky plan, there were innumerable conferences called at various levels, in an endeavour to produce a plan in which the majority of commanders had some confidence. It would be pointless to describe this phase in detail. Senior officers and their staffs were forced to fly to and fro between the widely scattered headquarters wasting precious time which should have been used in assembling and training their assault forces. The main bone of contention was the estimate of the Axis— particularly the German—strength and intentions. If the Germans followed the Kesselring school, they would reinforce the Italian garrison of Sicily with strong mobile forces which would make the Husky planners' proposals hopelessly optimistic. The assault divisions would be too dispersed within each task force, and the task forces themselves would be out of supporting distance of each other. A strong German force could attack and eliminate each in turn. The plan, as it stood, could only succeed if the Rommel school won and the Italians were left on their own or with only marginal German support.

Allied intelligence of Axis dispositions was more sketchy than usual because they were not in direct contact with the Axis troops in Sicily. Thus they received none of the usual front-line intelligence reports, which are one of the main sources of information used in building up the picture of an enemy order of battle. The planners knew that there were about five low-grade, static, Italian coastal divisions covering the Sicilian beaches and that these were backed by three regular Italian mobile divisions. The Axis was bound to reinforce the garrison when Tunis fell. The planners estimated that the mobile force might rise to eight divisions, two of which could be German. Further reinforcements could be brought across the Straits of Messina at the rate of a division every three days once the Axis knew that Sicily was the next Allied target. The London planners had originally said 'we are doubtful of the chances of success against a garrison which includes German formations'. Alexander thought that this was overstating the case, but he and his principal subordinates all agreed that, if the Germans reinforced the island substantially, the Allies' task would be much more difficult, not only because of the Germans' superior fighting qualities but also because they would demand a greater say in the conduct of the defence of Sicily.

Alexander had misgivings about the plan when it was first explained to him by General Gairdner at the end of February. He instructed the planners to clear up a number of obvious weaknesses such as splitting divisions on too many diversionary tasks, over-dispersion of airborne forces, and lack of sufficient reserves afloat. When he suggested concentrating both task forces against the south-east corner of the island, General Gairdner persuaded him that port capacities would make this impracticable.

On 13 March, Eisenhower and his principal commanders, Alexander, Cunningham and Tedder, accepted General Gairdner's plan, but Montgomery expressed concern about the dispersed deployment of his Eastern Task Force. In his view, he did not have enough troops at Avola (one division) to capture Syracuse and Augusta, upon which the maintenance of his force would depend until Catania had been taken in the second phase. Availability of assault shipping precluded the addition of another assault division, so the only way to increase the force at Avola was to cancel one of the other landings. He proposed that the Gela assault should be dropped, thus uncovering a major part of the Ponte Olivio airfield complex. Tedder strongly objected to this from the air point of view, and he was supported by Cunningham who held the view that amphibious landings should be carried out on as wide a front as possible and that it would be dangerous to bring the mass of assault shipping near the coast as long as the Ponte Olivio airfields were unsubdued. It would take too great an air effort to keep these airfields neutralized by bombing alone.

Alexander agreed with Montgomery's objection, but realized that the air and naval commanders would not accept a plan which left the Ponte Olivio complex uncovered. The only alternative to Montgomery's proposal was to detach the American division, which was to have taken the Castelvetrano complex, from Patton's Seventh Army and to give it to Montgomery to take the Ponte Olivio complex. The American assault on Palermo would have to be postponed several days and would then be covered by Allied fighters operating from Ponte Olivio when it had been taken in the second phase of Montgomery's assault. This change of plan was only valid if Montgomery's Eastern Task Force was to be given operational priority over Patton's Western Task Force. The British members of the planning staff felt this was a logical thing to do. Eighth Army was a tried veteran force which could be trusted to do the job; Seventh (US) Army was still learning and, as Kasserine had shown, had some way to go before it reached Eighth Army standards. The Americans quite naturally saw this proposal in a very different light. This was the bombastic and swollen-headed Montgomery undermining Patton's chances of success. If the Ponte Olivio complex was essential to Montgomery, then the Castelvetrano complex was just as important to Patton for exactly the same reasons. Palermo, anyway, was a far better port than Syracuse and Augusta combined. It would be more logical to give Patton priority at Montgomery's expense. In Eisenhower's and Alexander's minds, however, there was little doubt about which attack had priority. The Catania–Gerbini area held the key to the conquest of Sicily. In it were the main German air installations and the ground which dominated the approaches to the Allies' ultimate objective, the Straits of Messina. Eisenhower, as an American officer, had the difficult task of overruling Patton in favour of Montgomery. He accepted the new plan reluctantly, and put in hand new studies to see if anything else could be done to avoid weakening Patton's task force.

The British Chiefs of Staff now took a hand. The problem was not so much how to find another division for Montgomery, but how to find more shipping in which to carry it. This was eventually solved by staging an extra British division from the Middle East through Malta, thereby saving shipping in the assault convoys. Alexander was thus able to restore the detached US division to Patton, but he kept the idea of staggered assaults. Patton's attack on Castelvetrano would go in on D + 2 and his main assault on Palermo on D + 5. All seemed to have come out well in the end, although the seeds of discord between the Seventh and Eighth Army headquarters had been sown and were to germinate very quickly.

Montgomery had won extra weight for his Avola assault but he still disliked the plan. He had sent his Chief of Staff, General de Guingand, back to Cairo to work with General Dempsey's XIII (Br) Corps Headquarters which he had made responsible for the detailed planning of the Eastern Task Force operation. De Guingand studied the plans and came to the conclusion that his master was right. If the scale of opposition proved as tough as Eighth Army had been experiencing in their drive into Tunisia, the assault might still fail through lack of concentration, even though an extra division had been added to the order of battle. De Guingand had been Montgomery's Chief of Staff throughout all the desert battles from El Alamein to Tunis and so had plenty of first-hand experience to back his judgment. On hearing that his Chief of Staff strongly endorsed his own impression of the plan, Montgomery left his Army while it was regrouping in front of the Axis' final defensive positions in Tunisia and flew back to Cairo to study the plan carefully himself. On 24 April he voiced his further objections to the plan in what can only be described as a tactless signal* to Alexander. This caused great embarrassment and annoyance in Allied circles in Algiers. In the signal he bluntly said that the planners had assumed too light a scale of opposition. If he was to carry the war into Sicily, he must do it in his own way. The whole of his task force must be concentrated for a landing on a much narrower front between Syracuse and the southern tip of the island. The first thing to do was to secure a lodgement and then he would operate outwards from a firm base—a favourite expression of Montgomery's. He maintained that he was not in a position to judge the effect of these changes upon the operation as a whole. In his view, however, should the Axis reinforce the island heavily before D-day, the forces available would be inadequate for their task if deployed in the way in which the assault plan suggested.

This signal confirmed the Americans' worst fears about Montgomery. It seemed to say 'the Eighth Army can do no wrong—it is the only real fighting organization on the Allied side—it must be allowed to play the game in its own way and be given everything it wanted; else it would not play, and the Allied cause would be that much the worse off in consequence!' The Americans were not the only people to be annoyed. Cunningham and Tedder were drawn together in opposition to this

* Printed in full in Hugh Pound, *Sicily*.

demanding Army Commander. The only thing to be said for Montgomery's handling of the situation was that he had the confidence of his convictions and he won what he wanted for his own Army. Whether or not this was for the good of the Allies, events were to show.

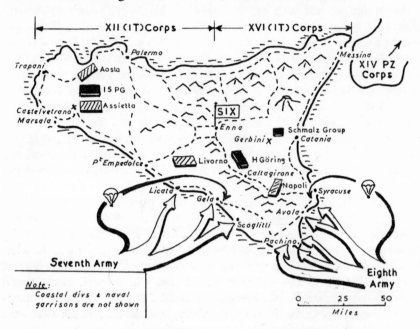

3 The final Allied plan for Husky and the
deployment of Axis forces on Sicily

Alexander called a conference on 27 April to resolve this new conflict. De Guingand was hurt in an air crash on the way to the meeting and so General Oliver Leese, Commander of the British XXX Corps, came instead. Leese presented to the conference an entirely new concept on behalf of his master. He proposed that the Eighth Army should confine its attack to the stretch of coast from just south of Syracuse to the Pachino Peninsula, the southern tip of the island; while the Seventh (US) Army assaulted the southern coast between Gela and Licata and covered Eighth Army's flank and rear as it advanced on Catania. Cunningham objected because the assault would be too concentrated and his ships would be vulnerable to Axis aircraft flying from too many unsubdued airfields. Tedder objected because he would be left with far too many airfields to subdue by air action. The Americans, not unnaturally, objected to playing second fiddle to Montgomery. Furthermore, they would have to scrap weeks of detailed planning and training, and would have to assault over inferior beaches with no reasonable ports through which to supply their troops. They would be running all the risks while Eighth Army reaped the rewards of capturing the main objectives, particularly Messina.

Eisenhower then held a meeting at Algiers on 2 May at which Alexander could not be present but at which Montgomery presented his case in person—and won the day. Eisenhower accepted his contention that planning must be based on determined Axis opposition. The Allies could not risk failure. Both task forces would attack side by side astride the Pachino Peninsula in the same areas that had been allotted to the Eighth Army alone in the original plan. Both task forces would be in easy supporting distance of each other and divisions would be able to attack closer together. The Eighth Army would be the principal striking force and would advance northwards to capture Catania, Gerbini and Messina as quickly as possible while Seventh Army protected its flank and rear.

The air and logistic risks in this new plan would have to be accepted to achieve the necessary degree of land-force concentration which Montgomery considered to be essential. Two things could be done, however, to reduce these risks: first, extra fighter cover could be provided over Gela and Licata if the Italian fortress island of Pantelleria was taken and converted to Allied use before Husky was launched; and, secondly, the arrival in the theatre of the revolutionary American $2\frac{1}{2}$-ton amphibious truck, the famous DUKW, could be accelerated, making it easier to maintain the Seventh Army over its open beaches. Thus, in the final plan, Montgomery got everything he wanted, but Alexander was faced with accepting three risks. First, two sets of airfields—Gerbini and Castelvetrano—would be uncovered for some time. Secondly, the port capacity would be quite inadequate: if the DUKWs failed or bad weather intervened, there might be a logistic breakdown. And thirdly, he risked an Anglo-American rift. Patton loyally accepted the change of plan but many of his staff did not.

The final plan was approved by the Combined Chiefs of Staff on 12 May. Detailed planning could now start in earnest for a D-day which was fixed for 10 July, less than two months ahead. The naval and air plans to support the landings were simple and straightforward. Admiral Cunningham intended to cover the Eastern Task Force by sailing his main fleet of four battleships, two carriers, eight cruisers and 18 destroyers to the eastward in the Ionian Sea so that he could intercept any Italian naval force which came out of the Adriatic or through the Straits of Messina. He placed a smaller force of two battleships and six destroyers to the westward to cover the narrow passage between Tunisia and Sicily. He provided the

Eastern Task Force with four cruisers and six destroyers for close support and shore bombardment; and the Western Task Force with five American cruisers with their escorts and the British Monitor HMS *Abercrombie*.

Tedder's air plan had four phases which started as soon as Tunis fell. The first phase was to be sustained operations to win general air superiority without disclosing the point of attack. The intensity of these preliminary operations would be only moderate so that the Allied air forces could build up their strength for the intense second phase. Targets were mainly strategic and covered the whole sweep of the Mediterranean. The second phase was designed to destroy the enemy air forces on and within striking distance of Sicily and the proposed routes of the assault convoys. It was to last from D − 7 (3 July) to D-day, taking the form of intense bombing of Axis airfields and radar installations, and massive fighter sweeps to clear the skies. The third phase would be the close cover of the assault convoys and offensive air support during the landings. The fourth and last phase was to be the continued close support of the land battle and the concurrent naval operations.

The first phase of Tedder's air plan was interrupted for a short time by the decision to seize Pantelleria. It was a small operation but important for two dissimilar reasons. The first reason was historical. It was the first time in history that a major fortress was to be reduced almost entirely by air action. Mussolini had fortified the island as a rival to Malta in the 1930s. It was given deep underground hangars and gun emplacements, and was stocked to stand a long seige. The air bombardment of the island started on 10 May and steadily increased in intensity until 7 June when the weight of attack was raised to a crescendo for four days. From 7 to 11 June, 5,000 tons of bombs were dropped. The island was summoned to surrender on 8 and 10 June, and when no answer was received a force from 1 (Br) Division arrived off the island in assault craft and started its run in towards the harbour covered by a precision bombing attack by US Fortress bombers. By noon on 11 June the force was ashore and the garrison had started to surrender without offering any co-ordinated resistance. 4,600 prisoners were taken. In spite of the intensity of the bombardment, the garrison had only lost about 200 killed and 200 wounded. The Allied air forces were naturally delighted with this startling proof of the efficacy of air power. The rebuff was not to come until the battles of Cassino and Caen showed what might have happened if the island had been garrisoned by Germans instead of Italians.

The second reason why this apparently minor triumph was important was its effect on Axis morale and future plans. The Italian people were deeply depressed by this example of the apparent ruthless use of Allied air power. Here was one of Italy's strongest fortresses crumbling into ruins and abject surrender after only four days of all-out attack. It showed what would happen to the Italians if they went on fighting much longer. Mussolini was as depressed as his people. He had always believed that artillery fire conquered ground for the infantry to occupy. Here was air power doing the same thing; and as the Allied air supremacy was obvious for everyone to see, there could be only one conclusion in the minds of his people—the war was lost. The Germans viewed the loss of Pantelleria quite differently. They were astonished that the Italians should give up so easily. It was as unthinkable to them as the garrison of Heligoland surrendering while there were still rounds to be fired. If this was to be the Italian standard of resistance in defence of their homeland, Rommel and not Kesselring would be proved right.

The immediate effect of the fall of Pantelleria was to make both Mussolini and Ambrosio more willing to seek German help. Little by little, Ambrosio brought himself to accept the German domination of Italy. The Italian commanders in Sicily, Sardinia and southern Italy were all pressing the Commando Supremo for more and more German assistance, and Kesselring was always there with ready offers of just the kind of help for which they were asking. In the middle of June Ambrosio accepted the fourth German division, which Mussolini had previously turned down. This was 3 Panzer Grenadier Division whose arrival enabled Ambrosio to agree to the transfer of the Hermann Göring Division to Sicily. By the end of June he had accepted two more divisions—29 Panzer Grenadier Division and 26 Panzer Division—together with another corps headquarters—General Herr's LXXVI Panzer Corps. The total German contribution to the defence of Italy and its major islands was now two corps headquarters and six divisions. Before long Kesselring would be pressing for an Army HQ to command the two corps.

Sicily was garrisoned by the Italian Sixth Army (*see* fig. 3). Its Commander had been the efficient General Roatta who had brought all Italian army, naval, air and militia units under his command but, in doing so, had offended the Sicilians in a speech which cast doubt upon their patriotism. He had been replaced by 66-year-old General Guzzoni, who had been recalled after two years' retirement! His Chief of Staff, Colonel Fadella, was able and energetic but he was new to Sicily, as were the commanders of the two Italian corps—XII (It) Corps holding the west of the island and XVI (It) Corps holding the east. Under these two corps came the coastal divisions and garrisons, and each corps had two regular Italian mobile divisions; XII (It) Corps commanded the Aosta and Assietta Divisions, and XVI (It) Corps the Napoli and Livorno Divisions. Superimposed on the Italian garrison were two German divisions—15 Panzer Grenadier and the Hermann Göring. In theory, the German divisions were under Guzzoni's operational command, but, in fact, they were closely controlled by Kesselring through his liaison officer attached to the Italian Sixth Army—General von Senger und Etterlin. General Hube, Commander of XIV Panzer Corps stationed in southern Italy, was in charge of their training and administration. The Hermann Göring Division had another master as well. Reich Marshal Göring, who took a personal interest in 'his' division, at times interfered directly in its operations, sending personal instructions to its Commander, General Conrath.

On the naval side, the Italian Fleet lay in La Spezia undermanned, lacking modern radar, short of fuel and at least 24 hours' steaming away from the Sicilian beaches. The Commando Supremo had no intention of hazarding one of their few remaining trump cards in future peace negotiations with the Allies, by sending the fleet to sea unless there was a real chance of success. The navy was making a small contribution to the defence of Sicily by manning the fortifications of the naval ports of Messina, Augusta, Syracuse and Trapani. The most important naval contribution was German. A highly efficient ferry service had been organized across the Straits of Messina by Captain von Liebenstein,* and the defences of the Straits were in the capable hands of Colonel Baade† who deployed some 70 anti-aircraft batteries, making the Straits the hottest anti-aircraft zone in Europe. The efforts of these two men were to be outstanding in the last days of the Sicilian campaign.

In the air, co-operation between the Luftwaffe and the Regia Aeronautica, which had never been close even at the height of the Axis successes in the Mediterranean, had almost ceased. The Germans acted as if the Italian airmen did not exist; and the Italians, in their turn, placed every possible bureaucratic obstruction in the way of the Germans. The German Luftwaffe reinforcements, which flowed into the Mediterranean during May and June, failed to halt Tedder's preparatory air offensive. Relentless Allied bombing of the forward Sicilian, Sardinian and Greek airfields forced von Richthofen to withdraw his bombers to Italy and France. Only his fighters and fighter-bombers could be left on forward airfields. In 21 major engagements over the Mediterranean in May and June the Luftwaffe lost heavily. Hermann Göring did not help matters by sending a special message castigating the pilots of the Second Air Force.

> Compared with the fighter pilots in France, Norway and Russia, I can only regard you with contempt. I want an immediate improvement and expect

* After the successful evacuation of Axis forces from Sicily, von Liebenstein was equally successful in ferrying all German troops out of Sardinia and Corsica.

† Colonel Baade later commanded 90 Panzer Grenadier Division in its successful defence of Cassino in the second battle.

that all pilots will show an improvement in fighting spirit. If this improvement is not forthcoming, flying personnel from the commander down must
expect to be reduced to the ranks and transferred to the Eastern Front to
serve on the ground.

Weak at sea and overwhelmed in the air, Guzzoni could only depend
on the Italian and German land forces. Fortunately there was more
co-operation between the army formations than there was in the air.
Kesselring's example of genuine concern for his allies was reflected down-
wards. The majority of Italian commanders welcomed German help, and
the Germans did their best for their allies. The Sicilian civil population,
however, did its best to break up this co-operation by openly resenting
the presence of German units and by clearly showing a defeatist attitude
to everything that the Italian regular divisions and the German units tried
to do to strengthen the island's defences. In planning these defences there
was no difference of opinion between Guzzoni and von Senger on the
disposition of the coastal divisions, nor in the poor estimate which they
both had of the degree of resistance they were likely to offer. Their men
were mostly locally enlisted Sicilians. They could only be relied on to
report the Allied landings and to inflict a few casualties by covering
beach minefields and obstacles with rifle and machine-gun fire. The
deployment of the mobile divisions was not so easily settled. Behind the
disagreements lay the genuine tactical quandary which was to beset the
Germans in Normandy as well as in Sicily. Should the enemy be defeated
as he approached the shore and while he was trying to establish himself?
Or should the shore be defended only lightly and reliance placed on
well co-ordinated counter-attacks by mobile formations held some way inland ready to move forward when the actual location and size of the landing had been established by the coastal units? Guzzoni and von Senger,
like von Runstedt in Normandy, believed in the latter school of thought—
light beach defences with strong reserve forces held in rear ready to launch
co-ordinated counter-attacks. Kesselring believed in the orthodox
German tactical doctrine of holding forward with the aim of destroying
the enemy before his tanks, anti-tank weapons and artillery could be
landed. This was Rommel's theory as well. Unfortunately for the Axis,
Kesselring's views prevailed in Sicily, as did Rommel's in Normandy.
Both misappreciated the strength and weaknesses of an amphibious
opponent. Guzzoni and von Senger wished to hold the four Italian mobile
divisions well back from the sea and deployed across the island so that
they could reach the Allied beachheads relatively quickly to contain them
and push them back if this proved possible. They wanted the two German
divisions concentrated in a central position from which a decisive counter-
attack could be launched at the right moment. Kesselring refused to accept

this deployment. He wanted both the Italian and German divisions deployed quite close behind the coastal divisions. In his view, and there is much to be said for his reasoning, the German divisions would never be able to move forward quickly enough over the narrow Sicilian roads under Allied air attack. Guzzoni cynically accepted Kesselring's views without demur; he did not believe that the Axis could hold Sicily anyway whichever policy was adopted, so there was no point in opposing a German field-marshal.

The final dispositions agreed between Guzzoni, von Senger and Kesselring are shown in fig. 3. Guzzoni's headquarters was placed centrally at Enna. The western XII (It) Corps placed its two Italian mobile divisions close behind the Palermo–Castelvetrano Sector. The eastern XVI (It) Corps held its Napoli Division behind the Syracuse–Pachino sector and the Livorno Division on the high ground above Licata. Von Senger intended to leave 15 Panzer Grenadier Division in the eastern Corps' area where it had been since it formed in Sicily in May, and to send the newly arrived Hermann Göring Division to the west. Kesselring would not agree—probably at the Reich Marshal's prompting—and insisted on the Hermann Göring Division concentrating on the high ground behind Gela. The division, however, had only two instead of three regiments, and so 15 Panzer Grenadier Division was ordered to detach one of its three regiments to form a special battle group under Colonel Schmalz to cover the Catania–Gerbini area. The rest of 15 Panzer Grenadier Division was sent westwards in late June to take up a position between the Aosta and Assietta Divisions in XII (It) Corps area. Guzzoni knew that the German divisions had orders to launch immediate counter-attacks irrespective of what action the Italians took, so to give himself some reserve, he withdrew the Livorno Division from XVI (It) Corps' control into Army reserve, but left it sited above Licata.

On 26 June, Kesselring and Guzzoni held what was to be their last co-ordinating conference before Husky was launched. Kesselring summarized his concept of operations: the enemy must first be opposed by the coastal divisions; the Italian mobile divisions must attack as soon as they knew where the landings had occurred; and the German divisions would do the clearing up. The Allies would probably land on a wide front at many different points. The aim must be to wipe out each beachhead before it could link up with its neighbours to form into a solid front. The Allies had missed their chance when they did not follow up quickly after Tunis. The defences of Sicily were now much stronger. The Allies would not attack until they had elaborated their plans. They were unlikely to be ready before the middle of July—a reasonably accurate forecast.

To the south, across the Mediterranean, the Allied troops detailed for the assault forces had been moving away from Tunis and back to their training and assembly areas. The Eighth Army went eastwards to Sousse, Sfax and Tripoli, and the American units went westwards to the Algerian ports. All units were given as much amphibious training as time and availability of craft would allow. Full-scale rehearsals were carried out and then final loading began.

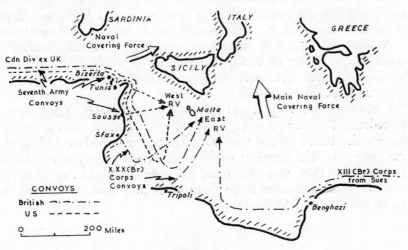

4   *The sea approach*

The Eastern Task Force under Admiral Ramsay sailed from three groups of ports: from Alexandria and Suez came XIII (Br) Corps under General Dempsey with 5 and 50 (Br) Divisions; from Sfax, Tripoli and Malta came XXX (Br) Corps under General Leese with 51 (Highland) Division; and from the United Kingdom came the 1 Canadian Division. The Canadians were to come under XXX (Br) Corps on landing. The Western Task Force under Admiral Hewitt, US Navy, came from the Algerian Ports: II (US) Corps under General Omar Bradley contained 1 and 45 (US) Divisions;* 3 (US) Division, which was to land to the west of II (US) Corps, was under direct Seventh Army control, and 2 (US) Armoured Division and parts of 9 (US) Division were in floating reserve. All the convoys hugged the North African coast and arrived at their rendez-vous south and west of Malta on the evening of 9 July (D−1). Losses on passage were surprisingly light. Three ships were lost in the

---

* 45 (US) Division came direct from the United States, but staged through Oran where it carried out a dress rehearsal before sailing for Sicily.

Canadian convoy from the United Kingdom, and one in the Alexandria convoy; all four to U-boats. The Luftwaffe failed to score any successes.

Allied strategic deception plans were bearing fruit. These had been designed to suggest threats to Sardinia, Sicily and Greece with the emphasis on the last of the three. At tactical level the plan was to suggest that Palermo was the most likely target, being closest to Tunisia. All preliminary air and naval action was designed to heighten the illusion. Air and naval bombardment was directed against western Sicily until the very last moment when the concentration of convoys around Malta would give the point of attack away. From then on eastern Sicily would suffer most.

As dusk fell on 9 July, there were some nine divisions afloat off the south-eastern corner of Sicily, of which seven would be in the assault wave—two more than were deployed in the assault wave against the Normandy beaches a year later.

It was the largest amphibious operation yet undertaken. There were no precedents. The shadow of Gallipoli fell only faintly across the minds of some senior British officers who had taken part in or had carefully studied that operation. The questions which no one could answer were: Will the Italians fight? How many Germans will appear? Would any of the five German divisions known to be stationed in Italy move southwards and across the Straits of Messina?

3

The Invasion of Sicily

'Up to that moment no amphibious attack in history had approached this one in size. Along miles of coast line there were
hundreds of vessels and small boats afloat and antlike files of
advancing troops ashore. Overhead were flights of protecting
fighters.'

General Dwight Eisenhower, *Crusade in Europe*

Field-Marshal Viscount Montgomery has described the phases of a
successful land battle as the 'break-in', the 'dog-fight' and the 'break-
out'. The attacker must win all three phases before he can claim the
victory. In Sicily the Allies broke in successfully; they fought a 30-day
dog-fight; but they did not break out. They could claim a victory over
the Italian Sixth Army, which disintegrated, and over Mussolini, who
fell from power during the campaign, but their real opponents, the
Germans, slipped away with their forces damaged but intact. It is true
that Kesselring's policy of immediate counter-attack upon the Allied
beachheads failed; on the other hand, the two German divisions, reinforced to the equivalent of three and a half during the fighting, withstood the attacks of twelve Allied divisions and the collapse of their
Italian partners, and yet still managed to withdraw at a time and pace of
their own choosing across the Straits of Messina in the face of Allied air
and naval supremacy. The Allies cleared Sicily in 38 days, but they could
only claim a drawn match with the Germans.

THE ALLIED BREAK-IN
10–12 July

'Then shortly before midnight that evening, as though in answer
to our prayers, the wind dropped and the sea levelled into a broad
swell: whilst the gale had frightened us badly, it had also helped
to keep the secret of our invasion.'

General Omar Bradley, *A Soldier's Story*

The preliminary Allied air, naval and deception plans were very successful.
At sea, the assault convoys formed up unscathed in their rendez-vous
around Malta where six months earlier even a single convoy would have
had to fight hard to survive. In Malta itself, the Grand Harbour was being
used once more by major units of the British Fleet for the first time since
1940, and the airfields were packed with fighters and fighter-bombers in
numbers which must have seemed miraculous to the island's most recent
defenders. Eisenhower and his senior commanders arrived to take advantage of the excellent communication system which the island could offer.
As they made their final preparations all seemed to be going well. The
safe concentration of the assault convoys indicated that strategic surprise
had been won. Intelligence reports of the move of 15 Panzer Grenadier
Division towards Palmero and away from the assault area suggested that
tactical surprise might be complete as well. The only worries left were
the weather and the difficulty of controlling such a vast enterprise once it
was launched.

During the afternoon of 9 July the wind rose and the sea became choppy.
Back on the airfields in Tunisia, where the airborne divisions were getting
ready to emplane, reports came in of rising wind speeds. Betting amongst
the parachutists swung heavily in favour of postponement. In Malta,
Eisenhower and his three senior commanders had difficult decisions to

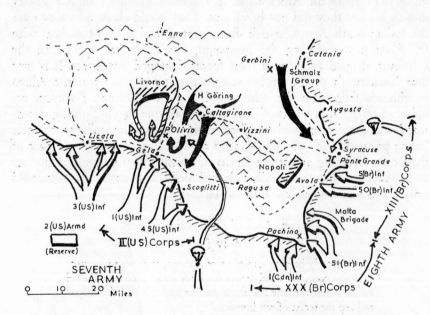

5   *The D-day landings and first Axis counter-attacks*

1 Field-Marshal The Earl Alexander of Tunis, Commander-in-Chief,
The Allied Armies in Italy and 15th Army Group

THE PROTAGONISTS

2 Field-Marshal Albert Kesselring,
Commander-in-Chief, German Army
Group 'C'

3 Field-Marshal Erwin Rommel,
Commander-in-Chief, German Army
Group 'B'

4 Eighth Army landing at Avola

THE INVASION OF SICILY

5 The RAF using Comiso airfield soon after its capture

make. Postponement at this late stage would cause confusion and would jeopardize surprise. Fortunately the meteorologists were able to predict that the storm should subside in the evening, and so no postponement was attempted. Even with everything going according to plan an amphibious landing is the most difficult military operation to control. So many echelons of commanders, all from different services—sea, land, air, logistic, technical—are involved. The scope for misunderstanding is infinite and the degree of control which can be exercised by the commanders is very tenuous. Success depends on the sum of the actions of hundreds of junior officers and NCOs: the junior naval officer trying to steer his heavily laden landing craft in pitch darkness through a choppy sea to the right beach; the infantry subaltern landed dripping wet on a shore whose landmarks he cannot recognize, and faced with machine-gun fire before he can collect his wits; or the pilot of a parachute aircraft groping his way through enemy anti-aircraft fire to the dropping zone whose outline he has only seen so far on air photographs. To most of the men taking part everything seems to go wrong from the start and it is not until some hours later, as the enterprise unfolds, that order starts to appear out of apparent chaos. The invasion of Sicily was no exception in this respect; the two hazards of weather and difficulty of control combined to provide greater opposition to the British and American assaults than did the Axis forces.

Both army commanders had decided to use their airborne troops to capture tactical features which would help their assault divisions reach their objectives more easily. Montgomery had chosen the seizure of the Ponte Grande bridge on the southern approach road to Syracuse as the task for the Airlanding Brigade of 1 (Br) Airborne Division; and Patton had decided to use a parachute regiment of 82 (US) Airborne Division to take the high ground behind Gela to loosen up the enemy defences in front of 1 (US) Division's assault and to ease its passage through to Ponte Olivio airfield. The American aircrew, who were to tow the British gliders and drop the American paratroops, did not arrive in North Africa until April and had only been trained in daylight operations. Further training after their arrival had been too sketchy and too hurried. The high winds on the evening of D-day made matters worse. Inexpert navigation, unexpected anti-aircraft fire—some from Allied ships as well as Axis shore batteries—and in some cases the timidity of the inexperienced pilots, conspired to scatter both forces all over Sicily and in the sea off the east and south coasts. In the British force, out of 134 gliders which took off, 47 were released too early and fell in the sea, 75 landed somewhere in Sicily and a mere 12 reached the area of the Ponte Grande. Eight officers and 65 men instead of a brigade of three battalions took and held the bridge until they were reached by the leading troops of XIII (Br) Corps the following afternoon. By then only 19 men were left but the bridge, whose destruction would have halted XIII (Br) Corps' advance on Syracuse, was still intact. The Americans fared no better. Only one of the four battalions which were dropped landed in any semblance of order and that was 25 miles from its target. The rest of the force was scattered far and wide: 33 loads landing in Eighth Army's area; 127 behind the 45 (US) Division's beaches; and only 53 anywhere near 1 (US) Division which they were intended to support. It has often been claimed that the panic and confusion caused behind the Axis lines by reports of parachute landings over such a wide area accounted for the ease with which the landings from the sea were made the following day. An honest analysis would suggest that this is wishful thinking, trying to find a silver lining in a very black cloud. The airborne operations were a fiasco in which the most carefully selected and highly trained soldiers from both armies were literally thrown away by inexperienced and inadequately trained aircrews.*

The landings from the sea went better but far from smoothly. Strong headwinds delayed the final approach of the convoys. Some ships were late; others anchored too far off shore before lowering their assault craft; and some had difficulty in getting their craft loaded and away on time. The choppy sea made handling craft difficult and their marshalling into orderly assault waves almost impossible. Navigational errors on the run-in did not help the assault troops, who were all too often landed on the wrong beaches.

On the Eighth Army front the landing was remarkably successful in spite of these difficulties. Opposition was very light. More casualties were caused through the leading troops stumbling into anti-personnel mine-fields in the dark than from the Italian coastal divisions' active opposition. There was some artillery fire on the beaches and a few air attacks developed as the first day wore on. Losses in craft amounted to a mere dozen instead of the three hundred forecast by the planners. By the evening of 10 July XIII (Br) Corps had taken Syracuse and was just making contact with Battle Group Schmalz on the road to Augusta. XXX (Br) Corps had consolidated its bridgehead across the Pachino Peninsula and its engineers were already repairing the Pachino airfield which had been ploughed up before the landings. Eighth Army's logistic units were having some difficulty in unloading supplies but with the capture of Syracuse they would become less dependent on the beaches. Montgomery had every reason to be pleased with the first day's work.

* The US account in *The Army Air Forces in World War II*, vol. II, blames the British glider pilots, but this is not supported by other accounts.

Seventh Army had a more difficult time. Their beaches were exposed to the swell and were obstructed by sand-bars on which landing craft tended to broach before they reached the shore. The Italian coastal troops put up a slightly better performance than those on Eighth Army's front, and the Luftwaffe concentrated its attention on the American convoys rather than the British. The US destroyer *Maddox* and a minesweeper were lost to air attack, and a number of landing craft were capsized in the swell off the beaches. The American sailors and soldiers complained that the arrangements for air cover over their beaches were not as good as Eighth Army's, and that the system of calling for close air support for the troops fighting in the beachhead was inadequate. The Allied air forces deny both these charges, but the fact remains that the enemy air attacks did do more damage to the Americans than to the British, and if it had not been for naval gunfire support 1 (US) Division might have been driven back to its ships by counter-attacks launched by the Hermann Göring and Livorno Divisions early on D-day.

On the Axis side Guzzoni and von Senger were fully alive to the possibility of Sicily being the next Allied target. They were supplied with adequate air reconnaissance reports and had correctly assessed the dispositions of Allied shipping as pointing to an attack on Sicily, and not Greece as OKW still believed. On 8 July Guzzoni ordered the obstruction of the west- and south-coast ports. Early on 9 July reconnaissance reports showed landing ships and transports off Pantelleria; and that evening more convoys were sighted heading for Sicily. Guzzoni ordered the preliminary alert at 7 p.m. and the full alert at 10 p.m. Hitler, back at OKW, alerted the 1 Para Division in France at about the same time.

At midnight Guzzoni heard of the glider and parachute landings. He ordered the immediate demolition of all the threatened ports and alerted his two Corps HQs to expect landings in the Gela-Licata and Avola sectors. Reports of landings began coming in from all over the island and for some time it was difficult for the Sixth Italian Army staff to assess what was happening. Guzzoni, however, was remarkably accurate in his assessment of the situation. He soon appreciated that the Syracuse-Augusta area was one Allied objective and Gela-Ponte Olivio another. He decided that as Syracuse and Augusta were well defended with naval fixed defences, and as the Napoli Division and Battle Group Schmalz were near at hand, this sector needed less attention than the Gela landings. Moreover, Guzzoni knew that the Gela defences were weak and, as the greater mass of shipping was reported off Gela, it seemed to suggest that this was the more dangerous assault. He released the Livorno Division from Army Reserve and ordered the XVI (It) Corps to mount an immediate counter-attack against the American beachhead around Gela, using the Livorno and Hermann Göring Divisions. With even greater clear-sightedness, he recalled 15 Panzer Grenadier Division from the west and ordered it into a central position west of Enna as fast as its Commander, General Rodt, could arrange its march.

The Napoli Division failed to achieve anything against the two British corps, and Colonel Schmalz was hard pressed slowing down XIII (Br) Corps' advance northwards. The naval garrison of Syracuse surrendered without firing a shot, and the garrison of Augusta started evacuating the port and destroying the naval guns which should have defended it before the British even appeared. The Livorno and Hermann Göring Divisions, however, were made of sterner stuff. They launched a number of strong infantry and tank attacks converging upon 1 (US) Division's beaches in and to the east of Gela. Only the determined resistance of General Allen's 1 (US) Division—the 'Big Red One'—and the accurate and sustained fire of the supporting US cruisers and destroyers saved the day. By evening, both Axis divisions had suffered severely and had pulled back to positions from which they could renew the attack next day.

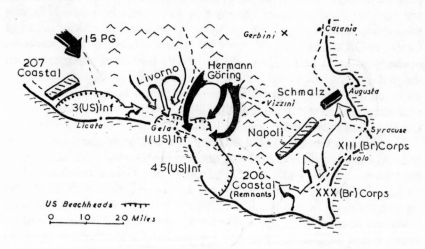

6   *The defeat of the second Axis counter-attack, 11 July*

During the first night, 10–11 July, Guzzoni heard of the fall of Syracuse and began to realize that the British thrust towards Catania, and thence to Messina, was the more serious threat. He had already instructed XVI (It) Corps to launch a carefully co-ordinated counter-attack against Gela early next day, so he now instructed the Hermann Göring Division to exploit success in an easterly direction rolling up 45 (US) Division and linking up with Schmalz as soon as this was practicable. The Livorno Division was to swing westwards towards Licata to link up with 15 Panzer Grenadier Division as it arrived opposite 3 (US) Division's beach-head. The Luftwaffe was to support the counter-attacks by bombing the American beaches and shipping lying off.

The Hermann Göring attack started at 6 a.m. on 11 July and was followed soon after by the Livorno attack. Both made excellent progress at first while they were out of range of the US naval guns. As they approached the beaches American resistance stiffened and naval broadsides started to take their toll. About midday the German tanks were within 2,000 yards of 1 (US) Division's beaches and were turning their fire on to the unloading parties. Reports sent by the Hermann Göring Division, suggesting that the US troops were being forced to re-embark, caused jubilation in Rome, but the Axis triumph was short-lived. Determined resistance by every American gun crew, tank troop and infantry platoon under the massive covering fire of their supporting naval ships again proved too much for the attackers. The Livorno Division suffered terrible losses from naval gun fire and from the fire of American Ranger battalions holding the town of Gela. The Hermann Göring Division lost about a third of its tanks in its effort to break through 1 (US) Division east of Gela. Both Axis divisions were forced to give up and by evening were pulling back to their start lines. It had not been practicable to wheel outwards to roll up the 3 and 45 (US) Divisions. The American divisions had withstood the main weight of the Axis counter-attack and in so doing had proved themselves to themselves, though not as yet to 15 Army Group and Eighth Army.

Guzzoni was disappointed at the failure of this attack which had seemed to be going excellently. Kesselring had some extraordinarily rude things to say about the handling, training and tactics of the Hermann Göring Division which led to Conrath replacing a number of senior officers responsible for the failure. Von Senger could fairly claim that, if 15 Panzer Grenadier Division, which knew the country, had been left in this vital sector instead of being sent westwards just before the invasion, the outcome might have been very different. Omar Bradley could also claim that, had Eisenhower not agreed to his suggestion of replacing the new 36 (US) Division with the more experienced 1 (US) Division, Conrath might have won the battle and forced the Americans to re-embark. As it was, the fighting on 11 July in the Gela area was, to use Wellington's expression, 'a close run thing'.

Kesselring's policy of forward defence and immediate counter-attack had proved a failure. Guzzoni had now no fresh troops with which to renew the attack. The gap between the Schmalz Group and the Hermann

Göring Division was widening as the Eighth Army developed its north-ward thrust. There was only one course open to Guzzoni—try to stabilize the front and withdraw to a shorter line, hoping for reinforcements from Italy and Germany now that the true direction of the Allied strategic thrust was clear. The Anglo-Americans were unlikely to have the strength or enough shipping to open another campaign in Greece or Sardinia. If Guzzoni were lucky, he could expect the Messina ferry to work overtime bringing him reinforcements to block the Allies' approach to the Italian mainland.

When the Germans and Italians pulled back to reorganize after their failure at Gela, Patton could not be sure that they would not renew the assault the following day. His 1 (US) Division was almost exhausted and there were no more troops readily available at sea. His nearest reinforce-ment was the balance of 82 (US) Airborne Division in North Africa. He decided to bring in the rest of this division by air during the night 11–12 July. The drop was to start at 10.45 p.m. Precautions were taken to warn ships and army units that Allied troop carriers would be flying in at this time. General Ridgeway, Commander of 82 Airborne Division, was in the beachhead during 11 July to co-ordinate the operation. He checked personally a number of AA gun positions to see if the gunners had been told. Out of six sites which he visited, one had not received the order, and so fresh warnings were sent out. During the day the ships off the beaches had been suffering Luftwaffe attacks which were part of the support given to the Livorno and Hermann Göring Divisions. In the afternoon an ammunition ship had been hit and had blown up in an awe-inspiring way. Just before 10 p.m. another Axis air attack came in and several ships were damaged. As the anti-aircraft fire died away the first hum of the approach-ing American troop carriers was heard and the first flight of paratroops was dropped safely into the beachhead. The second flight was just coming in when a solitary gun opened fire; whether from the land or from the sea no one will ever know. Within seconds, every anti-aircraft gun on ship and shore opened fire as if by sympathetic detonation. Some pilots wisely turned back and returned with their loads to North Africa; others tried to thread their way through the fire; others jettisoned their load anywhere on dry land and others let them go over the sea; and others were shot down with their paratroopers on board. The exact cause of this disaster was never established. Admiral Cunningham was utterly forthright in defence of the ships' crews. After years of air attack by Axis aircraft in the Mediterranean every plane approaching a ship was con-sidered hostile. Too many ships had been lost by opening fire too late to take chances. The rule was 'shoot first, ask later'; and such habits die hard. Few sailors had, as yet, fully recognized the change in the air situation in the Mediterranean. The fault clearly lay in inadequate 'guns tight' procedures which had proved unnecessary until then.

THE GERMAN RECOVERY

13–28 July

> 'I gave General Hube, the commander of XIV Panzer Corps, detailed instructions on the spot. His mission was to dig in on a solid line even at the cost of giving ground initially . . . . I also told him that I was reckoning with the evacuation of Sicily, which it was his job to postpone as long as possible.'
>
> Field Marshal Kesselring, *Memoirs*

The Allies, particularly Montgomery, who had forecast stiff initial resistance, were surprised how easily they had prized open the Sicilian oyster. The Axis partners were correspondingly depressed by the failure of their defence plans. In both camps there was debate and disagreement about future policy at different levels. The Axis was in disarray at strategic level, but acted with remarkable harmony at tactical level. The Allies were in the opposite position, having firm strategic direction but suffering tactical discord in Sicily itself.

Guzzoni appreciated that his task now was to buy time. His first step

7   Axis plans for stopping the Allied advance on Messina

must be to contain the Allied beachheads. Then he would withdraw slowly to a shorter line behind which he would construct a last ditch position covering his main reinforcement and main escape route through Messina. His orders on 12 July were to secure the line Augusta–Calta-girone–Porto Empedolce. The Schmalz Group was to hold the coast road to Catania; the Napoli Division was to cover the gap between Schmalz and the Hermann Göring Division, which was to side-step eastwards from Caltagirone towards Schmalz's position; and 15 Panzer Grenadier Division was to cover the western half of the Allied beachhead with the remnants of the Livorno Division and the local coastal troops. This containing line followed the high ground overlooking the Allied beachheads and covered the Catania plain with the Gerbini airfields which Guzzoni hoped to hold as long as possible. When he was forced to give up this line, he would pull back slowly to his main line of resistance running from the mouth of the Simeto River just south of Catania, along the Dittaino River to Leonforte and thence to the north coast at San Stefano. This line became known as the San Stefano Line. During the withdrawal to this line the road centre at Enna was to be strongly held to keep the door open for units withdrawing from the western end of the island. A longstop line would run from Acireale on the east coast just north of Catania, round the southern slopes of Mount Etna to Troina and to the north coast at San Fratello, which gave its name to this line. There were two critical manoeuvres upon which the success of this plan would depend. First, the wide gap between the Hermann Göring Division and the Schmalz Group, which was only partially covered by the dispirited Napoli Division, must be closed, otherwise the initial containment line could not be held and withdrawal would become difficult if the British broke into the Catania Plain before the Hermann Göring Division and Schmalz Group joined hands. And secondly, the areas around Enna and Leonforte must not fall before the Aosta and Assietta Divisions in the west had withdrawn into the San Stefano Line.

Kesselring visited Guzzoni at Etna on 12 and 15 July, and agreed substantially with his plans. In his usual way Kesselring was more optimistic than Guzzoni and von Senger, and his optimism was reinforced by a visit which he made to the sterling Colonel Schmalz. Augusta had fallen, but Schmalz was still holding the southern rim of the Catania plain at Lentini against XIII (Br) Corps. While he was with Schmalz he witnessed the arrival of 3 Para Regiment of 1 Para Division on dropping zones south of Catania. The German transport aircraft came in under heavy fighter escort and dropped the regiment with great precision, in marked contrast to the amateur airborne efforts of the Allies. The drop convinced Kesselring that this was a practical method of reinforcement and that, given the type of determination which Schmalz was displaying, at least the north-east of Sicily could be held for some time.

The only tactical difficulty on the Axis side was the cumbersome performance of the Hermann Göring Division. Guzzoni and von Senger had the utmost difficulty in persuading Conrath to move faster. After his unsuccessful counter-attack on 11 July, he pulled back to Caltagirone and then side-stepped very slowly eastwards, admittedly holding 1 and 45 (US) Divisions in check at the same time. He did not reach Schmalz's flank until Guzzoni was forced to order the withdrawal to the San Stefano Line on 13 July.

In Rome and at Hitler's headquarters in East Prussia, opinions varied from deep pessimism to unrealistic optimism. Events in Sicily had confirmed Ambrosio in his view that the war was lost and served to stiffen his determination to save Italy from further humiliation. Kesselring seems to have been unaffected by Ambrosio's pessimism and still clung to his thesis that given loyal German support Italy could be kept in the war. He accepted that Sicily could not be held indefinitely but he saw great advantages in not giving up the island without a struggle. Jodl, Hitler's Chief of Operations in OKW, leaned towards the Rommel school of thought and advised Hitler to force the Duce to hand over operational control to German commanders or, at least, to Italian commanders trusted by the German staff in Italy. He suspected Italian defection was being discussed behind closed doors in Rome and instructed his staff to check all arrangements for Plan Alarich.* Hitler had few illusions about the weaknesses of the Italian Fascist regime and of the Italian armed forces, but he was still unready to let down his fellow dictator. He preferred Kesselring's advice to Jodl's, not so much because he thought Kesselring right and Jodl wrong, but because he disliked surrendering territory until he was forced to do so and because he equally disliked being disloyal to Mussolini. The Duce, for his part, was not nearly so loyal to Hitler. If he had dared to break the unpopular German Alliance, he would have done so long ago. Fear, not loyalty, held him to his partnership with Hitler. He was sick and undecided as depressing reports from Sicily came crowding in upon him. He was torn between Ambrosio's unpalatable but realistic advice to break the alliance and his own reluctance to take the opposite course which meant crawling to Hitler for help.

The main decisions were, as usual, taken by Hitler in far-off East Prussia. He decided to take personal charge of operations in Sicily. Since the fall of Stalingrad and Tunis he had begun to realize that manpower was now Germany's most precious asset. It would be cheaper in terms of

* The German plan to take over Italy by force if she defected (see p. 27).

German soldiers to defend southern Europe with the Italians rather than without them. If Italy was to be held even with Italian help, he would have to find more German troops to strengthen the Axis forces fighting in Sicily and Italy, and also to build up a new and powerful striking force with which to implement Alarich if Italy defected. Operation Zitadelle, the offensive against Kursk on the Eastern Front, had started on 5 July, but had soon run into heavy Russian opposition and was showing no signs of gaining decisive results. On 13 July Hitler ordered it to be stopped and told Zeitzler, the Army Chief of Staff who controlled the Eastern Front, to be ready to release troops for the Mediterranean. He altered Kesselring's directive and instructed him 'to delay the enemy advance as much as possible and to bring it to a halt in front of Etna on the San Stefano–Catania line'. He then approved certain tactical moves: the despatch of Hube's XIV Panzer Corps Headquarters from southern Italy to Sicily to command all German troops on the island; the move of the balance of 1 Para Division to Sicily; the reinforcement of the Second German Air Force with three extra bomber groups; the stand-by of 29 Panzer Grenadier Division and one more bomber group with an extra torpedo squadron for Sicily; and finally, the strengthening of the Messina defences with eight 210-mm. guns. Secret instructions were sent to Hube which were not to be disclosed to the Italians. Working closely with von Senger, Hube was to take over as unobtrusively as possible all operations in the Sicilian bridgehead. This should be done by first claiming command of sectors in which German troops were predominant and as more Germans came into the line taking over complete operational command. He should exclude Italian officers from his operational and planning staffs so that his intentions would not be reported to Guzzoni. The keystone of his conduct of operations should be maximum delay consistent with conservation of German manpower. These may seem cynical instructions to issue secretly to the German Corps Commander, but they were no worse than the Italians expected. Remarkably little friction seems to have arisen between the Sixth Italian Army and XIV Panzer Corps, which says much for the spirit of co-operation between the Germans and Italians at the lower tactical levels. Guzzoni was equally cynical and just accepted the inevitable.

On the Allied side, the clash between the two army commanders and their staffs soon reopened. Montgomery took it upon himself to decide how operations should be developed. Knowing Alexander's 15 Army Group Headquarters staff much better than Patton did, he decided what he was going to do and started doing it before he had gained Alexander's approval or discussed it with Patton. On 13 July the right wing of the 45 (US) Division and 51 (Highland) Division on the left of XXX (Br) Corps found that they had both been directed to clear the same town, Vizzini, and use the same road, Route 124.

Montgomery appreciated that the key to tactical manoeuvre in the difficult mountain country of Sicily was control of the few main state routes. He had only one good road up the east coast (Route 114) and this was not enough for the quick and effective deployment of two corps with all their artillery, tanks and logistic support. He, therefore, decided that he would develop two thrust lines: his main effort would be up the coast road with XIII (Br) Corps, which he intended to help forward with a Commando attack from the sea to secure the Leonardo Bridge on the main coast road five miles behind the Schmalz Group holding Lentini,

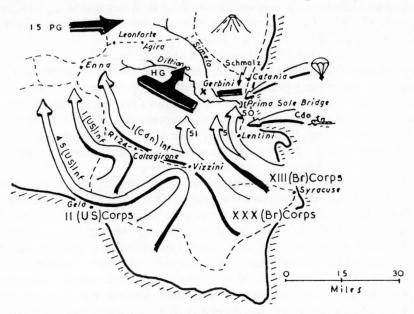

8 *The development of Eighth Army's operations, 13–19 July*

and with a parachute drop by a brigade on to the Prima Sole Bridge over the Simeto just south of Catania. His second thrust would take the form of a wide left hook by XXX (Br) Corps along Route 124 to Caltagirone, Enna and Leonforte, outflanking all German positions in the Catania Plain.

Unfortunately Route 124 lay within the American boundaries and General Bradley had intended to use it for his II (US) Corps advance towards exactly the same objectives as Montgomery had prescribed for XXX (Br) Corps. The Seventh Army staff were not unnaturally annoyed when not only did they find 51 (Highland) Division on their road, but also when at about midnight they received a directive from Army Group to hand over the road to XXX (Br) Corps. What made matters worse was that Alexander had been at Seventh Army Headquarters that morning and had restrained Patton from attempting to break out westwards to take Agrigento and Porto Empedolce to ease his logistic problems. Alexander had reiterated that Seventh Army's job was to protect Eighth Army's flank and rear. He would allow Patton to reconnoitre Agrigento in force but he stressed that Patton must not get involved in heavy fighting which would jeopardise his primary role. He said nothing about any change of boundary between the two armies. Montgomery had put his ideas to Alexander on his return from Seventh Army and was given the go-ahead without anyone in the 15 Army Group staff really considering the effect on Bradley's II (US) Corps.

·Nothing more need have been heard of this incident if it had not been symptomatic of something much deeper. It was, after all, just a misunderstanding over boundaries which occur in most operations and which it is the routine task of staff officers to sort out as they happen. In this case, however, the change of Route 124 reopened the wound in Anglo-American relations caused by the substitution of Montgomery's plan for the original Husky concept. It seemed clear to Patton, and more especially to Bradley, who was the quicker and deeper thinker of the two, that Montgomery was bent on hogging the whole campaign for himself and his Eighth Army. They resented the implication that the Americans should be nursed along while the veteran British reaped the spoils of victory. Patton could not stand the idea of Montgomery entering Messina in triumph when he was not even allowed to grab Palermo. Bradley had his eyes on breaking out through Enna to the north coast and then swinging eastwards to share Eighth Army's advance on Messina. Now he was having his 45 (US) Division squeezed out of the line by XXX (Br) Corps taking 'his' route. 45 (US) Division would have to be withdrawn back to the coast and passed round the rear of 1 (US) Division before it could get back into the race for the north coast. This may seem rather childish, but fighting men live for the glory of great achievements which make world headlines. Generals hope for personal victory and their juniors for the honour of being able to say they have taken part. If friction is to be avoided in an Allied force the spoils as well as the risks must be equally shared. In Sicily they were not and so trouble arose. Patton's Seventh Army resented playing second fiddle to Montgomery's Eighth Army.

It was not until the night 13–14 July that Montgomery was ready to start his advance on Catania. The move of Eighth Army north from its

beachheads, which should have been rapid in view of the poor performance of the Napoli and coastal divisions and of the smallness of the
Schmalz Group, was limited by lack of troop transport. Montgomery's
assessment of stiff enemy opposition to the landings had been reflected in
the loading tables of the assault ships. Priority had been given to guns,
tanks and ammunition. The speed of advance was thus limited to the
endurance of the infantry marching along the hot dusty Sicilian roads
under the scorching July sun. Although the Augusta garrison started to
evacuate the port on 11 July, counter-attacks by the Schmalz Group had
delayed matters. 5 (Br) Division of XIII (Br) Corps had not entered the
town until 12 July. Schmalz had then withdrawn slowly to Lentini where
he had been reinforced by the parachute troops whose drop Kesselring
had witnessed. 50 (Br) Division, now leading XIII (Br) Corps advance,
found progress slower and tougher during 13 July and by that evening
was up against Schmalz's position at Lentini. One bright spot in the day's
events had been the capture of the Napoli Division's commander and his
staff by the Durham Light Infantry of 50 (Br) Division. Little was heard
or seen of the Napoli Division thereafter; it seems to have disintegrated
and faded away. Its loss, however, was more than adequately made up by
the arrival of 1 Para Division's MG battalion, pioneer battalion, four
batteries of parachute artillery and two German infantry battalions from
southern Italy, all of which reinforced the Schmalz Group, blocking XIII
(Br) Corps' route to Catania. Thus instead of being opposed by the
Napoli Division, whose Commander they had captured, and by one
German Panzer Grenadier Regiment under Schmalz, XIII (Br) Corps was
beginning to meet the best part of a German Division, including hard-
bitten paratroopers, all under the ubiquitous Schmalz.

The fates were playing into Patton's hands. Montgomery's drive
towards Catania was proving more difficult than he had expected. The
Commando attack on the Leonardo Bridge was not strong enough and
failed. The parachute brigade attack on the Prima Sole Bridge, although
an epic in airborne histories, could hardly be classed as a success. All three
attacks—Commando, parachute and 50 (Br) Division's advance along the
main road—ran into heavier opposition than the Eighth Army staff
anticipated. The Commandos and parachutists would have had difficulty
in overcoming the enemy resistance if they had landed at full strength,
but neither did so. The Commandos were delayed by a series of mishaps
and reached the bridge in such a piecemeal fashion that they were not
strong enough to hold it in daylight. The parachute attack was a repetition
of the earlier airborne failures. It suffered heavily while still airborne. Its
aircraft had been carefully routed through lanes supposed to be clear of
allied shipping, but over half the troop carriers were fired on by friendly

ships. Two were shot down and nine were forced to turn back because of injury to the air crews or damage to the aircraft. Over the coast they ran into the Catania and Gerbini airfield complex anti-aircraft fire. Ten more aircraft were forced to turn back. Eighty-seven flew on, but only 39 dropped their loads within a mile of the bridge. Four loads landed on the slopes of Etna. Out of 1,900 men of 1 (Br) Para Brigade who set out, only 200, with three anti-tank guns, reached the target. They were welcomed by a savage reception committee from the German 3 Para Regiment which had landed on almost the same dropping zones only 36 hours before. The British parachute troops took and held the bridge all 14 July. When they were forced to withdraw, they managed to keep it covered from the south bank until 50 (Br) Division reached them the following morning—15 July. By this time, the Schmalz Group had joined hands with the Hermann Göring Division behind the Simeto and Dittaino Rivers. Guzzoni's main line of resistance was beginning to take shape. Attacks by 50 (Br) Division during 16 July resulted in the final capture of the Prima Sole Bridge and a bridgehead 3,000 yards beyond, but a further attack on 17 July made little further progress. The road to Catania was firmly blocked by first-class German troops and a few of the more stalwart Italian units which were prepared to fight on under German command.

The XXX (Br) Corps' left hook did not sweep round the German flank as Montgomery had hoped. 51 (Highland) Division, leading the Corps advance, ran into parts of the Hermann Göring Division at Vizzini and only managed to clear the town with the help of 45 (US) Division by 15 July. The 1 (Cdn) Division then took the lead from the tired Highlanders to continue the advance up Route 124 to Enna. 51 (Highland) Division, after a short rest, was turned due north on an axis across the Catania Plain with two aims in view: to keep a link between XIII (Br) Corps in front of Catania and the Canadians; and to threaten the Gerbini airfields. On 16 July opposition to XXX (Br) Corps lessened and both of its divisions found themselves delayed mainly by mines and demolitions covered by small rearguards. Guzzoni had given the order to withdraw to the main line of resistance on 15 July. XXX (Br) Corps' gain was XIII (Br) Corps' loss because the Hermann Göring Division had withdrawn north-eastwards into XIII (Br) Corps' sector and the Canadians had not yet come up with the main body of 15 Panzer Grenadier Division around Enna and Leonforte.

Guzzoni's decision to abandon his containment line was forced upon him by XIII (Br) Corps' advance to the Prima Sole Bridge and by the pressure of 45 (US) Division and XXX (Br) Corps upon the Hermann Göring Division. There is a possibility that, if XXX (Br) Corps had been

directed northwards on a parallel axis to XIII (Br) Corps across the
Catania Plain, its thrust line would have led it between the Hermann
Göring Division and the Schmalz Group. If this had happened Guzzoni
might not have been able to consolidate the San Stefano Line. Montgomery's 'theft' of Route 124 may have let the Hermann Göring
Division escape. This, of course, is mere speculation; on the other hand,
there is no gainsaying the fact that Eighth Army was beginning to show
signs of fatigue and over-extension. XIII (Br) Corps brought up 5 (Br)
Division between 50 and 51 (Br) Divisions. Both these divisions fought
their way over the Dittaino River, but could get no further. The
Canadians took Caltagirone without much difficulty and were then
directed on Leonforte and Agira, by-passing Enna to the east. Enna was,
however, still within Eighth Army's boundaries and should have been
cleared by the Canadians to protect the flank of Bradley's II (US) Corps.
Bradley was not told of the XXX (Br) Corps' change of direction. When
he found out about it, he ascribed it to another high-handed action by
Montgomery. General Leese persuaded him, with a case of champagne
to help, that this time it was only an error in staff work, and gave him
every facility to take Enna with his 1 (US) Division. The XXX (Br)
Corps' advance was beginning to slow down. In front of it were units of
the 15 Panzer Grenadier Division who knew they had to hold the
Leonforte–Agira area as long as possible to enable units in the west of the
island to withdraw. The Canadians did not reach the outskirts of Leonforte until 19 July. The gap between them and 51 (Highland) Division

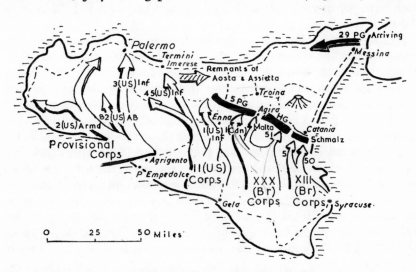

9   *Patton's conquest of western Sicily*

had widened so much that this had to be filled by 231 (Malta) Brigade★
which was directed on Agira from the south. Thus, as Eighth Army
approached Guzzoni's main line of resistance with the Seventh Army
theoretically protecting its flank and rear, all four of its infantry divisions
were deployed in the line with no reserves available with which to break
into the San Stefano position. In front of these four divisions lay the
equivalent of three German divisions holding ideally defensible ground
around the base of Mount Etna.

Meanwhile Patton had been reorganizing his army, hoping that events
would turn in his favour. He formed a new corps—the Provisional Corps
—under General Keyes, his deputy commander. He then divided his
front into two, giving Bradley's II (US) Corps the northern sector and
Keyes' Provisional Corps the west. Bradley was to keep his two divisions
—1 and 45 (US) Divisions; and Keyes was to have 9 (US) Division plus
82 (US) Airborne Division. 2 (US) Armoured Division was to stay in
Army reserve. Patton took Alexander at his word and restricted his
operations to an advance by Bradley to protect Montgomery's rear and
a reconnaissance in force towards Agrigento. A reconnaissance in force
was all that was needed to topple the coastal division defending Agrigento
which fell on 16 July, but Bradley had to contend with 15 Panzer
Grenadier Division which made him fight for every mile of his advance
northwards. Bradley's 1 (US) Division ran into the extreme western
flank of 15 Panzer Grenadier Division withdrawing on Enna and Leonforte, but his 45 (US) Division struck beyond the German flank and found
itself in the open with only Italian troops between itself and Palermo on
Route 121.

By now Alexander was becoming increasingly nervous about the
strong enemy line which was clearly forming across the north-east of the
island. It looked very much like Wellington's Lines of the Torres Vedras
in Portugal, behind which he resisted Massena's attacks until he was
strong enough to turn the tables on the French. If the Germans consolidated their positions across the Messina Peninsula in the same way, they
too might be able to reinforce Sicily sufficiently to stage a come-back. On
16 July Alexander issued a new directive which spelt out what Patton and
Bradley had always feared. Montgomery was given the job of breaking
into the Messina Peninsula while Patton was to continue protecting his
rear. There was no mention of any compensating American drive on
Palermo. Patton saw red. He had so far always accepted Alexander's orders
without complaint, but this was more than he could stand. He flew back
to Alexander's headquarters in Tunisia to put his case personally. None of

★ 231 (Malta) Brigade was composed of British units which had been part of the Malta
garrison during the siege from 1940 to 1942.

the British staff at Army Group Headquarters were aware of the American bitterness. They thought that the Americans had accepted the overall strategy as sound and believed that all the orders issued to Seventh Army had been in conformity with that strategy. They were taken aback by what appeared to them to be a sudden wave of American resentment. There is no doubt that the British staff officers had underestimated the strength and striking power of Patton's Army.* The American officers in the Army Group Headquarters were also at fault in not reflecting the opinions of Patton's staff. Eighth Army was becoming an experienced but cautious force. The Seventh was bursting to show what it could do. Alexander appreciated the position as soon as it was put to him forcefully and clearly by Patton, who was thus able to fly back to Gela with Alexander's blessing on his plan to seize Palermo.

Patton's drive on Palermo started on 18 July and turned out to be a brilliant cavalry-type action. Cynics may say that it was nothing more than a fast route march against reluctant Italians, but this decries the splendid dash and brilliant organization which led to Patton's triumph. When Guzzoni heard of the fall of Agrigento, he had ordered his XII (It) Corps to withdraw eastwards into the northern sector of the San Stefano Line. The Aosta and Assietta Divisions, mobile only in name, started a slow and dangerous flank march across the American front late on 16 July, leaving the unfortunate coastal divisions to oppose Patton's advance. General Marciani of the 208 Coast Division was left to hold Palermo with naval help. It took Keyes' Provisional Corps only four days to reach Palermo which fell without much resistance on 22 July. Two days later the last remnants of the coastal garrisons around places like Trapani and Marsala surrendered. The operation cost the Americans only 272 casualties in return for 52,000 Italian prisoners and a further 3,000 Italian battle casualties. This was just what Patton's Army needed: they had beaten back the Hermann Göring Division's counter-attacks at Gela and had now made a spectacular advance which had captured the head-lines of the world press. Patton was now ready to turn eastwards, deter-mined to rub in his victory by getting to Messina before Montgomery. It would take him a few days to transfer his logistic base from the southern beaches to Palermo; then, Alexander willing, the race would be on.

While Keyes' Provisional Corps managed Patton's dash for Palermo, Bradley's II (US) Corps was directed due north to protect Eighth Army's rear and to cut the north coast road. 1 (US) Division carried out the

* The degree to which the British were unconscious of American feeling is shown by the fact that in Montgomery's Chief of Staff's book (*Operation Victory*, by General de Guingand) no mention is made of any difficulty with Seventh Army over boundaries, tasks or roles.

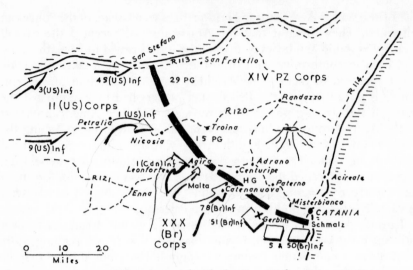

10   *Operations to break the San Stefano Line*

former task by advancing northwards in step with the Canadians. They had to drive in the rearguards of 15 Panzer Grenadier Division who were holding open the escape route for the Aosta and Assietta Divisions. After stiff fighting 1 (US) Division reached Petralia on Route 120 by 23 July. This was to be as far north as it was to go. 45 (US) Division moved faster because it was beyond the flank of the German covering positions. Opposed only by Italians, it cut the north coast road just east of Termini Imerese on 23 July as well, but when it turned east along the coast road it ran into a battle group of the newly arrived 29 Panzer Grenadier Division.

All this time Eighth Army had been meeting with little success. Further efforts by XIII (Br) Corps led nowhere in the Catania sector. XXX (Br) Corps was still making some progress, but the pace was slow and the fighting severe. 51 (Highland) Division took Gerbini airfield on 20 July, but was thrown back to the south of the airfield by determined counter-attacks from the Hermann Göring Division. The Canadians had to fight 15 Panzer Grenadier Division for every feature on the road to Leonforte which fell on 21 July. Between the two divisions, the Malta Brigade was stopped by heavy opposition three miles south of Agira.

21 July was a day of decision. Montgomery finally acknowledged that he was over-extended. He ordered XIII (Br) Corps to go over to the defensive in front of Catania, while he shifted the weight of his attack to XXX (Br) Corps. Although this decision enabled his staff to shift the army artillery and air support from Catania to Leonforte, there were no

66

fresh troops with which to mount an offensive to break Guzzoni's line. Montgomery, therefore, summoned 78 (Br) Division from North Africa. This could not arrive before the end of the month so in the meantime the Canadians were directed to turn due eastwards to attack Agira in conjunction with the Malta Brigade, as a preliminary operation to a major XXX (Br) Corps offensive directed on Adrano, which Montgomery considered to be the key to the Axis position. This change of direction freed the two northern roads (Routes 120 and 113) into the Messina Peninsula for Patton's Army.

On 25 July Alexander held a conference with his army commanders to co-ordinate the final offensive towards Messina. Seventh Army was to drive eastwards on the coast road and Route 120 aiming for San Stefano and Nicosia. The operation would be carried out by II (US) Corps. 1 (US) Division would wheel eastwards along Route 120 from Petralia against 15 Panzer Grenadier Division, and 45 (US) Division would continue along the coast road pushing back 29 Panzer Grenadier Division. In order to ensure a continuous and sustained effort two fresh US Divisions were to be brought up behind the leading divisions of II (US) Corps. 9 (US) Division would arrive behind 1 (US) Division, and 3 (US) Division behind 45 (US) Division to take over advance whenever this proved necessary. The divisions on each route would leap-frog each other to keep up the momentum of the advance. Eighth Army would make its main effort in the centre, using the fresh 78 (Br) Division, supported by the Canadians, to attack Adrano through Catenanuova and Centuripe; 51 (Highland) Division would aim for Paterno; 5 and 50 (Br) Divisions of XIII (Br) Corps would make a feint at Catania, but would not press their attacks until XXX (Br) Corps' operations forced the Germans to withdraw all along the front. Alexander set 1 August as the target date for the resumption of the offensive.

In the north the two leading American divisions and the Canadians had some way to go before they could close up to the main Axis positions: 45 (US) Division had to fight hard to throw back 29 Panzer Grenadier Division on the coast road to reach San Stefano, and 1 (US) Division had an equally tough struggle with a battle group from 15 Panzer Grenadier Division to reach Nicosia. It took five days hard fighting before the Canadians and the Malta Brigade managed to drive the Germans out of Agira. On 28 July the two US divisions and the Canadians took their objectives with sudden and surprising ease. Mussolini had fallen on 26 July and by 28 July new directives had reached the German commanders.

The break-in and dog-fight phases were almost over. The stage was now being set by both sides for the final phase of the Battle for Sicily.

4

The Conquest of Sicily

'I believe, Führer, the time has come for us to examine the situation together attentively, in order to draw from it the consequences conforming to our common interests and to those of each of our countries.'

Mussolini to Hitler, 18 July 1943

As the news from Sicily deteriorated, Mussolini finally accepted Ambrosio's defeatist advice and telegraphed Hitler asking for a meeting between the two dictators. In this telegram he gave a clear indication that he was giving up the struggle. Hitler reacted swiftly and arranged to meet the Duce at Feltre in northern Italy. Hitler used the meeting for one purpose only: to put new heart into his old friend. He was so successful in this that Mussolini failed to mention any of the demands for German help which Ambrosio had put into his brief for the conference. While Hitler was haranguing the meeting in his usual way, news was brought in that Rome was being bombed. Even this dire news did not stir Mussolini into action. Ambrosio realized that Mussolini was a spent force and was no further use to Italy. On his return from Feltre he offered Mussolini his resignation. When this was refused, he threw in his lot with the high-ranking military officers in the Commando Supremo who were preparing for Mussolini's overthrow. Ambrosio realized better than most of the conspirators, because he had the necessary information, just how difficult breaking the German Alliance was going to be. He could not risk the Germans learning what was afoot, so he had to play a double hand: one with the King and Field-Marshal Badoglio (Mussolini's successor designate) and the other with Kesselring and the Germans. He co-operated fully with OKW in transferring 29 Panzer Grenadier Division to Sicily because he had agreed to this some time before. He also accepted in principle the transfer of 71 and 305 German Infantry Divisions from France

68

to Italy and the strengthening of Baade's anti-aircraft defences at Messina. He was not, as yet, ready to resist further German reinforcements.

Mussolini's failure to put Italy's case to Hitler at Feltre and the bombing of Rome's railway marshalling yards persuaded the King, as well as Ambrosio, to act against him. The King asked Mussolini in an indirect way to resign, but the Duce failed to realize what was expected of him; and so the King instructed his staff to arrange for his arrest when he came to the palace for his next audience, which was due on 26 July. The Commando Supremo was fully aware of the plot and arranged for two reliable divisions—the Piave and the Ariete—to move into Rome to neutralize any counter-action by the Fascist Militia. Mussolini then unwittingly stage-managed his own overthrow. Grandi and Ciano, leaders of the dissident Fascists, realizing something was afoot, were determined to make their own claims to the succession. On their advice, Mussolini called the Fascist Grand Council for a meeting on 24 July at which he was decisively outvoted for the first and last time in his career as Duce. When he reported the results of the meeting to the King at his audience on 26 July he tried to brush this defeat aside as a minor issue, but the King firmly demanded his resignation. As he left the palace Mussolini was arrested and driven away—ostensibly for his own safety—in an ambulance. Badoglio, and not Grandi or Ciano, was summoned to the Palace. The people of all Italy rejoiced and the Germans, for a time, disappeared from public view.

Both the Allies and the Germans were taken by surprise. The Allies had no agreed armistice terms available if the new Italian Government decided to seek peace. Hitler and OKW had been so satisfied by their efforts at Feltre that they had stood down the units alerted for Alarich. Rommel had been sent off to command the Army Group in Greece and the Balkans, and was now in Salonika instead of standing by with Army Group 'B' for the invasion of northern Italy. Hitler's first impulse was to seize Rome, the King, the Badoglio Government and even the Pope. His military advisers, for once, managed to persuade him to think twice before taking precipitate action and in the end he accepted the wisdom of making thorough preparations before attempting to re-establish Fascism by force.

Once more the Rommel and Kesselring schools of thought on Italian policy vied with each other. The first orders issued by OKW bore the Alarich stamp. Rommel was recalled to take command of Army Group 'B' at Munich. Von Rundstedt, C.-in-C. West, was ordered to despatch two divisions immediately to Italy and to earmark four more. 11 SS Panzer Corps with two Panzer divisions was to be withdrawn from the Eastern Front. General Student, Commander of XI Para Corps (1 and 2 Para Divisions), was to fly to Rome to take charge of 3 Panzer Grenadier

Division which was already there and 2 Para Division which would be flown into the Rome airfields from France as soon as possible. He had two tasks: to seize Rome and the Italian Government if ordered to do so, and to find and rescue Mussolini. For the latter task, Hitler sent him the famous Otto Skorzeny. Kesselring was to contact the new Government and to find out all he could about its policies, but he was also to prepare to evacuate all German troops south of Rome. If and when their withdrawal was complete, he would hand over command to Rommel who would be in overall charge of the defence of northern Italy and the southern approaches to Germany.

Kesselring saw Badoglio and Ambrosio on 26 July and was assured that Italy would remain faithful to her alliance with Germany and would continue with the war. Kesselring was convinced that they were telling the truth as, in fact, they were. Badoglio's policy was to try to persuade Hitler to make a joint effort for peace; only if this failed would he consider making a separate peace. Hitler did not accept Kesselring's appreciation of the situation, but it served his purpose to appear to do so. Kesselring was just the right person to sway the Italians into a false sense of security for long enough to enable Hitler to infiltrate enough German troops into Italy to overpower the Badoglio Government. Kesselring was instructed by special liaison officer on the part he was to play in the new plan to take over Italy by force if she defected—Plan 'Achse'. He was to assure Ambrosio of Germany's continued support and to offer him more German divisions to hold southern Italy. He was also to make plans for a quick withdrawal from Sicily and southern Italy in case Italy defected. He was thus given the incentive to prove his pro-Italian theories correct while at the same time carrying out the preliminary moves which would be needed if his appreciation of Badoglio's intention was proved wrong. Although he was not told what the future might hold in store for him he must have realized that, if he was right, he would remain C.-in-C., South, and Rommel would go back to Greece; and, if he was wrong, Rommel would replace him as soon as the withdrawal to the north was complete.

Badoglio's attempts to persuade Hitler to open a joint peace offensive met with no success. Like Mussolini before him he telegraphed Hitler asking for a meeting of Heads of Government to discuss joint policy, but he was rebuffed. The only concession he could obtain was an agreement for the Foreign Ministers and Military Chiefs of Staff to meet at Tarvis on 6 August. In the meantime, a dangerous situation was developing on the northern Italian frontiers. Ambrosio had accepted 26 Panzer Division in the middle of June, but it was only just beginning to move into Italy. In its wake there appeared 305 Infantry Division at Nice and 44 Infantry Division at the Brenner Pass, both intent on entering Italy. Although

Ambrosio had agreed in principle to two infantry divisions entering Italy, no dates had been fixed so far. The Italians started prevaricating, saying that there would be no trains available for at least ten days to move these extra divisions south. The Commander of 26 Panzer Division reported to OKW that his men had seen the Italians preparing the bridges in the Alpine passes for demolition. For several days the situation remained tense with Hitler determined to order Achse if he did not get his way. Only Kesselring's persuasiveness in the Commando Supremo and Badoglio's reluctance to break with Germany until he had given up all hope of a joint peace move prevented the crisis reaching breaking point. On 1 August Ambrosio authorized the entry of 44 Infantry Division. Hitler took immediate advantage of this concession and halted 44 Division in the Brenner to hold the pass open for the entry of the rest of Army Group 'B'. Kesselring played his part well by assuring Ambrosio that the hurried arrival of Rommel's divisions was necessary to forestall an Allied landing which the Germans thought might have been precipitated by the fall of Mussolini. Six German divisions marched into Italy in the next few days and 2 Para Division landed at Rome supposedly on its way to join 1 Para Division in Sicily. Four more divisions moved into the Italian Fourth Army area in southern France. Italy was fast becoming an occupied and surrounded country.

The ease with which Kesselring persuaded the Italians to accept these massive reinforcements should have allayed Hitler's suspicions, but they had just the opposite effect. He assumed, wrongly, that the Allies had rebuffed secret approaches which he was sure Badoglio had made when he became Prime Minister and, in consequence, Badoglio was now more willing to stay in the Axis camp. The reverse had, in fact, happened. Hitler's rebuffs had at last convinced Badoglio that there was no hope of a joint peace move. On 31 July the Crown Council had authorized approaches to the Allies. These approaches would take time to develop so the Germans would have to be placated for the time being—hence the fatal acceptance of 44 Division. Badoglio did not expect the flood which followed this minor concession but he had no means of stopping it as 44 Division was positioned to hold the gateway open.

When the Foreign Ministers met at Tarvis each side adopted a position which it did not mean and each knew that the other was lying. The Italians professed a determination to fight on but were already negotiating for peace; the Germans were eager to reinforce the defence of Italy, but were preparing to take Italy over by force of arms. The Italians accepted German reinforcements, but tried to have them deployed as far away from Rome as possible. The Germans accepted the continuation of the myth of Italian operational command, but strengthened their liaison staffs and brought in a further Corps Headquarters (LXXXVII Corps) to administer their units. The conference ended with both sides convinced that the dissolution of the Axis was not far off. No one on the German side had dared to mention that Rommel was the C.-in-C. (designate) for all German forces in Italy.

In Sicily, the immediate effect on the Axis side of Mussolini's fall was the disappearance of uncertainty and dual command. Hube had arrived in Sicily on 15 July with his XIV Panzer Corps Headquarters and had done as Hitler had ordered. He first claimed command over the Catania sector of the front where the troops were predominantly German. As 15 Panzer Grenadier Division fell back from Enna and Leonforte, XII (It) Corps could claim operational command with the Aosta and Assietta Divisions still in being, but both these divisions were gradually disintegrating and the arrival of 29 Panzer Grenadier Division enabled Hube to take over the northern sector as well. By the time Mussolini fell he was *de facto* commander of the whole front. Guzzoni still hoped to hold the San Stefano Line, but Hube received instructions from Kesselring on 27 July to prepare the evacuation of Sicily. And so it was that on 28 July the Germans pulled back abruptly into the main San Stefano positions, in some cases without telling those Italian units who were still loyally fighting with them.

Hube planned to withdraw in five phases. The first two phases were

11   *German evacuation plans and the Allied advance to Messina*

6 General George Patton with his escort in a Sicilian town

THE CONQUEST OF SICILY

7 Eighth Army enters Adrano, the key to the San Stefano Line

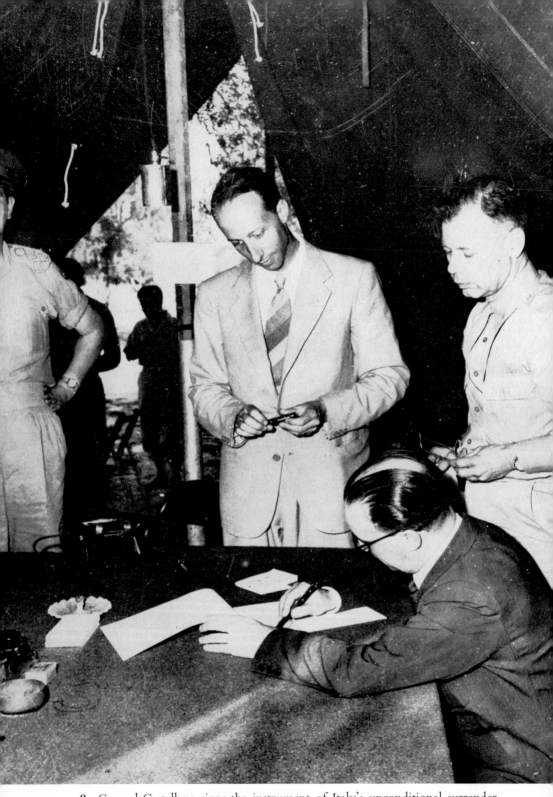

8 General Castellano signs the instrument of Italy's unconditional surrender in the presence of Brigadier Strong (*left*), Consul Montanari, Italian Foreign Office (*centre, standing*) and General Bedell Smith (*right*)

to be a continuation of Guzzoni's defensive battle and would be a slow withdrawal first to the San Fratello line, and then to a new and shorter Tortorici Line running from Cap Orlando on the north coast through Tortorici and Randazzo to Riposto on the east coast. The evacuation proper would then start using three phase lines which are shown in fig. 11. The evacuation itself was to take place over five nights. As each division retired from one evacuation phase line to the next, it was to despatch about a third of its remaining strength to one of five special ferries operated by von Liebenstein's German naval crews. The Italians had a similar plan for what remained of their Sixth Army and they had established four ferries at Messina for use of Italian troops. The chances of Hube's evacuation succeeding must have looked slender, even to Kesselring, when planning started on 28 July. Hitler expected only the men to get away and gave firm orders that men rather than heavy equipment were to be given priority.

Eighth Army reopened its offensive slightly earlier than Alexander's target date of 1 August. On the night 29–30 July, 78 (Br) Division with a Canadian brigade under command attacked Catenanuova to form a bridgehead over the Dittaino as a preliminary to their main attack on Centuripe. The attack was strongly resisted, but the well-trained and experienced 78 (Br) Division, who had fought in similar country all the previous winter in Tunisia, were not to be stopped. In four days brilliant fighting they cracked the centre of the German position between the Hermann Göring and 15 Panzer Grenadier Divisions, storming the heights of Centuripe on 3 August and forcing the Germans back to Adrano. Regalbuto fell to the combined efforts of the Canadian Division and Malta Brigade. Hube at once recognized that the San Fratello Line was now untenable and authorized a slow withdrawal to the Tortorici Line.

These XXX (Br) Corps successes soon had their effect on the Hermann Göring Division and Schmalz Group holding Catania and Gerbini. On 3 August XIII (Br) Corps detected withdrawals on their front and attacks by 50, 5 and 51 (Br) Divisions soon led to the capture of Catania, Misterbianco and Paterno. On 5 August, XIII (Br) Corps entered the narrow passage between Etna and the sea which the withdrawing Germans effectively blocked with mines and demolitions. XXX (Br) Corps found itself in a similar position forcing its way round the western side of the volcano. Both corps had more divisions than they could deploy on these narrowing fronts, so Eighth Army ordered the withdrawal of the Canadians and 5 (Br) Division into Army Reserve to refit for the invasion of Italy which was clearly imminent.

In the Seventh Army sector, Bradley's II (US) Corps never really halted. Its operations were continuous with regiments leap-frogging each other and divisions doing the same. 1 (US) Division had its hardest fight of the campaign when it broke 15 Panzer Grenadier Division's hold on Troina. It took six days hard fighting and the combined efforts of massed US artillery and the tactical air forces to make the Germans give way. Even then they withdrew in their own time to a new position at Cesaro on the Tortorici line which they reached on 6 August. 1 (US) Division was then relieved by 9 (US) Division whose objective became Cesaro. On the coast 45 (US) Division pushed 29 Panzer Grenadier Division back to San Fratello on 3 August when 3 (US) Division took over. Patton, however, was becoming agitated by the slowness of the advance. If he did not move quicker, Montgomery might break through and beat him to Messina. He decided to try a series of amphibious hooks behind the enemy on the coast road. There were only enough landing craft for one battalion group but this should be enough to hasten the German withdrawal. 29 Panzer Grenadier Division's stand at San Fratello gave him his first opportunity. He launched his first 'end run'* on 6 August when 3 (US) Division estimated that it was on the point of breaking through so that it could link up quickly with the amphibious force before the Germans could liquidate it. Unfortunately just as the battalion was about to embark the Luftwaffe raided the embarkation beaches and sank an LST. The operation had to be postponed 24 hours while a replacement was sailed from Palermo. When the attack did go in on the night 7–8 August, 29 Panzer Grenadier Division was already withdrawing and so only its rearguards were slightly delayed. The force was also landed on the wrong beaches, which did not help to make the operation a great success.

The losses of Catania, Adrano, Troina and San Fratello, convinced the Germans that the time had come to start the evacuation proper. Von Senger visited Kesselring and advised that it would be dangerous, and contrary to Hitler's orders to save manpower, to hold on any longer. Kesselring concurred, and, without consulting OKW, ordered the evacuation to begin as soon as Hube was ready. OKW heard the news on 9 August and for once Hitler accepted his subordinate's actions without demur.† Hube issued his evacuation orders on 10 August, naming D-day for Operation 'Lehrgang' as 11 August.

Alexander had suspected that a German evacuation was probable as early as 3 August and asked Cunningham and Tedder to co-ordinate plans

---

* Patton's expressive name for an outflanking attack from the sea taken from American football jargon.

† This incident should be noted because in the final Battle for Italy in the spring of 1945 Kesselring's successor von Vietinghoff failed to order a withdrawal in time and lost the battle. Kesselring would probably have ignored Hitler's orders to stand and fight in a hopeless military situation.

to take advantage of the situation. Cunningham replied that the operations of light naval craft would be intensified in the area, but that heavier naval units would not be able to intervene as they had done during the last days of the Tunisian battle unless the coastal batteries covering the narrow Straits of Messina were destroyed. This would take far too great an air effort to guarantee success, so he proposed that the main effort to stop the evacuation should come from the air forces who should be allowed to operate without restriction north of 38° north and east of Cape Milazzo on the north coast. Tedder agreed and directed General Spaatz, Commander of the Allied North West African Forces, to act accordingly. The subordinate air commands primarily involved were Air-Marshal Coningham's Allied North West African Tactical Force and General Doolittle's Allied Strategic Air Force. Working on the experience which they had gained in stopping the Axis evacuation from Tunis, the air commanders concluded that there would be no difficulty in preventing movement across the Straits in daylight. The problem was how to stop night traffic as well. Only a physical barrier such as a strong naval force across the Straits could make success certain in the dark, but the navy had already tried operating motor torpedo boats and motor gun boats in these narrow and heavily defended waters and had found that these craft were too slow to evade the fire of the coastal batteries. The only alternatives were to subject the embarkation and disembarkation points to steady bombing throughout the night and to depend on night fighters spotting the ferries in the moonlight. The final plan was to maintain constant air surveillance over the Straits to determine when the evacuation began. Coningham's tactical forces would then concentrate on keeping the Straits closed by day and the British Wellington night-bomber force would bomb the ferry terminals by night. Light naval forces would do what they could to help. The US Strategic day-bombers were to be on call for high level daylight attacks, but it was hoped that it would not be necessary to withdraw them from the strategic bombing programme aimed at disrupting Italy's communications before the next stage of the campaign. Most of the Allied commanders—land, sea and air—believed the evacuation would be spotted easily and would take place by night. There was thus little pressure to have the US Fortress bombers taken off the strategic programme to attack from high level during daylight. Hube, Baade and von Liebenstein had good reason to thank the Allied commanders for their complete misappreciation of the problem.

Hube handled the final withdrawal of his XIV Panzer Corps with great skill. On 12 August he ordered the evacuation of the Tortorici Line and pulled 15 Panzer Grenadier Division out of Randazzo and straight back to the ferries that night. This left the 29 Panzer Grenadier and Hermann Göring Divisions to conduct the final phases of the withdrawal. 29 Panzer Grenadier Division tried to hold its Tortorici position until 13 August to give 15 Panzer Grenadier Division plenty of time to get away to Messina, but Patton made this difficult by landing a second 'end run' on the night 11–12 August. A battalion group was landed at Brolo just behind 29 Panzer Grenadier Division's positions on the north-coast road. It was not strong enough to cut off the German battle group opposing 45 (US) Division and soon found itself heavily attacked and in considerable trouble. Fire from US warships helped it to maintain its position throughout the 12 August, and, although it could not stop 29 Panzer Grenadier Division withdrawing, it did accelerate the German division's withdrawal by about 24 hours. The American battalion group which landed suffered severely, and 29 Panzer Grenadier Division made up the lost time by delaying for an extra day in its position on Line 1. On the other coast, which was far steeper and more rugged than the north coast, the Hermann Göring Division, which contained strong elements of 1 Parachute Division, had no difficulty in fending off Eighth Army with heavy mining and demolitions covered by well sited rearguards. Montgomery was forced to bring 5 (Br) Division* back into the line alongside 50 (Br) Division to make any progress. Orders then arrived from Army Group setting the date for Eighth Army's next operation—an attack across the Straits of Messina—for 1 September, and so Montgomery was forced to relieve 5 (Br) Division with 51 (Highland) Division and to withdraw XIII (Br) Corps Headquarters who were also wanted for the invasion of Italy. XXX (Br) Corps took command of all British operations east and west of Etna. On 15 August 50 (Br) Division passed through the German Line 1, 48 hours behind the Hermann Göring Division's main body, and reached Taormina. They found the corniche road so thoroughly destroyed that the only way round was by sea. Rather belatedly Montgomery ordered forward an amphibious force, consisting of 40 (Br) Commando with tank and artillery support, to land just south of Scaletta on the German Line 3 on the night of 15–16 August. Patton, on the north coast, was trying to launch his third end run, this time with a regimental- instead of battalion-sized force. His target was Barcelona on the German Line 2, timed also for the night 15–16 August, but, unbeknown to the Allies, Hube planned to be clear of Line 2 by 14 August. In consequence, Patton's force waded ashore rather ignominiously behind the leading elements of 3 (US) Division as reinforcements instead of as a cut-off force. Montgomery's end run was no more successful. It landed just in

* Withdrawn to refit for the invasion of Italy (*see* p. 73).

front of Line 3 on the same night but was so impeded by demolitions that it was beaten into Messina by 3 (US) Division's 7 Infantry Regiment which entered the town on the evening of 16 August and was there to welcome the British Commandos as they drove in on the following morning. Patton had won his heart's desire—he had beaten Montgomery to Messina!

Baade and von Liebenstein had achieved the German 'miracle of Messina'. In the first two days of the evacuation they did as the Allies expected and tried to move everything by night, but heavy bombing by the British Wellingtons and the difficulties of directing units to the ferries in the dark made progress too slow. On 13 August von Liebenstein decided to risk daylight working to catch up his schedule. To the Germans' surprise losses were remarkably light and ferrying much swifter than by night. Baade's anti-aircraft batteries kept the low flying tactical air forces in check and as the American Fortress bombers had not been targeted on Messina there were no high-level attacks during daylight. Von Liebenstein continued ferrying in the dark during the night 13–14 August but found the Wellington attacks too persistent and so he went back to daylight ferrying for the rest of the operation. Alexander's headquarters were not sure that the evacuation had begun until 14 August—three days after it did in fact begin. By then it was too late to extricate the Fortresses from their strategic tasks to neutralize Baade's anti-aircraft guns, and it was also too late to stop Hube's force slipping away. All his men and heavy equipment was ferried over successfully, and he had sufficient capacity left over to give substantial help to the Italians. Much Italian equipment was, however, commandeered by the Germans and used to replace their losses suffered during the Sicilian campaign. Most German units re-entered Italy more mobile than when they left for Sicily some months before.

At 0635 hours on 17 August Hube reported to Kesselring and OKW that Lehrgang was complete. He, and not Montgomery or Patton, was the real winner of the race to Messina.

The Sicilian campaign was over. The island had been conquered in a mere 38 days. The Allies had achieved the three strategic aims which they had set for Husky. First, the Mediterranean sea-lanes had been cleared. No greater proof of this is needed than the unmolested concentration of the Husky assault shipping around Malta before D-day. Secondly, German pressure had been diverted from the Russian Front. The cancellation of Zitadelle only a week after it started showed the success of Husky in this respect. And thirdly, pressure was applied so effectively to Italy that the Allies gained the greatest prize of all. The fall of Mussolini was to lead to the total collapse of Italy and the diversion of a steadily increasing number of German divisions into Italy and away from Russia and North-West Europe.

Husky also laid two ghosts of the past. The spectre of Gallipoli was finally exorcised. The Allies had learned how to handle the vast concourse of ships and aircraft needed for a modern amphibious operation. They had proved techniques for handling men, equipment and stores across open beaches and they now had concrete experience upon which to base future landing operations. They knew where the main hazards lay and had good reason to know how much they had still to master in the techniques of airborne operations and close air support. The other ghost which was laid was the American feeling of inadequacy left by the battle of the Kasserine Pass. Sicily gave the American commanders and troops back their confidence and disproved the slighting criticism which this minor Tunisian failure had invoked of their fighting abilities.

The British staffs had a tendency to under-estimate the striking power, organizing ability and keenness of their American partners. They correspondingly over-estimated the abilities of their experienced but now cautious British divisions. The Americans, for their part, were apt to look for hidden British motives in many of 15 Army Group's orders which did not exist. Both Allies had learned more about handling the other. Both came to realize the differences of outlook and method, and both came to accept the need for equal shares in risk and glory.

The main strategic lesson of Sicily remained unnoticed at the time. The conquest of the island in little over a month obscured the sterling qualities of the Germans in defence and withdrawal. The performance of Hube's hard-pressed Panzer Corps in the ideal defensive country which abounds in southern Europe should have made the strategic planners pause for a moment. The military signs that the soft under-belly of Europe might turn into a crocodile's tail were already visible, but political events were to draw the Allies remorselessly on towards the frustrations of the Gustav Line, Cassino and finally the Gothic Line battles.

September–November 1943

THE FIRST BREACH IN FORTRESS EUROPE

'You are to plan such operations in exploitation of Husky as are best calculated to eliminate Italy from the war and to contain the maximum number of German forces.'

*Combined Chiefs of Staff Directive to Eisenhower
after Trident Conference, 26 May 1943*

5

Planning the First Breach

'... the alternative between Southern Italy and Sardinia involved
the difference between a glorious campaign and a mere convenience.'

W. S. Churchill, *The Hinge of Fate*

The Casablanca conference had set the Husky planning in train long
before the Allies could be certain of clearing the Axis out of North Africa.
The next Allied conference—'Trident', held in Washington in the first
weeks of May—set the stage for post-Husky operations six weeks before
Husky itself was launched. The Husky planners had been faced with many
imponderables, none of which could be answered until the operation
started. How would the Italians fight in defence of their homeland?
Would the Germans come to their aid in a determined way or would they
cut their losses and withdraw to the northern Apennines? Could the
Allies maintain their forces over open beaches? How many of their
precious landing craft would be lost? These questions were still unanswered
when the Trident conference began and so most of the arguments and
debating points were a repetition of Casablanca—with one essential
difference. The Americans felt that they had been overrun at Casablanca
by the large and well-prepared British team and that their case for the
cross-Channel strategy had been inadequately stated. At Trident they
were determined to do better and in this they succeeded. They restated
their case with great frankness and let it be known that, if the British
were not prepared to accept whole-heartedly the cross-Channel concept,
then the Pacific theatre would receive priority in the allocation of
American resources. The British delegation had no alternative but to
bow to this strategic blackmail. They were, however, determined not to
waste the great opportunities which seemed to be opening up before the

Allies in the Mediterranean. If these were seized with both hands, German strength would be diverted southwards away from North-West Europe and away from Russia in the most effective way open to the Allies in 1943. To the Americans, the Mediterranean was still a secondary theatre which, if not kept in check, would drain resources from the primary operations in North-West Europe. To the British, the Mediterranean operations were now an essential preliminary to the main cross-Channel assault; without them the Germans might never be weakened enough to make landings in northern France practicable. The outcome of Trident was a compromise biased towards the American position. The cross-Channel operation, now named Overlord for the first time, was to have first call on all Allied resources. The target date for the operation was fixed for 1 May 1944. Operations in the Mediterranean were to continue with the aim of driving Italy from the war, but the resources allotted to the theatre were to be reduced by transferring seven veteran divisions (four American and three British), together with most of the theatre's landing ships and craft, to the United Kingdom for Overlord. The last date for this transfer was to be 1 November 1943. Major amphibious operations in the Mediterranean would have to be completed by this date. What these operations should be was left to Eisenhower who was directed 'to plan such operations in exploitation of Husky as are best calculated to eliminate Italy from the war and to contain the maximum number of German forces'.

Churchill was far from satisfied with the outcome of Trident. His heart was already set upon the glittering prize of Rome, whose seizure might lead to far-reaching political consequences. The allegiance of many of Hitler's Eastern European satellites would be shaken; the subject Balkan peoples would be encouraged to redouble their efforts to regain their freedom; and it might be that the Allies would find the back door to Germany ajar. With Roosevelt's concurrence, he set off with General Marshall to discuss future plans for the Mediterranean personally with Eisenhower in Algiers. There were two broad alternatives; the eventual choice between them would depend on the outcome of Husky. If the Italians fought hard in defence of their Sicilian home island and the Germans helped them to do so, then it would be unwise to press on into Italy proper. Once committed to an invasion of Italy there could be no pulling back until Rome fell. Allied resources would be drained away from Overlord and the chances of releasing the seven divisions by 1 November would become very slender indeed. The alternative was to attack Sardinia and Corsica. This could be an operation of limited liability and was well within Allied resources even if Italian resistance in Sicily proved tenacious. From these islands the Allies could develop a threat to southern France and northern Italy which would pin down German divisions and prevent them moving towards Overlord. Furthermore, the Sardinian and Corsican airfields could be used to increase the weight of air attack on northern and central Italy. To Churchill, the Sardinian operation, which was codenamed 'Brimstone', was a poor second to Rome. To Eisenhower's planners, Brimstone seemed the only sensible course to take in view of the Trident limitation which would bring amphibious operations in the Mediterranean to a halt by 1 November.

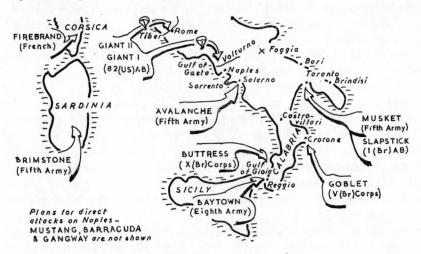

12   Post-Husky contingency plans

At General Marshall's suggestion Eisenhower set up two groups of planning headquarters to explore both possibilities. He gave General Mark Clark with his Fifth (US) Army Headquarters the task of planning the seizure of Sardinia (Brimstone) in conjunction with the French General Giraud who was to plan the re-entry of French North African troops into Corsica (Operation 'Firebrand'). Planning the invasion of the Italian mainland was given to two uncommitted British corps headquarters. General Horrocks' X (Br) Corps was to work out an attack on the 'Toe' of Italy, landing in the Gulf of Gioia (Operation 'Buttress'); and General Alfrey's V (Br) Corps was to plan a landing on the 'Ball' of the Italian 'Foot', aimed at seizing the port of Crotone and the nearby Axis airfields (Operation 'Goblet'). At this stage in planning it was impossible to forecast the state of divisions fighting in Sicily and so all these plans were to be based on using fresh divisions uncommitted to Husky. In the case of the British plans, Buttress and Goblet, it was to be assumed that there would be about a month's gap between the two to allow time for reassembly of assault shipping. Buttress would be launched first and, as X (Br) Corps fought its way northwards up the Toe, it would be helped forward by the landing of V (Br) Corps at Crotone in the German rear about a month later. From Crotone the Allied air forces would be able to cover the further advances of both corps towards Naples or Taranto.

These first tentative ideas for attacking the Italian mainland were very cautious and conservative. The Mediterranean planners envisaged such stiff resistance in the difficult mountain country of the Toe of Italy that they did not expect the two corps to fight their way much further north than the Castrovillari isthmus by Christmas. It is not surprising that the Sardinian and Corsican operations looked the more promising. Tentative plans were, of course, made for a sudden Italian collapse. In the first of these, Operation Mustang, the aim was to advance up the Toe with light forces to seize the port and airfields of Naples through which to land a force of six divisions and 43 squadrons of aircraft for a rapid advance on Rome. All subsequent plans to exploit an Italian collapse* envisaged taking Naples with an overland advance and landing only follow-up forces direct into the port. No one at this stage envisaged a direct amphibious assault into the Bay of Naples.

The keynote of all post-Husky planning had to be flexibility because the planners could not forecast the Axis reaction to the invasion of Sicily. Plans had to be ready to take quick advantage of any change in the strategic situation which everyone could sense was loosening up; and yet it was equally important not to have too many plans nor to leave the choice of plan too late for the executive staffs to mount the operations properly. There had been almost six months in which to get Husky ready. The post-Husky operations might have to be mounted in less than six weeks. Some nine different plans were worked out in detail between June and September of which only three were eventually used. As events unfolded these plans became more ambitious until in the end the Allies nearly over-reached themselves and came close to giving Hitler the decisive victory which he needed to restore his waning fortunes.

The news of the successful Sicilian landings and the collapse of Italian resistance transformed the planning atmosphere and swung the emphasis from excessive caution to galloping optimism. Three days after the assault Montgomery signalled to say that he would be in Catania by 14 July and should be in Messina soon afterwards. Hasty plans were made to hurry forward X (Br) Corps' Buttress plan on an *ad hoc* basis. Kesselring's rapid reinforcement of the Schmalz Group in front of Catania soon brought the planners back to a greater sense of reality. The Italians might be

* 'Gangway' and 'Barracuda'.

giving up, but the Germans certainly were not. Even so, it was clearly time to consider bolder operations to avoid being penned up in either the Calabrian Peninsula or Sardinia for the winter. Rome might be beyond the Allies' immediate reach, but Naples and Taranto offered promising targets. Taranto seemed the better of the two because, by seizing the Heel of Italy, the Allies would gain a defensible bridgehead with good ports and airfields from which to develop operations towards the great Foggia airfield complex and later to Naples and possibly Rome. An additional advantage of an attack on Taranto was that the operation could be covered by fighters based on the Crotone airfields, V (Br) Corps' target for Goblet, whereas Naples lay outside the range of shore-based fighters on Crotone.

Eisenhower held a senior commanders' conference on 17 July at which he decided that operations had gone so well in Sicily that he could drop the Sardinian operation in favour of an invasion of the Italian mainland. Mark Clark's Fifth Army was told to give up Brimstone and to hand its plans over to Giraud who would take on both Sardinia and Corsica with French troops. Fifth Army was to plan a new operation called 'Musket' aimed at the seizure of the Heel of Italy east of the line Taranto–Bari. Montgomery's Eighth Army was to plan an assault crossing—'Baytown' —over the Straits of Messina to clear the Toe. This operation was expected to run into very stiff opposition in the heavily defended area of the Straits and so X (Br) Corps' Buttress landing in the Gulf of Gioia was to be retained for the time being. V (Br) Corps' Goblet would still be needed to take Crotone, both to help Eighth Army's advance northwards and to provide fighter cover for Fifth Army's Musket attack on Taranto.

In Washington the success of the Sicily landings, while welcome, caused some re-thinking amongst the American strategic planners. The British plans for a methodical advance up the Toe seemed far too slow. General Marshall rightly suspected that, if Churchill did not get Rome before the winter, the British would insist on keeping all their resources in the Mediterranean at the expense of Overlord until Rome did fall. Encouraged by the poor Italian showing in Sicily, he proposed a major amphibious operation to capture Naples by direct assault. Churchill was delighted with this turn of events. It seemed to him that the Americans were at last coming round to his way of thinking. Nothing could have been further from the truth as far as Marshall was concerned; he was interested in finishing with the Mediterranean as quickly as possible. The British Chiefs of Staff, goaded no doubt by Churchill, seized their opportunity. Not only did they produce a previously prepared plan for an assault in the Naples area, called 'Avalanche', but they offered Eisenhower one extra fleet aircraft-carrier and four escort-carriers to ease the problems of fighter cover until shore-based fighters could be established within range of Naples. They also offered him 40 extra cargo ships to help lift vehicles and stores. Furthermore, they ordered a stand fast on all withdrawals of ships and men from the Mediterranean until Eisenhower was able to state exactly what he needed for Avalanche. These British measures made Marshall hesitate. It was quite clear that he was being dragged head-first into an enlarging Mediterranean commitment of the type which he had resisted for so long. The US Chiefs of Staff, unlike their British counterparts, decided that Eisenhower already had enough resources to mount Avalanche and would receive no more ships, troops or aircraft from American sources. This meant that the assault wave for Avalanche would be limited to a maximum of four divisions as opposed to the seven used in Husky.* Any doubts that the British or American staffs had about this limitation were soon swept aside by the startling news of Mussolini's fall. A new wave of optimism swept through the planning offices.

On 27 July, while Hitler was ordering the preparation of Plan Achse, Eisenhower was issuing orders for a new series of contingency plans. Mark Clark was to give up Musket which was cancelled and instead to plan Avalanche. As the operation involved a high degree of risk he was to have under his command one US and one British corps, each of one armoured, one airborne and two infantry divisions, of which only a maximum of four could be in the assault wave. There were three possible approaches: from the north over the beaches of the Gulf of Gaeta and across the flat plain of the River Volturno; direct into the Bay of Naples; or from the south from the Gulf of Salerno over the rocky Sorrento Peninsula. A direct attack was ruled out because of the strength of the enemy defences around the Bay. The flat northern approach was ideal for the Allied armoured formations, but the beaches, although practicable, were not good and were obstructed by sand-bars rather like Seventh Army's Gela beaches in Sicily. Intelligence reports also suggested that there were at least two German divisions within striking distance of this approach. By contrast, the Salerno beaches had steep underwater gradients and were excellent for landing men, tanks and vehicles dry shod. The beachhead at Salerno, however, would be closely overlooked by the surrounding hills and the approach to Naples over the Sorrento Peninsula would be difficult. Intelligence reports, on the other hand, showed that as yet there were no German divisions covering the area. The advantages

---

* Baytown, Buttress and Goblet would absorb at least two divisions' worth of assault shipping and losses since Husky was launched, due to enemy action, wear and tear, and to diversions to the Indian Ocean, accounted for a further division's worth of assault shipping.

and disadvantages of the northern and the southern approaches were thus evenly balanced.

The deciding factor which led to the choice of Salerno was air cover. Two-thirds of the Allied fighter force were Spitfires and Mustangs which, when fitted with long-range drop tanks, had a radius of action of 180 and 200 miles respectively. The remaining third consisted of longer-ranged Lightnings but there were not enough to give adequate cover beyond the Spitfire and Mustang range even when helped by the extra carrier-borne fighters provided by the British Chiefs of Staff. Tedder advised that he could cover Salerno but not the beaches north of Naples. Even over Salerno, Spitfires could stay over the beaches for a bare 20 minutes and Mustangs for about half-an-hour. If the northern approach had offered overwhelming advantages from other points of view, then some risks might have been taken with air cover. Remembering the criticism levelled at the air forces by Patton's Seventh Army during the Husky landings, Tedder naturally preferred to play safe and to press for the Salerno approach.

Montgomery was far from happy about the choice of Salerno. In his view the chosen landing area was too far north for the Fifth and Eighth Armies to support each other if either ran into trouble. He had forced the change in Husky plans for just this reason, but the situation was now different. Before Husky the Allies could not afford to gamble; now they were playing for higher stakes—Rome before Christmas—and against one opponent whose nerve was clearly shaken. They were ready to accept greater risks to exploit the obvious Axis weakness. After weighing the conflicting arguments carefully Eisenhower decided that Salerno should be the chosen site for the Allies' first major breach in Hitler's 'Fortress Europe'.

On 16 August, the day before Hube left Sicily, Eisenhower finalized his post-Husky plans as far as it was possible to do so at the time. Badoglio's announcement that 'the war goes on' fooled no one, least of all the Germans. Plans had to remain flexible to take advantage of a sudden Italian collapse and to avoid a German trap. Eisenhower was not certain whether Avalanche would prove practicable but he decided to go all out on the most ambitious plan. His decisions were:

1 Montgomery would launch Baytown across the Straits of Messina between 1 and 4 September using existing Eighth Army resources only. He would have to accept some degree of improvisation so that Avalanche could have as much assault shipping as possible.

2 Mark Clark would land at Salerno with the Avalanche Force

a week later on about 9 September. Fifth Army would consist of General Dawley's VI (US) Corps and General McCreery's X (Br) Corps.*

3 X (Br) Corps would be so loaded that it could take part in either Avalanche or Buttress.

4 Eisenhower hoped Buttress would not be needed and that Eighth Army would get across the Straits by itself without X (Br) Corps' help.

5 V (Br) Corps' Goblet would be held in abeyance.

The orders of battle for these operations are in Appendix D (*see* p. 330).

Everything seemed to be shaping well and the executive staffs were about to implement the latest version of the post-Husky plans when news reached Algiers that an Italian general called Castellano had appeared at the British Embassy in Madrid asking to make arrangements for Italy to change sides and join the Allies.

After the Crown Council in Rome on 31 July, Badoglio's Foreign Minister, Guariglia, despatched two emissaries to make tentative approaches to the Allies. The Marchese D'Ajeta was sent to the British Ambassador in Lisbon and Alberto Berio, a former counsellor in the Italian Embassy in Turkey, went to Tangiers to contact the British Consul. Both men described Italy's unhappy position, giving excellent reasons why she wished to change sides and stressing how difficult it was to do so with so many German troops in the country. Neither emissary offered unconditional surrender; on the contrary, in their view, Italy was doing the Allies a great service for which she would expect to be well rewarded. She had much to offer—a fleet, a large army and an air force with which to embarrass her former ally, Germany. D'Ajeta had memorized the complete German order of battle and dispositions in Italy and to show his good faith repeated them to the British ambassador. News of these peace feelers reached Churchill and Roosevelt on their way to the third Allied strategic conference—'Quadrant'—held in Quebec between 14 and 24 August. Neither of the Allied leaders received the news very warmly. Why should the Italians expect the Allies to help them break with the Germans and escape the just retribution of both sides? They must first accept unconditional surrender; then the Allies would state their terms. Churchill expressed Allied feelings at the time when he said 'Badoglio admits he is going to double-cross some one'. The Allies were not prepared to be his victims.

* General Horrocks had been wounded and was replaced as Commander X (Br) Corps by General McCreery.

Back in Rome, the Commando Supremo waited for the outcome of these feelers with increasing nervousness. German troops were moving into the country far quicker than was ever intended when Ambrosio sanctioned the entry of 44 Infantry Division through the Brenner. General Castellano, head of the plans and operations staff in the Commando Supremo and one of the principal military conspirators in Mussolini's overthrow, persuaded Ambrosio and Badoglio to let him go to Madrid with full powers to arrange a military *volte-face*. The King, however, was not prepared to give Castellano the necessary credentials until he was sure that the Allies would intervene in sufficient strength to save Italy from German reprisals. Castellano had to set off for Madrid as a representative of the Commando Supremo and not as a full plenipotentiary. To escape the Germans, he had to travel under an assumed name as part of an Italian diplomatic party going to Lisbon to meet the returning Italian Ambassador from Chile. During the delegation's stop in Madrid he presented himself to the British Ambassador, Sir Samuel Hoare, as an official emissary of the Italian General Staff. He explained Italy's plight and the possibility of the Germans re-establishing a Fascist regime by force if Italy did not make peace in time. Like D'Ajeta he gave exact details of the German dispositions and plans which, as a member of the Commando Supremo, he knew in greater detail than D'Ajeta. When asked by Sir Samuel Hoare about Italy's reaction to the unconditional surrender formula, Castellano replied that Italy was in no position to stipulate conditions but she had much to offer and, provided she was allowed to join the Allies fighting against Hitler's Nazi tyranny, he was sure unconditional surrender could be made acceptable to the Badoglio Government and the King. Sir Samuel Hoare was without instructions and so could only cable London recommending that Castellano should be treated seriously even though he had no credentials. As Castellano had to leave for Lisbon with his 'cover' delegation, Sir Samuel Hoare gave him a letter of introduction to the British Ambassador in Lisbon so that negotiations could be re-opened when he reached there.

In Quebec the Allied leaders were faced with two difficulties. The first was the absence of any agreed surrender terms. During the Trident conference the combined Chiefs of Staff had approved a draft list of 12 military clauses which Eisenhower proposed should be used as the basis for a military armistice if the Italians suddenly asked for terms. These clauses were known as the 'Short Terms' and included such essential military conditions as the repatriation of Allied prisoners of war in Italian hands, the surrender of the Italian Fleet and Air Force, the free use of Italian ports and airfields, the withdrawal of all Italian armed forces from foreign territory, guarantees that the Italians would use the armed forces remaining to them to ensure compliance with the armistice terms, and reservation of the rights of the Allied Commander-in-Chief to protect Allied interests in Italy. The British proposed a comprehensive list of 44 articles which included political, economic and financial terms as well as Eisenhower's military clauses. These 'Long Terms', being political, had been more difficult to agree and were still being argued in the Combined Civil Affairs Committee. Thus the only agreed document which could be used in negotiations with Castellano was Eisenhower's Short Terms. The second, and much more embarrassing difficulty, was the overwhelming military strength with which the Italians were crediting the Allies in the Mediterranean. If Castellano were to find out that the Allies could not land more than about six divisions and no further north than Salerno, he would quickly realize that they could not save Italy from German vengeance if she defected. Faced with these difficulties, the Combined Chiefs of Staff advised their political masters that Castellano should be told that the Allies would accept Italy's unconditional surrender on the basis of the Short Terms and that full political and economic terms would be put to the Italian Government later. Eisenhower should be instructed to send one American and one British senior staff officer to Lisbon to put these terms to Castellano and to arrange details of a military armistice. On no account should Allied operational plans be revealed, and Eisenhower should insist on the announcement of Italy's surrender being made just before Fifth Army landed at Salerno.

Eisenhower's position in the negotiations which followed was extra-ordinarily difficult. He needed the Italian surrender to give Avalanche a fair chance of success, and yet he could not sway the Italians either by revealing an overwhelming military posture which did not exist or by offering them co-belligerent status against Germany because this was contrary to the unconditional surrender formula. The most that the Combined Chiefs of Staff would allow was a hint that the Allied terms might be softened in proportion to the amount of help the Italians gave to the Allies as the war proceeded. Castellano was in an even more difficult position. He was not sure whether he would receive the support of his own Government in any agreement that he might reach; and, worse still, he was under the delusion that his task was to align Allied and Italian military policy for the defeat of Germany—a thing which the Allies were certainly not prepared to let him do. Castellano knew that Italy could break her German Alliance and change sides only when it was militarily safe for her to do so. Eisenhower, for his part, could only agree to her breaking her Alliance at one specific moment—when Fifth Army landed at Salerno on 9 September (a date not to be revealed to the Italians until the last possible moment to ensure no leak to the Germans).

The two staff officers who went to Lisbon were Eisenhower's Chief of Staff, the American General Walter Bedell Smith, and his Chief Intelligence Officer, the British Brigadier W. D. Strong. They arrived in plain clothes and met Castellano on 19 August. Bedell Smith informed Castellano with suitable abruptness that, assuming Italy was ready to surrender, he was authorized to present him with terms for a military armistice which must be accepted unconditionally. After studying the Short Terms, Castellano asked for clarification of a number of points and then came to the crucial issue. What were the Allied invasion plans and would they provide reasonable security for the Italian Government from German attack? Bedell Smith replied that, as a soldier, Castellano must know that such information could not be revealed. Brigadier Strong then questioned him closely on the German and Italian orders of battle. Castellano's replies were disquieting. The news he gave of German reinforcements showed that, if correct, the Allies had seriously under-estimated the opposition which Avalanche was likely to meet at Salerno. Castellano's knowledge of the military disposition in Italy seemed to corroborate D'Ajeta's information and be corroborated by intelligence from other sources. Bedell Smith and Strong concluded that he was genuine, but they could not help wondering why he carried no credentials. At the end of the meeting methods of secret communication, including a special wireless link and secret cyphers, were arranged with Castellano and it was agreed that if no reply was received from the Italian Government by 30 August the Allies would assume the rejection of their terms. If the terms were accepted Castellano should fly to Termini Imerse airfield on the north coast of Sicily on a pre-arranged course and at an agreed time on 31 August.

Castellano arrived back in Rome with the Italian Ambassador to Chile on 27 August. Having heard nothing from him for so long, the Commando Supremo suspected that he might have been caught by the Germans, so they despatched another emissary, General Zanussi; and with him they sent one of the most senior British prisoners of war in their hands, General Carton de Wiart, as further evidence of good faith. These two reached Lisbon on 25 August to find that Castellano was already on his way back to Rome with the Short Terms. The day before, in Quebec, the Allies had agreed to the Long Terms. These were cabled to Lisbon and handed to Zanussi. When Eisenhower heard this he realized that his task of persuading the Italians to surrender would be jeopardized if the Long Terms, with their harsh political interpretation of unconditional surrender, came into Badoglio's hands too soon. D-day for Avalanche was only two weeks ahead. Castellano was going to have a difficult enough time as it was persuading Badoglio, Ambrosio and the King to accept the

Short Terms. Eisenhower appealed to the Combined Chiefs of Staff and was fortunately authorized to proceed on the basis of the Short Terms. Zanussi had to be stopped sending the Long Terms to Rome. This was done by inviting him to Eisenhower's headquarters in Algiers. He accepted and, as a precaution against loss during the journey, he handed back his copy of the Long Terms for safe transit to Algiers. Once in Algiers he was closely interrogated to find out why a second emissary without credentials had arrived. It soon became clear that he represented a different and perhaps rival faction in the Commando Supremo. Eisenhower decided not to risk sending him back to Rome with his knowledge of the Long Terms. Instead Zanussi was allowed to send back his interpreter, Lieutenant Lanza, with a letter for Ambrosio urging the acceptance of the Allies' terms and suggesting that Ambrosio could depend on the Allies' good faith to ease the harshness of unconditional surrender if Italy co-operated to the best of her ability.

Castellano did not receive a warm welcome in Rome when he described the terms. The Allies' insistence on announcing the armistice just before the invasion was no good to the Italian Government. They would be behind German bars or in front of a firing squad before the Allies could reach them. They did not object to the Short Terms as such; it was the timing of their implementation which caused the difficulty. Badoglio was about to send a message to Eisenhower over Castellano's secret link asking for reconsideration of the timing of the announcement when Zanussi's letter arrived urging surrender. Badoglio decided to make one more effort by negotiation before finally accepting these dangerous terms. Castellano was given a written memorandum to take to Sicily explaining very fully the Italian difficulty in breaking the German Alliance. In his own hand, Badoglio wrote out strict guide lines for Castellano's last effort to sway the Allies. Amongst these instructions was the following paragraph which shows Badoglio's frame of mind: 'In order not to be overwhelmed before the English are able to make their action felt, we cannot declare our acceptance of the armistice except after landings have taken place of at least 15 Divisions with the greater part of them between Civitavecchia and Spezia.'

Castellano flew to Sicily on 31 August and was taken to Alexander's headquarters where he met Zanussi who had been flown there from Algiers. He read Badoglio's memorandum to the Allied delegation headed by General Bedell Smith, stressing that the Allies must make their main landing near Rome and with at least 15 divisions. Bedell Smith bluntly rejected this Italian condition. There were only two alternatives open to the Italians: accept or reject the Allied terms. He explained that Eisenhower had met with the greatest difficulty in persuading the Allied political leaders to allow him to offer a military armistice at all. This opportunity would not occur again. Next time the Italians would have to deal with the Allied political authorities and the terms would be far harsher. Whatever happened, Italy would be a battlefield between the Allies and the Germans; but, if the Italians co-operated now, the duration of operations would be far shorter and the damage to Italy much less than if she prevaricated. The Italian generals were in a cruel dilemma, but so were the Allies. Alexander, who was present at these talks, felt that the landings at Salerno were gravely threatened by the German military build-up in Italy and would only be worth risking if they coincided with the confusion caused by a sudden Italian capitulation. Much as the Allies might like to stick to the political formula of answer 'Yes' or 'No', to do so would jeopardise their chances of breaking into Fortress Europe without heavy casualties. As the parley progressed it became clear that some concession would have to be made by the Allies. Castellano was asked what he needed to make the terms sufficiently acceptable for him to sway his Government. In reply, he suggested an airborne division should be dropped near Rome and an armoured division should be landed at the mouth of the Tiber. After consulting Eisenhower by radio, Bedell Smith agreed to the former but could not promise the latter. This concession helped Castellano who then agreed to urge his Government to accept. With this the meeting broke up and the Italians returned to Rome.

Castellano's return to Rome with this minor concession did not help Badoglio. General Carboni, who was in command of the Italian Motorized Corps in the Rome area and upon whose shoulders would fall the responsibility for defending the King, Government and City of Rome from the Germans, advised against acceptance because he considered his task was impossible. The King unexpectedly bowed to the inevitable and despite Carboni's views authorized Badoglio to accept. A signal was sent to Sicily late in the evening of 1 September agreeing to the terms. Castellano flew back once more, thinking that Badoglio's signal of acceptance finalized the armistice and that his task was now to arrange the details of Italian military co-operation to ensure the success of the invasion and the safety of the Italian Government and Commando Supremo. He was taken aback when General Bedell Smith confronted him with an instrument of surrender and asked him whether he had Badoglio's authority to sign. He had not. The Allied officers gathered to witness this historic scene withdrew abruptly and left the Italians in their tent to think things over. Later in the day Bedell Smith returned and asked if Castellano wished to signal Badoglio for fresh instructions. This he agreed to do. Badoglio had been hoping that the Allies would not insist on the humiliation of a public acceptance of unconditional surrender.

In his view Italy's military co-operation with the Allies in their invasion of Europe would provide *de facto* recognition of Italy's surrender and acknowledgment of her break with Fascism. Castellano's signal showed that all hope of this had gone. The Allies were determined to stick to the letter of the Casablanca declaration and would divulge nothing of their plans until Italy signed the unconditional surrender documents. News was now coming in of Montgomery's successful Baytown operation. Eighth Army had crossed the Straits of Messina and was advancing up the Toe, meeting no Italian resistance and very few Germans. The time had come for Badoglio to make his final painful decision. At about 5 p.m. on 3 September his authority reached Castellano who then signed the instrument of surrender on Badoglio's behalf. Bedell Smith signed for Eisenhower in the latter's presence, and in the presence of Alexander, Cunningham and Tedder.

As soon as the brief surrender ceremony was over, the executive staffs set to work with feverish haste to send out instructions to implement the armistice. Detailed orders were given for the surrender of the Italian Fleet and Air Force, and arrangements were made for warning the Italian Government of the exact date of G-day (Great Day, i.e., D − 1 day of Avalanche). The BBC was to broadcast two short talks on Nazi activities in the Argentine between 11.30 a.m. and 12.45 a.m. on G-day. Eisenhower and Badoglio would announce simultaneously the armistice at 6.30 p.m. the same evening. Mark Clark's Fifth Army would land on the Salerno beaches in the early hours of the following morning. A much more difficult task was to work out the landing of 82 (US) Airborne Division on airfields near Rome on the evening of G-day which Bedell Smith had promised Castellano during the final phase of negotiations. General Ridgeway, the Divisional Commander, arrived at Alexander's headquarters with his staff during the afternoon of 3 September and worked all through that night making plans with the Italians for a parachute landing on the Rome airfields. 82 (US) Airborne Division had been scheduled to land on the bridges over the Volturno River in the Plain of Campania to stop German reinforcements rushing south towards Salerno. There had been some doubts about the wisdom of this plan because the Volturno was so far away from Salerno and on the far side of the city of Naples which would make a junction between the airborne troops and the main body of Fifth Army a very doubtful proposition. 82 (US) Airborne Division was taken off this dubious operation and given the even more risky task of helping the Italians to hold their own capital. Castellano gave a number of specific guarantees, such as the silencing of all anti-aircraft fire in the Rome area during the drop, the marking of the dropping zones with agreed light signals, and the provision of transport for the division at the dropping zones. The original Volturno landing had been called 'Giant'; the new operation became known as 'Giant II'.

By the time that the planning of Giant II was nearing completion on 4 September, General Ridgeway had begun to feel that his division was being thrown away on an impracticable adventure. He was almost certain that Castellano was offering more than he could reasonably achieve. In particular Ridgeway doubted if the Rome anti-aircraft defences could be silenced. Memories of Gela made him very dubious of the validity of the plan. He protested to Alexander and Bedell Smith, and it was agreed that two officers from the division and the supporting troop carrier force should go to Rome, ostensibly to finalize details with the Italians, but, in fact, to assess the feasibility of the operation. They were to travel with Castellano on his return to Rome that evening. Before they could leave it was decided that Castellano should stay with the Allies as head of an Italian military mission to Eisenhower's headquarters. Ridgeway selected his Artillery Commander, General Maxwell Taylor, and Colonel W. T. Gardner of the American Air Force Troop Carrier Command to travel by British motor torpedo boat to a rendezvous with an Italian corvette which would land them on the Italian coast near Gaeta. From there they would be taken to Rome in an ambulance, looking as if they were survivors from a crashed American aircraft. If Taylor decided that the operation was impracticable, he was to radio the single codeword 'Innocuous'.

As Castellano would not now be returning to Rome, he sent back written reports of his negotiations together with the instruments of surrender by air on 5 September. In these reports he made his own guess at the Allied timing of G-day. Quite incorrectly, he deduced from snatches of conversation that the main landing would take place between 10 and 15 September with 12 September as the most likely date. This guess was to have the most disastrous consequences for the Italian Government, the Italian armed forces and the Italian people.

By 5 September the Allies began to feel that, at last, they knew where they stood. Montgomery was across the Straits and was advancing northwards, impeded mainly by German demolitions, mines and small aggressive rearguards. The Italians had agreed to announce the armistice as the Avalanche force approached Salerno. The airborne operation against Rome was a grave risk, but its promise to Castellano had swung the balance at the crucial moment in negotiations. It could always be cancelled if Maxwell Taylor thought Italian reception arrangements inadequate. There was just time before G-day to exploit the Italian armistice in other directions. The Allied planners had for some time been considering snapping up the outlying Aegean Islands and also Crete if Italy surrendered.

This was a course which most armchair critics would have expected them to pursue, but the necessary troops and ships were just not available. There had been no replacement of assault shipping in the Mediterranean since the Trident conference decision to give Overlord priority. Moreover, some ships had been withdrawn for use in the Indian Ocean against the Japanese. Almost every available man, ship and craft was committed to Avalanche, Goblet and Montgomery's advance up the Toe. There were, however, two other tempting targets for which it might be possible to scrape together *ad hoc* forces. Sardinia and Corsica contained only one-and-a-third German divisions which should be hard put to it to contain the four Italian divisions in the islands if these were reinforced by the Allies. General Giraud was ready to use *coup de main* tactics to take both islands with his French North African divisions. He would have to use whatever French shipping he could scrape together but he was more than willing to do so. He was, therefore, given the 'go ahead'. The other target was the Italian Heel, with the large ports of Taranto, Brindisi and Bari as attractive prizes. If these could be taken, Eighth Army could be given its own ports on the east coast of Italy while Fifth Army operated up the west coast based on Naples. There was just one available Allied division uncommitted—1 (Br) Airborne Division which could not be used for Avalanche due to shortage of troop-carrying aircraft. Admiral Cunningham would be able to release warships as soon as the Italian Fleet surrendered and so a plan, appropriately codenamed 'Slapstick', was hurriedly put together to land the British parachute troops in Taranto from the cruisers and destroyers of 12th British Cruiser Squadron. The chances of success seemed reasonable now that Italian co-operation was assured. Taranto itself was held by the Italian Navy and there was not more than one German regiment—a parachute regiment—in the whole of the Heel area. If Taranto fell easily, V (Br) Corps could be diverted from Goblet and landed dry-shod from merchant shipping in the captured port.

Thus by 8 September, the eve of the Salerno landing, Montgomery had made a diversionary breach in Fortress Europe at the tip of a remote bastion. Mark Clark was now about to make a main breach and 1 (Br) Airborne Division another secondary breach, this time with the help of the local inhabitants of the Italian part of the Fortress. The Allies knew that the German garrison would react strongly; just how strongly only time would tell.

6

The Breach is Made

'How easily this critical time—"a dramatic week" even according
to the English—might have led to a decisive German victory if
Hitler had acceded to my very modest demands.'

Kesselring, *Memoirs*

On the day that Hube left Sicily with the rearguard of his XIV Panzer
Corps, Rommel moved his headquarters from Munich to Lake Garda,
well inside Italy, close to the vital Brenner Pass road and rail links with
the Reich. On the same day, 17 August, Hitler briefed another senior
Wehrmacht officer destined for Italy. He had appointed General von
Vietinghoff, a steady and reliable but thoroughly non-political infantry
officer of the Prussian Guards, to command the newly raised Tenth
German Army which was to control the two German corps in southern
Italy under Kesselring's overall command. The German forces in Italy
had risen in the first few weeks of August to 17 divisions including one
division in Sardinia. Five of these divisions were reformed Stalingrad
units which should have gone back to the Eastern Front, one was an
Eastern Front unit and the rest had been sent to Italy from North-West
Europe. The Allies were already achieving their strategic aim of drawing
forces from the Eastern Front and from the Overlord area.

The dispositions of the German divisions in Italy on 3 September when
Castellano signed the Armistice terms are shown in fig. 13. Each Army
Group had eight divisions which were deployed with three requirements
in mind. First and foremost, Rommel's Army Group 'B' was to ensure a
firm German grip on northern Italy which served as the glacis protecting
the southern approaches to the Reich. Its main defensive position would
be on the northern sweep of the Apennines between Pisa and Rimini
which became known later as the Gothic Line. Behind this line Rommel

was ordered to build up logistic facilities for a prolonged defensive battle and to pay particular attention to the defence of the two main passes into northern Italy—the Brenner from Germany and the Ljubljana Gap from Austria.

13   German dispositions, 3 September 1943

The second requirement was to be able to attack any Allied landing in its earliest stages and not to wait until sufficient forces had been gathered together for a major counter-attack. The German reading of the lessons of Sicily was that it was futile to counter-attack Allied beachheads once they were firmly established. The aim of all German commanders should be the disruption of the landing itself. If this failed, then it was better to carry out a methodical withdrawal to ground of German choosing to fight a normal land battle away from the broadsides of Allied battleships. The German operational staffs considered that there were five possible areas for an Allied landing: the Calabrian Toe, which was nearest to the Allies in Sicily; the Heel, covering the ports of Brindisi, Bari and Taranto; the Naples area; the Rome area; and finally the Gulf of Genoa. They eliminated the Heel and the Gulf of Genoa as most unlikely and concentrated upon the defences of the Toe, Naples and Rome.

Each of the potential Allied landing areas was made the responsibility of a German corps commander who was to co-operate with the Italian troops in the area as far as practicable. The Toe, together with the low-priority Heel, was given to General Herr's LXXVI Panzer Corps which was responsible for all of Italy south of the line Salerno-Bari. Kesselring believed it would be dangerous to hold the Toe in strength because the garrison could be cut off so easily by an Allied landing in its rear. There were advantages, however, in trying to entice as large an Allied force as possible into the Calabrian cul-de-sac where it could be contained with very few troops at the Castrovillari isthmus. The topography of the Toe was ideal for defensive fighting and so Herr was given only three weak divisions for his task of luring the Allies into this inhospitable area. 29 Panzer Grenadier Division was deployed in southern Calabria. It had suffered severely in Sicily and needed rest, but it did possess all three of its panzer grenadier regiments. 26 Panzer Division, an ex-Stalingrad unit, was positioned behind 29 Panzer Grenadier Division to support it and to ensure the defence of the Castrovillari isthmus. 26 Panzer Division had left its panzer regiment behind in the Rome area to help overawe the Italian capital, and so had reached Calabria with only its two panzer grenadier regiments. Herr's third division was 1 Para Division which could muster barely one parachute regiment and was stationed at Alta-mura within reach of the Heel ports of Bari and Taranto. Thus Herr had just six regiments in his three divisions to cover the vast area of the Toe and Heel with their long and vulnerable coast-lines. If the Italians fought as badly as they had done in Sicily, his chances of stopping an Allied landing were small, so he was instructed to make no attempt to hold the Straits of Messina but to withdraw under pressure to Castrovillari. The country was so mountainous and so easily defended that very few troops, well supported by sappers to blow and mine the roads, should be able to, and did, hold up an Army—the Eighth Army.

The Naples Area was made the responsibility of Hube's XIV Panzer Corps when it returned from Sicily. Like Herr, he was given a slice of the Italian Peninsula east and west through Naples but his primary responsi-bility was the defence of the Port of Naples which he entrusted to his well-tried Sicilian divisions—the Hermann Göring and 15 Panzer Grenadier. 16 Panzer Division was already stationed on the Adriatic side of his sector near Foggia. The Germans appreciated, as the Allies had done, that there were the three approaches to Naples: from the Gulf of Gaeta; through the Bay of Naples; and from Salerno. In their view the northern approach was the most likely. The direct approach was too heavily fortified and the southern approach seemed to them to be so easily defensible as to make it unlikely. If it were attempted, an Allied landing at Salerno could be quickly blocked. In consequence, Hube disposed his two divisions in and to the north of Naples. Salerno was left to the Italians.

The Rome area presented rather a different problem. There were two different contingencies and a combination of the two to consider. The Allies might land astride the mouth of the Tiber, hoping to reach the Italian capital before the German forces could intervene, but this did not seem very likely to Kesselring who, as an airman, appreciated the Allies' problem of fighter cover. The second contingency was an Italian rising in the city concurrent with an Allied landing further south. Or thirdly, it was just possible that the Allies might attempt a landing in the Rome area in conjunction with a revolt in the city, but Kesselring thought this less likely than the second contingency. General Student's XI Parachute Corps was made responsible for the area with the primary task of preventing or snuffing out a revolt in the city; defence of the coast was to be only a secondary consideration. His divisions were 2 Para and 3 Panzer Grenadier Divisions reinforced by 26 Panzer Division's panzer regiment. Student's Corps came directly under Kesselring. Hube and Herr were commanded by von Vietinghoff's Tenth Army which was responsible for what the Germans expected to be the main operational front if the Allies landed in Italy.

The third principle led from the second. The ground of the Germans' own choosing, to which they would withdraw if they failed to defeat the Allies on the beaches, consisted of a series of defensive lines stretching across the peninsula upon which they could block the Allies' advance northwards and, if a suitable opportunity arose, from which they could mount a counter-offensive.* Under the most favourable circumstances they would try to hold south of the Port of Naples and the Foggia airfield complex. The next line, which had been surveyed in detail by the Italian General Staff, was designed to cover Rome and the Rome airfields. It ran from Gaeta to Isernia and then to Vasto on the Adriatic, and became known as the famous Gustav Line centred upon Cassino. North of Rome there was a third line from Grosseto through Lake Trasimene to Ancona. And finally there was the Gothic Line in the northern Apennines. The German policy was to give nothing up until they were forced to do so, but to be prepared to withdraw gradually northward under pressure, abandoning southern and central Italy. This unusual and, as it turned out, short-lived German policy was accepted by Hitler through two misappreciations. The first was an over-estimate of Allied strength and intentions in the Mediterranean; and the second was an under-estimate of the German ability to deal with Italian treachery. OKW

* See map of Southern Italy, front end-paper.

felt that Italy south of the Gothic Line had far too long a coast-line to be defended successfully against Allied amphibious attack. They did not believe that Eisenhower's forces would be content to fight their way laboriously up the peninsula. As soon as the Allies had established air bases on the Italian mainland they would work their way north using sea and air power. The German divisions must be ready to pull back swiftly if their flanks were turned from the sea. The danger of Italian defection increased the risks of keeping forces in central and southern Italy. OKW had no high opinion of Italian fighting ability, but Italy still had a very large number of men under arms and the Germans knew that the Italian people believed that Germany stood between them and the peace for which they longed. An Italian rising could have disastrous consequences for their troops in the south. Rommel would have his hands full dealing with the turbulent people of the north. Kesselring would have to do the best he could to keep his communications open through Rome so that Tenth Army could withdraw if either an Allied landing, or an Italian revolt, or both, made it necessary.

What turned out to be the final revision of Plan Achse was issued by OKW on 30 August. It now contained instructions on how to treat the Italian units if Italy defected. The Germans were to disarm their former allies, by force if need be, and to offer their soldiers the choice of joining German units or of going home. The German Navy was to take over the Italian Fleet, and the Luftwaffe was to seize the Italian aircraft. The division of opinion between the Rommel and Kesselring schools still remained. Kesselring was optimistic about the outcome and believed that there would be no need to evacuate central Italy although he conceded the loss of the extreme south. He also felt that, with careful handling, many of the Italian divisions could be kept on the German side. Rommel still held to his strong conviction that Kesselring was wasting German time and effort on the worthless Italians. In his orders to his Army Group for Achse the Italian units were not only to be disarmed but were to be taken prisoner ready for transfer to Germany as a labour force.

Montgomery's attack across the Straits of Messina started at 4.30 a.m. on 3 September to the accompaniment of a full orchestra of naval guns, air bombardment and a field-artillery barrage. Destroyers lay off the coast bombarding; the Desert Air Force flew offensive patrols overhead; and 630 guns belonging to Seventh and Eighth Armies fired a heavy programme in support of the leading troops of XIII (Br) Corps, as they landed just north of Reggio de Calabria with 5 (Br) Division on the left and 1 (Cdn) Division on the right. No Germans were met and the few Italian troops in the area made no attempt to resist. The Eighth Army had struck air. 29 Panzer Grenadier Division had wisely retired north of Reggio two days before the attack and escaped Montgomery's preparatory bombardment. Most of the Italian coastal units surrendered themselves intact to XIII (Br) Corps without even a show of resistance. The people of Calabria cheered the arrival of the British and Canadian troops. At last they would be free from the constant air attacks.

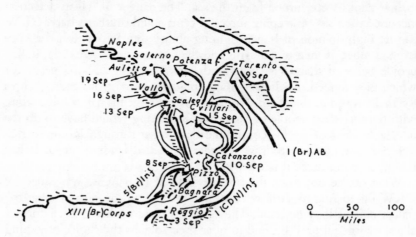

14 *Eighth Army's operations in Calabria, 3–19 September*

Eighth Army's advance north was delayed more by demolition and mines than by enemy resistance. Most of the troops were moved up the coast in a series of amphibious hooks, but even so progress was slow. The first real contact with 29 Panzer Grenadier Division occurred at Bagnara during the night 3–4 September when the Special Air Service Brigade landed on the coast ahead of 5 (Br) Division. The Germans soon withdrew and, by 9 September, D-day for Avalanche, XIII (Br) Corps was approaching Eighth Army's first major objective—the Catanzaro Isthmus.

We must now return to the crucial events which had been taking place in Rome since the secret signing of the Armistice on 3 September. Eisenhower had every reason to expect the Italians to be working feverishly and covertly to give his invasion, when it came, all possible help. They had been so keen in the early negotiations to change sides and they now had the added incentive to soften the harshness of the unconditional surrender terms by giving the Allies really effective help. Just the opposite was happening in Rome. Castellano's inaccurate guess about the Allied timings and his over-optimistic military undertakings began to have their effect. Ambrosio noted Castellano's estimate of 12 September as the Allied G-day but did not appreciate the flimsy nature of the evidence upon which it was based. He reported the date to Badoglio and other senior officials and in so doing gradually sanctified 12 September as a firm Allied undertaking. The Italian officials in Rome were thus basing their policies on acting three days later than the Allies intended. Secondly, General Roatta, the Army Chief of Staff,* and General Carboni, commander of the Italian Mobile Corps defending Rome, were not kept informed of Castellano's military arrangements for 82 (US) Airborne Division's drop on Rome's airfields. When they heard the details, they advised Ambrosio and Badoglio that they were not prepared to carry them out because they were quite impracticable. Carboni knew his divisions would be no match for Student's Parachute Corps if the only help he was to receive from the Allies was to be one American airborne division. Roatta, however, had been arranging the concentration of two more Italian divisions in the Rome area and these would be in position by 15 September. He advised Badoglio to ask Eisenhower for a postponement of G-day from 12 to 15 September at the earliest. Badoglio accepted the force of Roatta's arguments and early on 8 September, thinking there were at least four more days before G-day, signalled Eisenhower on Castellano's secret wireless:

> Due to changes in the situation brought about by the disposition and strength of the German Forces in the Rome area, it is no longer possible to accept an armistice as this could provoke the occupation of the Capital and the violent assumption of the Government by the Germans . . .

General Taylor and Colonel Gardner, who were in Rome and had taken part in the final discussions within the Italian hierachy, realized that the situation in the Italian capital was hopeless and so sent the Giant II cancellation codeword 'Innocuous' at about 1130 on the morning of 8 September, hoping it would reach the division in time to stop the troop carriers taking off.

The arrival of Badoglio's signal caused consternation in Algiers. Eisenhower was on his way to his advanced headquarters at Bizerte. His Algiers staff relayed Badoglio's signal straight away both to Eisenhower and to the Combined Chiefs of Staff requesting instructions. Eisenhower's reactions can be imagined. Furious with Badoglio for what appeared to be a double-cross and equally annoyed with his own staff for signalling Washington for instructions, he drafted a curt reply to Badoglio to the effect that he was going to announce the armistice as originally planned

---

* Roatta became Army Chief of Staff when he was relieved by Guzzoni in Sicily. The post of Army Chief of Staff should not be confused with Ambrosio's post of Chief of Staff of the Armed Forces. Roatta administered the Army only; Ambrosio was military adviser to the Italian Government on land, sea and air policy.

and if the Italian armed forces failed to comply he would publish the full record of the whole affair to the world. Plans had been made on the assumption of Badoglio's good faith. If he did not carry out the full obligations of the signed agreement no future actions of his would restore confidence and the downfall of his government and country would ensue.

Eisenhower informed the Combined Chiefs of Staff of his action and received their full support. At 6.30 p.m., as planned, Eisenhower announced the Armistice over Algiers Radio, but no corresponding announcement came from Rome. After waiting ten minutes Eisenhower ordered the agreed text of Badoglio's announcement to be broadcast in English. An hour later, at 7.45 p.m., Badoglio was heard announcing the surrender over Radio Roma. Eisenhower's threat to publish the story of the armistice negotiations had proved decisive. However much the Italians might wish to repudiate their agreement with the Allies, it would do them no good because Hitler was more likely to believe the Allies than the Badoglio Government. Whatever course Badoglio took, Rome was bound to fall into German hands. Badoglio himself refused to make the final decision. He offered the King his resignation so that the agreement could be repudiated if the King so wished, but Victor Emmanuel realized that he could not change sides again. He refused Badoglio's resignation and authorized him to broadcast the announcement.

The full folly of the Italian Government and Supreme Command was yet to be revealed. The original decision on 3 September to allow Castellano to sign the instrument of surrender seems to have robbed them of power of decision and sense of reality. Unlike the Germans, who had made meticulous plans to protect themselves against Italian treachery, they had made no attempt to work out how they were going to throw off the German yoke or even how they proposed to help the Allies to do so for them. The Fleet and Air Force received their instructions on how to surrender when the time came because these instructions were part of the Short Terms which Castellano had accepted. The actual details had been worked out by the Italian naval and air force liaison officers belonging to Castellano's mission in Algiers. The Italian Army and Civil Government departments received no instructions at all. Badoglio was frightened that a premature leak might occur and Ambrosio felt there would be time to issue instructions just before 12 September. The Army Chief of Staff, Roatta, had issued a directive at the end of August giving instructions on action to be taken if the Germans tried to reimpose a Fascist regime by force. He intended to amplify these instructions for use in the new circumstances, like Ambrosio, just before 12 September. Eisenhower's announcement took everyone by surprise. By dawn on 9 September, it was clear that the Germans had reacted strongly to the Badoglio announcement and were attacking Rome. The King, Badoglio and all the high-ranking military staff officers abandoned their headquarters and escaped in a convoy of cars to Pescara on the Adriatic coast, leaving no instructions and no one in charge of affairs in Rome. Their deputies and junior staff were left to fend for themselves. It was assumed that Carboni would take charge but no instructions were left for him to do so. Contact with Rome was effectively lost when the royal party embarked in an Italian warship and sailed for safety behind the Allied lines.

Kesselring's reactions were very different. His Chief of Staff, Westphal, was conferring with Roatta at the Italian Army Headquarters when Jodl rang up from OKW to ask for confirmation of the Italian surrender which OKW had just picked up from Algiers Radio. Kesselring rang Westphal who was assured by Roatta that it must be an Allied trick to put the two Axis powers at each other's throats. Roatta probably said this in good faith because he knew Badoglio was actively engaged in delaying G-day to 15 September. His surprise was so genuine that he did not have much difficulty in convincing Westphal of his sincerity. An hour later, Badoglio's announcement made Kesselring realize that Hitler had been right in his suspicions of Italian treachery. Without any hesitation he ordered Achse, determined to make good the ground he had lost through trusting the Italians too far.

8 September had been a trying day for Kesselring and his staff. They had been keeping a careful watch on the courses of the approaching invasion convoys which the Luftwaffe had been shadowing since 5 September. It was still not clear where the landing would be made. At about midday, his headquarters at Frascati was heavily bombed by Allied aircraft. Kesselring and his principal staff officers were shaken but unhurt. His communications were severed for a short time but, thanks to the efforts of his chief communications officer, these were soon restored. It was clear that the Allies had something big afoot and someone had given away the exact location of his headquarters. Achse went into operation with the smoothness associated with most German General Staff contingency plans. The Italian commanders, being without instructions, could only place their own interpretation on Badoglio's broadcast which had ended with the words, 'The Italian armed forces will therefore cease all acts of hostility against the Anglo-American forces wherever they may be met. They will, however, oppose attacks from any other quarter.' They had not been instructed to attack the Germans. Unless the Germans attacked them they had no need to react. To most of the Italian commanders, the humiliation of their position was such that they were prepared to hand over their arms to the Germans when asked to do so and even go

so far as to wish them luck in their continued fight with the Anglo-Americans. In the north, Rommel's Army Group 'B' had little difficulty in disarming the Italians in his area. Much to Kesselring's annoyance, he wasted time and effort taking them prisoner instead of dispersing them to their homes. The Italian Fleet escaped because the Italian Naval Chief of Staff, Admiral de Courten, had persuaded the Germans the day before that it should put to sea to attack the approaching invasion convoys. Admiral Bergamini sailed the La Spezia and Genoa Divisions of the Fleet southward along the western coast of Corsica as instructed by the Allies, but before he could reach the safety of Allied air cover Achse was ordered and his ships were attacked by German aircraft using the new wireless-controlled glider bombs. The flagship, *Roma*, was sunk taking the Admiral and most of her crew with her. The rest of the fleet escaped damage and joined the other division of the Fleet from Taranto in their surrender to Admiral Cunningham in Malta—a very proud day for the Royal Navy. The Italian Air Force reacted half-heartedly. About 300 pilots took their planes to Allied airfields; the rest dispersed to their homes or were taken prisoner.

In the south, the German Tenth and Italian Seventh Armies had been collaborating closely in their plans to defend Italy. There was mutual respect between the two staffs, who were both taken by surprise when they heard Badoglio's announcement. Arisio, the Seventh Italian Army Commander, felt utterly humiliated by his Government and willingly turned over vehicles, equipment, supplies and installations to von Vietinghoff. Most of his subordinates followed his lead and gave up their defensive positions and equipment to the Germans. Von Vietinghoff pursued Kesselring's policy of sending the disarmed soldiers back to their homes instead of taking them prisoner. He needed every German soldier to oppose the Allies and could not afford the extra burden of finding prisoner escorts as Hitler and OKW would have liked.

Kesselring heard of the Allied landings early on 9 September. His worst fears were now over. Rome was not the Allies' immediate objective. He had been wrong about the Italians but he had been right about the Allies' military planning. The factor of fighter cover had, as he thought, dominated their thinking. He now knew exactly where he stood. Moreover, he was free from OKW interference because Hitler was so sure that Kesselring would not be able to extricate Tenth Army that he abandoned him to his fate and turned to Rommel to stabilize the situation. Kesselring had two immediate tasks: to clear his communications through Rome and to support von Vietinghoff at Salerno. He could see no reason to abandon southern Italy until he was sure that the Allies could not be forced into another Dunkirk.

In Rome, Student lost no time in putting Achse into effect. The German ambassador and diplomatic staff all left for the north with indecent haste, but military commanders soon gripped the situation. A parachute battalion from 1 Para Division at Foggia, implementing a pre-arranged plan, dropped on the Italian Army Headquarters at Monterotondo, outside Rome, but were just too late to catch Roatta. 2 Para Division and 3 Panzer Grenadier Division advanced on the city from south and north, calling upon the Italian divisions not to fire on their former comrades. Some of Carboni's Corps opposed the Germans and fought well. Others gave up without a show of resistance. By the evening of 9 September the Germans had persuaded a number of Italian commanders to open negotiations for a cease-fire. Kesselring left the arrangements to his able Chief of Staff, Westphal, who used a mixture of sympathy for the Italian Army in its predicament and open threats, including the bombing of Rome, to induce surrender. The leaderless Italians argued amongst themselves for a time and in the end one of Badoglio's rivals, the aged Marshal Caviglia, took the responsibility on his own shoulders and authorized the capitulation of the city. Kesselring was master of Rome, and of his lines of communication with the north and the south, by nightfall on 10 September. He could now turn his full attention to defeating the Allies and proving the Rommel school wrong.

Unbeknown to the Germans the shadow of the Trident conference decisions was already falling across Allied operations in the Mediterranean. Husky had been mounted with seven divisions in the assault wave. Shortage of shipping eventually reduced Avalanche to three divisions in the assault wave with two in the follow-up. Admittedly Eighth Army was bringing two more divisions up the Toe, but there would not be more than seven Allied divisions operating against the eight German Divisions in Kesselring's Army Group. Had it not been for the British Admiralty's unilateral action in sending back ten large troop ships to the Mediterranean and allowing the retention of British assault craft which should have gone elsewhere, Avalanche would have been weaker still. If the Italians did not oppose the Germans as strongly as Eisenhower hoped, Fifth Army's five divisions might well be faced with a superior German force before Eighth Army could reach Salerno.

In the air a similar situation had arisen. Eisenhower had been forced to surrender three medium-bomber groups to North-West Europe. Tedder had asked for more Fortress bombers and Lightning fighters, but these were refused because the combined bomber offensive against Germany, which needed heavy fighter escorts as well as bombers, had overriding priority. Thus the Allied air effort before Avalanche was weaker than it had been before Husky and, to make matters worse, operations were now within range of a greater number of German air bases. Tedder's ability to create a favourable air situation was correspondingly reduced as events were to show. Again, if it had not been for the British Admiralty providing the extra fleet carrier and escort carrier group, fighter cover over the beaches would have been very sparse.

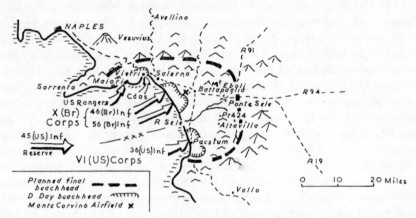

15   *The Fifth Army landing at Salerno and its progress up to the end of D-day*
(*9 September*)

Mark Clark's plan for Avalanche was to land McCreery's X Corps, consisting of 46 and 56 (Br) Divisions, on the northern half of the Salerno beaches, and Dawley's VI (US) Corps with only 36 (US) Division in the assault wave on the southern half. Two regimental combat teams of 45 (US) Division were to be in floating reserve and 7 (Br) Armoured Division would follow up into X (Br) Corps' sector after D+4 for the subsequent advance on Naples. The northern flank of the beachhead was to be secured by three battalions of American Rangers and two British Commandos, who were to land ahead of the main force to block the passes on the two roads leading south from Naples, by which the first German reinforcements were expected to arrive. After establishing their initial beachheads both corps were to exploit forward to establish a firm perimeter on the arc of hills which overlooked the beaches. The boundary between them was to be the Sele River and the Ponte Sele bridge on Route 19 was to be the junction point between the two corps on the perimeter. X (Br) Corps had the specific tasks of seizing the small port of Salerno and the Montecorvino airfield from which it was hoped to operate fighters by D+1. In the subsequent operations it was planned that X (Br) Corps should break out northwards and seize Naples by

21 September, when the first major follow-up convoy of troop ships was due to arrive.

Avalanche planning was bedevilled, like Husky, by wide dispersal of headquarters, troops and mounting ports. There was less absentee landlordism because Mark Clark and his subordinate corps commanders were free from current operations. In its place came the rush and confusion caused by last-minute uncertainty about which of the many plans would be implemented and what shipping would be available when the order to start loading was given. Mark Clark himself did not help matters by making changes up to the last moment such as advancing H-hour by 30 minutes on 24 August, and so upsetting all the detailed timings of convoys and assault waves. The haste with which orders had to be transmitted is illustrated by the state of Admiral Cunningham's copy of the Operation Order which is heavily amended in manuscript—the amendments not always coinciding with those on Admiral Hewitt's copy.[*]

The naval plan was very similar to the Husky deployment. The covering force which might be needed if the Italian Fleet did not surrender, was to be Admiral Willis' powerful Force 'H' with four battleships and two fleet carriers and 12th Cruiser Squadron with four cruisers. Force 'H' was to block an Italian approach from La Spezia and Genoa. A separate force of two battleships was to watch Taranto and the Adriatic. Inshore support for X (Br) Corps was to be given by 15th Cruiser Squadron of three cruisers, the anti-aircraft ship HMS *Delhi* and the monitor HMS *Roberts*; and for VI (US) Corps by four US cruisers and the British monitor HMS *Abercrombie*. Admiral Hewitt was in command of the naval assault force and flew his flag in the US Headquarters Ship *Alcon*, which carried Mark Clark as well. Submarines, which had reconnoitred the Gulf of Salerno, reported the bay to be mined and so the assault force was to be preceded by minesweepers to clear safe anchorages and lanes to the beaches.

The air plan was based on the three principles which were becoming standard in all Allied operations. First, the Luftwaffe was to be neutralized and driven back from its forward airfields by bombing and fighter sweeps; secondly, the Germans' ability to move up reinforcements was to be reduced by bombing vulnerable points in his road, rail and coastal shipping networks; and finally, fighter cover was to be provided over the assault area until such time as the Army broke out of its beachheads, the assault shipping dispersed and the whole area offered a less attractive target to the Luftwaffe. Close support to the Army would be provided from resources left over after these three primary tasks had been fulfilled.

[*] *The War at Sea*, Vol. III, Part I, p. 155.

Until D—7 attacks would be over a wide area to avoid disclosing the point of attack; thereafter they would be concentrated in the Naples area to drive the Luftwaffe northwards and to cut all routes leading into the battlefield.

One grave mistake was made during planning. It was decided not to carry out a preliminary bombardment of the defences covering the Salerno beaches. Experience in Sicily led commanders to believe that with such a long coast-line to defend the enemy beach-defences could not be strongly held unless surprise had been lost. The critical period in an assault landing occurred when the enemy had found out where the landing had taken place and was able to launch a strong counter-attack. The longer this counter-attack was delayed, the stronger the Allies would be to receive it. If a preliminary bombardment was carried out, minesweepers would have to clear a way for the bombarding ships and point of attack would be given away some 24 hours before the landing took place. There was also the consideration, perhaps only a minor one, that, if Italy had surrendered just before the landing, the worst thing to do would be to blast the towns and villages in the assault area. Mark Clark decided that he would rely on surprise and the assistance of the Italians rather than upon preliminary softening up by naval and air action. McCreery's (Br) Corps wisely took the precaution of laying on a close naval support programme in case surprise was lost. VI (US) Corps did not make such detailed arrangements and depended upon the ships firing on an as-required basis.

At the end of August Hube seems to have sensed that Salerno might be used by the Allies after all and so he brought over 16 Panzer Division from the Adriatic side of his sector to strengthen the Italian defences. This was a reformed Stalingrad division and had within its ranks about 4,000 survivors of the original division which had fought in Poland and France as well as in Russia. Its morale was exceptionally high and it had adapted its tactics to its new theatre very quickly. It could not hold the whole 30 miles of the Salerno beaches in strength, so it established a series of strong points from which it could command the most likely landing areas. It relied on strong mobile patrols of tanks, self-propelled guns and infantry to cover the gaps which were also obstructed by mines and wire. The Italian 222 Coastal Division was left holding the least likely sectors of the bay.

During the afternoon of 8 September reports of enemy shipping 25 miles south of Capri brought the whole of Hube's XIV Panzer Corps to the highest state of readiness and the codeword meaning a major landing was imminent was flashed to all troops. Preparations to meet a landing were well advanced when at about 8 p.m. codeword Achse reached the

Corps Headquarters and was interpreted to divisions with the appropriate sub-codeword *'Ernte Einbringe'*—'Bring in the Harvest'—meaning disarm all Italian troops immediately. One German officer of 16 Panzer Division recorded in his diary: 'As I expected, the Italians threw down their arms and showed their joy that the war was over for them and they could go home.' The only real trouble occurred at the headquarters of 222 Coastal Division. There the Divisional Commander, General Gonzaga, refused the German request to lay down his arms and was shot instantly by the German major sent to demand his surrender. 16 Panzer Division had just enough time to complete the disarmament of all Italians in their area when the American Rangers and British Commandos landed on the northern shores of the bay. There was going to be no tactical surprise; the German defenders were alert and ready.

Out at sea the Allies' approach passage to Salerno was a happier affair than the voyage to Sicily. The sea was calm and the night clear. The tension which should have existed below decks had been dissipated by the news of the Italian surrender. Few troops could be made to believe that the landings might be anything more than a walk-over. The minesweepers did their work creditably well and the marker ships found their positions accurately off-shore without arousing German suspicions. The landing craft were lowered and formed up with far less difficulty than in Husky and the direction-keeping on the run-in was much better. The great difference between the two landings was the reception of the troops on shore. The Germans reacted in a very different way to the Italians.

In the British sector surprise was lost before any assault craft started for the shore. Some Italian coastal batteries, which had been taken over by the Germans only a few hours before, opened accurate fire on the ships carrying the Rangers and Commandos. Full fire support was authorized in support of the landings in the northern half of the bay. Mark Clark, however, did not authorize fire to be opened in the American sector, hoping that VI (US) Corps might still gain surprise on its beaches. The British bombarding ships took on each enemy battery as it opened fire. The supporting destroyers moved in behind the assault waves to give close fire support and the landing craft, fitted with special rocket salvoes, opened fire with brutal effect on the front of each assaulting battalion. Unfortunately one of these craft mistook its target and so the infantry following behind it landed on the wrong beach causing some confusion. The Rangers and Commandos landed against light opposition and secured their objectives. The Commandos being closer in to the main German positions suffered more quick counter-attacks than the Rangers but managed to hold their positions successfully. 46 (Br) Division was lucky enough to land clear of major German strong points, but 56 (Br) Division ran into heavy opposition soon after landing. As first light came up 16 Panzer Division started launching a number of small but determined and highly skilled counter-attacks with groups of tanks and infantry. 56 (Br) Division bore the brunt of these attacks and was given magnificent support in repelling them by the destroyers off-shore. By the end of the first day neither British division had secured its D-day objectives. Salerno port lay just beyond 46 (Br) Division's reach, and although 56 (Br) Division arrived at the edge of Montecorvino airfield it could not secure it against enemy fire. 56 (Br) Division also managed to reach the outskirts of the important road and rail junction of Battapaglia, but was far from firm in the town. The British troops, who had been so elated the previous evening when they heard of the Italian surrender, were now in a grimmer mood. Their losses had been high and the German resistance tough.

In the American sector there was an ominous silence before the leading assault craft touched down. As the infantry emerged they were met by a hail of fire from concealed positions. Much of the fire was too high to do real damage, but even so 36 (US) Division's losses began to mount. Lack of close fire support from the ships, confusion amongst the landing craft coxswains and the alertness of the German defence nearly spelled failure on the American beaches. The superb training of this new 36 (US) National Guard Division and many acts of great bravery made up for its lack of battle experience and enabled it to win through to most of its D-day objectives. By dusk on 9 September it was holding a shallow beachhead around the ancient Roman ruins of Paestum.

At the end of the first day it was clear that the Avalanche gamble had not come off. The Italians had failed utterly; they had given the Allies no support whatsoever. The Germans were free to concentrate the weight of the Tenth German Army against Fifth Army and might well be able to destroy it before Eighth Army could reach it from the south. Von Vietinghoff had been presented with one of those situations which the German commanders loved and which they were so good at using. Eighth Army could be held at arm's length in the Toe by a comparatively small force while every available German unit was rushed to Salerno. If Fifth Army could be crushed quickly enough, they could then turn on the Eighth Army. Everything depended on the relative speeds of reinforcement; the Germans by road and rail in the face of Allied air superiority and the Allies by sea hampered by shortage of shipping. From the tactical point of view the Germans held a very great advantage. When daylight came up on the first day at Salerno, the full horror of the Allies' tactical position was revealed. They lay like two Christian captives in either corner of a great Roman amphitheatre. Every move they made could be seen by the Germans sitting on the surrounding terraces of hills which were

9 16 Panzer Division anti-tank gun crew covering the beaches at Salerno

THE BATTLE OF SALERNO

10 The Fifth and Eighth Army Commanders meet at Salerno

11 General von Vietinghoff,
Commander German Tenth Army

GERMAN COMMANDERS

12 (*bottom left*) General von
Mackensen, Commander German
Fourteenth Army

13 (*below*) General von Senger und
Etterlin, Commander XIV Panzer
Corps

just beyond the Allies' reach. There were three entrances into the amphitheatre. From the north over the passes in the Sorrento Peninsula which
were held by the Rangers and Commandos; from the south over a
difficult, tortuous road easily blocked by VI (US) Corps; and from the
east where, through a gap in the hills, ran Routes 19 and 94, along which
the attacking German gladiators would rush as soon as they were ready
for the kill. Unless Fifth Army could clear German observation off the
surrounding hills and unless they could block the eastern entrance to the
amphitheatre near the Ponte Sele bridge, their hold on the Salerno
beaches would be tenuous. The German artillery could command all
unloading and the destructive German tanks would be able to enter the
arena whenever they chose.

The nine-day battle of Salerno falls into three phases: the landings
which were an Allied success; the build-up and consolidation phase which
the Allies lost; and the German counter-offensive which the Allies
survived just long enough to enable Eighth Army to reach the battlefield
and turn the scales. Alexander appreciated the dangers of the situation
very quickly and bent all his efforts on speeding reinforcements to Salerno.
Montgomery was ordered to hasten his advance, taking operational and
logistic risks to do so. Eighteen American LSTs, which were in the North
African ports awaiting transfer to other theatres, were released by the
Combined Chiefs of Staff to speed the build-up at Salerno; Admiral
Cunningham offered all available warships to ferry troops; and 82 (US)
Airborne Division, now released from Giant II, was put at Mark Clark's
disposal with the necessary airlift. Von Vietinghoff was making similar
arrangements on the German side. General Herr was ordered to break
contact with Eighth Army and move the bulk of his LXXVI Panzer
Corps toward Salerno. His 26 Panzer and 29 Panzer Grenadier Divisions
were to leave only small rearguards behind and to move at best speed in
daylight over the 125 miles of winding mountain road which lay between
their present positions and the beachhead. Hube's XIV Panzer Corps was
ordered to leave the Gulf of Gaeta uncovered and to despatch the 15 Panzer
Grenadier and Hermann Göring Divisions south to block any attempt by
the Allies to advance northwards to take Naples. Kesselring ordered
Student to release 3 Panzer Grenadier Division from Rome as soon as the
Italians capitulated, and he also asked OKW for Rommel's two panzer
divisions. This request was sharply vetoed as OKW policy was still to
withdraw northwards under pressure without committing any more
troops to the south where they might be cut off by Allied landings
further north. Hitler and Jodl were frightened of an Allied trap. Rommel
was also in some difficulties in the north-east of Italy where the Slovenes
tried to profit by Italy's surrender. They helped themselves lavishly to

Italian equipment and threatened the German line of communication through the Ljubljana Gap. Trieste was threatened and Fiume was occupied for a time. The German Adriatic Command eventually re-established control but it was a long and stubborn business. Guerilla warfare continued in the area until the end of the war. Even without Rommel's two panzer divisions, von Vietinghoff would have six experienced mobile divisions concentrated around Salerno before Mark Clark would have four ashore.

10 and 11 September were the days of build-up and containment for both sides. The German effort was concentrated primarily against X (Br) Corps which presented the most dangerous threat to Naples. The Rangers, Commandos and 46 (Br) Division were attacked by the leading elements of 15 Panzer Grenadier and the Hermann Göring Divisions and just managed to hold their ground though with some difficulty. Salerno fell to 46 (Br) Division but the Germans could still bring observed fire to bear upon the harbour which remained unused for most of the battle. 56 (Br) Division failed to clear German artillery observation from Montecorvino airfield and was involved in heavy fighting around Battapaglia when it tried to force its way forward to Monte Eboli. The American VI Corps, by comparison, was left free to expand its bridgehead and secured two key points overlooking the Ponte Sele Bridge area. These were the village of Altavilla (see fig. 15) and the nearby Point 424. Realizing that there was a large yawning gap between his two corps, Mark Clark ordered his floating reserve to land astride the Sele River. One regimental combat team was directed up the south bank to seize the Ponte Sele and the other was to advance along the north bank to make contact with X (Br) Corps in the Battapaglia–Eboli area. If these moves had been completed the Fifth Army bridgehead would have been tolerably secure by 12 September. The first moves of the German counter-offensive on the evening of 11 September caught Mark Clark unbalanced.

The first signs of the German counter-offensive appeared towards evening on 11 September. 56 (Br) Division was hit by the leading elements of 26 Panzer Division which arrived up Route 19 and attacked off the line of march almost without a pause. The Royal Fusilier battalion in Battapaglia was surrounded and lost 450 prisoners to the elated Germans. At about the same time the 45 (US) Division's thrust towards the Ponte Sele was stopped by 29 Panzer Grenadier Division and sent reeling back towards the American beachhead. Overhead the Luftwaffe increased its efforts to break through the flimsy Allied fighter cover and managed to damage one British and two American cruisers with glider bombs. The German aircraft were operating from 18,000 feet, at which altitude only the Lightnings could intercept.

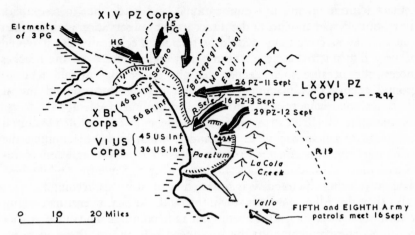

16   *The German counter-offensive at Salerno, 11–17 September*

The German plan was to maintain pressure on X (Br) Corps by attacks from the north while moving most of their reinforcing units round through the Ponte Sele Gap into the Eboli–Battapaglia area. From there they intended to attack due west along Route 19, to crush X (Br) Corps against their forces attacking from the north, and south-west astride the Sele River, to break through to the sea between the two Allied corps and thereby force their re-embarkation or annihilation. During 12 and 13 September the British lost heavily in the fighting around Battapaglia and Montecorvino airfield, but managed to hold their ground thanks to the excellent air and naval gunfire support. 36 (US) Division was forced off the key features of Altavilla and Point 424 during 12 September. The critical moment of the battle came during the afternoon of 13 September when a mixed force of tanks, self-propelled guns and infantry from 16 Panzer Division smashed through 45 (US) Division on the Sele and came within two miles of the beaches. The German attack was only just stopped by two regiments of American field artillery firing over open sights at the advancing tanks and infantry. General Dawley had no reserves left and was forced during the night 13–14 September to draw back his perimeter to the La Cola Creek not far from his D-day beachhead line.

Fifth Army's position looked so precarious to its Commander on 14 September that he ordered his staff to draw up contingency plans to re-embark either of his two corps and to use it to reinforce the beachhead of the other. The naval commanders soon pointed out how impracticable such a plan would be. It was difficult enough to disengage a corps in close contact with an enemy in a conventional land battle, but to re-embark the troops off open beaches under direct artillery observation with German guns within effective range would be suicidal. Technically also it would be very difficult to load the landing craft and retract from the beaches successfully because their deeper draught under load would tend to ground them. This planning exercise was soon discontinued but it illustrates how dangerous the situation had become. General McCreery, commanding X (Br) Corps, opposed the scheme and enlisted Admiral Cunningham's help to kill it. Alexander, when he heard about it the following day, was equally strongly opposed to any suggestion of re-embarkation. Unloading, which stopped during 14 September while these plans were being discussed, was restarted again towards evening.

By then the Allies' position was improving. In fact, events had begun to turn in their favour on the evening of 13 September. The quickest way to bring reinforcements into the beachhead was by air. There were no airfields on which to land them, so Mark Clark ordered 82 (US) Airborne Division to drop one regimental combat team into the American sector on the night 13-14 September and another on Avellino behind the German lines to disrupt their reinforcement plans. The Avellino drop was postponed 24 hours but the beachhead drop went ahead as planned. Great care was taken this time to ensure that the Allies did not shoot down their own troop carriers. A strict 'guns tight' order was enforced and, as luck would have it, a Luftwaffe raid on the anchorage came in just before the parachute force was due over the beaches. This time the 'guns tight' order was obeyed and the Luftwaffe bombed undisturbed. A few minutes later the parachute regiment landed accurately in VI (US) Corps beachhead. Allied airborne techniques were improving.

Back in Bizerte, Eisenhower asked for—and received—permission from the Chiefs of Staff to use the Strategic Air Forces in the tactical battle and Cunningham ordered the battleships HMS *Warspite* and HMS *Valiant* north from Malta to support Fifth Army with their 15-inch guns. Churchill signalled Alexander: 'Ask for anything you want and I will make allocation of the necessary supplies with highest priority irrespective of every other consideration.' In the same signal the ghosts of Gallipoli appear: 'I hope you are watching above all the Battle of Avalanche, which dominates everything. None of the commanders engaged has fought a large scale battle before. The Battle of Suvla Bay was lost because Ian Hamilton was advised by his CGS to remain at a remote central point where he would know everything.' Alexander did not need this direction. He was already at Salerno when Churchill's signal arrived. The reinforcing moves laid on two days before and in the original plan were beginning to take effect. 7 (Br) Armoured Division's units started to land in X (Br) Corps sector on 14 September. The third regimental combat team of 45 (US) Division arrived in VI (US) Corps' sector. 3 (US) Division was on its way from Sicily. A second regiment of 82 (US) Airborne Division landed the same evening in the beachhead and a third dropped at Avellino. Due to the mountainous nature of the area, the Avellino parachute drop had to be made from 3,000 feet and so was very dispersed. It caused the Germans little trouble and seems to have been a misguided operation. Most of the men were forced to hide in the farms and villages until the eventual Allied advance reached them.

Fighting during 14, 15 and 16 September was dominated by the massive naval and air support given to Fifth Army. The accuracy of the 15-inch salvoes from the battleships demoralized the Germans who felt they had nothing with which to strike back. Added to this came the carpet bombing by the strategic bombers in the confined Battapaglia–Eboli–Ponte Sele area. The Luftwaffe did have one fleeting success. HMS *Warspite* was hit and badly damaged by a glider bomb on 16 September and had to withdraw to Malta. This success, however, was more than offset by the arrival of Eighth Army's leading reconnaissance patrol at Vallo 20 miles south of Paestum, where it joined hands with a patrol from VI (US) Corps. The two Allied armies were in contact. The Germans had lost the race thanks to the support given to Fifth Army by the Allied navies and air forces.

Von Vietinghoff advised Kesselring on 16 September that the Allies were now too firmly established to be ejected. He recommended disengagement to save his troops from further punishment from naval gunfire and to give him sufficient time to redeploy before Eighth Army could threaten his rear. Kesselring agreed and authorized a slow withdrawal to the River Volturno north of Naples, which was to be held until 15 October to give his Chief Engineer, General Bessel, time to fortify the Gustav Line. In true German military tradition, von Vietinghoff decided to attack once more on 17 September to mask his disengagement and possibly to make sure that he was not mistaken about the strength of the Allied beachhead. His final attack was to be against X (Br) Corps only. Hube's corps was to strike from the north and Herr's corps from the east to crush the British divisions between them. Both attacks came under crippling bombardment and were soon brought to a halt. The Germans went over to the defensive and started to disengage on the southern extremities of the beachhead. The Battle of Salerno was over.

Before concluding this Chapter, we must look briefly at four other events: the occupation of Taranto; Montgomery's advance; the rescue of Mussolini; and the German evacuation of Sardinia and Corsica. As soon as it was clear that the Italian Fleet was on its way to surrender, Admiral

Cunningham released the 12th Cruiser Squadron to pick up 1 (Br) Airborne Division for the Slapstick attack on Taranto. The paratroopers were rapidly embarked and when the cruisers entered Taranto on 9 September they were unopposed. The only mishap was the tragic loss of the fast minelayer *Abdiel* with heavy loss of life. After anchoring in the harbour, she swung over a mine while still crowded with her load of parachute troops. The Germans made no attempt to recapture Taranto and the lightly-equipped airborne troops found no difficulty in holding the Italian Heel until 24 September when 8 (Indian) Division arrived from the Middle East.

The Eighth Army has often been accused of making a laboriously slow advance up the Toe and of failing to use the sea power to full effect. Both accusations are usually overstated. The original Baytown crossing of the Straits was undoubtedly a ponderous affair in which thousands of tons of steel and high explosive were flung at the luckless Italian inhabitants without doing any damage to the Germans. Thereafter the advance of 5 (Br) Division up the west coast and 1 (Cdn) Division up the east was as fast as its meagre allotment of shipping, and its sappers' ability to overcome the blown bridges and mined roads, would allow. Only one battalion group of each division worked its way over land. The rest were shipped round the coast, first to the Catanzaro isthmus and then to the Castrovillari isthmus (*see* fig. 14). By 19 September 5 (Br) Division had reached Auletta and 1 (Cdn) Division was in Potenza, both due east of Salerno, ready to continue their advance northward as Fifth Army broke out of its beachhead.

The rescue of Mussolini need not detain us long. Otto Skorzeny, who had been sent by Hitler to rescue his friend, eventually located Mussolini in a ski-lodge high up in the Gran Sasso in the central Apennines. In a daring rescue bid he landed a company of paratroopers by glider on a mountain ridge near the lodge and successfully abducted the Duce under the noses of his Italian guards. The Duce was flown off the hill in a small Storch aircraft, which only just managed to lift Mussolini, Skorzeny and the pilot. Hitler was delighted with this coup, which he used for propaganda purposes, but he was aghast to see the mere shell of a man which appeared at his headquarters in East Prussia. The Duce was broken in spirit and could no longer be trusted to show much determination, but his re-establishment as the puppet ruler of German-occupied Italy saved Hitler the trouble of creating a new Italian government. The Allies were not so lucky in the south. They had to establish an Allied military government to ensure the administration of their half of Italy. The King and Badoglio were more a liability than an asset.

The last event of importance in this period was the evacuation of

Sardinia and Corsica. On 7 September General von Senger und Etterlin, who had been Guzzoni's German liaison officer in Sicily, arrived in Sardinia with secret orders to prepare the evacuation of the islands. He did not have much time to make his preparations. Achse was ordered the following day and OKW decided to evacuate the islands so as not to lose 90 Panzer Grenadier Division in Sardinia and the SS Reichsfuehrer Brigade in Corsica. If OKW had waited a few days, they might have realized that the Allies did not possess as large an amphibious capability as German intelligence estimates suggested and they would not have surrendered the islands so precipitately. Von Senger's force was too small to attempt the disarmament of the Italians. He was only too thankful that the Italians allowed 90 Panzer Grenadier Division to withdraw from Sardinia to Corsica without fighting, but he was not so lucky in Corsica. The Italian commander there was unwilling to co-operate and the French partisans rose to make the German position more difficult. Von Senger had to fight a withdrawal action to a bridgehead around Bastia from which he organized the evacuation by sea and air between 16 September and 3 October. The Germans suffered some losses in the process, Allied submarines and aircraft catching several ships and shooting down a large number of Junkers transport planes into the sea. General Giraud's French Forces landed on 20 September and pressed the German withdrawal. The last airfields were given up on 2 October and von Senger left Bastia with the rearguard late on 3 October. The Allies had gained both strategic objectives which had been alternatives during post-Husky planning: Sardinia and Corsica had fallen as well as a foothold being won on the Italian mainland.

The first breach in Fortress Europe was now wide open. It is interesting to speculate what would have happened if OKW had released the two panzer divisions from Rommel's Army Group when Kesselring asked for them. They could not have arrived in strength in much less than six days. By then Eighth Army would have been nearing Potenza and 7 (Br) Armoured Division and 3 (US) Division would have reached the beachhead. The struggle might have lasted longer but the issue would have probably been the same at Salerno. The difference would have occurred slightly later. Kesselring would probably have stood south of Naples and have been able to hold this important port and the Foggia airfields until winter came to his assistance. The Allies might then have been so discouraged as to give up trying to force the issue in the Mediterranean. The British Chiefs of Staff would have lost their case and the Americans would have been in the ascendant. Kesselring's decision to withdraw to the Volturno drew the Allies on like a magnet and created the situation that General Marshall had always feared. The Germans would be containing the maximum number of Allied divisions instead of *vice versa* as the Combined Chiefs of Staff intended.

As for Avalanche, the landings this time were against determined German troops who taught the Allies four more lessons in amphibious warfare. Firstly, do not choose a beachhead overlooked by ground which you cannot be sure of taking early in the operation. Secondly, if the assault area is defended by first-class troops, preliminary bombardment is essential. Thirdly, air action alone cannot stop the reinforcement of the enemy's containing forces. Even though the Italian road and rail communications were very vulnerable to air attack, von Vietinghoff's divisions were not materially delayed by the Allied air attacks as they raced to Salerno. Fourthly, a landing force once committed cannot be withdrawn in the face of the enemy. The Allies were also confirmed in their views in three other respects. First, general air superiority was not enough in a landing operation; effective air cover over the beaches was also essential. At Salerno it was only just adequate. Secondly, large forces could be supplied over open beaches, at least in the tideless Mediterranean. Ship and craft handling had made great strides since Husky and the techniques of parachute reinforcement had improved. And thirdly, and probably unfortunately as later events were to show, they were convinced that the greatest danger in an amphibious operation lay in the enemy's ability to counter-attack before they could be ready to receive him. II (US) Corps had suffered at Gela, and VI (US) Corps was hit so hard that it nearly collapsed at Salerno. In the American commanders' minds, if not in the British, the first essential in an amphibious operation was a secure beachhead with a complete concentration of troops, tanks and guns within it before any attempt should be made to exploit inland. This 'Salerno' mentality, as it was called later, may have cost the Allies dear at Anzio.

7

The Breach Closes

'The Tenth Army Staff were the best that I ever encountered in this war.'

Von Senger und Etterlin, *Neither Fear nor Hope*

The third great Allied conference, Quadrant, drew to its close as Mark Clark's Fifth Army sailed for Salerno. At Trident the British had accepted Overlord as the primary operation for 1944, but between the Trident and Quadrant conferences the Americans began to suspect that the British were paying lip-service to the Trident decisions while looking for ways of exploiting the opportunities opening up before them in the Mediterranean. The relative ease of the Sicily landings and the short 38-day conquest of the island delighted the British planners as much as they depressed their American colleagues. At one stage, a school of thought emerged in Washington which suggested that the British might be right after all, and that the Overlord build-up should not be allowed to prejudice operations in the Mediterranean. If need be, Overlord could be relegated to the status of a contingency plan designed to take advantage of a sudden and unexpected deterioration of the German position in Western Europe. Roosevelt himself seems to have had doubts about the sanctity of the Trident decisions. He proposed to General Marshall that the seven veteran divisions destined to leave the Mediterranean in November should be replaced by seven new divisions from the United States. Marshall, however, stood firm in his belief that the cross-Channel strategy was still the correct course. He pointed out that Eisenhower—another strong advocate of the Overlord concept—had reported he had sufficient resources left to him in the Mediterranean to achieve the objectives set for him by the Combined Chiefs of Staff. If seven new divisions were despatched, as the President suggested, then not only would they and the shipping which carried them be lost to the Overlord build-up, the British would also be able to launch their cherished operation against the Balkans. No assurances which Churchill could give—and he gave them on several occasions—would convince the Americans that he was not bent on pouring troops into South-Eastern Europe. They were utterly unconvinced by his statements that he only intended to pose a threat to the German position in the Balkans by minor peripheral operations. Marshall's argument won the day. The President said he knew the British wanted to forestall the Russians in the Balkans but he did not understand the logic of their thinking. He did not believe that the USSR wished to take over the Balkan States; it only wanted to establish kinship with other Slav people. He would support Marshall at Quadrant in advocating the firm acceptance of Overlord as the prime operation for 1944.

At Quebec, Alan Brooke confirmed that the British still accepted Overlord as the major US-UK effort; nevertheless there were three conditions which must be fulfilled before it could be undertaken. First, German fighter strength must be drastically reduced; secondly, there must not be more than 12 German mobile divisions in France and the Low Countries on D-day; and, thirdly, the problems of maintenance over tidal beaches must be solved. The only area in which the Allies could mount diversionary operations to achieve the first two conditions was in the Mediterranean. Marshall countered by saying that he could not agree with the logic of supporting the main effort by withdrawing troops from it to reinforce the diversionary operations in the Mediterranean. The secondary theatre's strength must be pegged and the theatre commanders must draw as much German strength southwards as they could within the limits of these fixed resources. In the end, the Americans accepted something less than overall priority for Overlord, and the British confirmed their reluctant agreement to the withdrawal of the seven divisions with the assault shipping and troop-carrying aircraft approved at Trident. Neither side was wholly satisfied. The British feared that opportunities would be lost in the Mediterranean; and the Americans feared that these very opportunities, if they occurred, would destroy Overlord. Neither really appreciated the effect of the Italian winter. Had they done so the British would not have been so sanguine about success and the Americans would have clinched their case. The desert war had made men forget the mud of Flanders. In their minds, the advent of tanks, motor vehicles and aircraft had solved all that. Modern equipment had reduced the ability of the weather to interfere with a modern battle. First Army's experience in the Tunisian mud had been exceptional; it was an inexperienced army which would have bogged down anyway in front of von Arnim's veteran troops. The important thing was to keep the large Allied armies in the Mediterranean engaged with the Germans. No one at this stage really worried about the effect of winter in 'Sunny Italy'.

The instructions sent to Eisenhower after Quadrant had given him three tasks: eliminate Italy; capture Sardinia and Corsica; and maintain unremitting pressure on the Germans to create the conditions required for Overlord and for the eventual entry of Allied forces into southern France. Within a month of Quadrant the first two tasks had been performed. Eisenhower was now faced with carrying out the last and most arduous task of the three. Would the Germans allow themselves to be contained? Or would the Allies find themselves contained instead? The topography of Italy suggested that, if the Allies confined their operations to the Italian Peninsula, this is exactly what would happen. The narrow mountainous Leg of Italy was ideal for defence. Its only weakness lay in its vulnerability to amphibious attack, but if the Germans chose to retire slowly north this advantage would disappear as they approached the northern Apennines. The Allies would then be faced with trying to breach a major defensive position high up in the mountains in the depth of winter—not an enviable task. The Allies were about to put themselves in the position of the Germans at Verdun or the British on the Somme, attacking impregnable positions in order to draw the enemy's strength. Looked at another way, the Germans would be in Wellington's position in the lines of the Torres Vedras, holding superior Allied armies with great economy of effort. They would do this best if they stuck to the Rommel school of thought and did not allow themselves to be drawn southwards by Kesselring's successes.

Alexander issued his first directive to Fifth and Eighth Armies for the development of the campaign in Italy on 21 September when it was clear that the Germans were retiring from Salerno. He indicated four very broad phases: the consolidation of the breach from Salerno to Bari; the seizure of the port of Naples and the airfields at Foggia; the capture of Rome, its airfields and the road and rail centre of Terni; and, in the distant future, the occupation of the port of Leghorn and the communication centres of Florence and Arezzo.* During the advance he planned to take full advantage of Allied sea and air power to mount amphibious operations behind the German flanks to hasten their withdrawal and, if possible, cut off some of their divisions. He was to be hampered in this last intention by a shortage of ships and troop carrying aircraft; a limitation which vied with shortages of gun ammunition and infantry reinforcements as the most critical items in the Italian campaign.

The German withdrawal from Salerno was superbly organized by von

* See map of Southern Italy, front end-paper.

Vietinghoff's Chief of Operations, General Wentzell. XIV Panzer Corps held firm in the Sorrento Peninsula, blocking the advance of the British X Corps on Naples. LXXVI Panzer Corps withdrew north-eastwards to join 1 Para Division which was pulling back slowly in front of 1 (Br) Airborne Division advancing from Taranto. The whole German line unfolded from around the Fifth Army beachhead and then, pivoting on Sorrento, swung back like a folding door to form a continuous line from the Gulf of Salerno to the Adriatic. At the end of the first week of their

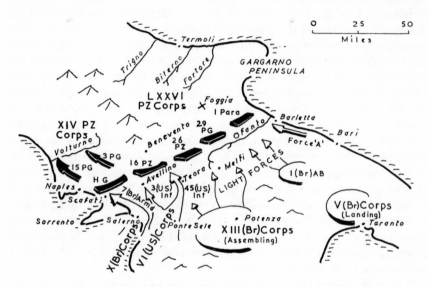

17   The German withdrawal and Allied advance from Salerno to the
Volturno–Termoli Line

withdrawal the Germans were on the line Sorrento–Melfi–Ofanto River. Behind XIV Panzer Corps, German engineers were destroying the port of Naples with ruthless efficiency. Every berth was obstructed by block ships; all tugs and harbour craft were sunk; all cranes and cargo handling gear were destroyed; pipe lines and power cables were ripped out; power stations were blown up; and the harbour was liberally strewn with mines. Ashore, time bombs were hidden in such places as the main post office, barrack blocks and hotels—anywhere likely to be used by Allied soldiers and Italian civilians after the fall of the city. The clockwork fuses had up to 42 days delay set on them. Many exploded with deadly effect; particularly the one in the main post office which was crowded when it went off.

It took X (Br) Corps two days to regroup before it could start to attack northwards towards Naples. When it attacked on 23 September it met bitter resistance and could make no headway against the Hermann Göring Division supported by detachments of 3 and 15 Panzer Grenadier Divisions. The main bodies of the two latter divisions were withdrawn to the Volturno to start preparing the river for defence. The Hermann Göring Division acted as the rearguard for XIV Panzer Corps. The VI (US) Corps, now reinforced by 3 (US) Division from Sicily and under command of General Lucas, who had relieved Dawley on 20 September, attacked on two axes almost due north. 3 (US) Division advanced through the ruins of Battapaglia and over the mountains towards Avellino. 45 (US) Division advanced in a wider turning movement from the Ponte Sele towards Teora, aiming ultimately for Benevento. Their advance was impeded by rearguards of 16 Panzer Division which opposed VI (US) Corps while 26 Panzer and 29 Panzer Grenadier Divisions made their way north-eastwards to stabilize LXXVI Panzer Corps' front against Eighth Army. 16 Panzer Division, which had borne the brunt of the Salerno fighting, was to be withdrawn into Tenth Army Reserve as soon as a continuous line was established from coast to coast. In a similar way the 36 (US) Division and 82 (US) Division were brought into Fifth Army Reserve.

On the Eighth Army front, XIII (Br) Corps at Potenza had over-reached its supply system and would not be able to advance in force again much before 1 October, by which time its line of supply would have been switched to Taranto. Headquarters V (Br) Corps, 78 (Br) Division and 8 (Indian) Division started landing through the Heel ports on 18 September, but could not be fully organized for an advance much before 1 October either. Montgomery, therefore, gave orders for light forces only to push forward to Foggia to keep contact with the German withdrawal. The Canadians were to advance from Potenza towards Melfi and the upper reaches of the Ofanto River, while advanced elements of 78 (Br) Division and 1 (Br) Airborne Division were to move on Barletta and the lower reaches of the Ofanto. A special force, known as Force 'A', consisting of parts of 78 (Br) Division with tank and Special Air Service support, landed at Bari on 22 September and pushed up the coast to the Ofanto which it crossed on 24 September. The German 1 Para Division abandoned Foggia to Force 'A' on 27 September, and on the same day the Canadians entered Melfi. German accounts speak of heavy fighting for the Foggia airfields before 1 Para Division gave them up, but there is very little mention of any real resistance in the British accounts. The area was far too large even for German parachute troops to make a significant contribution. Resistance did not start to stiffen in

front of 78 (Br) Division's reconnaissance in force until 29 September. By
then the whole of the Gargarno Peninsula was clear of German troops
and there were signs of the German resistance beginning to harden on
the Fortore River. Force 'A' was not strong enough to go further until
Eighth Army's main body was ready to advance.

VI (US) Corps, in the meantime, had made rapid progress on Fifth
Army's inland flank threatening the junction between the two panzer
corps. By 28 September 3 (US) Division was overlooking Avellino and
45 (US) Division was in Teora. The time had come for the Hermann
Göring Division to give way in front of X (Br) Corps if it was not to be

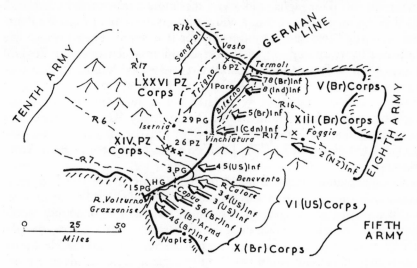

18   *German and Allied dispositions on the Volturno–Termoli Line*

cut off before it could escape through Naples. On 29 September 7 (Br)
Armoured Division passed through 46 (Br) Division to break out into
the plain leading to Naples. The bridge at Scafati was seized intact before
the German rearguard could fire its charges, but the narrowness of this
bottle-neck slowed the British advance. The Hermann Göring Division
had no difficulty in making good its escape and abandoned the shattered
port and city of Naples to 7 (Br) Armoured Division on 1 October. The
port which had once handled 8,000 tons a day could now handle less
than 1,000 tons. By superhuman efforts American and British naval
clearance parties and army engineers raised the capacity to 3,500 tons by
the end of the first fortnight of Allied occupation. On 14 October Fifth
Army was able to give up landing supplies over the Salerno beaches and
rely entirely on the port of Naples.

XIV Panzer Corps made no attempt to stand between Naples and the Volturno. The reconnaissance units of X (Br) Corps reached the river on 5 October. 46 (Br) Division moved into the coastal sector; 7 (Br) Armoured Division entered Grazzanise in the centre; and 56 (Br) Division took Capua on X (Br) Corps' inland flank. VI (US) Corps found their advance through the hills east of Naples impeded by demolitions. 3 (US) Division came through quickest and arrived alongside 56 (Br) Division on 7 October. 34 (US) Division, which had arrived at Salerno from North Africa after 3 (US) Division, had joined 45 (US) Division in its attack on Benevento on 2 October and had then advanced up the west bank of the Calore River to its junction with the Volturno. 45 (US) Division crossed the Calore at Benevento and advanced up the east bank. 45 (US) Division's advance was soon halted, however, by German defences running north-east from the river junction which were designed to continue the Volturno Line over the Apennines to the Biferno River and Termoli on the Adriatic.

The main body of Eighth Army had by now resumed its advance up the Adriatic coast. Montgomery gave XIII (Br) Corps responsibility for leading the advance with 78 (Br) Division on the coast road (Route 16) heading for Termoli and 1 (Cdn) Division inland on Route 17 directed on Vinchiaturo. The corps' objective was the main lateral road from Termoli to Vinchiaturo and the Biferno River which lay just beyond. V (Br) Corps with 5 (Br) Division and 8 (Indian) Division under command was to move behind XIII (Br) Corps, ready to move forward quickly if major opposition was met or if the Germans mounted a dangerous counter-attack. 1 (Br) Airborne Division was withdrawn into reserve ready to return two of its brigades to England (though not as one of the seven Overlord divisions). Once the Termoli–Vinchiaturo line was reached, Montgomery proposed to pause again to allow his logistic services to catch up. During the pause he would again push on with light forces towards Pescara and the lateral road leading from Pescara *via* Avezzano to Rome.

XIII (Br) Corps was helped by a very successful Special Service Brigade and Commando landing at Termoli on the night 2–3 October. The German garrison was surprised and lost its commander and headquarters. The town and port were taken undamaged and by early afternoon the Commandos had linked up with the leading brigade of 78 (Br) Division and had secured a crossing over the Biferno River. During the night a brigade of 78 (Br) Division was landed in the port, but by the middle of the next day signs of a strong German reaction became evident. Kesselring was determined not to relinquish the Volturno–Termoli line before 15 October. He issued orders personally to von Vietinghoff to move 16 Panzer Division out of reserve over to the east coast to counter-attack the landing. 16 Panzer Division made a long 95-mile march over difficult mountain roads and came into action piecemeal during 4 and 5 October. Heavy attacks developed against 78 (Br) Division's bridgehead over the Biferno, which it had been impossible to reinforce with more than a few tanks because the sappers had not as yet managed to build a secure tank crossing. The Luftwaffe made one of its rare appearances in strength to support 16 Panzer Division. For a time the issue was in doubt, but during the night 5–6 October a second brigade of 78 (Br) Division landed in the port and the sappers completed the tank crossing over the Biferno. Fighting during 6 October swung in favour of the British and 16 Panzer Division was forced to withdraw to the next river line, the Trigno. Meanwhile, on Route 17, the Canadians had been forced to fight for every mile in their advance on Vinchiaturo which did not fall until 15 October. By then the thrust lines of the two XIII (Br) Corps divisions were becoming dangerously far apart, so Montgomery regrouped his Army bringing V (Br) Corps up to take charge of operations on the coast road, while XIII (Br) Corps confined itself to the inland advance on Route 17. V (Br) Corps was given 78 (Br) Division and 8 (Ind) Division, and XIII (Br) Corps received 1 (Cdn) Division and 5 (Br) Division. The newly arrived 2 (New Zealand) Division was held in Army Reserve. The next Eighth Army objective was to be the lateral road running from Vasto to Isernia on the far side of the Trigno. Operations could not start in earnest against the Trigno until supplies had been built up. Montgomery intended to move forward in strength again on about 22 October to undertake the first of many opposed river crossings carried out by Eighth Army in Italy. On the west coast, Fifth Army were already engaged in their first opposed crossing—over the Volturno. Two new factors were emerging which were to have a profound effect on the campaign.

The first factor was the weather. The autumn rain started as X (Br) Corps was forcing its way round Mount Vesuvius into Naples. By the time Fifth Army reached the Volturno it was wallowing in thick yellow mud. The weather broke at about much the same time on Eighth Army's sector adding to the difficulties of moving tanks and ammunition forward over the long supply route from Taranto. Even under summer conditions the road network in southern Italy was barely adequate for two armies of some 11 modern mechanized divisions. Given the demolition of practically every bridge and culvert, add water in gushing torrents from each river and rivulet, churn up the improvised crossings over them with tanks and heavy vehicles and you have a morass where roads used to be. The task of the engineers became impossible while the rain lasted.

There was only one answer—wait until it stopped—but few commanders were willing to do so. Men and vehicles struggled on until they were eventually forced to halt. The rain then stopped, the sun dried out the tracks for a time and the commanders pushed their units forward once more full of hope. Down came the rain again and the whole disillusioning process would be repeated. Only when the units were too exhausted to move any further was a halt called—but for only just as long as it took to dry out the ground. The strategy of the campaign, however, was simplified because as long as winter lasted the only thrust lines which could be used were the main State Routes.

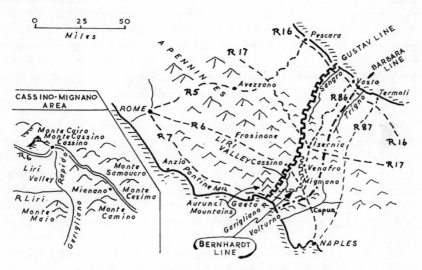

19   *Kesselring's plans for his winter Line 1943–44*

Running north from Naples was Route 7 which crossed the Volturno at Capua and then divided into two alternative roads to Rome: Route 6 *via* Cassino and the Liri Valley, and Route 7 *via* Gaeta and the Pontine Marshes, passing close to the beaches of Anzio. On the Adriatic side of the mountains there were two routes; Route 16 on the coast and Route 17 parallel to it but some distance inland, running through the foothills on the northern side of the Apennine chain. There were, of course, many smaller roads between these four major State Routes, but none were strong enough to carry the centre line of a modern corps in winter. Linking the four routes there were three important lateral roads. Route 87 from Termoli through Vinchiaturo to Naples; Route 86 from Vasto through Isernia to Mignano; and Route 5 from Pescara through Avezzano to Rome. The autumn, winter and spring battles were strongly influenced by these seven major roads.

The second factor was a sudden and quite unexpected change in German strategic policy. On the Eastern Front, Hitler's abortive operation Zitadelle against Kursk, which had to be broken off when the Allies landed in Sicily, was followed by massive Russian counter-offensives either side of the Kursk salient against Orel in the north and Kharkov in the south. In these great battles the Germans were soundly beaten and their armies were sent reeling back to the last good defensive position in Russia proper—the Dnieper River. Military logic suggested that every available German division should be moved eastward to stem the Russian tide, leaving only a minimum force to hold the Allies in the Mediterranean. Almost the opposite happened. Kesselring's success in saving Tenth Army from what Hitler believed was almost certain annihilation gave him new hope. A successful defence of the Gustav Line south of Rome, where the Italian Peninsula is at its narrowest, would need fewer divisions than the longer Gothic Line between Pisa and Rimini in the north. By holding the Gustav Line he would be able to cover Rome and its airfields, and he would be holding the Allies further away from Germany's back door. The only serious weakness of the Gustav Line was its greater vulnerability to Allied amphibious attack, but winter weather at sea would reduce this danger. What swayed Hitler most was the chance to hold on to more occupied territory. Kesselring, unlike Hitler's other senior generals in Russia, thought that he could halt the German retreat and so Hitler decided to give him every chance to set an example to the pessimists.

On 1 October Hitler ordered Kesselring to base his plans on holding a front south of Rome. It might not be practicable to hold the Volturno, but the Allies should be delayed there as long as possible to allow time for the Todt organization to complete the defences of the Gustav Line and to allow the effects of winter to cripple the Allies' material superiority. Thus the fateful decision was taken which resulted in the Allies succeeding in their purpose of containing the maximum number of German divisions in the south. Both sides were to fight each other to a standstill, using resources which they could have used to better effect elsewhere.

The Gustav Line on which Kesselring planned to hold the Allies for the winter ran along the Garigliano River and its tributary, the Rapido, to Cassino and then up and over some of the highest features in the southern Apennines until it reached the River Sangro on the Adriatic coast (*see* fig. 19). The main defensive positions were not on the river banks but were well back on the reverse slopes of the hills overlooking the river valleys. The river banks were held by light covering forces, helped by minefields and artillery fire from batteries positioned securely behind the hills. Only in the wide Liri Valley overlooked by Cassino were there any strong defences in the low ground.

The German appreciation of the Allies' plans led them to believe, quite rightly, that Rome was their immediate objective. There were four possible approaches which could be used during winter. The first was Route 7 up the west coast, but this was easily blocked where it passed round the Aurunci Mountains near Gaeta and later amongst the irrigation ditches of the Pontine Marshes. The second was Route 6 past Cassino and up the Liri Valley to Frosinone and thence to Rome. The weakest sector of the Gustav Line seemed to be the wide mouth of the Liri Valley which was only obstructed by the small Rapido River, although the strength of this small stream was greatly enhanced by the superb artillery observation afforded by the two 'gate posts' of the valley—Monte Cassino to the north and Monte Majo to the south. Some ten miles nearer Naples, however, Route 6 runs through several narrow defiles, starting with the one at Mignano. Between Mignano and Cassino the road is obstructed by what looks like a series of mountain baffle-plates, each of which affords a strong defensive position blocking the road as it approaches the Liri Valley's entrance. The third approach was up the Adriatic coast on Route 16, but, if the Allies used this, they would have to swing westwards at Pescara and fight their way over the Apennines on the lateral Route 5 to Avezzano and then Rome—not an inviting course. The inland Route 17 was so obstructed by mountain features that it could be disregarded as a route for a major attack. The fourth approach would be by sea to the mouth of the Tiber or further north. This possibility had to be guarded against at all times and meant positioning German divisions in depth behind the front to deal with this threat. In Kesselring's view, and in that of his subordinates, the most likely approach was up the Liri Valley, but if the Allies contemplated an amphibious assault during the winter they would also advance on Route 7 through the west coast sector.

Most of the German effort during October went into blocking Routes 6 and 7. Behind the Volturno positions Tenth Army had a tactical delaying line, known as the Barbara Line, which ran along the ridge of high ground between the Volturno and Garigliano Rivers and then over the Apennines to the River Trigno. Covering the Liri Valley entrance, Hube had reconnoitred a covering position called the Bernhardt Line (and sometimes the Reinhard Line), based on the Mignano defile, before he handed over command of XIV Panzer Corps to General von Senger und Etterlin. This was an immensely strong position which could be held in great depth and in many respects was better than the actual Gustav Line.

Its disadvantage was that it was just too far forward and could not be co-ordinated successfully with the rest of the Gustav Line which had to be based on the Garigliano and Sangro Rivers. It would, however, serve as an excellent addition to the defences of the Liri Valley. No OKW or Army engineers were available to prepare its defences, so they were built with XIV Panzer Corps' own resources and consisted of a series of strong points using the large number of excellent tactical features with which the area abounds rather than attempting to form a continuous line. Depth was the main characteristic of Hube's Bernhardt Line.

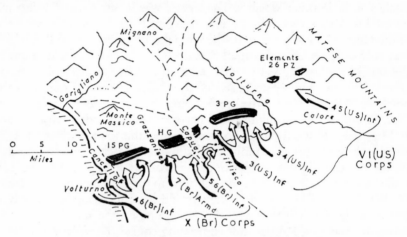

20   *The crossing of the Volturno, 12–15 October*

In the first ten days of October Tenth Army deployed all its divisions along the Volturno–Trigno Line. The only reserve in Kesselring's Army Group was 2 Para Division near Rome. Orders had, however, been issued for three infantry divisions to move southwards from Rommel's Army Group. 305 Infantry Division was on the way, and 65 and 94 Infantry Divisions had received warning orders. On XIV Panzer Corps' front, von Senger had disposed his three divisions forward on the Volturno. 15 Panzer Grenadier Division held the lower reaches; the Hermann Göring Division the centre; and 3 Panzer Grenadier Division the Upper Volturno Valley which ran back northwards into the heart of the German defences. The most westerly division of Herr's LXXVI Panzer Corps, 26 Panzer Division, joined hands with 3 Panzer Grenadier Division over the Matese Mountains.

Fifth Army reached the Volturno with six divisions abreast. Only 36 (US) Division and 82 (US) Airborne Division had been left in reserve. Mark Clark hoped that X (Br) Corps on the left would be able to bounce a crossing during the night 9–10 October, but heavy rain soon ruled this out. He then decided to attack simultaneously across the whole Fifth Army front on the night 12–13 October. All the Allied commanders felt fairly certain that the Germans would not stay long on the Volturno and would soon be pulling back again on their way to Rome and the northern Apennine Line. None of the Allied divisions had any experience of an opposed river crossing and very little floating bridging equipment had yet been landed in the theatre. For instance, there was only just enough bridging equipment in X (Br) Corps for one 30-ton tank bridge and one 9-ton vehicle bridge over a river as wide as the Volturno. In the light of subsequent experience, the crossing of the Volturno was an amateur performance which would have suffered a severe rebuff had it not taken place at just about the time that Kesselring had set as the target date for holding the Volturno.

In X (Br) Corps' sector, the river was a major obstacle about 200–300 feet wide with no obvious fords for men or waterproofed tanks. The flood plain was flat and, after the heavy rains, so soft that vehicles were forced to stay on the roads. This confined the possible crossing places to the sites of the demolished road bridges at Cancello, Grazzannise and Capua, the last being the main Route 7 bridge. McCreery's first idea was to attack in strength at Capua where the road network and the bridge site offered the best chance of deploying a sizeable force, but it soon became clear that the north bank at Capua was strongly held by the Hermann Göring Division. Patrols reported heavy opposition at Grazzannise as well, but near the coast the chances appeared better. Moreover, tanks could be ferried round the mouth of the river by naval craft and naval gunfire support would be available if this sector was chosen for the corps' main crossing. X (Br) Corps' plan was to attack with 46 (Br) Division on a two-brigade front between the mouth of the river and Cancello. The navy was to provide fire support and was to ferry two squadrons of tanks across the mouth of the river to support the infantry bridgehead when it was established. 7 (Br) Armoured Division would try to cross at Grazzanisi on a one-brigade front, and 56 (Br) Division would do the same at Capua with a feint attack near the next crossing at Triflisco in VI (US) Corps' sector. The 7 (Br) Armoured Division and 56 (Br) Division attacks were to be little more than feints as they were not to be pressed if strongly opposed.

The US (VI) Corps had a slightly easier task. The river was narrower, the ground was higher and therefore drier, and the 3 Panzer Division was not up to the standard of the two other divisions in XIV Panzer Corps. It was composed of East Europeans with only tenuous German ancestry who were not fired with the same determination that the native German divisions possessed.* A further factor was that 45 (US) Division had no river to cross as it was already over the Calore and the Volturno Valley swung northwards before it reached 45 (US) Division's sector. These considerations, however, should not be allowed to decry the very fine efforts of 3 and 34 (US) Divisions. 3 (US) Division planned to cross at Triflisco the next bridge site north-east of Capua, but, realizing that it was an obvious site and would be strongly held, put in its main attack further up river to turn the defences of Triflisco. 34 (US) Division attacked further up still into the great bend of the Volturno where it is joined by the Calore.

The crossings started after dark on 12 October. The American divisions both established bridgeheads which they expanded steadily in the next 48 hours. X (Br) Corps were not so lucky. 56 (Br) Division failed to form a bridgehead at all at Capua, and 7 (Br) Armoured Division gained only a toe-hold at Grazzanise. 46 (Br) Division was luckier and succeeded with both its assault brigades. As the 46 (Br) Division assault was the main corps effort, the other two divisions did not continue their attacks. Instead they kept up a steady pressure with patrols and minor crossings so as to be ready to take advantage of the first signs of an enemy with-drawal. With so little bridging equipment available, the reinforcement of 46 (Br) Division's bridgehead and 7 (Br) Armoured Division's lodgment was very slow compared with river-crossings later in the war. The two squadrons of tanks were ferried round by the navy on 13 October but found their advance from the beaches barred by minefields. These took a long time to clear because the sappers found they contained non-metallic mines which did not give a reaction in their mine detectors. Painfully slow hand-prodding had to be used which kept the tanks out of the battle until midday on 14 October. No bridges were built in the X (Br) Corps' sector in the first three days. All the heavy weapons were ferried across the river on rafts. By the evening of 14 October, 46 (Br) Division's bridgehead was firm but the division was making slow progress against 15 Panzer Grenadier Division. 7 (Br) Armoured Division's bridgehead was also very small. 56 (Br) Division had mounted a number of small attacks which revealed that the Capua area was still strongly held by the Hermann Göring Division. 3 (US) Division, by contrast, had all its infantry across and was building a 30-ton bridge at Triflisco. 34 (US) Division had been equally successful.

Mark Clark decided to reinforce success. He moved the inter-corps boundary eastwards to enable 56 (Br) Division to cross by the Triflisco

* Although 3 Panzer Grenadier Division was theoretically a mobile division its poor reputation resulted in it being used largely in infantry divisional roles and rarely to mount far-ranging counter-attacks like the other mobile divisions.

bridge to come up on 3 (US) Division's exposed western flank. Once across the river 56 (Br) Division was to swing westwards to take the defenders of the Capua site in the rear. 46 (Br) Division and 7 (Br) Armoured Division were to continue crossing but the main effort was to be made to clear Route 7 and to establish a bridge at Capua. This change of plan and the German willingness to withdraw, now that they had held the Volturno up to Kesselring's target date of 15 October, loosened up the whole battle. 56 (Br) Division crossed at Triflisco during the night 14–15 October and by the afternoon of 16 October the sappers were able to start a 30-ton bridge at Capua. By 19 October the whole of the Volturno line was in Fifth Army's hands, but German resistance continued all along the front making the advance to the Barbara Line tedious and exacting. The change in German strategy was becoming apparent at tactical level.

East of the Apennines, Eighth Army was experiencing the same stiffening of the German resistance. 78 (Br) Division's leading elements just failed to capture the Route 16 bridge over the Trigno intact when it was blown up in their faces. Although they established a small bridgehead across the river, they could make no further progress against 16 Panzer Division. The Trigno position would have to be attacked in strength, but Montgomery would not be ready to do so before the end of the month. It was time to review Allied strategy in the light of the new German tactics. Weather and German determination to hold firm south of Rome had closed the first Allied breach in Fortress Europe.

8

The Seeds of Disillusion

'Following the Armistice there had been a hope that to evict the Germans from Italy with the aid of the Italian Army would be a speedy matter. Events proved this impossible and we became involved in a major campaign lacking a predetermined plan of action.'

Montgomery, *El Alamein to the Sangro*

As autumn slowly turned to winter the Allied planners seemed to lose their sureness of touch. There were a number of reasons for this. They had become used to success. Husky had been planned on a 'no risks' basis with a preponderance of force and plenty of reserve in hand. Risks became fashionable with Avalanche as the Italian surrender offered great strategic opportunities, and, at first, these risks were justified and success continued. Then the Italians failed to play their part; the Germans, in their turn, exploited this failure by deciding to stand south of Rome; and the weather broke. Alexander's Army Group now faced larger German forces than it had ever met before; its logistic situation was tenuous; and its reserves inadequate. Over its planners' shoulders hung the shadow of the Trident decision to withdraw the seven Overlord divisions with assault shipping and troop carrier aircraft by the end of November. It is not surprising that a note of desperation crept into their appreciations. Their main objective, Rome, seemed so near and yet they knew that their strength would ebb away unless they could reach the city quickly. If 15 Army Group Headquarters had been a predominantly American staff, it would probably have accepted the situation and cast its plans within the straitened circumstances of a diversionary theatre. Alexander's staff were mostly British; and he and his subordinates treated strategic decisions in the traditional British way as a basis for continued

14   Scorching heat and billowing dust

DUST AND MUD

15   Blown roads and foul weather

16   A bridge over the Sangro destroyed by floods

RIVER AND MOUNTAIN

17   An Italian mountainside

discussion as winter unfolded. In their view strategy should be pragmatic and flexible enough to allow modification if some unexpected success, or failure for that matter, opened up new situations. They hoped that, if they could make decisive progress quickly enough, the Trident sentence might be softened, leaving them with at least some of the divisions, ships and aircraft earmarked for withdrawal. They were encouraged in this by the obvious over-insurance in the Trident decisions. Why return divisions, and more especially mobile items like ships and aircraft, to the United Kingdom in November for an operation in May of the following year? There was clearly scope for negotiation here. If the Overlord resources could be kept for just a short while longer, great results might be achieved. Thus wishful thinking was added to the feeling of desperation caused by the November deadline. These two evils conspired together to lead Alexander's staff into a series of unrealistic estimates, and Churchill and the British Chiefs of Staff into further clashes with their American colleagues, who were determined to stick to the letter of their strategic agreements.

The 15 Army Group Staff carried out a careful review of the situation in the last ten days of October. Alexander discussed his conclusions with his army commanders and with Eisenhower at a series of conferences stretching into November. The basic plan produced from this initial review remained unaltered throughout these discussions, so we need not follow each twist and turn in the arguments which ensued. The position at the end of October was summed up on the following lines. Eleven Allied divisions were attacking nine German divisions in country which offered the defender every advantage and under lowering winter skies which restricted Allied air operations. In northern Italy there were another eight German divisions and this number could be increased to almost any figure if the Germans wished to mount a counter-offensive. Moreover, they could relieve tired divisions facing the Allies in the south with Rommel's divisions from the north whenever they wished to do so.* The Allies, on the other hand, were limited in the forces they could deploy in Italy. Available shipping had to be shared between three tasks: building up the Fifth and Eighth Armies; bringing in the strategic air forces to operate from Foggia and later from Rome against targets in southern Europe—one of the principal reasons for invading Italy in the first place; and providing an amphibious assault force to turn the successive German defensive lines across the Peninsula. The first task entailed bringing in fresh divisions

* The figures quoted above were Allied estimates of German strength made at the time. In fact, only eight German divisions were south of Rome; one was in the Rome area; and there were ten in Rommel's Army Group. Two of the latter were under orders to move south.

from elsewhere in the Mediterranean and clearing the large backlog of logistic units and equipment which were needed to maintain the armies in Italy.* The shipment of the strategic air forces presented a multiple problem as well. The Foggia airfields were badly damaged by Allied bombing and German demolition, and were so far below the specifications needed for the heavy American bombers that enormous quantities of pierced steel plank had to be shipped in to strengthen and extend the runways. To make matters worse the Combined Chiefs of Staff accepted the American Air Staffs' plan to set up the XV United States Air Force in Italy instead of in the United Kingdom. Staff estimates showed that without allowing for amphibious shipping to lift one assault division, the Allies would have, at the most, 13 divisions in Italy by the end of November, 15 a month later, and 17 by the end of January. The Germans could match these figures with no difficulty at all.

The Allied Commanders appreciated that their primary task was to draw German divisions away from Russia and North-West Europe. In their view, there was only one way to do this—attack—and, as Alexander put it, 'keep the Germans on their heels'. If the Germans decided to mount a counter-offensive in the spring this should be welcomed because it would hand the advantage of defence to the Allies and draw German divisions away from the Overlord area at the crucial moment. Eisenhower expressed their feelings in a signal to the Combined Chiefs of Staff dated 15 October, forwarding Alexander's appreciation: 'If we can keep him on his heels until early spring, then the more divisions he uses in a counter-offensive against us the better it will be for Overlord and then it makes little difference what happens to us'.

This conclusion had an ominously self-sacrificing ring about it. Simple arithmetic showed how dangerous a policy of unrelenting offensive action would be in the Italian winter. Allied air and naval superiority would be at a discount. Allied superiority in tanks and vehicles would be useless as long as they could not be deployed off the roads. Alexander's attacks would have to depend on infantry, artillery and sappers, but these arms would need overwhelming superiority to overcome the German defensive advantages. The most optimistic estimates would not give them parity before the end of January. In spite of these gloomy facts, the Allied Commanders set about planning a series of offensive battles which were designed to give them Rome by Christmas; or certainly before the Combined Chiefs of Staff insisted upon the Overlord shipping being returned to the United Kingdom. They were no longer planning to attain objectives well within their resources; they were stretching their

* There was at that time a deficit of 10,000 vehicles belonging to unit establishments and maintenance reserves awaiting shipment to Italy from North Africa and Sicily.

resources to reach unattainable goals. It is true that by adopting this policy they achieved the overall aim of pinning down German divisions, but it was a costly method of doing so. The outline plan agreed at these conferences was for Montgomery to press northwards to Pescara, taking the Trigno, Sangro and Pescara Rivers in his stride, and then turning southwest along Route 5 across the Apennines to threaten Rome from the east (*see* fig. 19). Mark Clark was to advance up Route 6 through the Liri Valley to attack the city from the south. It was hoped that Eighth Army would be supported by a brigade-sized amphibious force and that Fifth Army would have at least one division afloat, but this would depend on whether the Chiefs of Staff would let the Overlord shipping stay in the theatre later than November. The staffs calculated that if the Combined Chiefs of Staff could be persuaded to postpone its departure until 15 December, then the amphibious forces could be mounted at the expense of delaying the build up of the strategic air forces in Italy. This delay to the air forces seemed to make sense because the heavy bomber squadrons could not be fully deployed until the Rome airfields were secured. If the Chiefs of Staff were prepared to leave the shipping until 5 January, then the air build-up could be completed as well.

Eisenhower signalled to the Combined Chiefs of Staff asking for this delay and thereby set off a chain reaction which reverberated through the Allies' plans for the rest of the winter. This request was the thin end of the Italian theatre's wedge and was to be driven home relentlessly with Churchill's connivance. As Marshall had always feared, the secondary theatre was starting to suck resources from the primary effort. How the Mediterranean commanders envisaged reaching Rome in a further eight weeks is difficult to understand. They would have to advance about twice the distance which Fifth Army had already taken some seven weeks to cover from Salerno to the far side of the Volturno, and they knew that there was now a major German defensive line between them and their objective. They were also aware that fresh German divisions were moving southwards and they had recent experience of the effect of the autumn rains on their speed of advance. From the parochial Italian theatre point of view, it was right to press for the retention of shipping, but the Combined Chiefs, in agreeing to delay its return until 15 December, committed themselves to the capture of Rome at almost any cost. It always seemed that just one more extension of the shipping time limit would bring the Italian capital within the Allies' grasp. Each new effort to reach it met with further frustration, but it did lead to more German units moving south. To this extent Alexander's policy of keeping the Germans on their heels paid off, but at a high price in life and resources.

There was one facet of the Trident decisions that no one tried to alter at this late date. The seven divisions had been nominated and knew they were due to go back to England. They were the British 7 Armoured, 50 and 51 Infantry Divisions and the American 2 Armoured, 1 and 9 Infantry and 82 Airborne Divisions. The British armoured and infantry divisions had come all the way from El Alamein and were longing to get home. A warning of what would happen if their return was delayed had occurred at Salerno. Amongst drafts hurriedly embarked from transit camps in North Africa to reinforce 46 and 56 (Br) Divisions in the beachhead were men who had belonged to 51 (Highland) Division. When they found themselves on their way to reinforce English divisions in Italy,

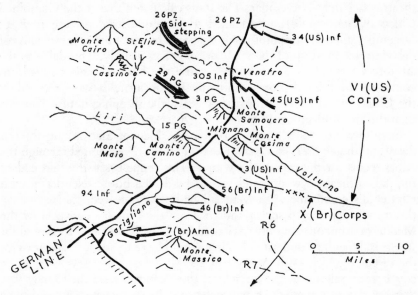

21   *Fifth Army's advance to the Bernhardt Line, 15 October–15 November*

instead of rejoining their units to go home, trouble started. When they reached Salerno, they mutinied. The authorities appreciated that a gross injustice had been done by the posting organization and so only the ringleaders were given long prison sentences.

Fifth Army continued its slow advance, pushing back the German rearguards covering the preparation of their main winter line. The Germans found no difficulty in keeping to their planned withdrawal schedule and bettered it in most areas. They had so much time in hand on the Barbara Line that this turned out to be something of a myth. When X (Br) Corps mounted its attack on the Monte Massico feature the

Germans withdrew without offering as much resistance as Allied intelligence staffs had led their commanders to expect. 7 (Br) Armoured Division was switched to the coastal sector to give its armour more scope for manoeuvre, and by 2 November it reached the Garigliano River with 46 (Br) Division on its inland flank. All the bridges had been destroyed and the river banks were heavily mined. All movement in the wide flood plain drew accurate artillery fire and there seemed little doubt about the enemy's determination to contest any attempt to cross.

Further inland 56 (Br) Division ran into the southern bulwark of the Bernhardt Line, Monte Camino. VI (US) Corps, advancing up Route 6 and the Volturno Valley, struck this grim mountain position at much the same time. 3 (US) Division's initial momentum enabled it to take Monte Cesima which was one of the forward ramparts of the Bernhardt Line covering the Mignano defile on Route 6. 45 (US) Division in a similar way won a foothold in the hills above Venafro and 34 (US) Division had some success on the extreme inland flank of Fifth Army, but all progress was soon halted by determined German counter-attacks. Von Senger, who now commanded XIV Panzer Corps, was ready to oppose Fifth Army in strength.

Now that the autumn rains had definitely broken, the German policy was to withdraw their mobile divisions, which had been in action almost continuously since Salerno and in some cases since the invasion of Sicily, and to replace them with infantry divisions more suited to protracted defence in mountain positions. Von Senger disposed 94 Infantry Division along the high ground overlooking the Garigliano. He kept the reliable 15 Panzer Grenadier Division in the line to hold the key feature of Monte Camino. The rather shaky 3 Panzer Grenadier Division was made responsible for the northern side of the Mignano defile, the security of which depended upon the defence of Monte Samoucro. Then came 305 Infantry Division holding the rest of the high ground up to the inter-corps boundary with 26 Panzer Division of Herr's LXXVI Panzer Corps above Isernia. The Hermann Göring Division was withdrawn into reserve for a well-earned rest and refit. Thus the four German divisions in the line and the fifth in reserve were opposed by only six American and British divisions—hardly sufficient superiority for an offensive in mountain country.

Fifth Army's first attempt to breach the Bernhardt Line failed. 56 (Br) Division and 3 (US) Division attacked Monte Camino on 5 November and after ten days hard fighting had to accept defeat at the hands of 15 Panzer Grenadier Division. It was so difficult to keep the forward troops supplied on the mountain side that Mark Clark authorized their withdrawal to the lower ground. 45 and 34 (US) Divisions made better progress against 3 Panzer Grenadier and 305 Infantry Divisions who allowed the Americans to overrun a number of their forward positions. The Germans had not expected a serious Allied attack in the mountains north of Route 6 but they reacted swiftly to VI (US) Corps' threat above Venafro. Thinning out the Adriatic sector in front of Eighth Army, they switched 26 Panzer Division across to von Senger's front to relieve 305 Infantry Division which had to be taken out of the line to reorganize. Shortly afterwards 29 Panzer Grenadier Division came up from Tenth Army Reserve and relieved 3 Panzer Grenadier Division. Von Senger's front began to take on a formidable appearance with three panzer and panzer grenadier divisions holding the Bernhardt positions. Attack and counterattack followed each other in rapid succession all along VI (US) Corps' front and by 15 November it was clear the Fifth Army had been fought to a standstill for the time being. Only a co-ordinated offensive, carefully planned, using both Fifth and Eighth Armies, was likely to prise the Germans out of their positions. Alexander authorized Mark Clark to halt his offensive and to regroup.

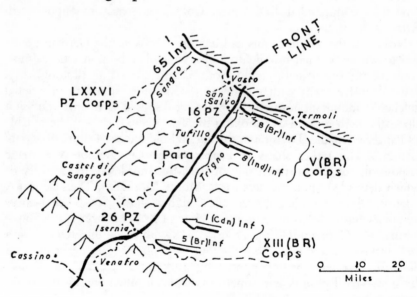

22   *Eighth Army's operations across the Trigno, 2–7 November*

Eighth Army opened its attack across the Trigno after several postponements due to bad weather on the night 2–3 November. V (Br) Corps attacked along the coast, using the experienced 78 (Br) Division with heavy air and naval supporting fire against the San Salvo ridge, while the less experienced 8 (Ind) Division started its first operation in the Italian Campaign by attacking across the river ten miles inland to take Tufillo. 78 (Br) Division was opposed by 16 Panzer Division and 8 (Ind) Division by 1 Para Division which was now three regiments strong. XIII (Br) Corps supported V (Br) Corps by attacking along Route 17 towards Isernia against 26 Panzer Division. 16 Panzer Division reacted strongly to 78 (Br) Division's attack and fought bitterly for two days, suffering heavy losses in the process. The weather remained fine and enabled the Desert Air Force and the Royal Navy ships off the coast to give excellent support. Weakened by two months' continuous fighting, 16 Panzer Division gave way late on 4 November and fell back behind 65 Infantry Division which was preparing the main Gustav positions behind the River Sangro. 8 (Ind) Division fought a brisk action with detachments of 1 Para Division who only withdrew when their flank was exposed by 16 Panzer Division's departure. XIII (Br) Corps, away inland, struggled forward as fast as its sappers could repair or cut their way round the demolished bridges on the mountain roads and entered Isernia unopposed as 26 Panzer Division moved across to strengthen XIV Panzer Corps' resistance to Fifth Army. 1 Para Division side-stepped to fill the gap left by 26 Panzer Division and had little difficulty in blocking further progress by XIII (Br) Corps.

78 (Br) Division reached the Sangro on 8 November and soon had patrols across the wide river bed and up amongst the main German positions on the high ground overlooking the north bank. 8 (Ind) Division took rather longer to close up to the river against 1 Para Division's rear-guards which made excellent use of the difficult mountain country in this sector. 8 (Ind) Division was not squarely up to the river until 19 November when the last parachute detachments withdrew to the north bank.

In the meantime planning had been going ahead to co-ordinate the next actions of Fifth and Eighth Armies. Hitherto they had fought separate campaigns either side of the Apennines. The lateral roads had been just as thoroughly demolished by the Germans as the main axis of advance. Engineer effort was naturally concentrated on the latter and so road communication between the two armies was precarious. 26 Panzer Division's sudden move from LXXVI to XIV Panzer Corps sectors showed that the undamaged lateral roads behind the German front were being used to switch reserves to and fro between the two panzer corps. Co-ordination of the Allied armies' thrusts was, therefore, essential. Alexander's favourite tactic was the two-handed punch: like a boxer he would hit with, say, his left until the German reserves had been drawn across the front and then strike with his right, and vice-versa, until he achieved a break-through. He decided early in November to adopt this policy with Fifth and Eighth Armies. Mark Clark was to prepare a new offensive to break the Bernhardt Line, which would not be mounted until Montgomery had smashed his way through the Sangro positions and had drawn units like 26 Panzer Division back to the Adriatic flank. Montgomery estimated that he would be ready to assault across the Sangro on 20 November, i.e., five days after Mark Clark stopped his first attempt to break through the Mignano defile. Fifth Army's offensive would reopen about 30 November and would be supported by a divisional landing on the coast south of Rome, timed to occur when Fifth Army reached a point 30 miles from the proposed landing area at Anzio. The amphibious operation was codenamed 'Shingle' and would have to take place, at the latest, by 15 January,[*] otherwise there would not be enough shipping left in the theatre. Allowing time for mounting the amphibious operation, a decision to go ahead with it would be needed not later than 20 December. Mark Clark had thus a bare three weeks from the start of his renewed offensive in which to break through the Bernhardt and Gustav Lines so as to be reasonably certain of linking up with the amphibious force. The weather would have to remain remarkably fine and the Germans suffer some unexpected reverse to make this plan even remotely possible. Wishful thinking was clearly at work. Churchill's goad, as will be seen in the next chapter, was adding to the staff's inclination to underestimate the problems facing both armies.

In the German camp, Kesselring at last won Hitler's wholehearted support. Hitler had agreed to hold south of Rome early in October. It was now essential to organize the whole of the Italian theatre under one commander-in-chief. Rommel's headquarters was to be replaced by a new headquarters called Fourteenth Army under General von Mackensen. Both von Vietinghoff's Tenth Army and the new Fourteenth Army were to come under Army Group 'C'—the new title for Kesselring's headquarters. Hitler was not sure whether to leave Kesselring as the theatre commander with the title of C.-in-C. South-West (a title chosen to avoid confusion with the C.-in-C. South on the Russian Front), or to give the command to his rival, Rommel. Hitler seems to have decided to give it to Rommel but at the last moment changed his mind and left Kesselring in command, sending Rommel off to organize the forces concentrating in northern France to oppose Overlord. Kesselring could now dispose all German forces in Italy, north and south, to suit his strategic plans. The only bar to his bringing down substantial reinforcements to the Gustav Line was the fear of Allied landings behind the main front and the need

---

[*] The extension of the previous 15 December and 5 January deadlines is explained on p. 168.

to keep a strong German presence near the main Italian cities in the north to discourage rebellion.

The stage was now set on both sides for the first round of the battle for Rome. Alexander struck first with his right and then with his left.

THE BATTLES OF THE SANGRO
AND THE MORO

'... we were running what was to prove a losing race with the winter weather.'

Montgomery, describing the Battle of the Sangro,
El Alamein to the Sangro

Hitler issued his order appointing Kesselring C.-in-C. South-West on 21 November, the day after Montgomery's assault on the Sangro had been due to begin. The Battle of the Sangro turned out to be the prototype of a series of disenchanting winter operations fought by both Allied armies. Montgomery had thought about this battle some weeks before his army closed up to the Sangro. The enemy's intention to stand on the river was well known and his fortifications had been repeatedly photographed from the air. The Eighth Army staff had designed all its preliminary moves in the advance from Foggia northwards with this battle in mind.

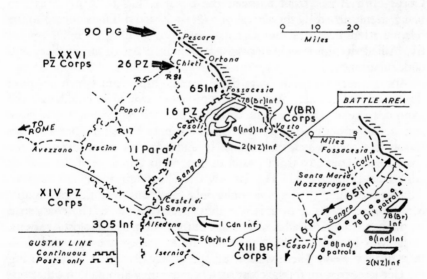

23   *Allied and German dispositions on the Sangro, 20 November, and Montgomery's first plan of attack*

Montgomery, the modern master of the set-piece battle, was determined to make the breaching of the Sangro positions yet another of his master-pieces. Weather, the Italian topography and the German Army were to decide otherwise.

The river Sangro runs in a wide gravel bed and is normally only a few feet deep. It is less of an obstacle than the soft fields on either bank which will only support wheeled and tracked vehicles in dry weather. The Germans decided not to defend the river itself; instead they developed their main line of resistance on the higher ground some three miles north of the river. The main feature was the Li Colli ridge running parallel to the river from the village of Fossacesia near the coast, through Mozzagrogna and Santa Maria to Casoli. Their positions then swung further away from the river to follow the line of the lateral Route 84 to Castel di Sangro and Alfredena. 65 Infantry Division was known to be holding the coastal sector with 16 Panzer Division in reserve behind it. 1 Para Division held the rest of the front stretching some 25 miles from Casoli to Castel di Sangro, most of which was impassable to anything but small lightly equipped columns using pack animals for supply. Unknown to Eighth Army, 90 Panzer Grenadier Division, which had been in Sardinia, was on its way south to reinforce Herr's LXXVI Panzer Corps. 16 Panzer Division was due to be withdrawn for transfer to Russia and was to be replaced by 26 Panzer Division as soon as the situation on the XIV Panzer Corps–Fifth Army front allowed the transfer. Eighth Army was also being strengthened by the arrival of 2 (New Zealand) Division and so the relative strengths were four German divisions holding 40 miles against five Allied divisions which possessed the advantage of air, artillery and tank superiority.

Montgomery's objective was the Avezzano area from which he could threaten Rome. There were four approaches which he could use: the main coast road which was the obvious approach but the only one large and strong enough to carry the Army's supply traffic; Route 81 from Casoli to Chieti which ran parallel to and some 15 miles inland of the coast road; Route 17 from Castel di Sangro to Popoli; and the narrow Alfredena–Pescina road. The last two ran through about 40 miles of difficult mountain defiles and could only carry one-way military traffic. Montgomery's choice of axis was thus severely limited. The coast road would have to be cleared at some stage of the operation for logistic reasons, so he was forced to accept the two routes nearest the coast, obvious though they were. There was little hope of any deception plan reducing the German strength on the coast road because they also had no other op-tion but to hold strongly on this obvious approach. All that could be done was to delay the move of German reserves to the point of assault by showing activity all along the front. Montgomery, therefore, directed XIII (Br) Corps to simulate the preparations for a major attack from Isernia towards Castel di Sangro and Alfredena. All the well-known tricks developed with such efficiency by the Eighth Army staff were to be employed. Elaborate wireless deception plans were made, simulating such moves as Montgomery's tactical headquarters to the XIII (Br) Corps area. Ammunition dumps and gun positions on the coast were concealed whereas those inland were allowed to show and were exaggerated in size by using dummies. 1 (Br) Airborne Division, which had not yet left the theatre for the United Kingdom, was to stage embarkation exercises at Barletta to create the impression of preparations for an amphibious right hook aimed at Pescara or Ancona. The Royal Navy was also to bombard the Pescara area.

Montgomery's first plan gave V (Br) Corps, with 78 (Br) and 8 (Ind) Divisions under command, the task of breaking through on the coast road. The New Zealand Division, direct under Army control, would attack along the inland Route 81 towards Chieti. XIII (Br) Corps with 5 (Br) and 1 (Cdn) Divisions was to divert attention and to pin down German reserves by attacking towards Alfredena and Castel di Sangro. In the coastal sector, where Montgomery intended to break through, V (Br) Corps was to attack in three phases: first, 78 (Br) Division would secure a bridgehead over the river below Mozzagrogna; then 8 (Ind) Division would break into the enemy position by taking Mozzagrogna; and finally 78 (Br) Division would exploit with 4 (Br) Armoured Brigade along the Li Colli ridge to take Fossacesia, thus opening up the coast road. The attack was to have heavy artillery and air support of the type that the Eighth Army was so adept at organizing. The success of V (Br) Corps' attack, however, would probably depend upon the surprise use of tanks. The Germans appeared to have left the steep slopes up to the Li Colli ridge uncovered by anti-tank guns, believing it was unsuitable for tanks. General Alfrey, commanding V (Br) Corps, thought that tanks could get up in strength and thus win surprise as well as saving the infantry making a frontal attack alone. The attack also depended on the river remaining fordable and the approaches firm enough for military traffic.

The New Zealand Division's plan was to attack by stealth astride the demolished bridge site near Casoli on Route 81, hoping that the enemy would be distracted by the noisy preparations to the north. Great pains were taken not to reveal the presence of the New Zealand troops. 78 (Br) Division stayed patrolling the whole front on which it had reached the river and 8 (Ind) Division left its 19 (Ind) Brigade opposite the Casoli crossing where it too had originally arrived. Behind this screen the rest of 8 (Ind) Division moved north into its attacking position behind 78

(Br) Division, and the New Zealanders assembled behind 19 (Ind) Brigade.

Preliminary operations were timed to start on the night 19–20 November and the main attack was to be made on 20–21 November. Rain fell intermittently from 9 November onwards. On 16 November the river was too high for patrols to wade across and the river banks too soft for vehicles. It looked as if the attack would have to be postponed, but on 19 November the weather improved and the river had started to fall. The preliminary operations went ahead that night in the V (Br) Corps' sector, but the river was still too high opposite the New Zealanders. 78 (Br) Division secured a bridgehead as planned through which 8 (Ind) Division would attack the following night. On 20 November it rained and rained. Rather than attacking when night came, every effort had to be made to ferry heavy weapons over to the forward troops of 78 (Br) Division who were now stranded on the far bank without support. For the next few days V (Br) Corps struggled to ferry over more troops, anti-tank weapons and tanks to secure a conventional bridgehead using troops of both its divisions. The high hopes of a great tank attack to clear the Li Colli ridge disappeared, it seemed for ever, when on 23 November flood water from the mountains swept down and submerged the three bridges which had been laboriously built by the sappers during the previous nights. A new plan had to be made with more limited objectives which did not depend on tank support. 8 (Ind) Division would take Mozzagrogna with an infantry assault on about 26 November and Santa Maria on 28 November. 78 (Br) Division would then clear the Li Colli ridge with or without tanks on 29 and 30 November. Timings were now only targets and 78 (Br) Division had to make two plans; one if the weather improved and enabled tanks to move and one if it did not.

The New Zealand attack started later than V (Br) Corps' and suffered the same fate. On 22–23 November, 19 (Ind) Brigade mounted a preliminary operation to seize some high ground on the flank overlooking the New Zealand crossing places. Although the Indians took their objective, they were then cut off by the rising flood water in the river behind them. A new plan had to be made, discarding stealth and using full air and artillery support timed for 28 November.

Bad weather had another effect. It reduced patrolling and prevented intelligence of enemy reinforcements reaching the British commanders. Kesselring had visited the front and had ordered the defences of Mozzagrogna to be strengthened. 16 Panzer Division moved one regimental group into the sector opposite the New Zealanders, allowing 65 Infantry Division to shorten and so strengthen its front opposite V (Br) Corps. The leading units of 90 Panzer Grenadier Division were also starting to arrive and 26 Panzer Division was on its way to relieve 16 Panzer Division. If the V Corps attack had gone in on 20 November, as planned, it would have hit only the inexperienced and relatively immobile 65 Infantry Division; it would now meet elements of three German mobile divisions as well. Weather had robbed Eighth Army of its chance to break through Kesselring's winter line.

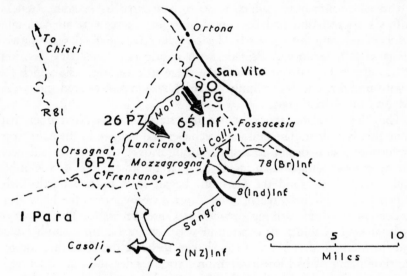

24   The Battle of the Sangro, 27 November–2 December

Between the flood of 23 November and the reopening of the Eighth Army offensive, the weather and the depth of the river varied from day to day. The Desert Air Force kept up a programme of some 400–500 sorties a day, deluging the enemy defences. On land, the battle against mud went on with all divisions trying to build up shallow bridgeheads on the far side of the river so as to be ready to attack when the ground dried. On 27 November things improved. About 100 tanks were moved successfully into the bridgehead in daylight and that evening 8 (Ind) Division attacked and took Mozzagrogna, but was driven out by units of 26 Panzer Division which had just arrived. During the following day, V (Br) Corps consolidated its gains and prepared to renew the attack on the night 28–29 November. A reconnaissance ordered by General Alfrey showed that it might still be possible to use tanks up and along the Li Colli ridge. A plan was made for 8 (Ind) Division to retake Mozzagrogna during the night and for 78 (Br) Division to mount a combined tank and infantry assault against the ridge early next morning, 29 November.

Unfortunately for the Germans the weather remained fine and enabled the two attacks to be given full air and artillery preparation and support. The German prisoners later complained that they had never suffered such bombing and shelling, even in Russia. The Indians took Mozzagrogna in their night attack and exploited along the road to Lanciano. 78 (Br) Division were equally successful. The tanks climbed the ridge and turned left to take Santa Maria which was firmly secured by evening. General Alfrey's appreciation had been proved right; there were no anti-tank defences covering this approach. The following day the attack was renewed using 4 (Br) Armoured Brigade with a brigade of 78 (Br) Division. It was directed northwards along the ridge to take Fossacesia which fell before midday, and by evening 78 (Br) Division had cleared the whole ridge to the Adriatic coast.

The New Zealand attack, which had started on 28 November, had gone slowly at first. The tanks and vehicles had bogged in the exits from the crossings and the New Zealand bridges over the Sangro had been damaged by shelling and an accurate Luftwaffe attack. On 29 November things went better and the Germans began to withdraw northwards. When 78 (Br) Division reached the sea on 30 November, the New Zealanders were within striking distance of Castel Frentano. The whole of 65 Infantry Division's main position was now in Eighth Army's hands and the German division was too shaken to be of much further use for the time being. It had lost its divisional commander and one of its regimental commanders, both seriously wounded, and had yielded over 1,000 prisoners. Counter-attacks by 26 Panzer Division and 90 Panzer Grenadier Division were launched piecemeal and were not strong enough to regain 65 Infantry Division's lost positions, but they were able to re-establish a new defensive line based on the high ground overlooking the north bank of the Moro River which screens the lateral route running south from Ortona to Orsogna on the New Zealander's road to Chieti. 78 (Br) Division took San Vito on the coast just south of the Moro and 8 (Ind) Division entered Lanciano, both divisions reaching the Moro itself on 3 December. The New Zealanders pressed on from Castel Frentano and attacked Orsogna, the next dominating feature blocking the road to Chieti. Their first attack reached the centre of the town but vicious counter-attacks by 26 Panzer Division drove them out again. This was the furthest into Orsogna that any Allied attack penetrated for five long wintry months.

German writers have suggested that the defeat of 65 Infantry Division should have led to a British break-through to Pescara if it had not been for Montgomery's logistic timidity. Under normal circumstances quick exploitation should have been possible and might have led to the destruction of LXXVI Panzer Corps—but conditions were not normal. The Germans were operating over unbroken roads and could move their troops and supplies quicker than the British even though they were harassed, on fine days, by the Allied air forces. They also had the ability to introduce fresh troops from the north to relieve tired or defeated units. British superiority lay in their armour, artillery and air power all of which were hampered by weather. When tanks could move, they were canalized into narrow approaches by soft ground and became easy targets for German anti-tank weapons. Although guns could be hauled into position, they still had to be supplied with large quantities of ammunition which took

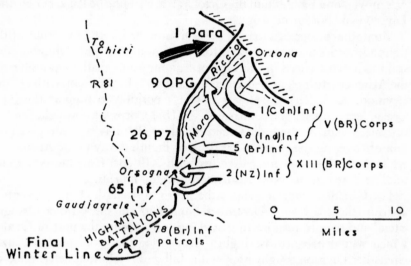

25 *The Battle across the Moro, 8–20 December*

days to bring up over the broken roads. When aircraft could fly, the Allied air forces were extremely effective but the number of flying days were shrinking as the winter deepened. Under these conditions a break-through was unlikely. Moreover, Montgomery would have been unwise to concentrate more than light troops forward of the Sangro until he had an all-weather supply line across that treacherous river. It took his engineers until 6 December to build a high-level bridge proof against floods. In the meantime both he and his opponent, General Herr, regrouped for the next round.

The pattern of fighting on the Adriatic coast was now established. Both sides realized that neither could make much headway in the mountains. XIII (Br) Corps had reached Castel di Sangro and Alfredena, but further advance was too easily blocked by small German forces holding the defiles on the few passable roads. On the coast, there were only the two axes of advance already used by Eighth Army in its Sangro battles—the coast road leading through the small port of Ortona to Pescara and the inland road to Chieti. Both commanders thinned out their mountain sectors and concentrated their troops near the coast. On the German side, 90 Panzer Grenadier Division held a six-mile front behind the Moro based on the Ortona–Orsogna lateral road. Then came 26 Panzer Division stretching as far as Orsogna. The remnants of 65 Infantry Division held Guardiagrele and beyond them 1 Para Division was being relieved by some newly arrived special 'high mountain' battalions. 1 Para Division was moved unit by unit into the Ortona area, enabling 90 Panzer Grenadier Division to shorten its front.

Montgomery decided that 78 (Br) Division had borne the brunt of the fighting on the main Army axis for long enough. 8 (Ind) Division were still too inexperienced in this type of fighting to be made responsible for the Army centre line, so he decided to relieve 78 (Br) Division with 1 (Cdn) Division. As V (Br) Corps was not in a position to support the New Zealanders properly, Headquarters XIII (Br) Corps was brought over to organize the drive along the Chieti Road. 78 (Br) Division was given the task of covering the extreme left flank of Eighth Army in the Apennines, while 5 (Br) Division moved across with XIII (Br) Corps to come into the line between the New Zealanders and the Indians.

The Canadians attacked across the Moro in strength about three miles in from the coast on 8 December hoping to cut the Ortona–Orsogna lateral and then to turn north-east along it to capture the port of Ortona which would help to ease Eighth Army's logistic problems. 90 Panzer Grenadier Division fought back with skill and resolution, determined to show what a real German division could do.* It took 12 days' hard fighting before the Canadians mastered the lateral road and managed to push patrols into Ortona late on 20 December. 8 (Ind) Division ably supported the Canadian's inland flank and tried to outflank Ortona, but without success. The New Zealanders made two more attacks on Orsogna on 7 and 18 December but were repulsed. The Moro, like the Sangro, had been cleared, but this time the Germans did not pull back to the next major river line; they opposed Eighth Army where they stood.

The fighting in Ortona has become a classic example in the art of street fighting. The German defenders were units of 1 Para Division which came into the town during the Canadian struggle for the lateral road. 3 Para Regiment was responsible for the Ortona sector and had made its 2nd Battalion under Captain Liebschev responsible for the town. Liebschev

* 65 Infantry Division contained mixed nationalities and was looked down upon by the pure German divisions.

had already won his spurs in street fighting when his battalion defended Centuripe in Sicily against 78 (Br) Division. He was about to add one more page to 1 Para Division's saga of ruthless actions. Liebschev prepared his defences with extraordinary thoroughness, choosing only to defend the northern half of the town. The southern half was turned into a nightmare of trapped and mined houses some of which were blown into the streets to form road blocks and others were blown up to clear arcs of fire. All his strong points were linked by what is best described as 'mouse holing' from house to house. All approaches to the defended sector were either heavily mined or under concealed enfilade fire. The main approach into the town square was left attractively unobstructed, an invitation which the Canadians managed to resist. The 2 Canadian Brigade was given the task of clearing a way through the town and was forced to fight its way from house to house on not more than a 250-yard front. Every building, when taken, had to be occupied to stop the Germans infiltrating back into it again after the leading troops had passed on. The fighting was at such close quarters that artillery support was impossible, and so ruthless that little quarter was given. One example of the type of fighting was the destruction of a whole Canadian platoon in one house under which a time bomb had been placed. The Canadians retaliated by trapping and killing a patrol of 20 paratroopers with a booby trap in the same area. It was not until 28 December that the first Canadians fought their way out to the far side of the town; by then Captain Liebschev had withdrawn his battalion back behind the small Riccio River two miles north of Ortona where the rest of 3 Para Regiment was waiting to block any further Allied advance.

Inland of Ortona, the Indians tried to work their way forward but suffered heavy losses and soon met the parachutists opposing them as well behind the Riccio. The New Zealanders and 5 (Br) Division further inland made one more despairing attempt to break through to the Chieti road past the Orsogna block on 23 December. Heavy air and artillery preparation failed to subdue the defenders and the XIII (Br) Corps' final effort was spent when rain started falling again on Christmas Day.

Montgomery reviewed the situation in the last week of December and advised Alexander that in his view the offensive should be stopped. There was no hope of breaking through to Rome from the Adriatic as long as Allied material superiority was hampered by winter weather. To go on would be to play into the Germans' hands. The Germans would be doing the containing and the Allies would be wasting resources which they would need in the spring. A new factor had also emerged; gun ammunition was running short. Shorn of tank and air support, the infantry needed very heavy artillery programmes to enable them to seize objectives without undue casualties. The current rate of supply could not keep pace with expenditure; if it went on there would be no reserves of ammunition available for the spring when the armies would have to attack hardest to prevent German divisions leaving to face Overlord. Alexander agreed with Montgomery's views as far as the Adriatic coast was concerned and authorized Eighth Army to stop fighting for a break-through. Instead it was to keep the Germans on their toes and do everything short of a major offensive to stop them withdrawing troops from LXXVI Panzer Corps.

On 30 December Montgomery handed Eighth Army over to General Leese and returned to England to take over 21 Army Group for Overlord.

BREAKING THE BERNHARDT LINE

'What I experienced has astounded and dismayed me. The northern slopes of Monte Cassino on the opposite side of the valley
was under bombardment of an intensity such as I had not witnessed since the big battles of the First World War.'

Von Senger und Etterlin, describing the Battle of Monte
Cassino, *Neither Fear nor Hope*

Mark Clark's Fifth Army spent the last days of November regrouping and preparing for their part in Alexander's first co-ordinated offensive. Its attack had been timed to start on 30 November. Bad weather delayed preparations and Montgomery's late start across the Sangro made further delay advisable. Alexander suggested 12 December but Mark Clark felt he could start on 2 December and thereby give the Shingle landing* a greater chance of being launched before its shipping was withdrawn. His army had been reinforced by a number of new formations. 7 (Br) Armoured Division and 82 (US) Airborne Division had left for Overlord. In their places had come the II (US) Corps from Sicily and 1 (US) Armoured Division, 1 Special Service Force (a mixed American and Canadian force of six battalions of specially trained commando-type troops) and the first of the American equipped French North African divisions, the 2 Moroccan Division. The first Italian formation, 1 Italian Motorized Group, to enter active operations against the Germans also came under command of Fifth Army.

Mark Clark's plan was to fold up the Bernhardt Line from the south in three phases: in Phase I, X (Br) Corps and II (US) Corps, which took over 3 and 36 (US) Divisions and 1 Special Service Force opposite the Mignano defile, would take Monte Camino, the southern bastion; in Phase II, X (Br) Corps would take over the whole of Monte Camino and leave II (US)

* The amphibious left-hook to Anzio (p. 144).

Corps free to take Monte Lungo in the centre of the defile and Monte Samoucro, the northern bastion, while VI (US) Corps with 34 and 45 (US) Divisions demonstrated in the hills above Venafro along the Colli-Atina road; Phase III would be exploitation to the Liri Valley once the door had been prised open.

Operation 'Rain Coat'—as the Phase I attack on Monte Camino was appropriately called—was preceded by a number of deception measures designed to direct the enemy's attention elsewhere. Dummy tank concentrations and gun positions were established opposite the lower reaches

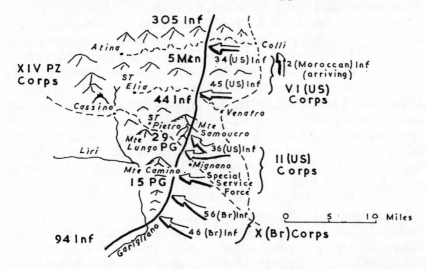

26   *Fifth Army operation to destroy the Bernhardt Line, 2–29 December*

of the Garigliano; naval ships and air forces bombarded the coast to the north of the river; landing craft were loaded with troops in Naples Harbour to worry the Germans about their seaward flank; and VI (US) Corps mounted demonstrations at the opposite end of the Fifth Army front. The attack itself was carried out by 46 and 56 (Br) Divisions from the south-east and the Special Service Force and 36 (US) Division from the north-east. In the preliminary bombardment directed at 15 Panzer Grenadier Division's positions on the mountain and against the main German gun areas in rear, some 4,000 tons of shell were fired. German prisoners reported that very little damage was done by either the accurate artillery shelling, which did not penetrate their dug-outs, or by the heavy air bombardment, which was too inaccurate on the mountain slopes to be effective. The Rain Coat battle itself lasted from 2 to 10 December. It consisted of hard climbing by the infantry, followed by a series of limited attacks from spur to spur and peak to peak until the German positions were finally eroded away. Difficulty in moving units and supplies up the mountain tracks and the courageous resistance of the Germans made progress slow and laborious. The key peak, Monte Camino itself, did not fall to 56 (Br) Division until 6 December and it took a further four days to clear the western slopes. Some German units left their withdrawal too late. The river rose behind them washing away their improvised bridges and ferries, forcing them to abandon their heavy equipment and swim the river. X (Br) Corps, who took the brunt of the fighting, lost over 1,000 men in this ten-day battle for one mountain feature.

The second phase of Mark Clark's plan started before Rain Coat was over. 36 (US) Division's first attack on Monte Samoucro opened on 7 December. The first objectives fell as planned, but determined counter-attacks by 29 Panzer Grenadier Division stopped any further advance. On the same day the Italian Mobile Group attacked Monte Lungo and was driven back. A fresh attack by II (US) Corps was mounted on 15 December this time with greater success, and by 17 December the whole of Monte Samoucro had fallen and Monte Lungo was in American hands. Casualties had been very high and 36 (US) Division's effort was exhausted by the time it took the village of San Pietro overlooking Route 6. In front of it stood another defended position around San Vittore which would have to be taken before Route 6 could be used.

To the north, VI (US) Corps had been no more successful. 26 Panzer Division, when it moved eastwards to oppose Eighth Army on the Sangro, was replaced by an Austrian-manned division called the 44 (Hoch und Deutschmeister) Infantry Division, which had been reformed after Stalingrad and was untrained in mountain warfare. To its north 5 Mountain Division arrived, but this formation had spent its war on the flat plains in front of Leningrad and had forgotten all it ever knew about mountains. Further north still, 305 Infantry Division sidestepped into Eighth Army's mountain sector. VI (US) Corps' American divisions, which were equally inexperienced in hill fighting, made little headway against these troops, but when 2 Moroccan Division, who were experts in mountain warfare, arrived under command, the tide turned against the Germans and they were steadily forced back towards the main Gustav Line. This Allied success, however, had come too late.

On 18 December Mark Clark realized that his army's progress was not fast enough. He could not reach even the entrance to the Liri Valley let alone a point 30 miles short of Anzio by the time the assault shipping for Shingle would have to be withdrawn. He signalled Alexander:

I reluctantly recommend cancellation of Operation 'Shingle' in early January. ... The limiting date of 15 January which has been set for return of craft makes it impracticable to launch this operation due to the fact that the remainder of the Fifth Army will not be in a position to support it. . . .

The moment of truth had come. The Germans had succeeded in stabilizing the front for the winter, and both Allied armies were exhausted. The point of diminishing returns had been reached; losses were mounting and the gains were falling to a few hundred yards per day. To continue attacking under these conditions seemed to be a policy as bankrupt as the Allied offensives on the Western Front in the First World War. There was no room for manoeuvre; the defence had the upper hand and the attacker's trump card of material superiority was to remain useless in their hands until the spring weather returned.

December 1943–April 1944

THE WINTER OF DISILLUSION

'. . . we cannot leave the Rome situation to stagnate and fester for three months without crippling preparation of Anvil [attack on the south of France] and thus hampering Overlord. We cannot go to other tasks and leave this unfinished job behind.'

Churchill's telegram to British
Chiefs of Staff, 25 December 1943

9

The Tyranny of Overlord

'Overlord remains top of the bill but should not be such a tyrant
as to rule out every other activity in the Mediterranean.'
*Churchill at the 24 November session of
Sextant conference in Cairo*

While the Fifth and Eighth Armies were feeling the first bite of the Italian
winter and the effects of Hitler's order to stand south of Rome, important
strategic decisions were being taken at the fourth great inter-Allied conference which was held in Cairo and Tehran under the codewords 'Sextant'
for Cairo and 'Eureka' for Tehran.* The strategic situation had developed
dramatically since Quadrant. Italy had surrendered, giving the Allies far
less help than they or she had hoped. The Russians had crossed the
Dnieper after a 250-mile advance since Hitler's abortive Operation Zitadelle. The tide was turning as well against Japan in the Pacific, bringing
plans for her decisive defeat nearer practical possibility and hence increasing the Pacific theatre's demands on American resources. The Americans
were becoming just as afraid of missing opportunities in the Far East as
the British were in the Mediterranean. There was little change in the
strategic arguments used by both sides, but there was now a need to
translate strategic concepts into actual tactical plans as the shadow of
Overlord grew shorter. As Roosevelt put it, the main issue before the
Sextant conference was how to resolve the conflict between the American
determination to maintain 'the integrity of Overlord' and the British
desire 'to keep the Mediterranean ablaze'. Although the Americans and
Russians suspected that the British were still paying lip service to Overlord,

* Churchill, Roosevelt and Chiang Kai-Shek met in Cairo from 22 to 26 November;
Churchill and Roosevelt went on to Tehran to meet Stalin on 28 November while the
Chinese went home; then on 3 December Churchill and Roosevelt returned to Cairo to
finalize their plans before dispersing on 7 December.

no one challenged the pre-eminence of the cross-Channel operation. The points at issue were the timing of Overlord and the direction which operations should take in the Mediterranean after the Pisa–Rimini Line had been reached.

The British position remained much as it had been throughout the previous conferences. In their view the key to success lay in stretching German resources to the limit by threats against Fortress Europe from the north of Norway all the way round to Turkey. It might be that, if this policy was successful, Overlord would become a mere *coup de grace* operation. The Germans were most sensitive to threats in the eastern Mediterranean as had been shown by their determination to recapture the Dodecanese Islands of Cos and Leros, which had been captured and held for a short time by British light forces when Italy surrendered. The island of Rhodes was the key to the German defences of the Aegean. If this island could be taken, the threat to southern Greece would draw large numbers of German troops into the Balkans at a minor cost to the Allies. There would be no need to press on into Greece; the threat would be enough. A similar threat could be created cheaply by establishing Commandos and Special Service forces on the eastern shore of the Adriatic to support the Yugoslav partisans. Here again no major landing would be needed to attract substantial German reinforcement. The local guerillas, if well supported with supplies of equipment, would do that just as efficiently as an Allied force landed on the Dalmatian coast. Finally there was the Italian campaign itself. This must not be allowed to languish. 'He who holds Rome, holds the title deeds of Italy', said Churchill when summing up the British case. If the needs of diversionary operations in the Mediterranean meant a few weeks' delay in mounting Overlord, then this should be accepted as a price worth paying for a reduction of German forces in North-West Europe. Churchill expressed this point by saying, 'Overlord remains top of the bill, but should not be such a tyrant as to rule out every other activity in the Mediterranean'.

The Americans were most uneasy about this British demand for flexible Overlord timings. They felt that the only way to ensure the integrity of Overlord was to fix its date, otherwise the diversionary theatre would triumph in the end. They also believed that the forces left in the Mediterranean should be concentrated on one main thrust line and should not be dispersed on a number of minor operations against islands in the Aegean. In their view, concentration of effort was the only effective way of destroying the German armed forces. The Americans became more uneasy when they heard rumours from Moscow that the Russians might press for a greater Allied effort in the eastern Mediterranean, thus supporting the British pressure for more action in the Balkans. It is not surprising that they approached the Tehran part of the conference with some trepidation.

Before the Western Allies could meet the Russians, it was essential to be clear amongst themselves what could and could not be done with the forces available. The limiting factor in ways and means was, as usual, shipping. Calculations showed that only two out of three potential amphibious operations could be mounted without delaying Overlord. The three were:

(a) The attack south of Rome to accelerate Fifth Army's advance —Operation 'Shingle'.

(b) The capture of Rhodes—Operation 'Hercules'.

(c) The capture of the Andaman Islands in the Indian Ocean, as a stepping stone to the invasion of Sumatra and Malaya—Operation 'Buccaneer'.

Both teams accepted Shingle as highly desirable. The British preferred the Rhodes to the Andaman operations. Churchill's views were expressed in a minute to the British Chiefs of Staff:

> The centre point of my thought is the capture of Rome at the beginning of January and the capture of Rhodes at the end. The capture of the Andamans is trivial compared with Rhodes and also it can be undertaken later in the year. In addition to the capture of Rhodes and all that follows from it, the surrender or destruction of 8,000–9,000 Germans will give us three times the German prisoners we have taken during all our operations in Italy.

The Americans were in a difficult position, because Roosevelt, as it transpired later in the conference, had already promised Chiang Kai-Shek that Buccaneer would be mounted as part of a combined Allied offensive to clear the Burma Road into China. Buccaneer was part of the price for Chinese support and was important to Roosevelt who wished to keep China in the war and to use Chinese territory later for offensive operations against Japan. The British saw little merit in helping feckless allies like the Chinese and were much more interested in damaging the German position in the Aegean and Balkans. No decision on which of the three operations should be cancelled, or whether Overlord should be delayed instead, could be taken until Stalin's views had been heard.

At Tehran Stalin was asked how he hoped to see Anglo-American operations developed to give Russia the greatest help. The first point made by Stalin in reply was of great significance, as will be seen later. Russia, he said, would join in the war against Japan as soon as Germany was defeated. His second point was that the Russians placed Overlord top of the list of Anglo-American operations but he wanted to know exactly when it was to be launched and who was to command it. His third point took the Combined Chiefs of Staff by surprise. He would prefer the Anglo-American forces in the Mediterranean to turn left into France instead of right into the Balkans and Austria. In his experience, major offensives launched on a single axis were rarely as successful as a pincers movement. Overlord should be supported by an attack on southern France carried out with the forces fighting in Italy. It has been suggested that this was Stalin's way of keeping the Western Allies out of an area which the Russians had pegged out as part of their post-war sphere of influence. There is little doubt, however, that the military reasoning behind the advice which he gave was sound. Moreover, it was well argued subsequently in staff meetings by Marshal Voroshilov, the Russian Chief of Staff. Germany was more vulnerable to an attack on her western frontier than she was in the south where the Alps gave her natural protection. Allied experience in Italy suggested that major operations through the Ljubljana Gap into Austria might well prove as difficult as opening up the entrance to the Liri Valley.

Stalin's views brought the Russians and Americans together against the British who were forced to seek new ways of gaining their ends. Churchill was quick to propose that enough assault shipping should be left in the Mediterranean to mount the two-divisional assault on southern France (code-named 'Anvil') as suggested by Stalin. With this shipping he hoped to be able to mount the Shingle operation in January to hurry on the capture of Rome and then to mount Hercules against Rhodes in February; the craft would thus be freed in ample time for Anvil which would take place concurrently with Overlord. If Overlord had to be delayed six to eight weeks in order to provide enough ships for Anvil he believed that the delay would be worthwhile. Delay would not affect Overlord materially while gains in the Mediterranean might give the operation a far greater chance of success. Stalin and Roosevelt, however, were adamant that there must be no delay to Overlord. The final Tehran decision was

> . . . that we will launch Overlord in May, in conjunction with a supporting operation against the South of France on the largest scale that is permitted by the landing craft available at that time.

Decisions on the actual size of the Anvil landing, and about which subsidiary operations should be mounted to help Overlord and Anvil, were left until Churchill and Roosevelt arrived back in Cairo. The British case against the Andaman operations had been decisively strengthened by Stalin's agreement to enter the war against Japan when Germany was defeated. Russia could provide far more help against Japan than China would ever be able to do. The President demurred for some time because to cancel Buccaneer would be to break his promise to Chiang Kai-Shek. Debates in the Combined Chiefs of Staff Committee on 4 and 5 December showed there was no way of avoiding delay to Overlord unless Buccaneer was dropped. The President reluctantly agreed and undertook to explain to Chiang Kai-Shek that the quick defeat of Germany would do more than anything else to help operations in the Far East, and that the demands of the European theatre for this purpose precluded major amphibious operations in the Indian Ocean for the time being. The way was now clear for the final decisions which were:

(a) Overlord and Anvil were to be mounted in May 1944 with priority over all other operations.

(b) Anvil would, if possible, be a two-divisional assault followed up by ten divisions from the United States.

(c) The immediate aim in Italy was to take Rome and then to advance as far as the Pisa–Rimini line; thereafter pressure was to be maintained on the Germans as far as the detachment of forces for Anvil would allow.

(d) The capture of Rhodes was desirable but not essential.

(e) The capture of the Andamans was cancelled.

(f) 68 LSTs, which were due to return from Italy to the United Kingdom on 5 December, could be held until 15 January.

Churchill had won as much as he could hope for in the face of combined American and Russian opposition. He had also won another battle which was to help him exploit the Mediterranean situation. Stalin had asked for the name of the Commander of Overlord. Churchill had accepted Roosevelt's nomination of Eisenhower, but he had opposed the American plan to place a Supreme Commander over both the North-West European and Mediterranean theatres. As the Mediterranean forces were predominantly British, Churchill won the Mediterranean Supreme Command for a British officer, General Maitland Wilson, who would henceforth command the whole Mediterranean area including the British Middle East Command.

And so Sextant ended with both sides pleased with the bargains they had struck. Churchill remarked, as the final report was initialled, 'When military historians come to adjudge the decisions of the Sextant Conference, they will find them fully in accordance with the classic articles of war.' Unbeknown to the Allied leaders much of their hard work in Cairo and Tehran was already being undone by the harder realities of the Italian theatre and the inaccurate estimates of the Mediterranean planners.

Churchill's forecast of Rome by the beginning and Rhodes by the end of January was doomed to disappointment. The basis of the Sextant calculations was being undermined while the conference was still in progress and was finally destroyed on 18 December by Mark Clark's signal to Alexander advising the cancellation of Shingle.

Neither Alexander's right- nor left-handed punches had landed with decisive effect. Far from being rocked back on his heels, Kesselring had stabilized his front and was forming a strong mobile reserve by bringing down two more infantry divisions from the north and by making those already in the line take over wider sectors to release 3, 29 and 90 Panzer Grenadier and the Hermann Göring Divisions from the line.

27   *Allied and German dispositions, early January 1944*

The opposing dispositions at the end of the year are shown in the sketch above. LXXVI Panzer Corps was holding Eighth Army's four divisions in the coastal sector with three divisions, and an independent force called 'Gruppe Hauck', composed of 305 Infantry Division reinforced by special mountain troops, was holding 78 (Br) Division in the mountain sector east of the Apennine watershed. XIV Panzer Corps was using only four divisions permanently in the line to hold Fifth's Army's seven divisions. Three mobile divisions (29 and 90 Panzer Grenadiers and the Hermann Göring) were held in Corps reserve behind the front, although most of these divisions had regiments forward blocking holes which appeared from time to time in the line as Fifth Army worked its way slowly towards the German main positions. In the Rome area a newly raised HQ 1 Para Corps had taken over from Student's XI Para Corps, which had been sent to Russia taking with it 2 Para Division. 2 Para Division left behind the cadres necessary to form a new division, 4 Para Division, whose formation was, as yet, only half complete. Another new division, 92 Infantry, was forming north of Rome and 71 Infantry Division was on its way southwards with orders to relieve 3 Panzer Grenadier Division, which was destined for the Adriatic sector. In the Fourteenth Army area, covering Rommel's old command in the north, there were still eight divisions but only one was a mobile division. The hard hitting Panzer formations, which had made up Rommel's Army Group in the Achse days, had moved off one by one towards the Eastern Front and to North-West Europe. Behind the Allied front, General Juin's French Expeditionary Corps was moving up with 3 Algerian Division to take over from VI (US) Corps in Fifth Army's mountain sector. I (US) Armoured Division had arrived in Naples, and behind Eighth Army four divisions were forming up ready to enter the line: 1 (Br) Division, which had been in North Africa since taking Pantelleria; 4 (Cdn) Armoured Division which was to join 1 (Cdn) Division to form 1 (Cdn) Corps; 4 (Ind) Division which last saw action in Tunisia; and the first of General Anders' Polish divisions, 3 Carpathian, had reached Taranto. Thus the total count at the turn of the year was 23 German divisions, of which two were just forming, to the Allies 18. Tenth Army alone had 15 divisions in the main operational area with which to oppose the Allies' 18, thus giving Alexander no more than marginal superiority with which to continue attacking through mountain country. If OKW decided to reinforce Kesselring for any particular operation, they could do so quite quickly whereas the Allies' shortage of shipping prevented any corresponding reinforcement on their side.

Churchill, on his way back from Sextant, decided to visit Eisenhower and Alexander at Carthage, where he arrived on 11 December only to fall ill with pneumonia. Alexander's report that Shingle could not be mounted before the assault shipping left the theatre came as a bitter but galvanizing blow just as he started his recovery. Here was his Mediterranean policy, which he had fought so hard to sustain, stagnating in just the way that his American critics predicted it would. Calling his senior Mediterranean commanders together, he started a rigorous search for ways of breaking the stalemate imposed by the mountains, the winter and the defensive abilities of the Germans. Alexander had already been working on similar lines and proposed the obvious solution. If Fifth Army could not reach the Anzio area in time to prevent the Shingle force being destroyed, then the landing force should be strengthened so that it could stand on its own feet against German counter-attacks and should not depend on an early junction with the main body of Fifth Army advancing overland. To bring the landing area nearer to Fifth Army than Anzio was impractical because there were no suitable beaches with adequate roads leading inland. Even the Anzio beaches were far from ideal. The coast south of Rome was too shallow in most places for LSTs to reach the shore. Strengthening the Shingle Force and making its landing a major amphibious operation appealed to Churchill's imagination: a 'wild cat' thrown on the beaches of Rome, clawing up the German communications and forcing Hitler to pull back north of the city, was just what he wanted. Sick though he was, he threw all his energy and persuasive powers into recreating Shingle as a corps assault of two divisions with a follow-up of two more divisions. Two limitations had to be overcome: provisions of extra assault shipping and for a longer period, and the old difficulty of giving the assault force a faster speed of build-up than its land-bound opponent. The success of the landing would depend initially on its shock effect, but, in the longer term, upon its strength growing faster than the defending forces which Kesselring could bring against it. Churchill set about finding the shipping, either ignoring or leaving the build-up issue to his military advisers. He beat his part of the problem, but the failure of the Allied staffs to solve their part cost him Rome as an immediate prize.

The shipping problem was how to assemble a minimum of 88 LSTs for the operation. There were 104 in the Mediterranean but 68 of these (12 American and 56 British) were due to return to England for Overlord by 15 January. Although 15 LSTs would be coming back from the Indian Ocean now that Buccaneer had been cancelled, they could not arrive in time. The Rhodes operation would clearly have to be cancelled, but, as this was to have followed and not been concurrent with Shingle, its cancellation produced no extra shipping; it only gave more time. The obvious answer was to delay the return of the 68 Overlord LSTs for a third time. The British Chiefs of Staff knew that to request this so soon after Sextant would rekindle American suspicions of a British anti-Overlord manoeuvre. Churchill was not prepared to be baulked by such fears and insisted on a thorough re-examination of the LST refitting and retraining programme, convinced that it contained the usual staff and administrative over-insurances. The British Chiefs were eventually persuaded that it would be practicable to hold the 58 British LSTs until 5 February* and then sail them back to England, in a series of convoys designed to bring them home at a rate which would make best use of the

---

* Most of the ships had been in action in the Mediterranean all summer and needed extensive refitting. Their crews also needed some retraining for the tidal conditions of the English Channel. It was the cut in the retraining time which enabled the greatest savings to be made in the programme. Some ships were refitted in Mediterranean yards to save time as well.

dockyard and retraining facilities. Having won his case, Churchill signalled Roosevelt on Christmas Day putting the whole position to him very frankly. On 28 December, the President's reply arrived accepting this third delay in the return of Overlord shipping. Time was short; the Fifth Army planning team which had worked out the one-divisional Shingle plan was quickly reassembled and instructed to revise their staff tables for a corps landing timed for the last ten days of January. Husky planning had taken five months, Avalanche six weeks, and now the enlarged Shingle had to be completed in three weeks.

Alexander's instructions to Fifth Army were short and to the point, covering just one page.

> Fifth Army will prepare an amphibious operation of two divisions plus to carry out an assault landing on the beaches in the vicinity of Rome with object of cutting the enemy lines of communication and threatening the rear of the German XIV Corps. This operation will take place between 20 January and 31 January but the target date should be as near 20 January as possible. . . .

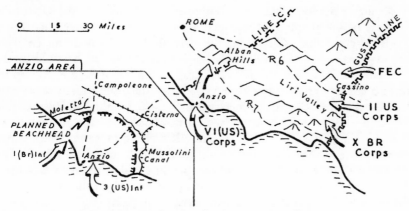

28 *Alexander's plan for the January offensive*

The forces allotted were General Lucas' VI (US) Corps with 1 (Br) Division, 3 (US) Division, two Commandos, a Ranger battalion and a US parachute regiment. 1 (US) Armoured Division and 45 (US) Division were earmarked for follow up purposes, the former being specifically included to give Lucas a hard hitting force with which to exploit any success he might have. On the naval side, Admiral Lowry, US Navy, would command the task force, and Admiral Troubridge RN would be responsible for the British element of the force.

The Shingle planners had very little choice in their selection of beaches and beachheads. There was a reasonable beach south of the small coastal shipping port of Anzio and another rather less suitable just to its north. Both were exposed to the winter gales and both were obstructed by German and Italian naval minefields laid off the coast which would have to be swept before the assault craft could approach the beaches. On land, air photographs showed a mass of field defences but intelligence resources revealed that the digging had been done some time before by Italian units which used to train there. Unlike Salerno, the beaches were not overlooked by a ring of hills. Both flanks were well protected; the right by the Mussolini Canal and the left by the Moletta River. Between these two obstacles, to a depth of about eight miles, the beachhead was flat and covered by woods and scrub which would provide some concealment. The ground beyond started to rise gently towards the dominating Alban Hills which were 25 miles inland and lay astride Routes 6 and 7, thus forming the natural objective for the landing. If the Alban Hills could be taken and secured, the German lines of communication to their Tenth Army would be cut. The crucial issue was whether this ground and the corridor to it could be secured with a force of only four divisions.

Detailed planning went remarkably smoothly under the pressure of the time factor but masked a fundamental difference of approach at various levels of command. Churchill, the driving force behind the concept, hoped to see a dynamic thrust towards the Alban Hills which would cut the German lines of communication and lead to the fall of Rome. Alexander was no less enthusiastic, but appreciated the difficulties more realistically. He saw the operation again in terms of left- and right-handed punches. The main body of Fifth Army would now become his right hand and would strike at the Gustav Line to draw Kesselring's reserves southwards. As soon as these reserves were committed in defence of the Liri Valley, the Shingle Force would land and compel him to shift them back to meet the left hand punch at Anzio. This loss of strength and the fear of being cut off should unsettle the German divisions in front of Fifth Army and might lead to a break-through. Mark Clark appreciated the aim of Alexander's strategy but had the memories of Salerno deeply imprinted on his mind and so he was more sceptical. His orders to General Lucas were 'to seize and secure a beachhead in the vicinity of Anzio . . .', whence he was 'to advance to the Alban Hills'. There were no references to rapid exploitation. Lucas, for his part, was worried about the inevitable German counter-attacks which his staff, though not he himself, had suffered at Salerno.* He envisaged building up a secure beachhead from which he would develop a thrust towards the Alban Hills as soon as he felt himself strong enough to do so. The British would hold the left side of the beach-

---

* Lucas relieved Dawley after the crisis had passed at Salerno.

head and would direct their main effort along the Anzio–Albano road towards Campoleone. The Americans would hold the right with their thrust line aimed at Cisterna on Route 7. Before any break-out was to be attempted a secure perimeter was to be established, based on the Moletta Stream and the Mussolini Canal. The gap between the two was to be obstructed with minefields.

Alexander appreciated that his attempts to draw the German reserves south could not by themselves prevent Kesselring building up his forces round the beachhead quicker than the Allies could land troops from the sea with the limited shipping at their disposal. The Allied air forces were given the task of reducing the German speed of build-up by attacking Kesselring's communications and destroying any German columns seen moving in daylight. He also appreciated that the whole operation could be endangered by bad weather at sea. His logistic staff arranged for stocks for 37 days to be landed as quickly as possible. To speed unloading, fully-laden lorries were to be embarked in LSTs. They would land, run ashore to the dumps, unload and return empty in the same ship to Naples, where they would refill and start the cycle again. This was wasteful in shipping space but reduced handling time. However carefully the operation was planned, the risks would still be heavy. Alexander rightly insisted on a mixed British and American force so that the dangers could be seen to be equally shared. There was to be no question of British commanders hazarding an American force.

The final 15 Army Group Operational Instruction was sent out on 12 January under the optimistic title of 'The Battle for Rome'. The picture painted was of a German Army tired and trying to rest and refit with only two divisions in reserve. It was thought to be incapable of offensive action and was likely to be caught unbalanced in the middle of a winter relief programme. The Allied winter offensive was to consist of five separate operations. First, II (US) Corps was to close up to the entrance of the Liri Valley by taking the last two hill features—Monte Porchio and Monte Trocchio—between its present line and the Rapido River. Two flank attacks would then be launched against von Senger's positions covering the Liri Valley. General Juin's French Expeditionary Corps (2 Moroccan and 3 Algerian Divisions), which had relieved Lucas' VI (US) Corps in the mountain sector, would threaten his northern flank by an advance through the mountains towards Atina, while X (Br) Corps would cross the Garigliano to attack his southern flank. When von Senger's reserves had been drawn away from his centre, II (US) Corps would open the main Fifth Army attack up the Liri Valley on about 20 January with an assault crossing of the Rapido River. As soon as the whole Fifth Army front was alight, VI (US) Corps would land at Anzio on 22 January to threaten the German rear. By then most of Kesselring's mobile divisions should have been drawn southwards to help hold the main Gustav positions and so the landing should not be strongly opposed. Kesselring would be forced to counter-march his mobile divisions to meet the Anzio threat and thereby weaken his main front enough to make an Allied break-through possible. If all went well, Fifth Army would link up with the Anzio force somewhere south of Rome and would destroy most of von Senger's XIV Panzer Corps in the process. Alexander realized that Kesselring was far too experienced to be trapped as easily as this and expected that he would withdraw slowly in front of Fifth Army to 'Line C' (or the 'Caesar Line' as it was also called) covering Rome. There were no fixed or prepared defences on this line; it was only a line marked on the German planning maps as a possible intermediate position between the Gustav and Gothic Lines to which the German divisions would be withdrawn if the former was breached. Eighth Army's part in these operations was to maintain pressure on the Adriatic front to stop German formations moving across the Apennines to oppose Fifth Army. It was, however, to surrender three divisions: 1 (Br) Division to VI (US) Corps for Anzio; 5 (Br) Division to X (Br) Corps to replace 7 (Br) Armoured Division which had left to join the Overlord forces in the United Kingdom; and 2 (NZ) Division which was to come into Army Group Reserve west of the Apennines ready to exploit up the Liri Valley if II (US) Corps broke through. In the paragraph dealing with future operations Fifth Army was directed to advance east of Rome because it was anticipated that all the Tiber bridges would be blown. Its objective was to be Pisa, while Eighth Army's was to be Rimini.

While planning and preparations were going ahead Fifth Army developed the first two operations. II (US) Corps worked its way steadily towards Cassino. The Mignano defile was cleared by the New Year and Monte Porchio and Monte Trocchio fell after hard fighting during the first fortnight of January. Juin's experienced mountain divisions made steady progress against the German 5 Mountain and 44 Infantry Divisions and drove them back some ten miles towards the back door of Cassino. Fifth Army thus arrived squarely in front of the main Gustav positions from Cassino to the sea on 15 January, only five days before it was expected to mount a major attack upon this heavily fortified position on which the Germans had worked with their Todt organization for nearly four months. Its divisions were dog-tired; they had lost about 26,000 men since the crossing of the Volturno, of which 16,000 had been lost breaking the Bernhardt Line.

VI (US) Corps had left the line on 9 January and retired to Salerno to carry out one hurried rehearsal before sailing for Anzio. 1 (Br) Division's practice landing went tolerably well, but the American 3 (US) Division ran into trouble. The weather was rough; many of their precious DUKWs, on which maintenance across the beaches would depend, were sunk, and few troops landed on the correct beaches—an inauspicious start. There was no time for further rehearsal; combat loading had to begin at once.

Kesselring's headquarters were fully alive to the danger of amphibious landings behind its front. It had made careful alarm plans to meet landings wherever they occurred. It was quite impossible to defend the whole coast-line now that the Italian Coastal Divisions had been dispersed. Each possible landing area was code-named and a staff table was drawn up showing what units would move to the area and by what routes as soon as the alarm was given. In most cases the German divisions detailed to find alarm units organized them around their divisional reconnaissance units which were not usually committed to the line in defensive fighting. The codeword for the Anzio area was 'Richard'. The Commander responsible for its defence was General Schlemmer, the Commander of 1 Para Corps. The only German unit actually in the area was a battalion of 29 Panzer Grenadier Division which had been sent there to rest and refit, and to practise demolitions at its leisure by blowing up Anzio Harbour. Heavy Allied air attacks on the Luftwaffe's long-range reconnaissance squadron base had effectively reduced German air surveillance and Allied deception plans had helped to baffle German radio interception. Admiral Canaris, head of OKW Intelligence, visited Kesselring's headquarters the day before the Anzio landings and advised his staff that a major amphibious assault was unlikely. Kesselring's commanders had been pressing him for some time to relax the states of readiness of the alarm units because of the exhausting effect it had on the troops. Hearing Canaris' advice, he reduced readiness but the effect of his order had not reached units when VI (US) Corps arrived off Anzio.

The backers of Overlord had been forced to give a little ground, but, as events were to show, not enough to enable the diversionary theatre to achieve a real success. The time limit for the release of shipping, though extended, was still far too tight for practical purposes. Fifth Army was forced to attack at Cassino before it was rested and VI (US) Corps was rushed to Anzio with only three weeks' planning and one unfortunate rehearsal. The tyrant Overlord still dominated every action in the Italian theatre, as if determined to prevent its rival winning the prize of Rome before it was ready to seize the limelight itself.

10

Costly Miscalculations

'If we succeed in dealing with this business down there [Anzio],
there will be no further landings anywhere.'

Hitler, as reported by Warlimont,
Inside Hitler's Headquarters

The early months of 1944 saw costly miscalculations by both sides. The
strategic thinking and tactical results had the ring of 1916 and 1917 about
them. The same ideas which led Von Falkenhayn to Verdun and Haig to
the Somme and Paschendaele drew the Allied and German commanders
in Italy to Anzio and Cassino. The Allies' task was to draw German
strength and the Germans' task was to teach the Allies such a lesson that
the whole idea of Overlord would be dropped or at least delayed for
many months. The Allies miscalculated the effect of the Anzio landings
upon the German High Command. They hoped to frighten the Germans
into withdrawing precipitately from their Gustav Line on which they
had spent so much effort and which was congealing satisfactorily under
the pressure of Fifth Army's attacks into an impregnable position. The
Germans, for their part, saw the Anzio landings as a heaven-sent opportunity to snatch just the type of victory which would damage Anglo-
American morale most—the destruction of an amphibious force. They
had failed to destroy the Sicilian and Salerno landings, because, in their
minds anyway, they were let down by the Italians. They were now free
from the need to pander to Italian susceptibilities and could handle the
Allied landings with a ruthlessness which should demonstrate conclusively
the hazards of a cross-Channel operation.

In the event, the roles of Anzio and Cassino were reversed. On the Allied
side Cassino became the rescuer of Anzio instead of Anzio helping to
create conditions for a break-through at Cassino. On the German side,
defeat instead of a decisive victory at Anzio endangered German morale,

and led to the debilitation of German strength and enthusiasm which victory at Cassino could not counteract. Neither side frightened the other in the way in which it hoped: the Germans clung to the Gustav Line in spite of the threat to their rear and the Allies defeated the German attempt to destroy the Anzio beachhead in spite of the crushing concentrations of troops which Hitler brought against it. Both sides acted like gamblers, throwing in more and more resources to win illusory prizes. The Allies were drawn on by the political mirage of Rome and the military creed of keeping the Germans on their heels. The Germans were drawn just as strongly by the fleeting political opportunity of a quick victory and the

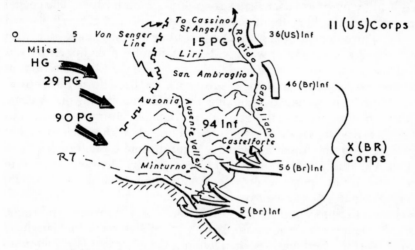

29 X (Br) Corps' crossing of the Garigliano River, 17–20 January

military need to hold on to the shortest and strongest line in Italy. Un-wittingly, the Germans helped Alexander to achieve his primary aim of drawing troops away from Overlord, while the Allies destroyed their own chances of mounting their high-priority Operation Anvil against southern France concurrently with Overlord. In short both sides miscalculated the odds and paid a heavy price for their miscalculations.

By 15 January the first two steps in the Allied winter offensive had been successfully completed. II (US) Corps was on the Rapido getting ready to break into the Liri Valley, and Juin's French divisions were causing von Senger considerable concern about his northern flank. It was time for the third operation—X (Br) Corps' attack over the Garigliano—to open.

The German positions on the Garigliano were held by the untried 94 Infantry Division, which had the difficult dual task of defending the river as well as the coast around the Gulf of Gaeta. General Pfeiffer, its

Commander, adopted the orthodox German stance on a major river line. He disposed the bulk of his division on the high ground some way back from the river with a strong outpost line on the river itself. One of his regiments held the Minturno ridge from the sea to the Ausente Valley, and another held the Castelforte ridge from the Ausente northwards to the inter-divisional boundary with 15 Panzer Grenadier Division on the southern edge of the Liri Valley. His third regiment was disposed in rear of his seaward flank to look after the coastal sector. 94 Division had been on the Garigliano for some weeks and had time to prepare its positions. All the obvious crossings over the river were heavily mined and held by outposts in fortified strong posts on both banks. The coastal beaches were also liberally mined and wired. General McCreery planned X (Br) Corps' attack against 94 Division using two divisions, each with two brigades in the assault wave. 5 (Br) Division from Eighth Army was to attack in the coastal sector astride Route 7 with the Minturno ridge as its objective. 56 (Br) Division was to attack the Castelforte positions to secure the high ground overlooking the road running up the Ausente Valley to Ausonia and the rear of the Gustav positions in the Liri Valley. 5 (Br) Division was given a fourth brigade with which to exploit northwards up the Ausente as soon as Minturno and Castelforte had been taken. The third division of X (Br) Corps, 46 (Br) Division, was not to take part in this operation. Its task was to support the flank of II (US) Corps when it attacked slightly later across the Rapido. 46 (Br) Division's target was to be the southern edge of the Liri Valley in the San Ambroglio area. As the appearance of Eighth Army's 5 (Br) Division on the Garigliano would alert the Germans, 56 (Br) Division was to cover 5 (Br) Division's front until the last possible moment.

Unlike the Volturno crossing, which had been an amateur affair, X (Br) Corps' assault on the Garigliano positions had all the hall-marks of a well-planned, professional river-crossing operation. There was now ample bridging equipment and more sappers to use it, but it was no easy task to cross this large fast-flowing river in winter with German artillery observers overlooking all the practicable crossing sites. The sappers had to use existing road approaches to the river because the fields either side were too soft to carry a large number of military vehicles in wet weather, and these roads were sure to be registered by German guns. To overcome this difficulty it was decided to use some 14 rafts, including two strong enough for tanks, in the early stages of the attack and not to try building bridges until direct artillery observation had been cleared off the bridge sites. On the seaward flank, landing craft and DUKWs would ferry tanks and guns around the mouth of the river and along the coast. Bridging, however, was not the only difficulty facing the X (Br) Corps' staff. The operation was further complicated by the difficulty of bringing up and deploying the Corps and Army Group artillery allotted to support the assault. There was only one good road, Route 7, along which all the guns and the vast quantities of ammunition needed for the artillery programme had to be moved. Once in the forward area the gun positions and ammunition dumps had to be hidden on the forward slopes of the south side of the valley in full view of the enemy. Furthermore, the German outposts on X (Br) Corps' side of the river had to be eliminated without arousing German suspicions that a major assault was imminent.

All the assembly, deception and preliminary logistic measures went well. Even the enemy outposts were forced to withdraw without alarming the Germans. When the attack started at nine o'clock on the evening of 17 January, Pfeiffer's 94 Division was taken by surprise. By dawn the following morning X (Br) Corps had ten battalions over the river with rafts working behind them to bring over anti-tank guns and other heavy weapons. During 18 January both divisions expanded their initial bridge-heads. 5 (Br) Division on the seaward flank had great difficulty with minefields on either side of Route 7 and on the beaches. Poor navigation by the leading wave of landing craft did not help as some of the skippers brought their tanks in on a beach south of the river mouth. By evening 5 (Br) Division was firmly established on the Minturno ridge and 56 (Br) Division was on the high ground either side of Castelforte although it could not take the town itself. The build up of both bridgeheads was slow because it depended on rafting troops and vehicles over the river. The first 9-ton bridge was over by dawn on 19 January, but was soon knocked out by German artillery fire. The first 30-ton bridge was not opened until the early hours of 20 January. Even then the bridges could only be used by night, because, although the bridges themselves were out of sight below the river's flood banks, the approach roads were under German artillery observation and were shelled whenever a vehicle attempted to move down to the river in daylight. This situation was to exist for the next three months as German observation was never cleared off the river line until the Gustav Line finally collapsed in May. X (Br) Corps' build-up, however, was fast enough to allow the troops in the bridgeheads to defeat 94 Division's immediate counter-attacks and the early counter-attacks by German reserve divisions which started to appear on 30 January.

Von Senger appreciated that the Allies were trying to turn both flanks of his XIV Panzer Corps. He had temporarily stopped Juin in the north with his own reserves, so he asked Kesselring to release 29 and 90 Panzer Grenadier Divisions, which were in Army Group Reserve south of Rome, to counter-attack the new threat posed by X (Br) Corps. Kesselring found himself in a quandary. These divisions were echeloned back behind XIV Panzer Corps ready to strike at any Allied landings behind the front. Kesselring's instincts told him that such a landing was bound to come sooner or later. German intelligence, however, had found no evidence that such a landing was imminent. If he ignored X (Br) Corps' advance on Ausonia, the Gustav Line would be rolled up from the south. At this stage the von Senger, or Hitler, Line, which ran across the Liri Valley some miles behind Cassino blocking the Ausente Valley approach, was not ready for occupation. Against his better judgment, he ordered

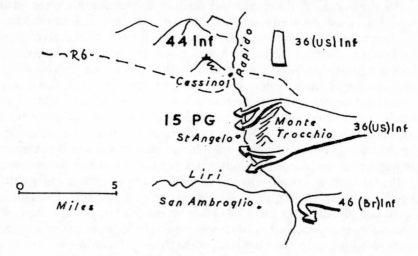

30 II (US) Corps' attack over the Rapido, 20 January

General Schlemmer, Commander of 1 Para Corps near Rome, to move south with 29 and 90 Panzer Divisions and elements of the Hermann Göring Division* to restore the situation in 94 Division's sector. Schlemmer's counter-attack started on 20 January and led to bitter fighting in which X (Br) Corps just held its ground, inflicting heavy casualties on the three German mobile divisions. Any idea of exploitation up the Ausente Valley faded as identifications of these German reinforcements reached Fifth Army. At 15 Army Group level the appearance of these divisions was welcomed as a sign that Alexander's strategy was working. If all went well there would be no German reserves left near Rome to oppose the Anzio landing. Jubilation, however, was muted by disaster which struck elsewhere.

---

* The Hermann Göring Division was under OKW orders to move to France but its move was delayed by the opening of the Allied winter offensive.

Fifth Army's fourth step, the attack in the centre across the Rapido, resulted in a costly and demoralizing defeat for II (US) Corps. In contrast to the professional performance of X (Br) Corps, the American Corps' first major river crossing was mismanaged and led, after the war, to a Congressional Enquiry into the handling of the operation. The Rapido is a fast-flowing stream, only about 30 feet wide, which is rarely noticed by travellers along Route 6 or on the new Autostrada which runs up the Liri Valley. It runs in a deep-dredged channel with flood-banks on either side and is unfordable. It flows so fast that swimming and handling cumbersome assault boats is very difficult, even without the added hazard of hostile artillery and small arms fire. 36 (US) Division was detailed to make the crossing and was oppposed by General Rodt's experienced 15 Panzer Grenadier Division, which for the first time since the Sicilian landings was occupying heavily fortified positions specially prepared for it. The flat fields of the Liri Valley were mined, wired and covered by carefully sited machine-gun positions, creating belts of inter-locking fire across the Rapido and the approaches to it. Artillery, mortars and Nebelwerfer batteries were registered on the whole length of the river, on the routes down to the river and on the likely assembly areas in the narrow stretch of ground between the abrupt slopes of Monte Trocchio and the river. All the German weapon crews were amply provided with deep dug-outs in which they could seek cover while Allied artillery searched their positions with preparatory bombardments. In the centre of the valley, on the German side of the Rapido, there is the small village of Saint Angelo which stands on a low bluff overlooking the river. It was clearly a key position in 15 Panzer Grenadier Division's defences as it gave observation along the river in both directions and could enfilade any crossing north or south of the village. It also provided a road along which 36 (US) Division could be supplied as it advanced up the Liri Valley until Route 6 could be opened. The importance of Saint Angelo, however, was dwarfed by the towering eminence of Monte Cassino and the massive Monastery which capped its peak. The Abbey looked down on every move made in the valley below. Allied soldiers, who were unlucky enough to arrive in the Cassino sector, were immediately aware of its apparently all-seeing eyes. Whatever they proposed to do, they had to think first, 'Can I be seen from the Monastery?' They soon found that there were very few places where they were hidden from its view. Only Monte Trocchio provided any cover and so behind it were crammed as many Allied batteries as the area of its shadow could hold.

When 36 (US) Division approached the Rapido after taking Trocchio, it had no reason to view its next operation with any more alarm than it had done before scaling the hills protecting the Mignano defile. It knew fighting would be tough because intelligence reports indicated that it was now up against the main German winter positions, but there was no evidence to show that it would be any worse than breaking through the Bernhardt Line. Given enough artillery support, the Rapido defences should be cracked fairly easily. The plan of attack was simple and direct. Two regiments were to cross the Rapido, one either side of Saint Angelo. 18 January was the original target date for the crossing, but wet weather, and need for more time for preparation led to a postponement until 20 January. The crossing started soon after dark to give the American combat engineers as much darkness as possible in which to construct bridges over the Rapido behind the assaulting infantry. Nothing went right from the start. The approach march to the river was a nightmare. Wet weather made the ground between Trocchio and the river a slippery, muddy slide, down which it was almost impossible to carry the heavy assault boats. A river mist came up, making it difficult for officers and NCOs to recognize landmarks and to find their correct routes forward. When the American artillery barrage started, the Germans replied with heavy defensive fire, which ripped into the boat-carrying parties, killing men and destroying boats; it tore up the white tapes marking the routes to the crossing places, making it even more difficult to find the way; and it created chaos amongst the assaulting battalions as they groped their way forward over unfamiliar ground in the swirling mist. Near the river bank they ran into a further hazard—uncleared anti-personnel mines—which took a further toll of men and boats. The crossing itself was even worse. The Germans had suffered little from the American bombardment, and were alert and ready to receive the assaulting battalions as they scrambled out on the far bank of the river. Only two companies of the northern regiment managed to struggle over, and, out of four footbridges carried forward, only one was successfully erected before dawn, to be destroyed itself as soon as German observers on Monte Cassino spotted its position. All contact was lost with the two companies on the far bank. The southern regiment fared better during the night and had one battalion over by dawn with two footbridges behind it. Daylight found the battalion in the open ringed by German tanks and self-propelled guns firing from concealed positions, methodically destroying the small American bridgehead. One bridge was soon destroyed and the other badly damaged. The battalion commander asked to withdraw to the east bank as his position was clearly untenable. Before the divisional commander's refusal reached him he found he had no option but to do so before the remnants of his battalion were overrun. Thus by midday, there were only the two American companies of the northern regiment on the far bank and these were cut off and out of communication with the rest of the division.

General Keyes, commanding II (US) Corps, ordered the assault to be renewed in daylight and General Walker, 36 (US) Division's Commander, ordered both regiments to try again with maximum artillery support at 2 p.m. This timing was too optimistic. The southern regiment organized its attack for 4 p.m. and again had some initial success in getting all three battalions across during the evening and the second night, but by midday on 22 January their position had again become untenable and they were forced back to the east bank with heavy losses. The northern regiment did not manage to attack until after dark. It succeeded in reinforcing the two original companies with the rest of their battalion and a second battalion. Fortunately the river mist hung in the valley until late the following morning and, reinforced by artificial smoke, enabled the engineers to start work on a Bailey bridge. In the afternoon the mist lifted and the smoke proved insufficient to prevent enemy direct observation. Monte Cassino towered ominously over the northern regiment's bridgehead. One by one the footbridges were destroyed and all work on the Bailey had to be stopped. By 4 p.m. contact with the far bank was again lost, and the sound of American weapons firing west of the Rapido died away until by dusk only German weapons could be heard. Forty men escaped to the east bank; the rest of those who had managed to cross had been killed or captured. 36 (US) Division's crossing of the Rapido was over. Not even a toe-hold had been won at the cost of almost 2,000 men. The division was temporarily reduced to the strength of one regiment—the reserve regiment which had not been committed. 15 Panzer Grenadier Regiment, by contrast, had added one more victory to its fine record and had avenged its defeat on Monte Camino. Von Senger found it quite unnecessary to reinforce General Rodt and was able to concentrate on counter-attacking X (Br) Corps' bridgehead over the Garigliano.

Many Americans had criticized Montgomery's careful, methodical preparations for a major river crossing. Eighth Army's ponderous build-up of guns and ammunition, its careful reconnaissance of the enemy positions, its deception plans and its rehearsals all seemed old-womanish. II (US) Corps approached the Rapido as if it was attacking enemy rearguards as had been the case on the Volturno. Through no fault of its commander or men, 36 (US) Division lacked the time needed for the careful preparation of what should have been regarded as a major set piece battle. They should never have been asked to carry out this attack on a major German position behind a river obstacle with only five days to prepare. The blame must rest with those who allowed the tyranny of Overlord to dominate the tactical as well as the strategic battlefield. 46 (Br) Division's attack on II (US) Corps' southern flank towards Saint Ambroglio fared no better than 36 (US) Division's. Its assault brigade managed to get just one company across the river and the attack was wisely abandoned. In the final battle of Cassino, 36 (US) Division's task was just accomplished by a whole British Corps supported by 1,000 guns after two months careful preparation and in hot spring weather which enabled men, tanks and guns to move freely over the open fields. One US division with five days' preparation, attacking in mid-winter, stood no chance at all. Unfortunately the commanders were not to know this at the time. The toughness of the Germans in defence with winter on their side was still underestimated.

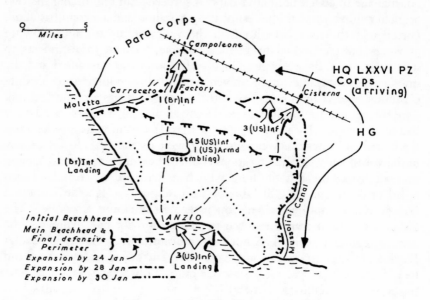

31   *The Anzio beachhead, 22–30 January*

As 36 (US) Division struggled to save its northern bridgehead, the Allied armada of 200 ships and craft was discharging VI (US) Corps over the Anzio beaches. Churchill's 'wild cat' was being thrown ashore behind Kesselring's lines just at the critical moment when all the German reserves were committed. The timing could not have been better. The approach of the Allied convoys went undetected by the Luftwaffe, whose main reconnaissance force had been neutralized by the heavy bombing of its airfields. The leading troops, who landed behind an impressive barrage of rockets from the specially-fitted landing craft, met practically no opposition. The two companies of Panzer Grenadiers resting in the area were quickly rounded up and the few coastal guns which opened fire were equally quickly silenced. Difficulties of unloading over very poor beaches caused more trouble than enemy reactions in the first few hours. Surprise was complete. Once again Kesselring had been caught off balance by Allied deception plans, but he was soon to demonstrate the resilience of the German operational staffs.

Codeword 'Richard' brought German counter-measures into play at once. The first troops to arrive were elements of the Hermann Göring Division which had not yet joined the rest of the division counter-attacking X (Br) Corps. General Schlemmer, Commander 1 Para Corps, returned from the Garigliano and took charge of the alarm units as they arrived from all over Italy and southern Europe to contain the beachhead. His first step was to order General von Pohl, the Commander of Rome's anti-aircraft defences, to ring the Allied beachhead with a screen of anti-aircraft guns deployed in an anti-tank role. Upon this anti-tank screen he built up a containing perimeter feeding in units piecemeal as they arrived. Colonel Gehricke, Commander 4 Para Regiment, acted as the commander of the western sector opposing 1 (Br) Division on the Anzio–Campoleone road, and the Hermann Göring Division took over the eastern sector blocking 3 (US) Division on the Anzio–Cisterna road. Kesselring did not for a moment consider abandoning the Gustav Line. He ordered Tenth Army to stop the counter-attacks on X (Br) Corps' bridgehead and to go over to a strict defensive all along the main Gustav positions so as to release as many troops as possible for Anzio. Even if Kesselring had hesitated, which he did not, he was to be left in no doubt about what Hitler wanted. A stream of signals flowed from OKW demanding the determined defence of the Gustav Line and the liquidation of the Anzio 'abscess'. Hitler's Order of the Day, which was to be read out to all troops, ran:

> The Gustav Line must be held at all costs for the sake of the political consequences which would follow a completely successful defence. The Führer expects the bitterest struggle for every yard.

Kesselring received authority to retain the Hermann Göring Division indefinitely and was told that two more divisions (715 Infantry from France and 114 Jaeger from Yugoslavia), three independent regiments including the crack Infantry Lehr (Demonstration) Regiment from Germany and two heavy tank battalions from France were being moved to his support as quickly as possible. He could also use any divisions he liked from northern Italy which were freed from all OKW strings.

Thus began the series of actions and reactions, calculations and miscalculations, which made up the complementary battles of Anzio and First and Second Cassino. Although the Allies started with the initiative, this soon passed to the Germans, and so it is easiest to trace the complex moves from the German point of view. The battles were fought in three phases: the containment of the Allied beachhead, the first and then the second German counter-offensives. The Allied attacks at Cassino, although intended as break-through operations, turned out to be relieving operations fought to save VI (US) Corps from the annihilation planned for it by Hitler.

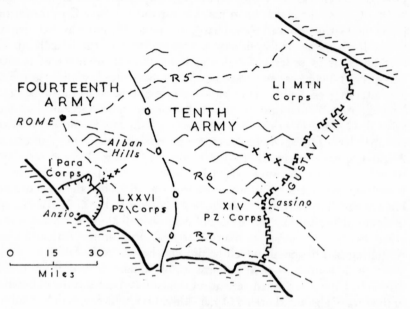

32   The German containment of the Anzio beachhead

In the first eight days after the landing, Kesselring managed to hold his main front and bring up the elements of eight divisions to surround the beachhead. Von Mackensen's Fourteenth Army Headquarters came down from northern Italy to take over the containment forces so as to leave von Vietinghoff's Tenth Army free to control the main front. Herr's LXXVI Corps Headquarters was brought over from opposing Eighth Army on the Adriatic coast to command the eastern half of the containment line and 1 Para Corps took over the western half. LI Mountain Corps moved down from northern Italy to take over the Adriatic sector vacated by LXXVI Panzer Corps. A new Army Group under General von Zangen replaced Fourteenth Army in the north. Thus the German chain of command was clear and simple. Two separate army headquarters controlled the two main battle areas, and each had two subordinate corps headquarters. More significant was the distribution of divisions, the total of which rose to 24 during the coming battles: eight surrounded the beachhead; seven opposed Fifth Army's main front and only three faced Eighth Army; the balance of six were under von Zangen holding northern Italy, Istria and the Ljubljana Gap.

On the Allied side, the vigour shown by the German defence seemed to the office-bound critics in London and Washington to be lacking in Lucas' handling of his VI (US) Corps. The divergent aims at the different levels in Allied planning soon became apparent. The Allied navies did better than their word. Unloading went quicker than expected and the ships of the assault convoy were on their way back to Naples by the evening of the second day to pick up the follow-up formations—part of 1 (US) Armoured Division and 45 (US) Division. Lucas' plan had assumed that there would be stiff opposition from at least one German division (29 Panzer Grenadier Division) reinforced by miscellaneous parachute units from the Rome area. His staff were told before the landing took place that 29 Panzer Grenadier Division had been identified on the Garigliano, but this information appears to have made no change in his or his staff's attitude. In Lucas' view, his primary tasks were to secure a defensible beachhead, fortify it, and stock it with the necessary stores and ammunition to sustain his force in case the winter storms disrupted his supply by sea. Not until he had a firm base ashore would he attack towards what was to him a secondary objective—the Alban Hills. Both Mark Clark and Lucas were strongly influenced by their experience at Salerno and were not in the frame of mind to operate as Churchill and, to a lesser extent, Alexander expected. Their attention was focussed on defeating the inevitable German counter-attacks and they were utterly sceptical about the Allied air forces' claim to be able to slow down the German rate of build-up by concentrated bombing on all road and rail links leading to the beachhead.

The planned beachhead perimeter* was occupied by the evening of the second day against only slight resistance. The first serious attempt to expand VI (US) Corps' foothold was made on 25 January by 3 (US) Division attacking towards Cisterna and 1 (Br) Division towards Campoleone. The former was stopped by the Hermann Göring Division and the latter by 3 Panzer Grenadier Division well short of their objectives. The chance of exploitation to the Alban Hills had gone; Lucas was too late. Subsequent events, however, cast doubt on the existence of this supposed chance of a break-out across the German communications. If Lucas had rushed forward to the Alban Hills to cut Routes 6 and 7 in rear of the Tenth German Army, his troops would have been hopelessly extended and exposed. He would not have been able to hold his objective and at the same time protect his supply lines back to Anzio. His force on the

* See fig. 31. The planned beachhead line equated to the main beachhead shown on the sketch.

Alban Hills would probably have been surrounded and forced to surrender before the main body of Fifth Army could do anything to help. The only chance which did exist was for a cavalry-type action by fast-moving armoured columns, striking across the German supply lines and possibly entering undefended Rome with the aim of raising the population and frightening the Germans into a precipitate withdrawal. Neither Lucas nor his force were suitable for such an operation. Lucas was no Sheridan or Jackson, and his armoured force, 1 (US) Armoured Division, was in the follow-up convoy. It was not Lucas' fault that Churchill's wild cat turned out to be a ponderous but well armoured tortoise. Mark Clark, who knew what Churchill wanted, chose the wrong man and accepted a wrong plan to achieve Churchill's aim.

Alexander, who visited the beachhead on D-day and on 25 January, urged Mark Clark to open a co-ordinated offensive to take Cisterna and Campoleone before the Germans could consolidate their defences in these important towns which blocked the two main roads out of the beachhead towards the Alban Hills. His intelligence officers believed that the German units holding the Cisterna–Campoleone Line were only a screen covering stronger positions which were being built up further inland. 1 (US) Armoured and 45 (US) Divisions were assembling in the beachhead and should be ready to support the attack. Mark Clark agreed and VI (US) Corps' first co-ordinated offensive started just after midnight on 30 January—a week after the initial landing. 3 (US) Division followed up a night attack by three US Ranger battalions on Cisterna. Two of these battalions fell into a well-laid ambush, and were surrounded and forced to surrender. The third suffered heavy casualties and 3 (US) Division itself was stopped with heavy loss without taking Cisterna. Further efforts on subsequent days were equally unsuccessful. 1 (Br) Division, supported by 1 (US) Armoured Division, renewed its attack towards Campoleone on the same day, 30 January. It was initially successful and reached the railway just south of the town, but that was as far as it or the American tank units could go. The Germans were in no mood to be pushed back any further and showed such strength that it was soon clear that the Cisterna–Campoleone Line was no screen; it had become a main defensive position on which the Germans intended to stand. 1 (Br) Division, like 3 (US) Division, was forced to give up its attempt to get forward and remained dangerously exposed in a narrow salient stretching up the Anzio–Campoleone road.

Thus at the beginning of February the Allied force, which was to have opened the way to Rome, was penned into a shallow beachhead, the whole of which was under German artillery fire. Fortunately the Germans did not possess sufficient artillery or aircraft to prevent unloading but they did stop the Allies' planned build-up of fighter aircraft in the beach-head. All fighter cover had to be flown from Naples which gave the Luft-waffe greater freedom for hit-and-run raids. These led to losses amongst the supporting Allied warships and assault shipping off the beaches. For the whole four months of its existence, the Anzio beachhead resembled a beseiged fortress in which no area was free from German artillery harassing fire or Luftwaffe raids.

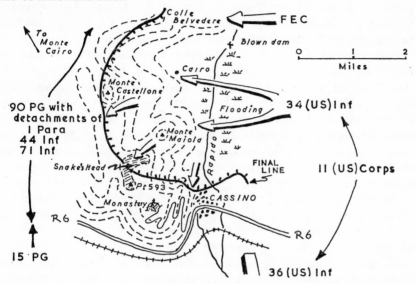

33   II (US) Corps' attempts to take Cassino, 24 January–11 February

Back on the main front, II (US) Corps was doing all it could to recover from its defeat on the Rapido and to open a way up Route 6 to reach VI (US) Corps as soon as possible. Juin's success in his advance towards Atina suggested that it might be possible to outflank Cassino from the north. 34 (US) Division was ordered to attack across the Rapido, this time north of Cassino, while Juin's 3 Algerian Division was directed to support the American attack by advancing through the hills still further north. The axis of 34 (US) Division's attack lay across the upper reaches of the Rapido where the stream was fordable, so, unlike its sister division, 34 (US) Division did not have to use boats. It was faced with two different but equally difficult problems. The Germans had blown a dam further up-stream, flooding the valley and making it too soft for tanks and vehicles to cross without laying a corduroy track to support them. The second problem was the German defences themselves which lay along the base of the great mountain wall which rose up on the far side of the Rapido towards the massive bulk of the snow-topped Monte Cairo, of which Monte Cassino is just the most southerly spur. The German positions lay behind wire and minefields as in the Liri Valley, but they were also tucked into the steep hillsides which provided even better observation over 34 (US) Division's approach than Monte Casssino had done over 36 (US) Division. In the first phase of the attack, 34 (US) Division was to cross the open valley, wade the Rapido and seize a shallow bridgehead at the foot of the mountains. Subsequently, the division was to scale the heights and to take the Monte Cassino spur from the rear. The French were to support the attack with similar operations to the north.

Both the American and French attacks were launched after dark on 24 January, the second day of the Anzio landing. As at Saint Angelo, the Americans lost surprise almost at once and heavy German defensive fire disrupted the attack before it had made much progress. On the first night no formed unit crossed the Rapido. It took two days hard and costly fighting to establish a small bridgehead over the river. Engineers worked under appalling conditions to create roadways for the tanks and it was not until 29 January, five days after the attack started, that any number of tanks reached the bridgehead. Operations then went faster as the tanks could crush paths through anti-personnel minefields for the infantry and could use their main armament in their support. The bridgehead was finally secured and the first phase of the operation completed when the village of Cairo fell on 31 January.

The French attack went better than the American. Two important hill features, the Colle Abati and Colle Belvedere, were taken, though with heavy losses. Abati was subsequently retaken by the Germans in a counter-attack, but Belvedere was held. Von Senger appreciated the dangers of the French successes and also the skill of Juin's North African troops who were more dangerous in the mountains than the Americans. He bolstered 44 Infantry and 5 Mountain Divisions with units of 71 Infantry Division as they arrived from Slovenia. 90 Panzer Grenadier Division moved north from the Garigliano and took over Cassino town and Monte Cassino. Under its command came three battalions of 1 Para Division which had been sent to Anzio from the Eighth Army's front as 1 Para Division's contribution to alarm scheme 'Richard'. These three battalions were given the task of defending the Monte Cassino spur within 90 Panzer Grenadier's Division's overall command. 5 Mountain, 44 and 71 Divisions were thus able to side-step northwards and shorten their frontages against 11 (US) Corps and the French.

By the end of January Alexander had a full picture of the German reaction. Kesselring's build-up around Anzio overshadowed everything. It was clear that a major counter-offensive was being planned. Two things

18 Aerial view of Cassino: top left, Route 6—the Road to Rome—in the
Liri Valley; centre, bombs bursting on the slopes of Monte Cassino, the hairpin bends on the road up to the ruins of the monastery showing to the left of
the bursts; foreground, Cassino town and the flat Rapido valley with Route 6
entering from bottom left

19 German command post overlooking the Allied beachhead at Anzio

ANZIO

20 German self-propelled guns in the ruins of Carroceto; Allied Sherman tanks lost in 1 (Br) Division's withdrawal lie at far side of the village square

had to be done: the beachhead had to be reinforced and the German pressure upon it had to be relieved by diversionary operations elsewhere. Whichever sectors of the front were not chosen for diversionary efforts would have to surrender troops for Anzio. The Eighth Army front was obviously a *cul-de-sac* from which Alexander had already taken three divisions in the New Year and from which the Germans had also withdrawn LXXVI Panzer Corps. Oliver Leese would certainly have to surrender more divisions. Of the two other sectors of the main front, the Garigliano sector seemed to lead nowhere. Its main route to Rome, Route 7, was obstructed by the Aurunci Mountains and the Pontine Marshes, and the significance of the Ausente Valley, the real key to Cassino, had not yet become apparent. This left only the Liri Valley and its Route 6 for major diversionary operations. II (US) Corps' progress north of Cassino was encouraging and it looked as if it would not be long before the Route 6 approach to Rome would be prised open. Alexander consequently decided to continue the operations to break through at Cassino. Eighth Army was ordered to surrender divisions to the Fifth Army's force attacking Cassino, and X (Br) Corps on the Garigliano was ordered to send units to Anzio.

The Eighth Army contribution to the Cassino sector was the formation of a new corps: the New Zealand Corps under General Freyberg* consisting of 2 (NZ) Division and 4 (Ind) Division. Freyberg was to assemble his corps behind the II (US) Corps ready to exploit up the Liri Valley when Cassino fell. If this did not happen before 10 February, Freyberg was to relieve the Americans and to burst open the gateway to Rome himself in addition to exploiting through it. To replace 2 (NZ) Division in Army Group Reserve, Eighth Army surrendered a further division, 78 (Br) Division, which moved across the Apennines in the middle of February and was delayed by heavy snow in the mountains on the way over.

The first units from X (Br) Corps started reaching the Anzio beachhead just in time. Von Mackensen had appreciated that he must stop the Allies expanding their perimeter while the large German forces were being assembled for Hitler's great counter-offensive. He also needed a suitable position from which to mount this offensive. 1 (Br) Division's salient offered an ideal target for both these purposes. Alexander had visited the beachhead again on 31 January where Mark Clark had now established an Advanced Fifth Army Headquarters. He had given him four tasks (*see* fig. 31) which, in order of priority were: take Cisterna with a corps attack; secure the flanks of 1 (Br) Division's dangerous salient; secure the line of the railway between Cisterna and Campoleone; and improve

* Lieutenant-General Sir Bernard Freyberg, VC, Commander of the New Zealand Expeditionary Force.

communications across the beachhead to enable counter-attack forces to be switched rapidly from one flank to the other. No further attempts were to be made to break out until these measures had been completed. Before any steps could be taken to put these orders into effect intelligence reports began to show the imminence of a German counter-attack. On 1 February VI (US) Corps ordered its divisions to prepare for defence. The ground already won would be held, but the corps ordered the preparation of a 'final' defensive position on the line of the original beachhead. In the fighting so far VI (US) Corps had lost 6,500 men and had taken some 1,500 German prisoners. Many units were a long way below strength when von Mackensen's preliminary containing attacks started shortly before midnight on 3 February.

The first German attack was designed to cut off 1 (Br) Division's salient and this it succeeded in doing. 1 (Br) Division only just managed to extricate its forward brigade after heavy fighting during 4 February in which the first brigade of 56 (Br) Division from the Garigliano had to be used to stabilize a new defensive line based on the Mussolini agricultural community centre, called the 'Factory', at Aprilia. Having forced the Allies on to the defensive, von Mackensen now turned his attention to seizing the start line to mount the main Hitler attack. In this he had little freedom of choice because everything was planned in detail back in OKW, where it was decided that the attack should be launched astride the Albano–Anzio road. For this to be successful the Germans considered they needed the Factory and the village of Carroceto, half-a-mile to the south-west. On 7 February von Mackensen launched a second preliminary attack to secure these objectives. Heavy fighting went on for three days before the Germans succeeded in wresting both from 1 (Br) Division's hands. They were forced to commit six regiments to gain this modest success. 1 (Br) Division's infantry strength was reduced to about a third of establishment while the Germans had lost even more heavily. Von Mackensen's attacks had been costly preliminary operations and both sides were forced to regroup before they could do any more. 45 (US) Division took over from 1 (Br) Division which was pulled back into reserve with 1 (US) Armoured Division. On the German side, their build-up continued in the face of heavy Allied air attacks, but it was only slowed and never halted by the efforts of the Allied airmen; nor was it affected by the Allies' diversionary efforts at Cassino.

II (US) Corps started the second phase of its attack through the hills behind Cassino on 1 February (see fig. 33). While von Mackensen's preliminary operations to take the Factory at Anzio were being fought out, 34 (US) Division, helped by the remnants of 36 (US) Division, fought its way up to the spur behind the Monastery. It took the two large features of Monte Maiola and Monte Castellone, but then its real difficulties began. The German positions were emplaced in the rocks on the tops and on the reverse slopes of the crinkled jagged ridges which formed this backdoor approach to Monte Cassino. The natural protection of the rocks and caves was given added strength by the liberal use of steel and concrete. The German positions on each high point could support several others with cross-fire, and the deep gullies behind them hid numerous mortars and nebelwerfers which could bring down devastating, searching fire on the rock-strewn slopes in front. In contrast, the Allied gunners found it difficult, due to crest-clearance problems, to give similar support with their conventional field guns dug in behind Monte Trocchio. All ammunition, defence stores and supplies had to be carried up the mountains by men and mules. The German positions had been stocked with ammunition long before the attack started, but the Americans had to haul up everything they needed during the battle. Working painfully from ridge to ridge the Americans reached the key feature of Point 593— nicknamed the 'Snake's Head' ridge—from which a col led directly to Monastery Hill on the end of the Monte Cassino spur. Point 593 was a rocky knoll halfway along the Snake's Head Ridge and was strongly held by the Germans who appreciated that it was the best position from which to block this Allied thrust. Between 4 and 7 February the Americans fought viciously to break through the last few hundred yards to the Monastery and the last half-mile to Route 6 some 1,500 feet below in the Liri Valley. They came within 400 yards of the former, the nearest anyone was to come to the Monastery from this direction until the final battle. Other units of 34 (US) Division fought their way into the outskirts of Cassino town from the north, but, like their compatriots on the mountain, they could not reach their final objective—Route 6 beyond the town.

General Keyes decided to have one more try before handing over to Freyberg. The New Zealanders came up and took over south of Cassino to release more Americans for a last attempt. This met with no success and by 11 February II (US) Corps was finally spent. Violent rain and snow swept the hills, making further efforts by its exhausted men impossible. Most of its infantry units were down to a quarter of their normal strength. As 4 (Ind) Division moved up to take over on the Snake's Head, they found many of the Americans too weak to walk back down the mountain. They had to be carried out on stretchers, such was their state at the end of the First Battle of Cassino, and at the end of the German containment phase.

Unbeknown to each other, both sides planned their next operations to begin on 16 February. On the Allied side, intelligence reports showed that Anzio would be attacked in great strength within the next few days. It was essential to hurry forward the New Zealand Corps' plans to take Cassino and to open up the route to Anzio and Rome. The Americans had come so near to doing so that it was felt that the fresh troops of the New Zealand Corps would be able to burst through the last few hundred yards.

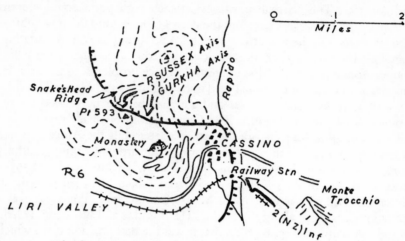

34 *The first New Zealand attempt to take Cassino, 16–18 February*

Freyberg's plan was far from original and was little more than an elaboration of the last American attacks which had failed. 4 (Ind) Division, which was as experienced in mountain warfare as Juin's North Africans, was to attack Monte Cassino from the Snake's Head Ridge. The New Zealanders were to break across the Rapido and enter Cassino town from the east, using the demolished railway as their axis of advance. General Tuker, the Commander of 4 (Ind) Division, tried to persuade Freyberg to make a wider encircling move over the lower slopes of Monte Cairo. He was encouraged in giving this advice not only by his own wide experience of mountain warfare, but also by Juin's similar belief that this would be a more effective way of opening up the Liri Valley. There was no point in battering away at the German defences where they were strongest and where the Germans had shown their determination to counter-attack any Allied gains. Up on Monte Cairo, the German positions were weaker; there was more room for manoeuvre by experienced mountain units like those of 4 (Ind) Division; and there was a very fair chance of surprising the Germans, whose defences there were manned by lower-grade infantry battalions rather than the first-class parachute and panzer grenadier battalions which were holding Monte Cassino. The main objection to Tuker's proposal was the difficulty of supplying a force up and over these mountain ridges and the time it would take to develop this axis of attack. The logistic problems could probably have been solved with French help and the time factor might have been brought into better perspective if General Tuker had not fallen ill at the crucial moment in planning and been unable to press his case as hard as he would have liked. He did his best from his sick bed, but the decision went against him. 4 (Ind) Division settled down to doing what it could with the plan as it stood.

It is doubtful whether the difficulties which faced 4 (Ind) Division relieving the Americans and preparing for this attack were ever really appreciated by the New Zealand Corps Headquarters, which had no experience of mountain warfare. Mule companies had to carry forward all supplies. Their columns had to run the gauntlet as they crossed the open Rapido Valley, which was still closely overlooked by Germans. They then had to make their way up the steep mountain tracks, long sections of which were harassed by German artillery and mortar fire. German fire and the natural hazards of the track took a cumulative toll of men and animals. When they at last reached the head of the track, their supplies had to be manhandled forward to the actual infantry positions. Everything had to be done in darkness which made stocking the necessary quantities of such vital items as grenades and mortar bombs a very slow business. If the Indians were to succeed where the Americans had failed, the one thing they needed most was time. Time to build up their supplies; time to patrol and fix the German positions accurately; time to make enough officers and NCOs familiar with the difficult routes they would have to follow to reach their objectives; and time to plan and co-ordinate their attack. The Americans had been unable to give them much information about the enemy positions except that the Monastery was the key to the whole area. The Americans did not know exactly where they were themselves—as the Indians soon found to their cost. The vital Point 593, which was shown on divisional and corps operations maps as in American hands, was in fact still held by the Germans some 70–100 yards in front of the positions which the Indians were taking over. Unfortunately the one commodity which the Indians were not going to be allowed was time.

It was not just the need to help Anzio which curtailed 4 (Ind) Division's preparations. That other special feature of the Cassino battlefield—the Monastery—played its baleful part as well. When Freyberg decided that a direct attack would have to be made, General Tuker rightly demanded the neutralization of the Monastery. No commander could have asked his troops to advance against that great building with a clear conscience unless he had done his utmost to ensure that they would not be mown down by German machine gunners in or on the slopes around it. It is quite academic to argue that the destruction of the Monastery was unnecessary or that it was a military mistake. The Indian Division was ordered to take Monte Cassino from Snake's Head Ridge. It was impossible to tell whether the Monastery was occupied or not. Even if it was not occupied—and the post-war evidence suggests that it was not—there were strongly fortified posts on the mountain side so close to its walls that they could not have been neutralized without hitting the building. If the Germans had wished to show their great respect for this Christian shrine, they should not have included it within the layout of the strongest section of their Gustav defences.* Their attempts to blame the Allies for the bombing is nothing more than propaganda. No divisional, corps, army or army group commander could have ordered men to advance along that ridge with the Monastery unscathed before them. To have done so would have invited pillory for a callous disregard for their men's lives. Even the argument, used by Mark Clark in trying to shift the blame on to the British commanders, that the Monastery when bombed served as a better defensive position for the Germans than when it stood intact, is invalid. If Fifth Army's co-ordination of the land and air action at Cassino had been more efficient, 4 (Ind) Division would have taken the ruins and occupied them in the wake of the bombing. The ruins would then have served the Indians instead of the Germans as an excellent defensive position from which to repel counter-attacks. That this did not happen was not the fault of 4 (Ind) Division, as this story will show. The crux of the matter was this. If political, humanitarian or aesthetic considerations precluded the destruction of the Monastery, then 4 (Ind) Division should not have been ordered to attack Monte Cassino from the Snake's Head Ridge. Some other road to Rome should have been sought or some other way of relieving pressure on Anzio should have been tried. There was in fact another road, which no one found until much later, when it opened up almost by chance in front of Juin's mountaineers in the last battle of Cassino.

Once the bombing of the Monastery was accepted by Alexander and Maitland Wilson as essential and it had been endorsed by the Chiefs of Staff, the Allied air forces took over. The Monastery had been rebuilt as a fortress in earlier times. The walls were immensely thick and rose up from the rock on which it stood presenting a sheer and unscalable face. The only entrance was through the main gate. Medium bombers could not carry heavy enough bombs to breach the massive walls, so Fortress bombers of the Strategic Air Force had to be used. These bombers had to attack from high altitude and so needed clear weather to bomb a pin-point target. The difficulties of co-ordinating the action of strategic air forces

---

* On the evidence of General Oster, who was on von Senger's Operations Staff, it appears that von Senger did not intend to include the Monastery in his lines. He proposed to block the Liri Valley further north but this was vetoed by OKW.

within a tactical land battle were fully realized, but, as yet, techniques for using them in this way had not been fully developed, and so it was decided to make the Monastery bombing an operation by itself in which no attempt would be made to co-ordinate it closely with the army's tactical plan. The timing would depend on the weather, rather than upon 4 (Ind) Division's readiness to follow up. The target date was set for 16 February, by which time the New Zealand Corps hoped to be able to take advantage of the bombing. The New Zealand Corps seems to have considered the bombing as a mere bonus which might or might not come off. In its operation instruction dated 11 February 4 (Ind) Division is instructed to capture Monastery Hill and to exploit down its southern slopes to cut Route 6 and to capture Cassino town from the rear. There is just one paragraph on the action of the air forces.

11 Air

Requests have been made for all buildings and suspected enemy strong points on and in the vicinity of the objectives including the Monastery to be subjected to intense bombing from now onwards.

Details of aircraft available in direct support will be issued later.

One tentacle* is with 7 Brigade and one with Main Divisional Head-quarters.

4 (Ind) Division completed its take-over from the Americans on 13 February and set about preparing to take Monte Cassino. Its leading brigade, 7 Indian Brigade, held the eastern end of the Snake's Head with only 70 yards between its leading platoons and the Germans on Point 593. Its second brigade was echeloned back behind the leading brigade ready to pass through when it was needed, and the third brigade was used up providing porters. 7 (Ind) Brigade's first task was to take Point 593 to secure a safe start line for the main attack to clear the rest of the Monastery spur.

In the valley below the New Zealanders were getting ready to seize a new bridgehead over the Rapido in the area of Cassino Station. The 28 (Maori) Battalion was to attack along the railway early on the chosen night to take and hold the station while the New Zealand sappers turned the railway into a tank route by clearing the ballast of mines and twisted railway lines and rebuilding a number of demolished bridges and culverts which blocked the track. Their work would have to be finished by dawn because they would not be able to work in daylight under German observation from Monte Cassino, and unless the tanks were into the station

---

* Tentacles were special communication teams responsible for passing air support demands from forward units to the air forces.

by daylight the Maoris would be in a worse position than the regiments of the 36 (US) Division had been at Saint Angelo.

A storm raged all 13 February. Next day the meteorologists forecast 24 hours' clear weather which would be followed by more stormy weather. It was now or never; and so the bombing of the Monastery was ordered for the next morning, 15 February, 24 hours earlier than the New Zealand Corps expected it. In all 142 Fortresses and 87 medium bombers dropped 450 tons of bombs with remarkable accuracy on the Monastery which was reduced to a great pile of rubble. There was no time to withdraw the troops of 7 (Ind) Brigade behind the bomb safety line but only about a dozen bombs fell wide causing some 24 Allied casualties. The walls of the Monastery were not completely breached and still presented a formidable obstacle to any infantryman who could reach them. The ruins also offered an ideal defensive position on the ridge to whoever got there first. Colonel Baade, commanding 90 Panzer Grenadier Division, did not hesitate and ordered their immediate occupation before the Indians could forestall him.

7 (Ind) Brigade were far from ready to follow up the bombing. It did not even know the Monastery was to be bombed that day. The Commander of the leading battalion, the Royal Sussex, commented 'they told the enemy, but they did not tell us!' The best that could be done in the time was to attack Point 593 with a company of the Royal Sussex that night. This attack failed due to lack of time to make adequate preparations and because the German strength on Point 593 was underestimated. The company was stopped by a deep gulley which they did not know was there and after losing half its strength had to withdraw before daylight.

The following day fighter-bombers pounded the Monastery once more, but the bulk of the Allied air effort had by then been switched to Anzio where von Mackensen had launched Hitler's great counter-offensive. That night the Royal Sussex were told to try again, this time using the whole battalion. Direct artillery support could not be given onto Point 593 because the Royal Sussex were too close to the enemy position; instead, supporting artillery fire was directed on neighbouring ridges which could enfilade the Royal Sussex attack. Unfortunately the crest clearance was insufficient for the artillery and the Royal Sussex were disorganized before they could get under way by shells from their own gunners bursting amongst them. Thanks to many feats of individual gallantry, several of the German positions were overrun and destroyed. Then hand-grenades, the most effective weapon in this type of fighting, began to run short, whereas the Germans still had ample supplies in their prepared positions. As daylight started to break, Point 593 was still in German hands, and so the Royal Sussex withdrew from the exposed positions which they had gained during the night's fighting. To have remained out on the forward slopes in daylight would have been to invite annihilation. As it was the Royal Sussex had lost 12 out of 15 officers and 162 out of 313 men who went forward on the two nights. An experienced battalion had been cut to bits for no material gain. 4 (Ind) Division had still not taken the part of the ridge which it needed to mount the main attack on the Monastery Hill called for in the corps plan. But the news from Anzio was alarming; there could be no pause. The main New Zealand Corps attack by the Indians onto Monastery Hill and the New Zealanders into the station would have to be made straight away without first securing Point 593.

The corps attack started at midnight on 17–18 February. 4 (Ind) Division used four battalions this time; a Rajputana Rifle battalion supported by the Royal Sussex against Point 593 and two Gurkha battalions across the arc of the Snake's Head Ridge—a more direct route as the crow flies, but far longer on the ground amongst the broken folds of rock and terraced fields. The Rajputana Rifles took Point 593 losing all but two of their officers in the process and found that their way along the ridge towards the Monastery was still blocked by further German positions in depth which they could not overcome. The first Gurkha battalion ran into difficulties from the start. Air photographs had shown a belt of low scrub across their line of advance, such as had been found on many of the Italian hillsides and which normally presented no difficulty to advancing infantry. In this case it turned out to be about five-foot-high thorn bushes liberally laced with wire and anti-personnel mines and covered by strong German positions which had not been detected before the advance. The Gurkhas fought on in spite of heavy losses in the scrub and overran several German positions, but could not break through and were forced to withdraw. The second Gurkha battalion was now directed to clear the ridge in front of the Rajputana Rifles instead of pressing on towards the Monastery. This they succeeded in doing only to find, as dawn came up, that they were completely exposed to fire from the Germans in the Monastery and from many unsubdued positions between them and the Rajputana Rifles on Point 593, who had been resisting a number of fierce counter-attacks by German paratroopers. The 7 (Ind) Brigade Commander decided rightly that he could not continue the attack in daylight and ordered a withdrawal to the best defensive positions his battalions could find before full daylight arrived. The Rajputana Rifles took up positions on the reverse slopes of Point 593 and the Gurkhas withdrew to the reverse slopes of the features on the Rajputana Rifles' left flank.

On the railway below, the Maoris took the station and the New Zealand sappers cleared most of the railway, completing all except the last two bridges. Dawn came just too soon. The battalion was isolated in the station without tank support. To protect it, the artillery laid a continuous smoke screen around it for most of the day. All seemed to be well until the middle of the afternoon when German tanks were heard coming into the station area through the smoke. The Maoris fought back but in the end had to abandon their bridgehead. The Second Battle of Cassino was over. The only gain was one new bridge over the Rapido which could not be used and about a hundred yards of rock strewn hillside. The crest of Point 593 was still in German hands.

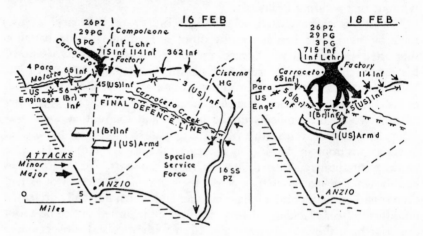

35   The first German counter-offensive, 16–20 February

After von Mackensen's preliminary offensive had succeeded in taking the Factory and Carroceto, General Lucas had relieved the battered 1 (Br) Division with 45 (US) Division. As 56 (Br) Division arrived from the Garigliano, he brought it into the line on 45 (US) Division's western flank so that the Albano road sector was held by completely fresh troops. 3 (US) Division remained holding the Cisterna sector which had not yet been seriously attacked. Kesselring and von Mackensen studied the front in great detail before they decided where to deliver their decisive counter-offensive. The two coastal sectors provided most cover, but the German experience at Salerno made them avoid an axis within easy range of Allied warships. Moreover, they wished to make the best use they could of the strong tank formations which Hitler had placed at their disposal. They decided that the best axis of attack was, as OKW believed, the line of the Albano–Anzio road. Their plan was to attack initially with the troops of four divisions on a very wide front either side of the main road and with two diversionary attacks on the extreme flanks of the bridge-head. As soon as they had achieved a break-in, they would exploit with a concentrated attack by 26 Panzer and 29 Panzer Grenadier Divisions. Hitler called for von Mackensen's plan and insisted that the main attack should be made on a much narrower front with the Infantry Lehr Regiment, in which he had great faith, leading. The Luftwaffe were to give maximum support and were heavily reinforced for this purpose. The unusually large concentrations of German field artillery were to be further augmented by anti-aircraft guns firing in a ground role. A new secret weapon, called the 'Goliath', was to be used for the first time. This was a remote-controlled, explosive-filled, miniature tank which was to help clear a way through the Allied defences. All units in the attacking force were to be specially indoctrinated with the great responsibility imposed upon them by the Führer. They were to be told that the chance for a decisive victory had come; the Führer had concentrated an over-whelming force to destroy the flimsy Anglo-American beachhead; nothing had been spared to ensure success; and, as a reward, the German units which broke through would have the honour of escorting the captured Allied prisoners through the streets of Berlin. This indoctrination was not difficult to make realistic; even Kesselring had not seen such an open-handed massing of German resources since the great days of 1940 and 1941, but it had two unfortunate results for the Germans. Over-confident prisoners gave away the date of the offensive to Allied interrogators; and when defeat ultimately stared von Mackensen's divisions in the face, the effect on their morale was deep-seated and lasting. Many German soldiers realized for the first time that the war was really lost.

The German attack started in daylight on 16 February because the newly-arrived divisions did not know the ground well enough to launch a night attack. Probing assaults came in all along 56 (Br), 45 (US) and 3 (US) Divisions' fronts. The Allied battalions withstood the intense pounding from German artillery and from the Luftwaffe, and drove off most of the tank and infantry attacks during the first day. German long-range guns and Luftwaffe bombers struck at the rear areas trying to panic the administrative echelons without success. In return, the Allied air forces were switched from Cassino and flew about 500 sorties mainly against Carroceto and the Factory which the Germans were seen to be using as main assembly areas. During the night the position changed dramatically. Infiltration either side of the Albano road led to a large gap appearing between the centre and left-hand regiments of 45 (US) Division. This was just what the Germans were looking for and they lost no time in widening the breach during the morning of the second day. By the afternoon von Mackensen judged the moment had come to attack in strength with fresh troops. The much-lauded Infantry Lehr Regiment was brought up and, supported by panzer grenadier battalions, launched an all-out attack down the Albano road. Some 14 German battalions were involved in widening the salient driven into 45 (US) Division's front. Packed into such a small area and unable to use their tanks much off the road, the Germans offered excellent targets to the massed VI (US) Corps' artillery, to naval guns off-shore and to Allied airmen. Their losses were appalling, but they continued to launch successive attacks in a desperate endeavour to break through and to give Germany another lease of life. Lucas ordered 1 (Br) Division to move out of Corps reserve into a block-ing position astride the Albano road on the 'final' defence line of the beachhead. He also ordered 45 (US) Division to counter-attack the salient during the night.

All through the second night the Germans moved up more units ready to make a decisive effort next day. They defeated 45 (US) Division's counter-attack and infiltrated in and around the American and British positions blocking their advance. At dawn, profiting by the confusion caused by their night's work and catching 45 (US) Division off-balance after its unsuccessful night counter-attack, five German regiments includ-ing the Lehr Regiment reopened the offensive. The sky was overcast and prevented the Allied medium and heavy bombers operating, but the artillery and fighter-bombers gave the American and British defenders effective support once more. The bulk of 45 (US) Division was forced back on to the 'final' defensive line east of the Albano road and 1 (Br) Division came under attack astride the road itself. That afternoon 26 Panzer Division was committed. Only a blown bridge over the Carroceto creek stopped a German break through. By evening the stubbornness of 45 (US) Division and 1 (Br) Division was rewarded. The Germans began to pull back to reorganize.

The fighting went on for two more days in which 1 (US) Armoured Division and 1 (Br) Division successfully counter-attacked. On 20 February a last despairing effort made by the panzer grenadier divisions came to nothing and marked the end of the Germans' first counter-offensive. They had learnt what the Allies had been experiencing for some time, but were refusing to admit; that attacking in winter, when tanks and heavy weapons are confined to the roads, is a frustrating and debilitating mode of warfare. Their ten divisions had failed to break through the four-and-a-half Allied divisions. They had again felt the crushing weight of Allied air and artillery superiority, and their morale had been seriously weakened. Never again did the German divisions in Italy attack with the dash that they displayed between 16 and 19 February at Anzio. They continued to defend as brilliantly as ever but they had lost the stomach for attack after this costly failure along the Albano road.

Ironically, the Allies owed their success to the one man who lost his command during the battle. Mark Clark eased General Lucas out of command, replacing him with 3 (US) Division's Truscott. If it had not been for Lucas' cautious handling of the initial landing and the care with which he built up stocks of artillery ammunition and defence stores, when everyone above was goading him to launch out towards the Alban Hills, the story might have ended differently. The German attack was broken by the stubbornness of the Anglo-American infantry and the overwhelming support they received from their gunners, airmen and tank crews. That support would not have been there, nor would they have had a tight defensible perimeter, if Lucas had dashed helter-skelter for the Alban Hills. It is difficult to escape the feeling that Mark Clark's sacking of Dawley at Salerno and Lucas at Anzio may have had a common factor—the need for a scapegoat. Someone had to be sacrificed to quieten Churchill's restless criticism of the tactical handling of his strategic brain-children. Mark Clark's orders endorsed Lucas' policy of consolidation before exploitation. He was dismissed just as his policy was proved by events to be right.

Both sides had failed to gain their objectives, the Allies at Cassino and the Germans at Anzio. Neither was prepared to give up and change its policy. They had both staked too much already, but they both needed to pause, rethink and regroup. The second German counter-offensive and its counterpart, the Third Battle of Cassino, were yet to come.

The Seeds of Victory

'... I was convinced that our Spring offensive would find him [the German] still offering a most determined resistance. It was for this reason that I considered regrouping absolutely vital to bring our full strength to bear at the critical point, while a continued attack in our present circumstances would merely weaken us to no good purpose. First, however, I would try once more to eliminate Cassino ...'

Alexander, in his Despatch

Great victories, when they occur, often appear to be the result of sudden inspiration, but in practice this is rarely the case. Able commanders, who seem so miraculously decisive at the crucial moment, have usually thought out and thought through the problems many weeks, if not months, ahead. When success comes it is more often than not because events have been set on their course by clear thinking at a time when everything seems to be going wrong. Moreover, successful plans are rarely the work of one man. They develop as many minds, looking at the problem from differing angles, are brought to bear upon it. During the anxious days of the first German counter-offensive at Anzio, Alexander's principal staff officers, ably led by his Chief of Staff, General John Harding,* were already elaborating plans for the spring. Harding's brilliant appreciation was forwarded to the Supreme Allied Headquarters on 22 February and became the basis for future planning in Italy. It contained many points which were unpalatable to Algiers, London and Washington, but, in the end, proved to contain the seeds of Alexander's spring victory before Rome. The train of thought is basic to the events of the next four months.

Harding did not argue about the strategic aim of operations in Italy.

* Later Field-Marshal Lord Harding who became Chief of the Imperial General Staff and Governor of Cyprus during the Eoka terrorist campaign.

This had been laid down by successive inter-Allied conferences as 'to force the enemy to commit the maximum number of divisions to operations in Italy at the time Overlord is launched'. For the first time he set out what this really meant. It was no use just pushing back the German front; nor had the capture of Rome any military significance. The tactical aim must be to destroy German formations in Italy to such an extent that they had to be replaced from elsewhere to prevent a disastrous collapse of Germany's southern defences. Three things were needed to accomplish this objective: first, the ability to gain at least a local superiority of three to one in infantry; secondly, fine weather so that the Allied preponderance in guns, tanks and air power could be brought to bear with maximum effect; and thirdly, time to rest, refit and retrain the divisions exhausted by the winter fighting. Staff calculations showed that the equivalent of an extra seven-and-a-half divisions would be needed and these, although available within the Mediterranean theatre and the British Middle East Command, could not be moved into Italy in the available shipping before mid-April. For the maximum effect on Overlord the destruction of the German armies in Italy should start some three weeks before Overlord's D-day. Most of the factors pointed to mid-April as the optimum date for a spring offensive in Italy; it would be right for Overlord; enough divisions could be concentrated in Italy by then; the weather should be fine and clear, and the ground hard; and provided—and this was an important proviso—operations were reduced to a minor key for the rest of the winter, the tired divisions should be ready to play their full part in an April offensive.

Harding envisaged three possible situations in Italy in April: 'Case A', the enemy driven northwards to the Pisa–Rimini Line as a result of the winter offensive, which was now clearly unlikely; 'Case B', a junction effected with Anzio, but the front stabilized south of Rome on the German Line 'C'; and 'Case C', little change in the current position. Taking each case in turn he showed that 'Case C' was not only the most likely because the Allies did not possess enough fresh troops to alter the current situation, but it was also the most advantageous to them. If the Germans stayed where they were, an attack by three to four divisions from the Anzio beachhead, in conjunction with a major offensive up the Liri Valley, would stand a reasonable chance of encircling and destroying a large part of the German armies in Italy. If there were sufficient troops available, subsidiary operations could be mounted up the Ausente Valley and along the west coast to help pin down and destroy the German divisions south of the Liri Valley. An amphibious force of one division might also be used profitably for operations in the Gulf of Gaeta. There were, however, three pre-requisites for this battle of annihilation: the

Anzio beachhead must be secured by retaking the Factory–Carroceto area and taking Cisterna; the German defences at Cassino must be cleared; and the troops must be given time to rest and reorganize after these preliminary operations were over.

The existing organization of the Army Group was unsuitable for decisive operations west of the Apennines. Unless changes were made in the inter-army division of responsibility, Fifth Army would be controlling over 20 divisions and Eighth Army possibly as few as four. The armies had also become hopelessly mixed in nationality and types of equipment. Ideally Eighth Army should command all divisions operating with British equipment and trained on British lines (e.g. all Commonwealth units and the Poles), and Fifth Army should command American and American-sponsored units such as the French. Harding proposed that the Adriatic sector should be reduced to a force commanded by a corps HQ direct under Army Group; Eighth Army should side-step across the Apennines to the Liri Valley sector; and Fifth Army's area of responsibility should be reduced to the Garigliano sector and the Anzio beachhead. The Poles would take over from the French in the mountains north of Cassino and the latter would move down into the Fifth Army sector on the upper Garigliano, to relieve the British corps (X Corps) in Fifth Army so that it could be brought back under British command. This regrouping would take some time and, although it had not been worked out in detail, Harding estimated that it could not be completed before 15 April—a further reason for timing the spring offensive for mid-April. A decision would be needed at once if all the moves were to be completed by this date (see fig. 37 for final grouping).

The tasks allotted to the Allied navies and air forces were simple. The navies were to accelerate the build-up of divisions in Italy and of the logistic stocks at Anzio. They were also to interfere with enemy coastal shipping and to support a divisional-sized operation in the Gulf of Gaeta. The air forces were to maintain air supremacy; sustain attacks on the enemy's rail communications; support the Anzio force if further counter-attacks developed; and be ready to concentrate total air effort against important land objectives in the preparatory operations leading up to the spring offensive whenever those objectives were found to be suitable air targets.

The most startling conclusion which Harding came to, and which caused most trouble, was that there would be no troops left for Anvil (the major amphibious attack on southern France which had been given co-equal priority with Overlord at the Tehran conference). He suggested that instead a simulation of Anvil should be used as the deception plan for the spring offensive in Italy with the object of holding German troops in southern France away from Overlord and away from the Italian front.

He envisaged the regrouping of Fifth Army would be carried out in such a way as to give the impression of the French Expeditionary Corps withdrawing from their sector north of Cassino to prepare for a return to their homeland. The actual embarkation of the division earmarked for amphibious operations in the Gulf of Gaeta would lend colour to this cover plan and would confirm the Germans in their suspicions that another Anzio, probably aimed at southern France, was being prepared.

Alexander put his proposals, based on this appreciation, to Maitland Wilson, who received them, if not coldly, with some reserve. He knew that the Combined Chiefs of Staff were still giving Anvil top priority with Overlord. Suggestions that Anvil should be cancelled had been mooted on a number of occasions since the Tehran conference and Maitland Wilson doubted whether the American Chiefs of Staff could be persuaded to drop one of their favourite operations, in order to help the Italian Campaign about which they had always had grave misgivings. He also disliked the idea of halting active operations until mid-April. Not only would such a suggestion bring down the wrath of Churchill on his head; it was also contrary to the views of the theatre air commanders. There was considerable optimism amongst the airmen that they could break the existing deadlock on land in two ways: first, by an operation, which was given the appropriate codename 'Strangle', designed to starve the German army south of Rome of vital supplies of ammunition, fuel, replacement equipment and reinforcing formations; and secondly, by mass bombing of German forces holding key points such as Cassino which were obstructing the advance of the Allied armies. It had been originally intended that Strangle should be based on persistent attacks on railway workshops and marshalling yards which appeared to be the Achilles heel of the German logistic system. On the advice of Alexander's staff, a broad interdiction belt across the Italian Peninsula was added to the Strangle programme. Within this belt all rail and road bridges would be destroyed. Marshalling yards could be repaired relatively quickly. Demolished bridges in mountain country presented the Germans with a much more difficult problem. Not only did they take longer to repair, but they also forced the Germans to use up precious stocks of petrol ferrying supplies round demolished bridges. As regards the mass bombing of major defensive positions, the reduction of Pantelleria and the destruction of the Monastery on Monte Cassino had shown what could be done by air action. The airmen were keen to extend this technique and show that they could win the land-battle in winter conditions even if the old-fashioned armies could not. Wilson replied to Alexander objecting to the pause in operations and adding:

As far as operations in Italy are concerned, these must be conditioned mainly by the air factor. My plan for Italy is to use the air to deprive the enemy of the ability either to maintain his present positions or to withdraw his divisions out of Italy in time for Overlord.

Alexander's reply pointed out that under his proposed plan pressure would still be maintained at Cassino and Anzio by the preliminary attacks aimed at capturing spring-boards for his April offensive. He was not over-sanguine about the air plan and he contented himself by saying that he hoped 'the weather will improve in time to give our air forces a chance to carry out their part of your plan. At present it is atrocious and shows no sign of change.'

Maitland Wilson also gave a serious warning about shipping. The Navy could not supply the tonnages which Alexander and Mark Clark believed were essential for Anzio. This problem and Alexander's wish to cancel Anvil reopened the whole difficult LST question at the highest level and with it the debate on Anvil itself.

Many of the assumptions on which the Tehran decision to give Anvil priority over Italy was based had been falsified by events. Anzio had taken far more shipping than expected; Rome had not fallen; the Allies were nowhere near the Pisa–Rimini Line which they had hoped to reach by March; and the Overlord plan had been found wanting in certain respects by Eisenhower and Montgomery when they took over executive responsibility for mounting that operation. In their view the assault force proposed by the planners, and upon which the Tehran calculations had been based, was inadequate. More ships and units were needed for the cross-Channel assault. Before Eisenhower left the Mediterranean he had said the same thing about Anvil—a larger assault force would be necessary. The margins in the assault shipping calculations had been pruned to a minimum during Churchill's Christmas conferences in Carthage when he was trying to find shipping for Anzio. Now Anzio was still not complete; and both Anvil and Overlord wanted more shipping than had been planned. Something would have to be cancelled; or the Americans would have to produce more shipping at the expense of the Pacific; or—and this was almost beyond contemplation at this stage—Overlord would have to be delayed to bring another month's production of landing ships into service.

There were three distinct views at the highest level on this strategic dilemma. The British Chiefs of Staff, advised by Maitland Wilson and Alexander, believed that Anvil should be sacrificed to produce the extra shipping for Overlord. Concentration of effort in Italy to destroy the German Armies south of Rome and the reduction of Anvil to a 'cover-plan' operation, as suggested by Harding, would help Overlord more than a full-blooded Anvil and half-hearted offensive in Italy. The American Chiefs of Staff held the opposite view. They were reluctant to change an agreed strategy to meet yet another shift in pragmatic British thinking. They hoped to find other means of strengthening Overlord which would not affect Anvil. They were even suspicious of the Overlord planners' calculations and believed that they were committing the usual planners' sin of over-insurance. The third view was that of Eisenhower, who had planned Anvil originally and was now responsible for Overlord. While he wished Anvil to survive to help his operations in North-West Europe, he believed that it should be abandoned if its continued existence meant weakening Overlord. General Marshall was not slow to appreciate the irony of the situation. Here were the Americans backing a Mediterranean operation at the expense of Overlord while the British were doing the reverse. A compromise was reached in the last week of February when Eisenhower proposed that operations in Italy should have priority over all other Mediterranean operations, provided the Supreme Commander Mediterranean continued to make plans and preparations for a seaborne diversion to help Overlord amongst which Anvil would be given prior consideration.* The theatre was to keep its existing fleet of assault shipping until 20 March when the situation would be reviewed. If, at this review, it was clear that a major amphibious assault to help Overlord could not be mounted, then all shipping over and above the one divisional lift needed for the cover plan would be withdrawn from the Mediterranean for Overlord. The Combined Chiefs of Staff agreed to these proposals on 25 February, just as the first indications of the second German offensive against Anzio were detected.

Hitler had been bitterly disappointed with the failure of his first counter-offensive and ordered the attack to be resumed as soon as regrouping could be completed. This time the 3 (US) Division's sector covering the Cisterna–Anzio road (*see* fig. 35) was chosen for the assault which was to be carried out by four infantry divisions with one mobile division in reserve. The start of the offensive was planned for 25 February, but bad weather forced successive postponements until 28 February. The weather was still poor, but the German commanders appreciated that low cloud would cloak their attack from the prying eyes of the Allied air forces and artillery observation planes and so they decided to go ahead rather than wait for an improvement. A preliminary diversionary attack was made against 56 (Br) and 1 (Br) Divisions west of the Albano road which made little progress

---

* There were a number of possible diversionary operations under consideration at this time. Amongst them were an attack on Bordeaux, an attack on the Gulf of Genoa and operations in the Adriatic including an attack on Istria.

and was not pressed. The German artillery then switched to 3 (US) Division to support a series of attacks launched on a wide front. By the end of the first day 3 (US) Division's front was still intact and no sign of a break-through had appeared. Attacks on the second and third days were no more successful. On 2 March the clouds cleared and the full weight of the Allied air forces came into play. On 4 March von Mackensen had to admit failure and ordered the German Fourteenth Army to go over to the defensive. His mobile divisions were gradually withdrawn into reserve; the 26 Panzer and 29 Panzer Grenadier Divisions moving into General Reserve between the Gustav and Anzio fronts; and the Hermann Göring Division pulling back to rest near Leghorn and to cover that area against possible Allied landings. VI (US) Corps was left facing not much more than its own strength of four to five infantry divisions. 56 (Br) Division was relieved by 5 (Br) Division from the Garigliano and the former went back to the Middle East for garrison duties in exchange for a fresh division. 3 (US) Division was relieved by 34 (US) Division but stayed in reserve in the beachhead.

The Third Battle of Cassino, which occupied the Italian stage next, cannot be linked directly to the second German offensive as it was planned independently of any Anzio considerations and was launched long after von Mackensen had given up. Like the second German offensive, however, it was the last attempt by the Allies to do something positive before the spring. Planning started as soon as the Second Battle of Cassino died away in early February. Alexander, Clark and Freyberg gave the problem detailed attention because in their view Cassino held the key to the Gustav Line and unless this strong bastion, which blocked the road to Rome, could be overcome in March, the scope for the spring offensive would be much reduced.

An attack up the Liri Valley had failed; the ground was still too soft for tanks, so this axis could be discarded. An attack round the extreme northern flank of Monte Cairo, which Juin always advocated, would be too difficult in winter and only lead into more tortuous mountain positions. Another attack along the Snake's Head Ridge would certainly be suicidal. There was just one other possibility. No really serious attempt had been made to fight a way through Cassino to clear Route 6 and to take the Monastery by direct assault from below. No one viewed this course with any enthusiasm, but it did offer one advantage which might be exploited. Cassino town was a possible target for heavy bombers which the airmen were keen to exploit. If the full weight of the Allied air forces from England as well as the Mediterranean were turned loose on the town, there should be very few survivors to oppose the New Zealand Corps when it advanced to attack. Any German soldier who did survive would be too shocked at the end of the bombing to offer much resistance. If any did survive and left their cellars to oppose the attackers when they advanced into the ruins they would be forced to cover again by a heavy artillery barrage. The square mile occupied by Cassino town would be hit by over 1,000 tons of bombs and 200,000 artillery shells. The concept was something new in warfare and would act as a guide to those who were busy planning the fire support for Overlord.

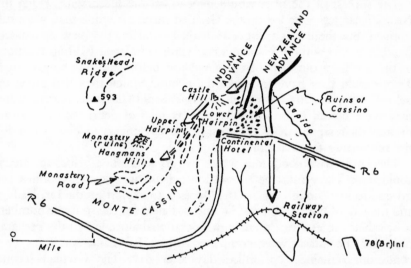

36　The Third Battle of Cassino, 15–23 March

Freyberg's corps plan was relatively simple. The New Zealand Division's task was to follow up the bombing and to clear the ruins of Cassino, opening a way to Route 6 through the town. 4 (Ind) Division was to take Monte Cassino and the Monastery from the town, attacking up the face of the mountain where the zig-zag road led up to what used to be the main gate. 78 (Br) Division and an American armoured force from 1 (US) Armoured Division were to be ready to exploit success up the Liri Valley once a way was opened for them. The New Zealanders would advance first with 6 (NZ) Brigade leading and would enter the town from the north behind the artillery barrage which would start as soon as the bombing was over. As they cleared the ruins from north to south they would detach a force to take the station and another to take Castle Hill. The latter was a prominent knoll above the town on which there stood a ruined mediaeval castle. This feature was part of a spur which ran up to the Monastery itself and formed the natural approach from the town. The Indian Division would be led by 5 (Ind) Brigade and would come into the town behind 6 (NZ) Brigade after dark, taking over Castle Hill and using it as a base from which to fight its way up to the Monastery via three intermediate objectives—the lower and the upper hairpin bends on the zig-zag road and Point 435, nick-named 'Hangman's Hill,' some 250 feet below the Monastery. The name of the latter came from the remains of a pylon which looked like a gibbet when seen from the Rapido Valley below.

The success of the plan would depend on the speed with which the New Zealanders mopped up the German survivors while they were still stunned, but there was a difficulty here. For safety, the New Zealanders would have to withdraw about 1,000 yards from their existing positions in the northern outskirts of the town just before the bombing started. They would then have to retake the ground which they had given up before they made any fresh gains and this would take time. Furthermore, they were bound to be slowed down by piles of debris and craters although their sappers had made careful arrangements to clear paths for the supporting tanks as quickly as possible.

There were two conditions which had to be satisfied before the attack could start. There must be at least three days' fine weather to allow the ground to dry enough for 78 (Br) Division to exploit up the Liri Valley; and the day of the attack must be fine and clear for the strategic bombers to see their target from their high operational altitude. All the preparations for the attack were completed by 24 February, but these two conditions remained unfulfilled day after day. The German second counter-offensive at Anzio came and went, and still the codeword 'Bradman', which was to signify bombing next day, could not be given. The Germans, freed from their Anzio commitment and unworried by Eighth Army on the Adriatic Coast, moved the whole of 1 Para Division into the Cassino sector to relieve the stalwart but now very tired 90 Panzer Grenadier Division. With the experience of the street fighting in Ortona behind them 1 Para Division were unlikely to surrender their new charge very easily. On 14 March the meteorologists advised that weather conditions were likely to meet the requirements of the airmen and the soldiers. The codeword 'Bradman batting tomorrow' was given during the afternoon, and that night the New Zealanders surreptitiously withdrew behind the safety line.

At 8.30 next morning, 15 March, Alexander and his senior commanders and staff officers together with many eminent journalists watched from a farmhouse some five miles away as the bombers arrived over Cassino. About 300 heavy bombers and 200 mediums dropped their thousand tons of high explosive on the town in three-and-a-half hours. The accuracy of bombing was not as good as the attack on the Monastery and several of the bomber waves mistook their targets. For instance, Eighth Army Headquarters at Venafro, a very similar town to Cassino, nestling under a large mountain, was hit. At midday the artillery barrage started and the leading New Zealand brigade moved forward on a one-battalion front with tanks and infantry working together. At first all went well: the force detailed to capture Castle Hill was detached and the rest of the brigade went on picking their way through the rubble. Before 1 p.m. they were well into the town but were meeting unexpected opposition from amongst the ruins and from the slopes of Monte Cassino and Castle Hill. They reached Route 6 but there they were held up by opposition which they could not clear without further help. There seems to have been some delay in moving the second and third battalions forward, and although the operation was still going to plan it was falling behind schedule.

Meanwhile the Castle Hill force fought a brilliant action seizing the Castle and reaching the lower of the hairpin bends. Here again, reinforcements were slow to arrive and the position was not as secure as the New Zealanders had hoped when dusk started to fall. The gods then interfered, as if displeased with the tardiness of the New Zealand reserves. The sky became overcast and, as darkness settled on the ruins, it started to rain. Torrential rain fell that first night. The huge craters left by the heavy bombers soon became lakes. The tracks winding through the rubble turned into quagmires and were often too slippery for fully armed men to negotiate. The moon, upon which the Indian Division had been depending, was drowned and the night became pitch. The second New Zealand battalion to enter the ruins took three hours to scramble a bare 600 yards. The sappers' task of clearing tank routes became impossible. They had hoped to bulldoze in the craters but when they filled with water this became useless and several craters had to be bridged before the tanks could move forward.

The three battalions of 5 (Ind) Brigade moved, as planned, into the town at dusk. They had to jostle and push their way up the few passable tracks which were also being used by New Zealand supply parties. The German artillery was back in action and was harassing the roads into the town with telling effect. The 1/4 Essex, the British battalion of 5 (Ind) Brigade took over the Castle and the Lower Hairpin Bend but the 1/6 Rajputana Rifles were repulsed when they tried to seize the Upper Hairpin Bend. The latter almost ceased to be an effective fighting unit; its battalion headquarters suffered a direct hit, killing the C.O. and all the headquarters officers, and the two rear companies were eliminated by German artillery fire. Only the two leading companies at the Lower Hairpin Bend were still a coherent force. The third battalion of the brigade, 1/9 Gurkha Rifles, lost touch with the two leading battalions. Its C.O. decided to push on alone to his objective, Hangman's Hill. One of his two leading companies was stopped by German opposition but the other disappeared into the night. He decided that the only thing to do was to take up a defensive position with the rest of his battalion so as not to be caught in daylight on an exposed hillside without cover. It was not until much later next day that artillery observers spotted his lost company on Hangman's Hill.

On the second day the Indians held the Castle and the Lower Hairpin but the Germans had a strong position on the Upper Hairpin and kept the lone Gurkha Company isolated on Hangman's Hill. In the town, it was clear that the Germans in the south-west corner had survived the bombing and had been reinforced during the night. They were occupying a number of buildings slightly higher than the rest of the town and were successfully blocking the southern exit of Route 6. The fighting in the town began to show the ruthless features of Ortona all over again with New Zealanders instead of Canadians fighting Heidrich's paratroopers.* The few tanks which had got through before the rain were able to help with their guns but could not move and reinforcements could not reach them. The infantry had to fight from house to house and cellar to cellar with grenade and rifle in the great jumble of mud and rubble.

How had the Germans survived? There seem to be four reasons why they had not been annihilated. First, they had been preparing their defences for a long time and these defences had been consolidated by practical experience in the first and second battles. Their strong points were constructed in the ground floors of key buildings and reinforced sufficiently to withstand the collapse of the building above. They had made extensive use of cellars for command posts and sleeping quarters and had shored them up to make them bomb-proof. They also made extensive use of two-man steel shelters called 'crabs', into which as many as six men could squeeze in an emergency. In a number of buildings tanks and assault guns had been run inside and bricked up to form concealed fortresses. These defensive measures accounted for some survival. Secondly, the number of troops in the town was not high. Cassino and Monte Cassino were held by one regiment only—Colonel Heilmann's 3 Parachute Regiment. His 1 and 3 Battalions were in the Monastery and on the slopes of Monte Cassino, and only his 2 Battalion reinforced by two companies of 3 Battalion was in the town. It was the 2 Battalion which took the brunt of the bombing. One company was completely destroyed; two others suffered serious losses; and the fourth withdrew

---

* Although both sides fought with great determination in the appalling conditions which existed in the town, they both behaved with conspicuous regard to the customs of war, particularly in respect of the Red Cross. Medical orderies on both sides were allowed to work freely without interference.

21 The ruins of the Monastery on Monte Cassino

CASSINO

22 A German mortar crew using the ruins of the Monastery after the bombing

23 Alexander with his Chief of Staff, General Harding

DIADEM

24 Mark Clark entering St Peter's Square in Rome

into some caves on the mountain-side when the bombing started and so survived. It was the return of this fourth company to its less damaged positions on the south side of the town which stopped the New Zealand advance. Thirdly, the bombing was too local. Colonel Heilmann still had a battalion in the Monastery which was untouched and a battalion on the hillside above the town which only suffered slight losses, mainly from the artillery barrage which supported the New Zealand advance. Heidrich, who was at Heilmann's command post during the battle, was soon able to intervene with his divisional reserves and his artillery. He moved up reinforcements from the rear and concentrated his artillery and mortars on the narrow front along which the New Zealanders and Indians were advancing. The fourth and final reason was the superb discipline and determination not to give way displayed by commanders and men alike in Heidrich's 1 Para Division. Their victory on the first day of Third Cassino must remain a memorial to the fighting qualities of the German Army. Allied psychiatrists who interrogated the prisoners taken in the town on the first day found no marked nervous disorders amongst them. They were proud of having survived such an attack. The morale of 1 Para Division rose still further as a result of the battle.

Looking at the situation at the end of the second day of the battle, the tasks of both sides were clear. On the Allied side the New Zealanders must break through along Route 6 and to do this they must turn Heidrich's paratroopers out of the Continental Hotel area which blocked the southern exit. The New Zealanders must also work their way into the station area to clear Route 6 into the town so that the Rapido could be bridged properly. The Indians must rescue their Gurkhas on Hangman's Hill and clear the rest of Monte Cassino so as to free Route 6 from German artillery observation. The German tasks were just the reverse. They must cling to their end of the town to stop a break-through to the Liri Valley and they must remove the Indian threat to Monte Cassino. The latter task could be achieved if the Germans could retake Castle Hill through which all supplies and reinforcements to the Indians on the Lower Hairpin Bend and Hangman's Hill had to pass. Thus the second phase of the Third Battle of Cassino became a struggle for two features—the Continental Hotel and Castle Hill. The Germans held the former and the Allies the latter; neither side released its grip in spite of every effort by the other to make it do so.

During the second night 1/9 Gurkha Rifles worked their way up the mountain-side platoon by platoon, until the whole battalion was on Hangman's Hill. The Upper Hairpin Bend was taken by 5 (Ind) Brigade and was lost again to a German counter-attack. The Germans, in their turn, failed to retake Castle Hill in spite of several determined efforts to do so.

The New Zealanders used most of the second night to reorganize and to bring tanks forward through the rubble. Two battalions worked their way towards the Continental trying to outflank the German positions but the streets were so badly cratered that the tanks could barely move and without their support the infantry found it difficult to penetrate the German positions. The third battalion had more success. It was ordered to capture the station. Its attack started at 11 a.m., but it was not until dusk that the station was firmly in its hands and the New Zealand sappers could start clearing Route 6 into the town from the east.

The third night and the fourth day followed a similar pattern—the Indians trying to secure a firmer foot-hold on Monte Cassino; the Germans trying to win back Castle Hill; and the New Zealanders painfully edging forward their tanks to come to grips with the Continental. None achieved what they wanted. It became more and more difficult to supply the Gurkhas on Hangman's Hill and in the end they had to be supplied by parachute drops. In the town the Continental resisted all the New Zealand attacks and it was found that the Germans had infiltrated back into the buildings at the foot of Castle Hill. Room for manoeuvre was shrinking as both sides brought more troops into the area.

On Saturday 18 March, the fourth day of the battle, Freyberg decided to prepare a co-ordinated corps attack for the following morning. The Indian Division was to reinforce the Gurkhas on Hangman's Hill and was then to assault the Monastery. The New Zealanders were to clear the Continental area. And, as a surprise element, a force of tanks was to make its way up a track laboriously and secretly constructed by the Indian sappers and miners, to appear on the high ground behind the Monastery. Heidrich had similar ideas. He now had a clear picture of the battlefield as well and decided to secure his positions on Monte Cassino by a strong counter-attack on Castle Hill. For this purpose he brought up a fresh battalion of 4 Para Regiment and timed its attack for first light on 19 March—the same day that Freyberg had chosen. The Germans struck first by about half an hour. Their men advanced under heavy covering fire helter-skelter down from the Upper Hairpin and reached the Castle but failed to take it. They tried again two hours later but again failed. They had, however, so dislocated the Indian Division's assault plans that it had to be postponed and was eventually cancelled. The New Zealand attack on the Continental fared no better than the German attack on the Castle. The tank forces' appearance on the Snake's Head Ridge caused momentary confusion amongst the German defenders. Point 593 was neutralized and it looked as though a break-through might occur. The Germans were overheard reporting by wireless that the tanks had broken through and that an infantry attack was expected any moment. Unfortunately 7 (Ind) Brigade was in no state to mount such an attack. It had been holding its positions ever since the end of the Second Battle of Cassino, losing about 60 men a week and was barely able to man its defensive positions let alone mount another attack. The possibility of attacking soon proved academic. The track leading towards the Monastery was found to be almost too narrow for the tanks. The leading tank struck a mine and effectively blocked the track. By then nearly a dozen tanks had been disabled and the order was given to withdraw. Freyberg's attempt to rejuvenate the battle had failed.

During the night 19–20 March the Allied position showed a marked deterioration. The Germans had moved up reinforcements and had infiltrated more men back into the ruins of the town and along the mountain-side. Their artillery and mortars were more active than ever and made the tasks of the New Zealand sappers, who were struggling to clear routes for the tanks, progressively more difficult. The battle was becoming a test of endurance.

On 20 March Alexander reviewed the position and decided that, if nothing more could be achieved within the next 36 hours, the operation should be halted and the ground gained consolidated as a useful bridgehead over the Rapido, which might be exploited in the spring offensive. Maitland Wilson would have preferred to go on but Alexander and Freyberg felt further efforts would be too costly and would lead to another Paschendaele. The Germans had enough reserves in hand now that they had gone onto the defensive at Anzio. If the Allied armies in Italy were to be ready in time for their spring offensive to help Overlord the Third Battle of Cassino must be stopped before it was too late. It would be better to concede Heidrich a temporary victory while losses were still manageable than to fight on and prejudice a greater Allied victory in the spring.

Freyberg tried for three more days to break the deadlock, but on 23 March he gave up and ordered the evacuation of the Gurkhas from Hangman's Hill and consolidation of the positions gained. Covered by a heavy barrage, the withdrawal was successfully carried out on the night 24–25 March.

The Third Battle of Cassino had ended. It had cost the New Zealand Corps about 4,000 men. 78 (Br) Division relieved the Indians on Monte Cassino and 1 Guards Brigade of 6 (Br) Armoured Division, which was just arriving from North Africa for the spring offensive, took over from the New Zealanders in Cassino's ruins. The New Zealand Corps' short life came to an end. It was disbanded and its units were dispersed to other corps.

The Allied and German winter offensives were over. Both sides began to prepare for the spring.

May–August 1944

THE SUMMER OF TRIUMPH
AND FRUSTRATION

'OBJECT

To give the greatest possible assistance to OVERLORD by destroying or containing the maximum number of German formations in the Mediterranean.'

British Chiefs of Staff Directive
to General Maitland Wilson, April 1944

Resetting the Stage

'The plan must envisage an attack on a wider front and with greater forces than Freyberg has been able to have for this operation. A little later, when the snow goes off the mountains, the rivers drop, and the ground hardens, movement will be possible over terrain which at present is impassable.'

Alexander to Churchill, 20 March 1944

As the winter of 1944 turned slowly into spring, an ominous silence descended in Europe. On all fronts men were getting ready for what they knew must be the decisive phase of the war with Germany. Unlike the other turning points of the war, there was no great Allied strategic conference to polish and finalize plans initiated at earlier meetings. This did not mean that there was complete strategic harmony between the Allies. As far as the Italian theatre was concerned, the divergence of view between London and Washington was deeper than ever, and led to one of the few curt and disagreeable exchanges between the British and American Chiefs of Staff.

The immediate cause of friction between the Allied high commands was the need to give firm direction to Maitland Wilson on Anvil. The decision had been postponed by Eisenhower's compromise (*see* page 207) until 20 March, and the British Chiefs had asked the Supreme Commander Mediterranean to furnish them with a new appreciation by that date. Successive postponements in launching the Third Battle of Cassino delayed the appreciation, which did not reach London until 22 March. In it Maitland Wilson went into the timings of future operations in some detail. Alexander now had adequate jumping-off positions for his spring offensive at Anzio, on the Garigliano and in the small bridgehead over the Rapido at Cassino. His regrouping could not be complete before the middle of April and it would be unwise to count on less than a month's hard fighting before a junction between the Anzio force and the main front could be accomplished. No troops should be withdrawn for Anvil before this junction was made, and thereafter it would take ten weeks to refit, rehearse and load them for the assault on the south of France. Thus, the earliest that Anvil could take place was the end of July—too late for Overlord in May. He concluded that his theatre could help Overlord most by continuing the offensive in Italy to take Rome and its airfields, turning Anvil into a threat to be launched in anger only if a German collapse seemed imminent. After the fall of Rome there were four possibilities: Anvil proper; continuing a full offensive in Italy with the help of small amphibious flank attacks; a major landing in the Gulf of Genoa or in the Po Valley; or, perhaps, a more ambitious landing in Istria to threaten the German communications through the Ljubljana Gap into Austria. He discounted Anvil because once it had been launched—however late—the Germans would realize that no other amphibious operations would be possible and the threat to their flanks would disappear. Continuing the offensive in Italy would maintain full pressure on the Germans, who had shown every inclination to reinforce Kesselring whenever he was in trouble. The use of smaller landings would maintain the outflanking threat and would not preclude any of the major landings if a suitable opportunity arose at a later date. Maitland Wilson much preferred the full-scale offensive in Italy, combined with the smaller threats to the German flanks. He asked the Chiefs of Staff to give him a new directive, cancelling Anvil and directing him to pursue the main battle for Italy. He would need enough assault shipping for a one-divisional force to threaten the German flanks and would prepare plans for an *ad hoc* Anvil in case Germany showed signs of collapse.

This appreciation was approved by the British Chiefs of Staff and was supported by a similar paper by Eisenhower, who believed that the Allies' failure to take Rome in the winter meant that they could not spare troops for the south of France. If this was so he would like all the surplus Mediterranean assault shipping transferred to Overlord. Everything seemed to point to the final burial of the Anvil plan, which Churchill and the British Chiefs of Staff had never liked and which had bedevilled operational planning in the Mediterranean for so long. The American Chiefs of Staff accepted the logic of Maitland Wilson's timings but not the final conclusion. On 24 March they consented to the transfer of shipping to Overlord but suggested that Anvil should only be postponed until 10 July. This gave the Mediterranean command the go-ahead for the spring offensive— codenamed 'Diadem'—but the battle for Anvil was not yet over. The new directive which Wilson had asked for had still to be drafted and this proved the stumbling block which led to harsh words across the Atlantic.

In essence, the argument between the two staffs over Wilson's directive amounted to the Americans demanding a firm date for Anvil without caring overmuch what that date should be, while the British steadfastly refused to be committed before the outcome of Diadem and Overlord was known. In spite of Stalin siding with the Americans at Tehran on turning left into southern France instead of right into Austria when the Allies reached the Pisa–Rimini Line, the British were still subconsciously wedded to turning right whereas the Americans were adamant that they would have nothing to do with Churchillian escapades in central Europe. Unless the British could be pinned to a target date for Anvil, the Americans feared that British inclinations would win in the end because they were predominant in the Mediterranean. To secure their position, the Americans tried what can only be described as blackmail. They offered to divert 26 landing ships and 40 landing craft from the Pacific to arrive in the Mediterranean in June provided their view on Mediterranean strategy was firmly accepted by the British. They proposed an all-out offensive to link the Anzio beachhead with the main front; thereafter operations in Italy should be geared to maintaining pressure during the Overlord D-day period and launching Anvil on 10 July. They would only release the Pacific ships if they were convinced that the British would honour a firm target date for Anvil. The British Chiefs of Staff were prepared to agree to postponement rather than cancellation, but, however much they might be attracted by the offer of additional assault shipping for the Mediterranean, they were not prepared to give an undertaking to pursue a strategy which they believed to be wrong. Two unfortunate things then happened. The British reply to the Americans' Chiefs' offer was unduly curt and annoyed the Americans; and then Maitland Wilson cabled to say that Alexander now found it impossible to complete re-grouping for Diadem before 11 May, which meant that Anvil could not be launched before late August. The Americans were thoroughly nettled by this delay and sent back an even curter rejoinder to the British Chiefs' signal, which annoyed the British; and so the argument, which we need not trace here in detail, escalated to the Churchill–Roosevelt level. Several long and carefully reasoned cables passed between the two leaders but no compromise could be found. Marshall, with Roosevelt's backing, adopted the attitude of no guarantee, no ships. Churchill, with the whip-hand because the Mediterranean was under British command, went ahead with a unilateral directive to Maitland Wilson, leaving the position much as it had been on 20 March. The object of operations in the Mediterranean remained to help Overlord by destroying and containing the maximum number of German formations in the Mediterranean. This was to be done by:

(a) launching Diadem;

(b) developing a threat to southern France;

(c) making the best possible use of the amphibious lift remaining in the Mediterranean to support operations in Italy or to take advantage of opportunities arising in the south of France;

(d) (b) and (c) were not to prejudice (a).

Thus, an unsatisfactory unilateral green light was given for Diadem; and Anvil was reduced, in spite of American objections, to the status of Diadem's cover-plan.

37   The Allied and German dispositions before Diadem, 11 May

In Italy preparations went ahead for Diadem which were an elaboration of Harding's February appreciation. He had stressed in his paper that the estimate of 15 April might prove too optimistic when the Army staffs had time to calculate the intricate redeployment of Eighth Army from east to west of the Apennines. In this he was proved right. Shipping shortages delayed the arrival of the extra divisions from North Africa and the Middle East, and the Eighth Army staff showed conclusively that it could not complete its redeployment before the end of April. These factors led to Alexander's request for the postponement of the offensive to 11 May which had so infuriated the Americans and had caused some alarm amongst the British Chiefs of Staff.

Diadem was based on the assumption that the Germans would fight stubbornly to hold the Gustav Line. When this was endangered, it was expected that they would fall back to the Hitler Line about six miles to the rear. Construction of the Hitler Line had started in December and consisted of a belt of strong-points whose novel feature was the emplacement of Panther tank turrets on concrete bases. The strongpoints were protected and linked by anti-tank ditches, mines and wire. When the Hitler Line had been breached, it was assumed that the Germans would then retire to their Line 'C'—now called the Caesar Line—covering Rome. Work had started on this line but it was not so formidable as the Hitler Line and appeared on air photographs to contain earthworks only. If Kesselring failed to hold the Caesar Line, he would probably fall back fighting to the main Gothic Line between Pisa and Rimini.

Alexander's intention, given in his Operation Order No. 1 of 5 May was: 'To destroy the right wing of the German Tenth Army; to drive what remains of it and the German Fourteenth Army north of Rome; and to pursue the enemy to the Rimini–Pisa line inflicting maximum losses on him in the process.'

Eighth Army's task was to break through at Cassino and advance up Route 6, passing east of Rome and aiming at Ancona or Florence; which of the two would be decided when the Combined Chiefs of Staff were agreed whether Alexander should turn left into France as the Americans wanted or east into Austria as the British hoped. Fifth Army had two tasks; to support Eighth Army's attack by seizing the Ausonia defile (*see* fig. 38) and advancing parallel with Eighth Army to a junction with the Anzio force; and secondly, to break out from Anzio to cut Route 6 at Valmonte and so seal the fate of von Vietinghoff's Tenth Army. Fifth Army would exploit through Rome to seize the Viterbo airfields and the ports of Civitavecchia and Leghorn. The Anzio break-out would not take place until Alexander gave the word, but VI (US) Corps was to be at 24 hours' notice from D+4. The corps detailed to look after the Adriatic coast, covering Eighth Army's old main-thrust line through Ortona, would come direct under Army Group and would follow up any enemy withdrawal.

The regrouping for Diadem was extremely complex as it involved not only the shift of corps headquarters and divisions all along the front, but also the relief of divisions with others from the Middle East and the arrival of extra divisions from the United States and from elsewhere in the Mediterranean. In broad outline the major moves were as follows: the Poles relieved the French north of Cassino; XIII (Br) Corps took over from the New Zealand Corps at Cassino when it was disbanded; Fifth Army's boundary was moved down to the south side of the Liri Valley; X (Br) Corps was released by Fifth Army and was replaced on the Garigliano by II (US) Corps on the coast and the French Expeditionary Corps in the hill sector of the upper reaches of the river; X (Br) Corps and 1 (Cdn) Corps were placed at Eighth Army's disposal; and Eighth Army's old Adriatic sector was taken over by V (Br) Corps. The final dispositions before Diadem are shown in fig. 37 and in Appendix F, Table 5.

Eighth Army's plan was to attack the Cassino sector with three corps, totalling nine divisions (see fig. 38). The Polish corps with its two Polish divisions was to neutralize, if it could not take, Monte Cassino using the old 34 (US) Division and 4 (Ind) Division approach over Snake's Head. XIII (Br) Corps, with four divisions—4 (Br), 78 (Br), 8 (Ind) Infantry and 6 (Br) Armoured Divisions—was to break into the Liri Valley attacking on the old 36 (US) Division axis either side of Saint Angelo. As soon as XIII (Br) Corps was across the Rapido in strength it would wheel half its force northwards to cut Route 6 behind Cassino and try to join hands with the Poles to force Heidrich to surrender Monte Cassino. The other half of XIII (Br) Corps would pass on up the valley. The Canadian Corps, with the Canadian infantry and armoured divisions working together, was to be ready to exploit the gap punched in the Gustav Line by XIII (Br) Corps. It was hoped that the Canadians would be able to advance quickly enough to burst through the Hitler Line before it could be fully manned by the retreating Germans. The newly-arrived 6 (South African) Armoured Division would be in Army reserve and X (Br) Corps with the New Zealand Division and a scratch force of independent brigades was to cover Eighth Army's inland flank, advancing behind Cassino towards Atina if the Germans withdrew. Thus Eighth Army would be repeating the manoeuvres used in the First and Second Battles of Cassino but would carry them out simultaneously and on three times the scale. XIII (Br) Corps would repeat 36 (US) Division's abortive attack on Saint Angelo, using four divisions instead of one; the Poles would emulate 34 (US) Division's attack on the Monastery with two divisions instead of one; and the exploitation force would consist of the two Canadian divisions and the South African division in the place of the lone New Zealand division which had waited to exploit in February. Moreover, the nine Eighth Army assault divisions would be supported by three corps artilleries, nine divisional artilleries and a larger proportion of the Army Group artillery— over 1,000 guns. But more important than all this massing of strength was the one factor which made the whole operation possible—summer weather. The ground would be hard and could carry tanks, guns and vehicles almost anywhere in the Liri Valley.

The scale of effort in Fifth Army's sector was increased in a similar way. In place of X (Br) Corps' three divisions, II (US) Corps would bring to bear two (US) divisions and the French Corps would launch the equivalent of five divisions. At Anzio the VI (US) Corps had grown from four to six divisions—1 and 5 (Br), 3, 34 and 45 (US) and 1 (US) Armoured Divisions. 36 (US) Division was to be in Fifth Army reserve ready to support II (US) Corps with an amphibious attack in the Gulf of Gaeta or, if this proved unnecessary, to move to Anzio to reinforce VI (US) Corps for the break-out.

The air plan was to continue Operation Strangle up to the last possible moment and then to switch to the now standard air tasks in any major setpiece battle—the maintenance of air supremacy over the battlefield, the interdiction of enemy reinforcements and the close tactical support of the armies. The Strangle attacks on the Italian railway system and the creation of the interdiction belt south of the Pisa–Rimini Line had been severely hampered by bad weather, as Alexander predicted when Maitland Wilson put the plan to him originally. Some 20,000 tons of bombs were dropped and railways were dislocated in ten different places but this was not enough. The Germans managed to bring their minimum requirements southwards and were never faced with the prospect of having to withdraw because they could not supply their troops. Strangle, though excellent in theory, was a failure in practice, because the Mediterranean air forces, though large, were not large enough for the task, nor was there long enough for the effects to become decisive. When faced with winter weather, the air forces' efforts were inconclusive.

Three other subsidiary plans are worth mentioning. To improve on the effects of Strangle, a sabotage operation was mounted to cut all road and rail communications in an interdiction belt across Italy on the line Spezia–Rimini between D−14 and D+14. Detachments of the Long Range Desert Group, Popski's Private Army, and French and Italian Special Forces, numbering 1,000 men, were dropped, landed from the sea or infiltrated through the front to increase confusion in the German rear at a time when Kesselring would need every man in the line. The second plan was for the capture of the island of Elba by French forces from Corsica. This was to be launched towards the end of May to take advantage of German preoccupation with the defence of the main front. And the third plan, and possibly the most important, was the preparation by both Fifth and Eighth Armies of a divisional-sized amphibious assault force each, targeted on Civitavecchia and Ancona respectively.

The tactical cover plan* for Diadem aimed at misleading the Germans in two ways. The first deception was to make it appear that regrouping would not be complete before June. No attempt was made to disguise the move of Eighth Army from east to west of the Apennines because it was realized that this was unlikely to be successful. Instead all the new

---

* The strategic cover plan was to suggest an early Anvil attack on southern France.

units west of the Apennines were held well back in training areas until the very last moment, apparently refitting and resting. At the front, where there was a danger that prisoners might be taken, only the existing units in the line were allowed to patrol. The attacking formations were restricted to viewing their future sectors from observation posts well behind the forward positions. These divisions were not to move forward until 48 hours before the attack. This meant intricate and careful movement planning, especially by Eighth Army who had to pass six divisions through the Mignano defile in the two nights and had to hide them in an area in which it had only been possible to conceal three divisions during the winter.

The second deception in the tactical cover plan was to make Kesselring think that the Allies were about to repeat the Anzio manoeuvre on a much grander scale. He had been caught in January when he moved his reserves down to the Garigliano too soon, and, in consequence, had denuded the Anzio area. The cover plan's aim was to play on this mistake by threatening a larger amphibious operation against Civitavecchia. It was hoped that, when the main attack opened at Cassino and on the Garigliano, Kesselring would believe that this was another holding attack. He would, therefore, hesitate to move his mobile divisions south until the Luftwaffe had located the main attacking force at sea. Steps were taken to simulate the Canadian Corps, reinforced by 36 (US) Division, rehearsing amphibious techniques in the Naples–Salerno area, and the intelligence services provided other false information to heighten this deception.

On the German side, Kesselring had become a prisoner of his own successes. He had proved the Rommel school wrong; he had held the Allies south of Rome; and he had become C.-in-C. South-West in consequence. He had then held the Gustav Line throughout the winter and had created two semi-sacred symbols which he could not abandon without a struggle. The importance of Cassino and Rome had been so magnified by their successful defence that they gave a rigidity to the German defence system which was to make it very brittle when the different operational conditions of summer weather arrived. Kesselring was also a prisoner in another sense. Hitler's idea of fighting for every acre of captured territory, which was only forming in the autumn, had now become an article of Nazi faith which no amount of military reasoning could sway. The days when Kesselring could withdraw on his own initiative, as he had done in Sicily and at Salerno, were over. Deliberate withdrawals, planned for well-founded strategic and tactical reasons, were becoming unthinkable. Kesselring, a born optimist, accepted this situation and put his heart and soul into defending the line which he had created and had managed to hold against Hitler's and OKW's expectations. Nothing succeeds like success, and success drew Kesselring on to tempt fate once too often.

When the Third Battle of Cassino had been won, Kesselring pulled back his mobile divisions to rest and refit, leaving his infantry divisions to share the front between them. So sure were the Germans that the Allies would not attack again before the summer that they allowed the infantry divisions to pull back a third of their strength to rest as well. OKW took advantage of the lull to order the Hermann Göring Division to France and 16 SS Panzer Division from Ljubljana to Hungary to help stop Hungarian defection from the Axis by force. Kesselring managed to delay the withdrawal of the Hermann Göring Division which OKW agreed should refit at Leghorn under his command while remaining under orders for France. The German drafting organization was working well and numerous large drafts arrived from Germany to bring most of his units up to establishment.

Kesselring appreciated that the Allies had three courses which they might adopt singly or in combination: a fresh attempt to break into the Liri Valley either from the Cassino or Garigliano bridgeheads or both; a break-out from Anzio to cut Route 6 in conjunction with an attack on the main front; or a new amphibious landing north of Rome aiming at Civitavecchia, Leghorn or Genoa. He feared the first possibility least. Tenth Army had proved itself quite capable of withstanding anything the Allies had been able to throw against it. It seemed unlikely that Alexander would repeat his earlier failures by making his principal effort against the main front, but Kesselring could take no chances. His intelligence staff had detected the move of Eighth Army across the Apennines and so he was free to reinforce his own western sectors at the expense of the Adriatic. He moved LI Mountain Corps across to face Eighth Army at Cassino where it took over 5 Mountain, 44 Infantry and 1 Parachute Divisions, the last still holding what had now become Heidrich's Monte Cassino. Von Senger's XIV Panzer Corps' front was thus shortened and much to his annoyance excluded the defence of Cassino. 15 Panzer Grenadier Division was at last relieved in the Saint Angelo sector after three months guarding the Rapido, overlooked by Allied observers on Monte Trocchio and constantly shelled as if in retribution for its defeat of 36 (US) Division. It was replaced by the Bode Blocking Group (part of 305 Division) from the Adriatic Mountain sector. As the Bode group was not strong enough for the job, 15 Panzer Grenadier Division had to leave a substantial detachment behind when it was pulled back into reserve. 71 Infantry Division, which had gained a fair reputation fighting north of Cassino, took over the Upper Garigliano, and 94 Infantry Division, with a less savoury reputation, continued to hold the Lower Garigliano. Kesselring left the Adriatic sector to the Commander of 305 Division, General Hauk, who disposed the balance of 305 which was not with Bode, the 334 Infantry and 114 Jaeger Divisions—all second-class troops—over 60 miles of front.

An attack from the Anzio beachhead in conjunction with a holding attack on the main front seemed to Kesselring more than likely. Anzio had been held by the Allies at great cost. They would certainly try to make use of this valuable threat to the rear of Tenth Army. On the other hand, von Mackensen's defensive positions surrounding the beachhead were strong and had proved easily defensible. His five divisions—4 Para, 54 Infantry, 3 Panzer Grenadier, 362 and 715 Infantry—seemed adequate for the job. What Kesselring feared most was the third alternative—another amphibious landing north of Rome. He could not believe that Alexander, with the mass of shipping which the Germans thought he possessed, would content himself with another frontal assault. The order of priority in which he placed the Allied threats was a new amphibious assault, a break-out from Anzio and lastly a major attack on the Gustav Line. He disposed his mobile divisions accordingly. The Hermann Göring Division covered the threat to Leghorn and Genoa. 29 Panzer Grenadier Division was pulled back to Civitavecchia. 26 Panzer Division stood behind the Anzio front in the Alban Hills. 90 Panzer Grenadier Division was split, half near the mouth of the Tiber at Ostia and the other half on Route 6 near Valmonte ready to move to the main front or the beachhead. Only 15 Panzer Grenadier Division, less its detachment with the Bode group, was anywhere near the main front. It, too, was positioned near the coast at Terracina with the dual role of stopping a short amphibious hook round the flank of the Gustav Line and of supporting 94 and 71 Divisions on the Garigliano.

Looking at these dispositions it is clear that Alexander's cover plan was working with remarkable precision. Tenth Army had no strong mobile reserves to support the Gustav Line other than 15 Panzer Grenadier Division, which was split between the coast and the Liri Valley. Fourteenth Army was lucky enough to have two mobile divisions—16 Panzer and 90 Panzer Grenadier Divisions. The other two mobile divisions—Hermann Göring and 29 Panzer Grenadier—were many miles to the north and out of supporting distance of either army. Alexander's deception plan was also working as regards timing. Hitler called an investiture at Obersalzburg at the end of April which was to be followed by a senior officers' indoctrination course. Von Vietinghoff, von Senger and Baade of 90 Panzer Grenadier Division, together with other important senior officers, were called away from the Italian front to attend, and several were still on leave when Diadem broke on 11 May. Von Senger had told his corps before he went on leave to be ready from 24 May onwards.

The stage was set. The weather was fine. Alexander had achieved a concentration of three to one in the vital Cassino sector and two to one on the Garigliano. The German mobile divisions were well back watching the coast and the Anzio beachhead. He was about to reap the harvest of a winter's hard work and unrelenting pressure upon his opponent. Diadem was to prove an appropriate codename.

13

The Triumph of Diadem

'All our thoughts and hopes are with you in what I trust and believe will be a decisive battle, fought to a finish, and having for its object the destruction and ruin of the armed forces of the enemy south of Rome.'

Churchill to Alexander, 11 May 1944

It is one of the tragedies of the Italian Campaign that the triumph of the Allied armies in Italy came just as the cross-Channel operation was launched. This was perfect strategic timing and was exactly what the Allied leaders had worked and planned for since Casablanca. It was nonetheless galling for the men who had fought so long and so hard to find their victory overshadowed by armies which, to them, had been sitting comfortably in England while they had been struggling through muddy rivers and over brutally jagged mountains in the foul weather of the Italian winter. Just as the world's press began to applaud Alexander's Diadem, Eisenhower's Overlord turned all attention northwards. Most people have heard of Overlord, but Diadem has disappeared into the official files as just one more military operation of the Second World War. Alexander's victory was as complete as any hard-fought battle can be. He surprised Kesselring; he defeated the German Tenth and Fourteenth Armies; and, most important of all, he achieved the aim set by the Allied Supreme Command of holding the maximum number of German divisions away from Overlord. By 4 June, when Rome fell, 26 German divisions had not only been contained, they had been routed. Only the great favours shown to the defender by the Italian topography saved Kesselring's forces from annihilation.

Diadem is most easily followed if we look at the battle in the phases in which Alexander visualized its progress. The first phase was the destruction of the Gustav Line, which he hoped to achieve before Kesselring realized that the amphibious threat was a myth. The second phase was the destruction of the Hitler Line. By then Kesselring would have realized what was happening and would, in all probability, be moving his mobile divisions southwards as fast as the Allied air forces would allow. Reserves behind Anzio front would be thinning out and the moment would come to launch the third phase—the breakout from the beachhead to cut Tenth Army's communications at Valmonte.

Few major battles go exactly as the commander has planned them; successes and failures occur where they are often least expected. Able commanders can profit by these unpredictable events provided they have thought the battle through its its conclusion; provided they keep their forces balanced and their reserves ready for the unexpected; provided news of what is happening reaches them quickly and accurately; and provided their subordinates all work to one common aim of implementing the commander's concept to their best ability. During Diadem the unexpected happened in each of Alexander's phases, but he was ready and balanced to profit by the changing tide of events. Information reached him quicker than it did Kesselring, but Kesselring had an easier task controlling his subordinates. The German commanders were all Germans whom he could promote or dismiss according to their performance. Alexander's subordinates were for the most part military prima donnas responsible to different national governments for the safety and fair treatment of their contingents. The most difficult subordinate was Mark Clark who, from his memoirs, appears never to have accepted Alexander as his real commander. He gives the impression of being suspicious of the British, always being ready to believe that they were working for their own ends at his expense. His pettiness during Diadem can be said to have robbed Alexander of his chance to annihilate the right wing of the Tenth German Army instead of merely routing it.

The first week of May was fine and sunny. The ground dried out, and tanks and vehicles could cross most of the ground leading down to the Rapido and Garigliano. The concentration of the attacking corps went smoothly. Instead of mud, the problem was dust. Every road and track was covered with a layer of fine white powder which billowed up behind vehicles as they moved, advertising their presence to watching artillery observers. On 11 May the day dawned ominously overcast. Some rain fell which laid the dust but also caused anxiety amongst the sappers of the attacking corps who saw all their weeks of hard work laying tracks and clearing mines disappearing once more in squelching Italian mud. By evening the sky was clear and a mist started to rise in the river valleys.

At 11 p.m. precisely 2,000 guns opened the artillery programme from
Cassino to the sea. Diadem had started.

Only one of the attacking Allied corps was successful during the
first three days of Diadem. On the coast Keyes' II (US) Corps was
resolutely opposed by 94 Division which withstood the attacks of the new
85 and 88 (US) Divisions far better than Kesselring and von Senger had
expected. In the Liri Valley, XIII (Br) Corps had to fight for every yard of

38   The first week of Diadem, 11–18 May

ground. 8 (Ind) Division attacked south of Saint Angelo and secured a
precarious bridgehead over the Rapido. Thanks to excellent work by its
Sappers, who had two 30-ton tank bridges in place before the dawn mist
rose, it managed to expand and consolidate its foothold against the
counter-attacks of the Bode Group and the 15 Panzer Grenadier detachment in the Liri Valley. 4 (Br) Division north of Saint Angelo, closer
under Monte Cassino, was not so lucky. It secured two small bridgeheads,
but had no bridges behind them because the bridge sites were so closely
overlooked by the Monastery that the Sappers were driven off before
they could start their work. It took the whole of the second night to
build a bridge in 4 (Br) Division's sector and even then this northern
bridgehead was tightly contained by detachments from 1 Para Division in
Cassino and from 44 Infantry and 5 Mountain Divisions brought down
from the north by LI Mountain Corps to protect its southern flank. By
the evening of 13 May, XIII (Br) Corps had linked up its two bridgeheads

and was secure on the far bank of the Rapido, but it was a long way from breaking through the German defence. The Monastery still dominated the battlefield and, although it was kept under a pall of artillery smoke all day, its screening was not completely effective and German artillery observers could still play havoc in the valley below.

The corps to suffer most was the Polish. General Anders decided that the only way to crush the defenders of Monte Cassino was to swamp all the German supporting posts simultaneously so that they could not give each other supporting fire as they had done in previous attacks. He would not attack the Monastery itself, but would break over the ridges behind the Monastery on a wide front using his two divisions, and would cut Route 6 below, hemming the garrison of Cassino and the Monastery in between himself and 4 (Br) Division in the Liri Valley. Unlike the Indians before them, the Poles had plenty of time to stock their positions with everything they wanted. The tracks were improved out of all recognition, allowing some tanks to reach supporting positions. They could not, however, patrol the sector thoroughly as it was essential not to reveal the presence of the Polish Corps. And, of course, the ground was just as rough, broken and difficult and the German positions were as strong, if not stronger, than ever. By unfortunate mischance the Germans chose the night of 11 May to relieve the units holding many of the posts in front of the Poles. The German garrison was thus, by chance, stronger than usual with more troops readily at hand. The Polish attack started well but the German paratroopers' machine guns began to take their toll as they had done with the Americans and Indians in earlier attacks. Both Polish divisions reached their first objectives. Far more of the German posts were overrun than had ever been before, but when daylight came the Poles found themselves exposed on the open slopes unable to get forward or back; unable to receive reinforcements or supplies; and unable to avoid the German fire which steadily reduced their numbers throughout the day. During the afternoon, General Anders decided to order their withdrawal and that evening, the Poles were back on their start-line, having lost half their strength and apparently gained nothing. They had, however, materially eased the problems of 4 (Br) Division who would have been far more heavily engaged if Heidrich had not had his hands full looking after Monte Cassino.

The only success came in the French sector. Accounts since the war have suggested that the positioning of Juin's corps opposite the difficult mountain features overlooking the Ausente Valley was a premeditated stroke of genius designed to profit by what was now obvious to everyone as the key to Cassino. Not only was it not obvious; it was not premeditated either. The French Expeditionary Corps were American-equipped and were therefore kept within Fifth Army when Alexander regrouped. II (US) Corps' new 85 and 88 (US) Divisions were unsuitable for a mountain sector, whereas Juin's divisions were at home in that type of country. Positioning the French on the Upper Garigliano was thus fortuitous and caused by the need to keep Juin's corps within the Fifth Army boundary. In all the appreciations and minutes of discussions held at 15 Army Group Headquarters during planning no stress is laid on the French contribution. Alexander was bent on achieving overwhelming superiority at Cassino and not on the Upper Garigliano. This was the first unexpected event of the battle. Juin and his North Africans were ideally suited for their sector of the front; the Germans did not expect a major attack against 71 Division; and von Senger, the corps commander responsible for the sector, was on leave and his deputy was not up to his job. The French attack took 71 Division by surprise. Working with pack transport and moving over country thought to be impassable, Juin's corps broke through and captured Monte Majo, the southern bastion of the Gustav defences in the Liri Valley, on 13 May.

Kesselring viewed the Allied attack as a holding operation designed to draw his reserves away from the coast north of Rome and away from the Anzio beachhead. The extent of the French success was not reported to him because the Germans themselves did not realize how deep the French had driven into their positions. The only mobile division ordered forward was 90 Panzer Grenadier Division which started moving along Route 6 toward the Liri Valley on 13 May.

14 and 15 May were dramatic days in the Fifth Army sector. Juin broke through into the Ausente Valley and took Ausonia. Keyes' II (US) Corps got into its stride and drove 94 Division, whose inland flank had been exposed by the French advance, back eastwards along the coast road towards Formia and Gaeta. The remnants of its neighbour, 71 Division, were also in full retreat in front of the French and were falling back northwards towards Esperia. The two most southerly German divisions were thus split by the mass of the almost trackless Aurunci Mountains. Juin seized his opportunity. He despatched his famous Goums, of which he had about 12,000, into the gap and across the mountains to cut the German lateral road from Pico to Formia behind the Hitler Line. The German right flank had collapsed. Only the efforts of the widely dispersed detachments of 15 Panzer Grenadier Division saved von Senger's corps from rout during his absence.

Back in the Liri Valley, the battles to the south in XIV Panzer Corps' sector had little effect on LI Mountain Corps, which was as determined as ever not to give up Cassino. 8 (Ind) Division was helped by the French successes, but 4 (Br) Division was still meeting stiff opposition. XIII (Br)

Corps ordered its reserve 78 (Br) Division into the bridgehead to pass through 4 (Br) Division and to cut Route 6 in conjunction with a renewed attack by the Poles behind the Monastery. The combined attack was timed for 15 May. 78 (Br) Division had difficulty crossing the Rapido bridges which were still under fire and frequently blocked, and so the attack had to be postponed. Oliver Leese, however, decided to move up the Canadian Corps as well in anticipation of a break-through. The Canadians started crossing the Rapido into 8 (Ind) Division's sector during 15 May. The following day, 16 May, 78 (Br) Division, now supported by the armoured brigade of 6 (Br) Armoured Division started a methodical attack in a great wheeling arc to cut Route 6 well to the west of Cassino. Each phase was a carefully-planned tank, infantry, artillery action of the classic type. 4 (Br) Division co-operated with a similar attack wheeling inside 78 (Br) Division's arc to cut Route 6 nearer to Cassino. Both attacks made steady progress and so Oliver Leese authorized General Anders to start the second Polish attack above Cassino for the morning of 17 May.

Between 12 and 17 May the Poles had reorganized their divisions to make good as far as possible the large gaps torn in their ranks by the first attack. They gave the Germans no respite while their reorganization was taking place. Frequent artillery, mortar and air attacks kept the German paratroopers pinned down, and, by extensive and aggressive patrolling, the Poles got to know the ground and the layout of the enemy posts far better than they had been able to do before their first attack. They studied the reasons for their first failure carefully and planned their second attack to reduce the chances of a recurrence. Even so, the battle, which was fought between Heidrich's paratroopers and the two Polish divisions on the ridges above Monte Cassino throughout 17 May, was far from one-sided. Heidrich's men fought back with just as great determination, but numbers began to tell. The Poles had the good fortune to take one key position during the night before the main attack as the result of a successful battle-patrol action. This success and their careful planning enabled them to eat away the German positions which had defied so many units before them. The threat posed by 4 and 78 (Br) Divisions in the valley below meant that Heidrich had fewer troops available for counter-attack. He was being swamped, as Alexander intended, by numbers. By dusk on 17 May, the tiresome Point 593 above the Monastery was in Polish hands but their attacking divisions were too exhausted and disorganized to mount another attack that night. 78 (Br) Division was stopped just short of Route 6, but 4 (Br) Division managed to get patrols across it. It was thought probable that Heidrich would attempt to pull out his battered, but still unbeaten, parachutists along the southern slopes of Monte Cassino during the night. Harassing fire was laid on the tracks which he might use, but there were not enough fresh troops left to close the trap during the night. Next morning the German rearguards were found to be still holding key features on the mountain side to the west of the Monastery. Its ruins and those of Cassino, however, were empty except for a few badly wounded Germans who had been left behind with medical orderlies. At 10.20 a.m. on 18 May, a patrol from the 12 Podolski Lancers entered the Monastery and raised the Polish standard over the ruins. The Fourth and last battle of Cassino was over. It had cost the Poles almost 4,000 casualties.

In the meanwhile Juin's attack had been making rapid progress. His 1 Motorized Division was advancing along the south bank of the Liri and reached the Hitler Line due south of Pontecorvo when Cassino was occupied. His 3 (Algerian) Division had taken Saint Olivia on the southern extremity of the prepared section of that line, and his Mountain Force of Goums and his 4 Moroccan (Mountain) Division were through the first half of the Aurunci Mountains and were overlooking the Pico–Formia lateral road. II (US) Corps were moving almost as quickly. Formia fell to 85 (US) Division on 17 May and Gaeta fell two days later. 88 (US) Division, fighting through mountains like the French, was threatening Itry on the Pico–Formia lateral, which it took on 19 May.

The battle for the Hitler Line was thus almost lost by the Germans before it started but not in the sector which Alexander had expected. The whole southern sector had been overrun before it could be properly manned and before the Canadian Corps, whose task it was to break the Line, had even sighted it in the Liri Valley.

The Hitler Line was in two distinct sections (*see* fig. 38): the northern section, which blocked the Liri Valley, was fully fortified and would be difficult to break if properly manned; the southern sector, called the 'Dora' extension was, as yet, only a staff planning line on which a few rudimentary defences had been started. The Hitler Line proper ran from the village of Piedmonte on the slopes of Monte Cairo through Pontecorvo to Saint Olivia on the south side of the Liri River. The Dora extension continued the line through the Aurunci Mountains to the coast.

Kesselring did not become fully aware of the disaster which had be-fallen XIV Panzer Corps until 17 May. At about that time a German radio interception unit identified the Canadians, who were thought to be embarking at Naples and Salerno for the amphibious attack north of Rome, in the Liri Valley. Kesselring could not be certain that the amphibious threat was over, but he was sure that if he did not block the French

advance round the southern end of the Hitler Line the greater part of
Tenth Army would be encircled. He ordered 26 Panzer Division to leave
its blocking position in the Alban Hills, where it was waiting to pounce
on any attempt by VI (US) Corps to break out of the beachhead, and to
move for the Pico–Pontecorvo area as fast as possible. He also ordered
305 and 334 Divisions over from the Adriatic coast, replacing them with

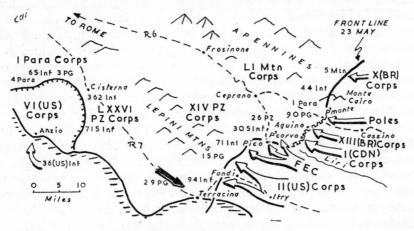

39 Breaking the Hitler Line, 18–23 May

237 Division from Istria. 305 Division was expected to arrive first and
would join 26 Panzer Division in trying to bring the French to a halt.

When the battle for the Hitler Line opened on 18 May, three out of the
five German mobile divisions had been committed. Due to Kesselring's
reluctance to believe that the attack on the Gustav Line was anything more
than a holding attack, he had made no attempt to mount the co-ordinated
counter-attack upon which German defensive policy is usually based.
These key divisions entered the battle piecemeal and were eaten up trying
to stem the waves of fresh troops which the Allies were committing.
15 Panzer Grenadier Division had been devoured first in small groups
trying to bolster up the defeated 71 and 94 Divisions. 90 Panzer Grenadier
Division had come next and had been sucked into the Liri cauldron and
into the desperate fight to stop the French breaking through the Esperia
defile. Now 26 Panzer and 305 Divisions were being drawn into the battle
in the same way, while 29 Panzer Grenadier and the Hermann Göring
Division sat coast-watching north of Rome, looking for an invasion force
which had never embarked. Few German armies can ever have been so
thoroughly hoodwinked and thrown off-balance by a deception plan.

As soon as Cassino fell, the Poles struck out along the southern spurs of

Monte Cairo to outflank and if possible take the northern pivot of the Hitler Line—the fortified village of Piedmonte. Alexander directed Juin to press northwards towards Pico to outflank the fortified section of the Line from the south. In the centre, Eighth Army directed XIII (Br) Corps on Aquino and the Canadian Corps on Pontecorvo. Both corps tried to rush the line but neither was successful. They had not been quick enough nor had the Allied intelligence staffs realized how many Panther turrets had been emplaced in the line's strongpoints. It was clear that a prepared assault would have to be launched. Responsibility for this was given to the Canadian Corps who had not so far been committed as a corps during the battle. XIII (Br) Corps was to maintain pressure on Aquino while the Canadians tried to breach the line at Pontecorvo.

While the Canadians were preparing their assault which was timed for 23 May, Juin's Frenchmen were closing in on Pico. The arrival of 26 Panzer and 305 Divisions slowed their advance. They captured Monte Leucio, which dominated the Pico–Pontecorvo area, but were thrown off it again by German counter-attacks. It took two more days hard fighting to take Pico which fell on 22 May. Opposition was now too great to allow Juin to cut in behind the Hitler Line so he was directed north-west towards Route 6 at Ceprano. On the other flank, the Poles broke into Piedmonte on 20 May but did not manage to clear it until 25 May.

The Canadians attacked early on 23 May and had to fight all day before a break-through occurred. The Germans lost heavily in the fighting, giving up some 500 prisoners. The Canadians lost as many men themselves and a large number of tanks, but the Hitler Line had been broken and Eighth Army could resume its advance up Route 6. Great events, however, were taking place elsewhere. Before we turn to them there is one interesting point to note in retrospect.

The greatest difficulty experienced by Eighth Army in the Liri Valley was one of its own making. To bring the necessary superiority in infantry, tanks and guns to bear, XIII (Br) Corps and the Canadian Corps advanced side by side in the narrow plain between Monte Cairo and the Liri River which is five miles wide at the most. The famous 'Gateway to Rome', which had figured so prominently in Allied appreciations in the autumn, was found to be far from ideal for an armoured break-through even in dry summer weather. It was cut up by a number of awkward streams and ditches which often had to be bridged to allow tanks and vehicles to move forward. These small bridges created hideous bottlenecks which led to endless traffic jams. The Eighth Army staff were at fault in not insisting that their divisions advanced with only the minimum transport. The French, using very few vehicles and depending largely on pack animals, moved far faster than the vehicle-clogged British divisions. No one seems to have appreciated that lavish-equipment scales appropriate to wide-ranging desert operations, or to operations on the wide fronts which existed earlier in the Italian campaign, were a hindrance to mobility when it came to fighting a classic set-piece battle in which overwhelming concentration of force was the key to success. There were many other instances of this type of misappreciation during the last two years of the Second World War. The Anzio beachhead suffered similar congestion and, later, in North-West Europe, the British Army slowed itself down by trying to force too many vehicles on to the roads. It is doubtful whether it has really learnt its lesson today.

The destruction of the Hitler Line lost importance as far as the opposing Army Group commanders were concerned some days before the Canadian attack. Kesselring's concern for his southern flank deepened as II (US) Corps and Juin's North Africans burst over the Pico–Formia lateral road during 19 May. 26 Panzer Division showed signs of stabilizing the front in the central Pico–Pontecorvo area, but 15 Panzer Grenadier Division could do nothing to stop the Allied onrush in the south.

Reluctantly he ordered von Mackensen to send 29 Panzer Grenadier Division down from Civitavecchia to block II (US) Corps' advance in the potentially strong defensive position along Route 7 between Fondi and Terracina. This was the last defile before Route 7 emerges in the flat Pontine Marsh area, leading straight to the southern edge of the Anzio beachhead. If 29 Panzer Grenadier Division could stop the Americans here, there was still a chance of preventing the two Allied forces from linking up. Von Mackensen did not agree and believed that 29 Panzer Grenadier Division should be held back to defeat a break-out which he was sure was coming from the beachhead. When he received Kesselring's order, his Fourteenth Army staff protested to the Army Group staff. Kesselring was visiting the main front at the time and when he returned to his headquarters he found that his orders had not been implemented. According to his memoirs this was the culmination of a long series of disagreements with von Mackensen, whom he relieved of his command after the battle. This disagreement did not help 29 Panzer Grenadier Division, which was so delayed in its move that it suffered the fate of the other mobile divisions. If it had come south when Kesselring originally ordered it to do so on 19 May, it would have had time to prepare its positions before the Americans reached the Terracina defile. As it was, it came into action off the line of march with no proper reconnaissance and found that it was too late to stop the Americans who were already on the high ground above the defile which should have been the basis of its defensive position. It did its best and managed to hold the town of

Terracina until the night 23–24 May and was then forced to pull back with the remnants of 94 and 71 Divisions through the Lepini Mountains towards Route 6 to avoid being cut off.

Alexander had a more agreeable decision to take. The time was approaching when VI (US) Corps should be unleashed from Anzio. As early as 18 May Alexander authorized the move of 36 (US) Division into the beachhead. II (US) Corps' success in the south meant that 36 (US) Division, Fifth Army's reserve division which was not to be committed without reference to Alexander, would not be needed on the main front.

40   The break-out from Anzio, 23–30 May

It would be more use strengthening the breakout force. Its move would take four days so the earliest that the break-out should take place would be 23 May. As it happened , the course of the battle made this a suitable date for other reasons. Eighth Army and the French would be attacking the Hitler Line on that day and II (US) Corps would be making for Terracina. There was thus no difficulty in deciding the date for the break-out, but the direction in which the break-out should be made was less easily decided and resulted in a clash between Alexander and Mark Clark and between their respective staffs. In his appreciations and orders for Diadem, Alexander had rightly stressed that the aim was to destroy German divisions. The capture of Rome was a secondary consideration and would probably occur as a by-product of the primary aim. Mark Clark saw the position in a different light and had his eyes fixed on Rome rather than on the German Army. He felt very strongly that his Fifth Army had struggled all winter for this prize. It had suffered grievous losses in its endeavour to give Churchill Rome by the end of January, and it was now the Fifth Army's right, and nobody else's, to enter the eternal city first. How much his personal ambition to go down in history as the Conqueror of Rome played in this argument is difficult to say. His own memoirs suggest that this may have been one of the predominant impulses which marred his judgment during this stage of the battle. This is unfortunate, though understandable, because there were sound military reasons for the course of action which he recommended and took in spite of Alexander's wishes to the contrary. Had it not been for his own utterances and the record of his own book, he might never have been accused of placing Rome before the destruction of Kesselring's armies. Unfortunately the evidence is too plain to allow the incident to be glossed over.

In Alexander's view, the VI (US) Corps' attack, for which there were five US and two British divisions available in the beachhead, should be made in the direction of Valmonte to cut Route 6 and so cut Tenth Army's main line of retreat. Mark Clark objected on two grounds. First, he would be executing a dangerous flank march across the front of the Germans holding the dominating Alban Hills; and secondly, when he reached Valmonte, Tenth Army could easily escape the trap by withdrawing up the two good roads and many subsidiary tracks leading north-westwards from Route 6 to the main Pescara–Rome lateral, Route 5, which had at one time been Montgomery's proposed line of advance on Rome. Once on this lateral, the Germans would have little difficulty in shaking out their divisions onto the Caesar Line. While Alexander accepted Clark's point about the Alban Hills, he did not agree with the second point. The fewer lines of retreat left open to the Germans the greater would be the execution done by the Allied air forces on their retreating columns. Alexander seems to have temporized and left Mark Clark with the feeling that it would not take much of a setback to the Valmonte thrust to make him change his mind and allow a direct attack west of the Alban Hills on Rome itself—which was Clark's aim. VI (US) Corps had a number of alternative plans worked out for the various contingencies, but it was finally agreed that the attack should be made as Alexander directed towards Valmonte. Mark Clark, however, seems to have made several mental reservations when he accepted this direction.

The break-out started, as planned, on 23 May with an attack on Cisterna by 3 (US) Division, 1 (US) Armoured Division and the Special Service Force. It was then intended to pass the fresh 36 (US) Division with 1 (US) Armoured Division through the breach in the German defences and on through the gap between the Alban and Lepini Hills to Valmonte, giving the Alban Hills as wide a berth as possible. 45 (US) Division would protect the northern flank by widening the breach towards the Alban Hills, while 1 and 5 (Br) Divisions held the northern perimeter against any relieving attack that the German 1 Para Corps might choose to make. When they attacked, 1 (US) Armoured and 3 (US) Divisions gained tactical surprise and blew a wide gap in the defences of the German 362 and 715 Divisions. 715 Division broke first and tried to pull back towards the Lepini Hills. 362 Division stood its ground and, helped by paratroopers from the northern side of the beachhead, held the northern shoulder of the American breach. Heavy fighting went on through 23 and 24 May, and on 25 May the leading elements of the Hermann Göring Division started to appear. Kesselring had been forced to commit his last reserve mobile division to stop the American break-through—a division earmarked by OKW to oppose Overlord. So desperate had the German position become that this division risked moving south in daylight and in consequence suffered heavy punishment from the air. During 25 May some of these German reinforcements were spotted moving south from Valmonte towards the American breach and were heavily bombed and straffed by Allied aircraft. VI (US) Corps claimed some 600 German vehicles destroyed and 400 damaged. The exact figures will never be known, but as the Americans advanced beyond Cisterna they found the roads blocked with burnt out German equipment. By dusk on 25 May a wide breach had been secured; Cisterna, Cori and the northern edge of the Lepini Hills were in American hands and the leading elements of II (US) Corps, advancing from Terracina, made contact with a patrol from the beach-head. Fifth Army was reunited after three and a half months. Two and a half thousand prisoners entered VI (US) Corps' cages at Anzio. 1 (US) Armoured Division's tank losses had been high and 3 (US) Division lost over 1,000 men on the first day but both divisions were far from spent.

It was at this stage that Mark Clark decided to change direction and to make his main effort along Route 7 and the Anzio–Albano road straight for Rome. To sugar the pill for Alexander, he proposed to go on attacking towards Valmonte with 3 (US) Division, while 34, 36 and 45 (US) Divisions and 1 (US) Armoured Division opened a direct attack on the Caesar Line west of the Alban Hills on 26 May. Alexander accepted Clark's plan on the assurance that he would maintain the Valmonte thrust. It would be overstating the case against Mark Clark to say that he paid only lip service to the Army Group Commander's instructions, but this is in effect what happened. By first-class staff work, VI (US) Corps started off on its new axis by midday on 26 May. 3 (US) Division, continuing the attack on the old axis, seized Artena only three miles south of Route 6 near Valmonte where it was brought to a sharp halt by a German force consisting of the Hermann Göring Division, 334 Division (ex Adriatic) and 92 Division (only just formed in the Rome area) which was firmly established in this key position, holding open Tenth Army's escape route. Mark Clark's main attack made progress at first and then ran into the main Caesar positions. For the next four days VI (US) Corps could make no impression on the German defences. It looked as if Kesselring had succeeded at long last in stabilizing his front. Mark Clark's change of direction brought agonized cries from Churchill who was briefed every day on the progress of operations together with the commanders' intentions for future operations. Looking at the arrows traced on his war room maps, he could see the chances of encircling the German XIV Panzer Corps slipping from Alexander's grasp as Mark Clark turned towards Rome. He signalled Alexander on 28 May suggesting that he should move the British armoured divisions round to the beachhead via Route 7 to add weight to Mark Clark's reluctant Valmonte attack.

> ... figures show that you have at least 2,500 [tanks] serviceable. Surely one half of these could be used and indeed used up, in making a scythe movement cutting off the enemy's retreat. ... I should feel myself wanting in comradeship if I did not let you know that the glory of this battle, already great, will be measured, not by the capture of Rome or the juncture with the bridgehead, but by the number of German divisions cut off.

What Churchill did not appreciate was that the ground was quite unsuitable for sweeping armoured warfare. The destruction of the German Army would have been more complete if the four Allied armoured divisions in the theatre had been equipped as mountain divisions like the French. There were enough independent armoured brigades to give the infantry all the tank support which they needed. The armoured divisions with their vast columns of supporting vehicles did more to slow down Eighth Army's pursuit up the Liri Valley than any other factor. Oliver Leese's desperate attempts to use the Canadian Armoured Division and 6 (Br) Armoured Division brought nothing but frustration. There was not enough room for tank regiments to deploy their squadrons nor enough road space to carry their supply columns without stopping all other movement.

Churchill and other armchair critics at home made another mistake. The Apennines to the north looked on the map like an impenetrable barrier against which the Germans could be pinned. In fact, they provided an excellent escape route. There were enough roads and tracks for an escaping army to withdraw through them and yet these hill routes were so easily blocked by rearguards that they served the double purpose of escape and protection for the exhausted German divisions.

The German plan was to withdraw Tenth Army as quickly as possible back into the Caesar Line alongside Fourteenth Army. To do this, von Senger fought a determined delaying action in the area Arce–Ceprano using 1 Para Division at the former and 90 Panzer Grenadier Division at the latter. So successful was he that Eighth Army failed to break through

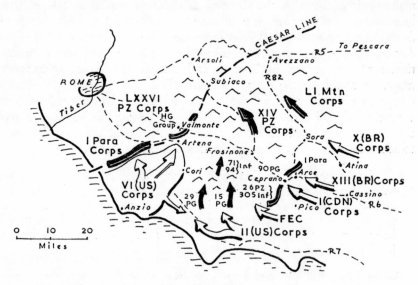

41   *The German withdrawal to the Caesar Line, 23–30 May*

his rearguards until the bulk of LI Mountain Corps and his own XIV Panzer Corps had escaped north-westwards. LI Mountain Corps, now consisting of 5 Mountain, 44 and 114 Divisions, slipped back along Route 82 pursued by X (Br) Corps' New Zealand Division, which had come round the north of Monte Cairo through Atina to Sora. 26 Panzer and 305 Divisions pulled back up the Frosinone–Arsoli road, and 29 Panzer Grenadier Division came back through the Lepini Mountains shepherding the remnants of 71 and 94 Divisions and making for the area north of the Hermann Göring Division at Valmonte. Von Senger gave up the Arce–Ceprano position on 28 May, sending 1 Para Division back direct to Subiaco and 90 Panzer Grenadier Division to Arsoli on the main Rome–Pescara lateral. He then opposed the advance of XIII (Br) Corps, the Canadian Corps and the French Corps with nothing much more than light rearguards, using the familiar German demolition and mining techniques at which his units were so expert. Eighth Army suffered from traffic indigestion and made very inadequate progress against this opposition. There seemed to be every chance that Kesselring would repeat his post-Salerno performance by re-establishing a continuous line across the Peninsula when an unexpected disaster destroyed his chances of holding south of Rome just as order began to appear out of chaos in the German lines.

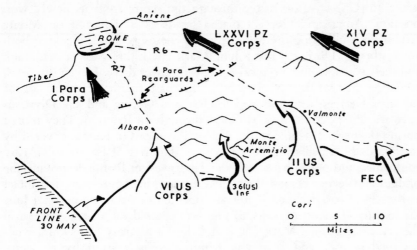

42   *The fall of Rome, 30 May–4 June*

On 29 May, Mark Clark regrouped his forces which were attacking the western end of the Caesar Line. He brought II (US) Corps up to take charge of 3 and 85 (US) Divisions which were to continue the attack on Valmonte; Juin's French divisions had followed 29 Panzer Grenadier Division through the Lepini Mountains and were approaching 3 (US) Division at Artena. VI (US) Corps was now very tired, but Mark Clark felt that one more effort might unnerve the Germans, who were equally exhausted. Then the unexpected occurred. 36 (US) Division, trying to outflank the German positions in the centre of the Alban Hills at Velletri (*see* fig. 40), had ordered vigorous patrolling during the night of 30 May. One of its battle patrols found the high ground behind the town—Monte Artemisio—unoccupied. Kesselring had also noted this weakness in von Mackensen's dispositions and had ordered the gap to be filled at once. Before this could be done 36 (US) Division had silently infiltrated first one regiment and then another onto this key feature. The third regiment of the division struck round behind Velletri cutting off the German garrison's retreat. A dangerous gap thus appeared in the strongest part of the Caesar Line. The Hermann Göring Division counter-attacked but failed to unseat 36 (US) Division. Mark Clark ordered immediate exploitation and a general attack by both of his corps next morning. II (US) Corps which now had both its original divisions, 85 and 88, plus 3 (US) Division, was directed to renew its attack round the northern side of the Alban Hills, cutting Route 6 and taking Valmonte on the way. VI (US) Corps was to advance round the south-western side of the hills, while 36 (US) Division drove through the centre from its newly won position. American observers placed by 36 (US) Division on Monte Artemisio could bring fire to bear on the enemy positions blocking both corps' thrusts. During 1 and 2 June Mark Clark threw every man, tank and shell available into a typical American power drive. Eleven divisions, including the two British divisions on the coast, smashed forward against the tired German formations. The Hermann Göring and 344 Divisions gave way first, letting II (US) Corps through on Route 6. They retired during the night 2–3 June to the Aniene River east of Rome, covered by rearguards provided by 4 Para Division. The rest of Fourteenth Army conformed and pulled back over the Tiber west of Rome destroying the bridges and ferries behind them. The bridges in Rome were left intact as Kesselring had declared Rome an 'open city'. At 7.15 p.m. on 4 June the leading elements of 88 (US) Division entered the Piazza Venezia in the centre of Rome. Mark Clark and the Fifth Army had won a well-deserved victory and crowning triumph, only marred by his petty behaviour in trying to exclude everyone else from sharing the honours with him.

The French Corps, which had joined II (US) Corps' right flank south of Valmonte, wheeled round close in to the eastern outskirts of the city. Eighth Army, as laid down in the original Diadem order, cut across the hills to continue its advance up the east bank of the Tiber, heading for Terni. It had two fresh armoured divisions in hand, but it was difficult to use them to effect the final destruction of the German Army. 'If only the country were more open we would make hay of the whole lot', Alexander signalled on 4 June. Until the three corps of Fifth Army, pressing down on the Italian capital, cleared Route 6 there was no way of moving these powerful formations through the traffic congestion, for all roads in this area certainly lead to Rome.

14

The Frustration of Anvil

'You will have heard of fresh enemy divisions which are on their way here. I hope our tap will not be turned off too soon as it was before, and prevent us from gaining the full fruits of our present advantageous position.'

Alexander to Churchill, 30 May 1944

Diadem could not have been better timed, nor so unjustly rewarded. By the time that Overlord was launched on 6 June the Fourteenth German Army had been routed and the Tenth German Army had been driven back with very heavy losses in men and material. Four German infantry divisions had been reduced to little more than cadres and had to be withdrawn to reform. The 1 Para Division and the six mobile divisions had been badly mauled. OKW's immediate reaction to Diadem had been to spring to Kesselring's aid although there were clear indications of the imminence of Overlord. During the battle Kesselring received four new divisions and a number of powerful tank and artillery reinforcing units. The 16 SS Panzer Division returned to Italy from Hungary; two Luftwaffe divisions arrived—19 Luftwaffe Division from Denmark and 20 Luftwaffe Division from Holland; 42 Jaeger Division came from Slovenia; and a heavy tank regiment equipped with Tiger tanks arrived from France. Alexander had achieved the primary aim of the Italian campaign in brilliant fashion, but before June was out he knew that he would have to surrender another seven divisions including all his French mountain troops to give Overlord further help. He was back in the position in which he had been in the autumn of 1943 when the first seven veteran divisions were taken from him just as Rome seemed to be within his grasp. This time it was the chance of taking Vienna and entering Germany through the back door which was snatched from him.

Kesselring was also back in the position in which he had been during the late summer of 1943, when Italy defected and the Allies landed at Salerno. Now, as then, he had two problems to solve; how to stabilize a continuous front across the Peninsula and how to gain time to create a new defensive position on which he could stand for the next winter. The great difference this time was that it was the beginning and not the end of the summer as it had been in 1943. He had to buy time for three more months before the autumn rains would come to his aid and give back to the German defence the degree of superiority it had enjoyed in the summer. Admittedly the Gothic Line had been under construction for much

43   *The pursuit of Army Group 'C' north of Rome, 5–20 June*

longer than the Gustav Line and so should be more formidable; on the other hand, he was now facing two experienced and victorious Allied armies backed by all the logistic resources they needed instead of the rather unsure and inadequately supplied opponents whom he had stopped in 1943.

In trying to stabilize his front, Kesselring's most pressing problem was how to rebuild the morale of his Fourteenth Army which had been badly shaken by Mark Clark's final break through before Rome. He had replaced von Mackensen with General Lemelsen after the fall of Rome, but it would take time to re-establish the confidence of the Fourteenth Army staff and of the corps and divisions under their control. Von Vietinghoff's Tenth Army could be trusted to check Oliver Leese's Eighth Army in the difficult mountain country east of the Tiber, but Fourteenth Army would have to face Mark Clark's thrusting Fifth Army in the open rolling country west of the Tiber. Kesselring directed the bulk of OKW's reinforcement to the Fourteenth Army's sector and built up a temporary covering position east and west of Viterbo through which the beaten and disorganized divisions of 1 Para Corps and LXXVI Panzer Corps could withdraw. He also directed Tenth Army to send three mobile divisions (26 Panzer and 29 and 90 Panzer Grenadier) to help Fourteenth Army to stabilize its line. Unfortunately these divisions had to move by a long circuitous route well to the north before they could turn westwards into Fourteenth Army's area because all the bridges over the Tiber north-east of Rome had been prematurely demolished in the first panic moves after Fifth Army's break through the Caesar Line.

In planning his delaying action Kesselring appreciated that logistic difficulties would slow down the Allied advance, provided he could destroy road and rail communications thoroughly enough as he withdrew. Although the Peninsula widens north of Rome there was a suitable position running east and west through Lake Trasimene which he considered was far enough north to allow his divisions time to regain their balance and to give his engineers sufficient depth of withdrawal to create a logistic desert to hamper the Allied advance with greatest effect. North of the Trasimene Line he intended to adopt his old tactics of falling back through a series of minor delaying positions until he reached the River Arno on which he would make his final stand before withdrawing slowly into the Gothic Line which he hoped to hold for the winter. In the first half of June few officers in either High Command would have credited him with much chance of success. In 1943 he had been lucky because the Allies had withdrawn seven of their best divisions and most of their landing craft for Overlord before they had inflicted a decisive defeat upon him. No one in OKW or in his own HQ Army Group 'C' knew at this stage that he would be saved in almost the same way again. At the highest levels of the Allied Command in the Mediterranean the chance of this happening was all too evident and had become the main preoccupation of Maitland Wilson, Devers,* Alexander and Harding.

The Allied pursuit north of Rome started at first light on 5 June, the day after Mark Clark had entered Rome. The Tiber valley formed the general boundary between the Fifth and Eighth Armies and between the two German armies which they were pursuing. Fifth Army sent VI (US) Corps up Route 1 to seize the port of Civitavecchia which was badly needed to supply Fifth Army in its further advance to the north. II (US) Corps went up Route 2 to seize Viterbo and its airfield complex which was needed by the Allied air forces. Both American corps met very little

---

* General J. L. Devers, American Deputy Commander to Maitland Wilson.

opposition. Civitavecchia fell after only a short fight on 7 June and Viterbo was in American hands as well by 9 June. VI (US) Corps was then relieved by IV (US) Corps, which had arrived in Italy at the end of March, so that the former could get ready for Anvil if the Chiefs of Staff ordered the attack on southern France. The French Expeditionary Corps relieved II (US) Corps which went into Army reserve. On the Eighth Army front the pursuit was conducted by XIII (Br) Corps with 6 South African Armoured Division west of the Tiber on Route 3 and 6 (Br) Armoured Division east of the river on Route 4. 4 (Br) Division was to follow up the advance in immediate support of the Armoured divisions. XIII (Br) Corps had to work harder than its American counterparts because it ran into the Hermann Göring and 15 Panzer Grenadier Divisions who were not prepared to give ground without a fight. In spite of this, progress was relatively rapid with 6 (SA) Armoured Division making 35 miles on the first day.

Alexander issued a directive for the continuance of the pursuit on 7 June. In this he ordered Eighth Army to advance to the general area Florence–Bibbiena–Arezzo using Routes 3 and 4, and Fifth Army to the Pisa–Lucca–Pistoia area using Routes 1 and 2. V (Br) Corps, on the Adriatic coast, was not to try to accelerate the German withdrawal, so as to economize in bridging equipment and transport which was badly needed by the main bodies of Fifth and Eighth Armies. If the general advance west of the Apennines did not persuade the Germans to abandon Ancona voluntarily, the Polish Corps would be brought forward over Eighth Army's main routes of advance on the west of the Apennines and would attack the port from the west. Both army commanders were told to take 'extreme risks' to reach their objectives before the German armies could recover their balance.

For the next ten days the advance of the Allied armies continued to be rapid, but as the days went by there was a noticeable stiffening of German resistance. The demolition of bridges and mining of roads became more thorough; fewer stragglers were caught; and each day's advance grew shorter. Fifth Army continued to use IV (US) Corps and the French along Routes 1 and 2. Eighth Army brought up X (Br) Corps on the eastern flank of XIII (Br) Corps and after some regrouping of divisions pressed forward in a more north-westerly direction aiming to pass both sides of Lake Trasimene in order to capture the important road and rail communication centre of Arezzo. By 20 June both Allied armies found themselves up against Kesselring's first main delaying position—the Trasimene Line. IV (US) Corps was meeting stiffer resistance on the Ombrone River and the French Expeditionary Corps was opposed on its tributary, the River Orcia. XIII (Br) Corps was stopped in front of Chiusi, west of

Lake Trasimene, and X (Br) Corps, having taken Perugia, was also brought to a halt east of the lake. On the Adriatic coast, V Corps followed up the enemy withdrawal into Pescara and Chieti (Eighth Army's old objectives in Montgomery's abortive Battle of the Sangro). The Polish Corps then took over on the Adriatic coast and advanced quickly to the Chienti River, the Adriatic extension of the Trasimene Line, which they reached on 21 June. Off the west coast, the operation against Elba, which should have been mounted during Diadem, at last went ahead. The operation had been postponed because it could not be given adequate air support and air cover until Diadem was over. The island fell to the French on 19 June, costing them 1,000 casualties in return for the island and 1,800 prisoners of war.

The pursuit phase of the advance behind Kesselring's withdrawal was over. The German line was now re-established as a coherent whole across the Peninsula. Kesselring had his formations under control and was more determined than ever to repeat his defensive successes of the previous year. The Allies would be made to pay in men and, more especially, time for every mile of their advance from Trasimene to the Gothic Line. In 1943, rain, mud and swollen rivers had slowed their advance to a crawl by the end of September. There was a chance that in the northern Apennines the autumn rains would begin earlier; possibly at the beginning of September. July and August would be dangerous months but if he could hold his front together until September he might well bar the door to southern Germany for another long winter.

On 6 June Alexander signalled Maitland Wilson giving his plans for exploiting the succcess of Diadem. The debate on Anvil had died away in Washington and London as everyone's attention was focussed on the battles in Normandy. After the British Chiefs of Staff had forced Anvil's postponement in April, Maitland Wilson had been instructed to study a number of post-Overlord amphibious operations using troops from Italy. His staff had produced three groups of plans: an assault on the west coast of France to seize the Biscay ports; similar attacks on southern France to seize the French Mediterranean ports; and a variety of attacks to help Alexander's operations in Italy. The American Chiefs of Staff were delighted with this apparent change of front by the British and agreed to supply the assault shipping from the Pacific which they had offered and then withdrawn when the British refused to accept a fixed target date for Anvil. Harmony seemed to have been re-established between the American and British staffs and all appeared to be going well on the battlefields and in the planning offices. Maitland Wilson warned Alexander that he would probably have to surrender one US Corps headquarters, three experienced

US divisions and two French divisions during the latter half of June, provided Rome had fallen by that date. By the beginning of June, Maitland Wilson, much to the Americans' delight, had made up his mind that Anvil was the most profitable post-Overlord operation and that he could mount it by 15 August. The arrival of Alexander's appreciation upset all these calculations as it threw a fourth set of plans into the arena; plans which matched Churchill's and the British Chiefs of Staff instinctive desires but were anathema to the Americans. Not only did they open old wounds at the highest level; they revealed a basic difference in thinking between the two major headquarters in the Mediterranean. Although Maitland Wilson was now Supreme Commander in the Mediterranean, his headquarters was still organized on American lines and was essentially American in its thinking. The advice he received reflected Washington's views more closely than London's. Alexander's headquarters, by contrast, was thoroughly British in organization and outlook and reflected Churchill's views more than anyone else's. Churchill was in close touch with Alexander, and the War Office was equally close to Harding and the Army Group Staff. The discussion, which began on 7 June and which lasted until 2 July, was one of the hardest-fought strategic debates of the war and was the culmination of the difference in strategic thinking between the British and American policy makers which had first shown itself at Casablanca.

In his appreciation Alexander stated his aim as to 'complete the destruction of the German armed forces in Italy and in the process to force the enemy to draw to the maximum on his reserves, whereby I shall be rendering the greatest assistance to the western invasion of which my armies are capable'. He suggested that Kesselring's armies had been so severely mauled that they would be unable to hold the Gothic Line without some eight to ten fresh divisions from elsewhere. In contrast, Alexander himself had two highly-organized, skilled and experienced armies capable of carrying out large-scale operations in close co-operation with their supporting Mediterranean air forces. On 6 June he signalled Wilson:

> Morale is irresistibly high as a result of recent successes and the whole forms one closely articulated machine capable of carrying out assaults and rapid exploitation in the most difficult terrain. Neither the Apennines nor even the Alps should prove a serious obstacle to their enthusiasm and skill.

He estimated that provided he was allowed to keep his two armies intact he would reach Florence in the second half of July and he would be ready to attack the Gothic Line, if Kesselring in fact managed to occupy it, by 15 August. These timings were based upon another of Harding's appreciations which had been drawn up soon after the Diadem plan had been completed in April.

Harding and the Army Group staff had made a very detailed study of the Gothic positions. There were three areas in which a major assault could be launched if Kesselring decided to stand. On the west coast, it would be possible to advance from Pisa to Genoa and then over the low Ligurian Hills, which Napoleon had crossed in his first invasion of Italy in 1796, but this would be a long way round into the Po Valley. On the east coast, the hills were lowest of all and an attack through Rimini would lead more directly into the Po Valley. Unfortunately the roads on the

44 *Alexander's first plan to breach the Gothic Line*

Adriatic coast ran across the grain of the country; that is to say they ran over the ridges and furrows of the rivers and spurs which ran down from the Apennines to the sea coast. The rivers present difficult military obstacles which can be covered from defensive positions on the ridges of high ground formed by the Apennines' spurs running parallel to, and in between, the rivers. An attack on this axis would probably meet the fate of Montgomery's Sangro offensive. The third alternative, an attack in the centre of the northern Apennines, seemed a formidable proposition at first sight. The mountains were high and steep, and looked like an impenetrable barrier, far stronger than the positions around Monte Cassino. Closer examination, however, showed that there were a number of good roads leading from the Florence area northwards to Bologna in the Po Valley which ran with the grain of the country (i.e. up the valleys instead of across them). Moreover, the preparation of the German defences appeared to be less advanced in this sector. Provided Alexander could

retain his highly-skilled French mountain troops to clear the hills methodically either side of these roads, it should be possible to burst through the
mountains where the German defences were weakest, and where a break-
through to the River Po might seal the fate of all German troops holding
the Ligurian and Adriatic sectors.

The plan which Alexander put to Maitland Wilson was based on this
appreciation. Provided he was allowed to keep his victorious armies intact,
and, in particular, retain the French mountain troops, he would secure
Bologna and then be ready to advance westwards into France or eastwards
into Austria. This would be a quicker, more effective and less hazardous
way of exploiting success than waiting for sufficient landing craft to be
released by Eisenhower for Anvil or any other amphibious operation. The
precious but delicate flower of close army–air co-operation which existed
within his Army Group would not be destroyed nor would the air effort
be split between Anvil and Italy. He suggested that there were two alternatives: adopt this plan or halt on the Pisa–Rimini Line to free resources for
other theatres. From his parochial point of view he could see nothing in
favour of the latter, but the former had two great advantages: the best
use would be made of the morale and momentum of his strong and successful ground–air team; and secondly, Hitler would be forced to reinforce
Kesselring during the next vital six weeks in which the exploitation of
Overlord would be hanging in the balance. Alexander estimated that, if
Hitler did not send eight to ten divisions into Italy, he would expose
Germany's southern frontiers to the danger of large-scale assault. Moreover, he would lose the industrial potential of northern Italy and surrender
airfields uncomfortably close to the southern cities of the Reich. It
might not be possible for the Allies to advance through the Brenner but
the Ljubljana Gap offered an alternative with Vienna as the ultimate
objective.

Maitland Wilson was personally inclined to favour Alexander's new
proposals but they ran counter to the advice of his American staff (particularly of General Devers, his American Deputy Commander) and
counter to the advice that he himself had only just given to the Chiefs of
Staff when he recommended launching Anvil on 15 August. He could not
reverse his position overnight and had to insist on the withdrawal of the
Anvil assault divisions from Alexander's Army Group while the pros and
cons of these new proposals were debated in London and Washington.
The VI (US) Corps was to be withdrawn on 11 June (*see* p. 251); 3, 36
and 45 (US) Divisions were to be pulled back before the end of June and
two French divisions would be withdrawn as well—one on 24 June and
the other in the first week of July. In the view of the Supreme Headquarters, Mediterranean, these withdrawals would not affect Alexander's

advance to the Gothic Line because he could only supply part of his Army Group during the pursuit phase until the ports of Civitavecchia and Ancona had been captured and his logistic position had improved. If the Chiefs of Staff favoured Alexander's new plan, then the Anvil divisions could be returned to him rested, refitted and ready for his assault on the Gothic Line. What was not appreciated in the rarified atmosphere of the Supreme Headquarters was the effect of this uncertainty on commanders and staffs in the field. It is not easy to look two ways in battle. The French were particularly affected. They were unlikely, and quite naturally so, to attack with enthusiasm in Italy when there was a chance of helping to free France by direct assault. Even in the Eighth Army the feeling that the Italian theatre was losing its importance and was becoming a backwater began to seep down from above. Fighting men's instincts are acute; any idea that their efforts are unlikely to have a decisive effect on the war soon destroys the willingness to take risks. Without taking risks, victories are seldom won and stalemates ensue. It was essential to decide for or against Alexander's proposals quickly and before the momentum and morale of his armies evaporated. Moreover, at lower levels in the staff, the Americans were already beginning to anticipate the Chiefs of Staff decision in favour of Anvil and had started withdrawing specialized logistic units needed for the invasion of southern France.

Alexander sent a copy of Harding's appreciation to Alan Brooke in London at the same time as he sent his new proposals to Maitland Wilson. As it happened the American Chiefs of Staff were visiting Europe at the time to see the Overlord beachhead at first hand. This opportunity was taken to discuss the development of operations in the Mediterranean. The stance adopted by the two sides remained as far apart as ever. The Americans were not prepared to give up the ideas of an amphibious assault and the British were not prepared to be tied, as yet, to any fixed plans. The discussion reduced the alternative courses to three: an assault on the Biscay ports; an assault on southern France; or an assault at the head of the Adriatic to help Alexander's advance over the Po. Each involved a major amphibious landing and so it was agreed to leave the choice of operation until it was clear how Overlord and the Russian summer offensive would develop. In the meantime Wilson's withdrawal of the Anvil divisions should be endorsed, but he should ensure that Alexander was left with whatever forces he needed to close up rapidly to the Pisa–Rimini Line. They hoped that this policy would allow them more time in which to make their choice of post-Overlord strategy. They also hoped that it would enable Maitland Wilson to launch the chosen operation by 25 July instead of by his estimate of 15 August.

Alexander and Harding were not prepared to give up their plan, in which they had great faith, without a fight. Their pursuit of Kesselring was going well and fresh calculations showed that it might be possible to be across the Po by mid-July and to be attacking the Lujbljana Gap by Mid-August. At a staff conference held at Maitland Wilson's headquarters, which had moved from Algiers to Caserta near Naples, Alexander developed his plans in greater detail. He was supported by the Mediterranean air and naval commanders, who were opposed to dividing their forces between Anvil and Italy. Wilson was won over, but his Deputy, Devers, remained opposed and took the American Chiefs of Staff line that Overlord was the primary Allied effort and that Anvil would be more use to Eisenhower than breaking the Gothic Line and advancing into Austria.

General Marshall visited Maitland Wilson's headquarters himself before returning to Washington after his visit to the Overlord beaches. He received Maitland Wilson's exposition of Alexander's proposals with no enthusiasm, pointing out that the one thing Eisenhower needed was more ports, through which to land the 40–50 US divisions waiting in the United States for shipment to North-West Europe. These divisions were to be used in France; on no account would they be used in southern Europe. He believed that the Germans in Italy would soon withdraw to the Alps and that OKW were unlikely to reinforce Kesselring with eight to ten divisions as Alexander postulated. Alexander's offensive would hit thin air. The Germans would withdraw to a shorter and stronger line, possibly on the Adige River covering the Ljubljana Gap and would be able to release a number of divisions to oppose Eisenhower. Furthermore, he doubted whether de Gaulle would be prepared to allow his best French divisions to move eastwards from Italy into central Europe instead of taking part in the direct liberation of France.

The turning point in the controversy came a few days later. Eisenhower stepped in and stated that in his view launching Anvil was the best way to speed up the destruction of the German forces opposing him in North-West Europe. The great Channel storm, which destroyed the American 'Mulberry' harbour on the Normandy coast, had seriously delayed his build-up and he was becoming alarmed at the prospect of the Germans being able to impose a stalemate upon him when the autumn rains began. The American Chiefs of Staff quickly supported him; this was just the card which they needed to trump Alexander's proposals. Churchill and South Africa's Prime Minister, Field-Marshal Smuts, however, entered the field to counter Eisenhower's intervention and raised the debate to the highest political level. The whole argument was set out with great clarity in a cable from the President to the Prime Minister on 29 June,* which

---

* Quoted in full in *Grand Strategy*, Vol. V, p. 353.

gave the American political and military case. In essence the cable was a detailed rebuttal of the British arguments. While the President agreed that the overall strategic concept should be to engage the enemy on the largest scale and with the greatest violence and continuity, he was not prepared to abandon the strategy agreed with the Russians at Tehran which relegated the Mediterranean to secondary importance. He accepted Churchill's political reasons for wishing to press on with the Italian Campaign but was not prepared to allow political considerations to dilute the military aim of striking at the heart of Germany by the most direct route. He was convinced that Maitland Wilson would be left with sufficient forces to chase Kesselring out of Italy and he was sure that Hitler would not waste an extra ten divisions, as Alexander suggested, to keep the Allies at bay in the south. The Allied air forces in the Mediterranean were powerful enough to support both Anvil and the Italian operations. It would be far more difficult and take much longer to attack through the Ljubljana Gap than it would be to advance up the Rhone Valley to threaten the southern flank of the German armies opposing Eisenhower. The quickest way to bring larger Allied forces to bear against the Germans would be to capture more French ports. The sting, however, lay in the last three paragraphs of the President's cable. If Churchill was not prepared to instruct Maitland Wilson to go ahead with Anvil, then the whole argument should be set before Stalin for adjudication. At Tehran a strategy had been agreed; nothing had occurred to make a major change necessary. History would never forgive Churchill and Roosevelt if they continued to waste time and lives through indecision and debate. Roosevelt's cable to Churchill concluded: 'Finally for purely political considerations over here I would never survive even a slight set-back in Overlord if it were known that fairly large forces had been diverted to the Balkans'.

The bitterness engendered in London by this cable was sharpened by reports from Italy that the Americans were already withdrawing front line units needed by Alexander in his advance to the Gothic Line. Alan Brooke advised Churchill to give way in the broader interests of Allied unity, but before he would do so Churchill made one more appeal to the President, who remained unmoved, ending up his second reply with the simple allusion which he had first used at Casablanca: 'I always think of my early geometry—a straight line is the shortest distance between two points'. Unfortunately the straightest and shortest line in military affairs is, more often than not, the most difficult and certainly the most heavily defended avenue of approach, but there was no point in arguing further; only events could prove which side was right. On 2 July, the British Chiefs of Staff directed Wilson to launch Anvil with three divisions in the assault wave on about 15 August. The Battle for Italy was to be continued with whatever forces were not needed for Anvil.

Alexander and his staff were disappointed by this decision, which reached them in the form of a new directive on 5 July. Anvil was given overriding priority for Allied army, naval and air resources. The VI (US) Corps and the three US divisions already withdrawn were now finally lost to Alexander. This was to be expected, but the directive also demanded the release of the four French divisions, about 70 per cent of the Army Group's air support, and a large number of logistic units such as American railway construction battalions which were essential for opening up supply lines into the Po Valley. 15 Army Group was reduced to 18 divisions and was left unbalanced operationally and logistically. Fifth

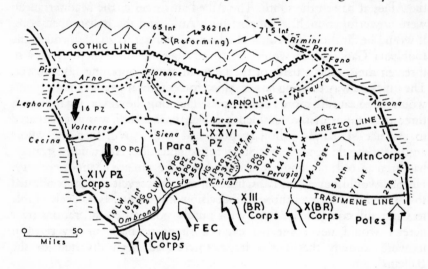

45   The Advance from Trasimene to the Gothic Line, 20 June–25 August

Army was worst hit and was reduced to only five divisions, losing many of its American specialist units which had been serving both armies. The only reinforcements offered to the theatre were the 92 (US) Negro Division, which would arrive in Italy in September, and a Brazilian division of unknown quality due at the end of October.

Meanwhile the Germans had taken the view which Alexander had forecast. It soon became known through Allied intelligence sources that Hitler had directed Kesselring to hold the Gothic Line 'as a final blocking line whose breach would have incalculable military and political consequences'. In addition to the four divisions already sent to reinforce his Army Group 'C' (see p. 247), Kesselring was to receive three more divisions intended for the Russian front and one from the Russian front itself. Thus while Alexander lost seven divisions and a large part of his air support, Kesselring gained a total of eight divisions together with substantial individual reinforcements to bring his battered divisions up to strength.

As Fifth and Eighth Armies were brought slowly to a halt in front of the Trasimene Line, they found the four German corps opposing them had been regrouped. In Fourteenth Army's sector, von Senger's XIV Panzer Corps had moved across to the west coast to stabilize the dangerous situation created by IV (US) Corps' rapid advance up Route 1, and the 1 Para Corps was holding the French advance on Route 2. In Tenth Army's sector LXXVI Panzer Corps was blocking Eighth Army's XIII (Br) Corps and X (Br) Corps, while LI Mountain Corps was opposing the Poles on the Adriatic coast. All the German mobile divisions were committed to holding the line as they had been during the withdrawal from Salerno.

The Trasimene Line had been well chosen. It covered the two important ports of Leghorn and Ancona which were needed by the Fifth and Eighth Armies respectively to ease their supply difficulties. Eighth Army's railhead was now some 200 miles behind the front and this was throwing a heavy strain on its road transport columns. The Trasimene Line itself was more a deep defensive zone using a number of obstacles than an actual fortified line based on one continuous obstacle across the front. It was situated in rolling hilly country and used several naturally strong positions blocking each of the north–south roads in depth. It was also well, if luckily, chosen from the point of view of timing. Kesselring did not know and could not have guessed that the Allies would withdraw a large part of their victorious striking force at such an opportune moment from the German point of view. He decided to stand just as the Allied advance lost its momentum.

The Trasimene battles lasted from 20 to 30 June and consisted of a series of isolated actions between individual Allied corps and their German opponents on each of the axis of advance. 16 SS Panzer Division arrived in time to make IV (US) Corps' progress up Route 1 slow and difficult, and it was not until 1 July that the Americans managed to force their way over the Cecina River, having suffered quite heavy losses. The French could not bring themselves to take their operations too seriously as their minds were fixed on preparations for Anvil. They were held up on the Orcia River until 27 June and made little attempt to get forward until the Germans withdrew on their own accord and allowed the French to enter Siena on 3 July. The hardest fighting of all took place in the centre, where XIII (Br) and X (Br) Corps tried to smash their way through on either side of Lake Trasimene. They were opposed by their old enemies, the Hermann Göring, 1 Para and 15 Panzer Grenadier Divisions, who were helped by a sudden spell of wet weather. Both British corps had to fight hard and were very relieved when they found early on 30 June that the Germans had withdrawn during the night. Kesselring had judged the moment had come to disengage and to slip back to another position which he felt he could hold before withdrawing to the Arno.

Kesselring withdrew from Trasimene fairly quickly until 5 July when the Allies again found themselves stopped all along the front on a new line running from a point six miles north of Cecina on the west coast, through Volterra to the heights south of Arezzo and across to the east coast south of Ancona. Fighting on this line proved to be a repetition of the Trasimene battles. Kesselring stood just long enough to force the advancing Allied corps to deploy and mount a series of co-ordinated attacks; then he slipped back once more on the night of 15 July. Thereafter he withdrew much more slowly than hitherto through a series of positions coded with girls' names in alphabetical order. Each day the reconnaissance elements of the advancing Allied divisions would push northwards up their centre lines looking for ways round the numerous blown bridges left by the German rearguards. About midday they would come up against the rearguards themselves. Sometimes these could be driven off and the advance resumed, but, more often, more and more of each division would have to be deployed to clear a way forward. If a division was lucky it would hear the German gunners increasing their harassing fire during the night, which was usually a sign that they were withdrawing again. Sometimes when the Germans found that they had a really strong position they would stand for two or even three nights. In this way they wore down the advancing Allied divisions and wasted the summer weather which was so precious to Alexander. It was not until 4 August that the German divisions consented to fall back into Kesselring's final delaying position in front of the Gothic Line—the Arno Line which ran from Pisa through Florence and then over the Apennines to the Metauro River. They had abandoned Ancona to the Poles on 18 July and Leghorn to the Americans on 19 July. On 4 August they retired to the north bank of the Arno blowing up all the bridges in Florence except for the historic Ponte Vecchio, which they blocked by demolishing and mining the houses at both ends of the bridge.

On the Allied side the moment had come to regroup and prepare for the battles of the Gothic Line, which now lay only about 15 miles ahead of their leading troops.

September 1944–May 1945

THE SECOND WINTER OF DISAPPOINTMENT AND THE SPRING OF FINAL VICTORY

'The Introduction of major forces into the Balkans as recommended by you . . . is not favourably considered at this time. Your first and immediate objective should be to capture Bologna, then secure the general line Ravenna–Bologna–Spezia and thereafter continue operations with a view to containing Kesselring's Army.'

*Extract from Combined Chiefs of Staff Directive
to Alexander, 2 December 1944*

15

One More River,
One More Mountain

'*Conclusions*
(a) The Italian offensive can continue to a limited extent with the forces that remain [after Anvil], but it will soon die out if the Allied Armies in Italy cannot be reinforced.
(b) The strategical advantages of continuing it to the logical conclusion of securing the Ljubljana Gap, preparatory to an invasion of southern Germany, are so great that supreme efforts should be made to find means to enable this to be done.'

General Harding, 1943

Alexander had always realized that the Anvil decision might go against him. On the day that the fatal decision was signalled to him, Harding produced a closely-reasoned appreciation of what could still be done within the Army Group's straitened resources. He estimated that the German strength would rise to between 18 and 21 Divisions. Kesselring would try to hold the Allies on the Gothic Line, but if he failed to do so he would pull back, fighting delaying actions, to the Po, from the Po to the Adige, and from the Adige to a line covering the Ljubljana Gap. His calculations showed that in each of these phases the Army Group would need about 18 divisions in the line to break each German defence line and another six in reserve, refitting, resting and getting ready to take the lead once more. Without this reserve, the momentum of the Allied Advance would be lost and the German front would congeal. After the Anvil withdrawals the Army Group would be left with just 18 divisions. Could the extra divisions be found? If they could then the Army Group might yet be able to reap the fruits of 18 months' desperate fighting and the brutal losses which it had suffered in Overlord's cause.

Alexander suggested a number of sources from which the extra divisions might come: the Middle East Garrison might be reduced; the Persia and Iraq Command might give up one division; India might surrender some troops during the Monsoon period; or the United States might spare some of the 50 divisions waiting to enter North-West Europe. The British Chiefs of Staff wished to do everything possible to help the Italian campaign but British manpower was dwindling after five years of war and no divisions could be spared from other theatres. The best they could do was to authorize Alexander to raise Italian divisions for which they authorized the issue of British equipment. The American Chiefs of Staff were convinced that Alexander's Army Group was correctly balanced; it had enough land and air resources for the limited role of containing Kesselring in Italy and not enough for any British adventures in the Balkans or central Europe. They remained firmly opposed to supplying any more troops to the Italian theatre, and in this they were ably supported by General Devers, who saw to it that General Patch's Seventh US Army received every unit it needed for Anvil at the expense of 15 Army Group.

The only course left to Alexander's Army Group was to make the best use it could of the existing resources. There were about two months of summer weather left and Germany was taking tremendous punishment on all fronts and from the air. Kesselring might have to surrender some of his divisions to the Eastern and Western fronts, and it might prove possible to hustle him out of the Gothic Line before his troops had time to settle down in its defence. And the unexpected might always occur; Germany might even collapse and the war end before winter—though the fighting spirit being shown by their soldiers in Italy suggested that this was unlikely.

The unexpected did occur but within the Allied instead of the German camp. Alexander and Harding met Oliver Leese on Orvieto airfield to discuss future plans on 4 August—the day that the Germans finally withdrew over the Arno. No record was kept of the discussion but a decision was taken then and there to change the whole plan of operations in Italy. Oliver Leese had been unhappy about Alexander's original plan for some weeks. It seemed to him that the loss of the French mountain troops made the attack in the high central sector of the Gothic Line much less attractive than it had been. Fifth Army was now so reduced that the bulk of the fighting would fall to Eighth Army, which had no proper mountain divisions and always relied on using its great superiority in armour and artillery. These two arms would be at a grave disadvantage in the Apennines. Accordingly he proposed that Eighth Army should be swiftly and secretly moved across to the Adriatic coast and should attack through the Polish Corps sector to break the Gothic Line where the hills were at their lowest. If he could break through to Rimini, his armoured divisions would then have the Plains of Lombardy before them and for the first time since they landed in Italy would be able to fight free from the cramping restriction of the Italian mountains.

Oliver Leese had a further reason for wishing to change the plan. He did not like working in close conjunction with Fifth Army. With the greatest good will on both sides, difficulties always arose when two armies of different nationalities, using different techniques, tried to operate side by side aiming for the same objective. Experience in Sicily* and in the

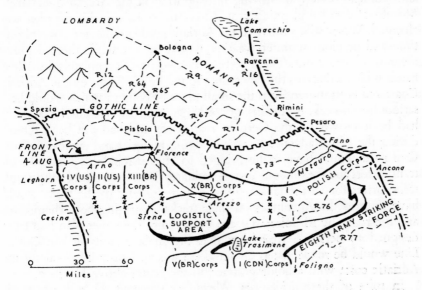

46   *Plan Olive suggested by General Leese, 4 August*

Liri Valley had led him to believe that operations would be easier if the two armies fought on quite separate axes. As it happened, Oliver Leese's proposal coincided with Alexander's favourite 'two-handed' punch technique. He would strike first with Eighth Army, drawing the German reserves to the Adriatic and then launch Fifth Army against the weakened German centre. As soon as Kesselring started moving his reserves back again to oppose Fifth Army, he would launch Eighth Army again in a decisive break-through in the Rimini area.

There were a number of serious difficulties to be overcome. The deployment of the Army Group had been designed to bring Eighth Army

* See p. 63 for Oliver Leese's previous difficulties with Bradley's II (US) Corps in front of Enna in Sicily.

straight from its line of pursuit into its assaulting position to breach the Gothic Line in the centre. The two pursuit corps, XIII and X (Br) Corps, had reached the Florence–Arezzo area as planned. The two assault corps, V (Br) Corps and the Canadians, with some seven fresh divisions, were concentrating around Lake Trasimene ready to move forward when everything was ready for the attack on the Gothic Line. The logistic plan was also in an advanced stage: the main army railhead was being moved forward and was almost ready at Arezzo; stocks of ammunition and supplies were building up south of Florence; and installations like hospitals and workshops were all moving into position in the Arezzo–Siena area. Months of detailed planning would have to be jettisoned if the plan was changed. Worse still, a move to the Adriatic could not be done overnight; time and precious summer weather would be lost while the redeployment was carried out. There were only two roads completely in Allied hands which led across the Apennines to the Polish Corps on the Adriatic Coast and both started from the small town of Foligno which would be a serious bottle-neck. All the bridges on these two roads (Routes 76 and 77) had been blown by the German rearguards and had not been rebuilt during the Allied advance to save bridging material and engineer effort. One road would have to be bridged to 70-ton standards for tanks on transporters and the other to 30-ton standards. There were not enough tank transporters for all the tank regiments and so many of the tanks would have to cross the Apennines on their tracks, damaging both themselves and the roads by so doing. To cap everything, the cover-plan had been designed to persuade Kesselring that the main assault on the Gothic Line would be made just as Oliver Leese was now proposing—along the Adriatic coast with a holding attack in the centre above Florence.

In spite of these difficulties, Alexander accepted the new proposals because it would enable him to use his two-handed punch technique and gave the Army Commander a plan in which he had full confidence. Furthermore, he appreciated Oliver Leese's reasoning. Eighth Army would be free to fight its battle in its own way: it would have fewer mountains to contend with for which it had no mountain troops; it could use its great weight of artillery in controlled and concentrated set-piece attacks—the techniques of which it had perfected ever since Montgomery had shown it the way at El Alamein; once it was through the Rimini Gap, the Plains of Lombardy would open before it and its desert-trained armour would do great execution; and, above all, it would not have to worry about close co-ordination with its sister army—or about rivalry for world-press headlines either. The decision was made on Orvieto airfield and the orders to change plan were issued immediately. The new operation was code-named 'Olive'.

In fairness to Eighth Army staff it should be recorded, in the light of subsequent events, that they did not favour the change of plan. Indeed, they advised strongly against it; not because it meant the loss of all their hard work but because they realized that instead of mountains they would be faced with a series of river lines. Operations during the previous autumn on the Sangro had taught them the difficulties of attacking up the Adriatic coast where the spurs of the Apennines run down to the sea, affording the Germans perfect defensive positions between each of the many rivers from which they could cover the crossings. They also appreciated that,

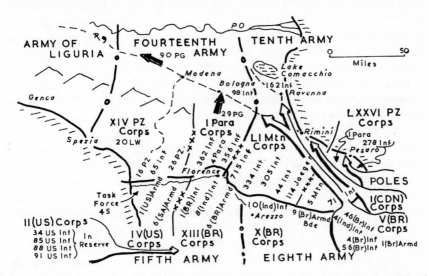

47   *Allied and German dispositions before Olive, and Eighth Army's plan of attack, 25 August*

as the Germans fell back, their line would shorten and grow stronger. Moreover, Route 9 would serve the Germans as an excellent lateral between the Fifth and Eighth Army sectors, allowing them to switch reserves between the two fronts far quicker than the Allies could hope to do. Few officers, however, in the Eighth Army staff appreciated the significance of the Romanga—the area of low flat ground north of Route 9 which fills the triangle Rimini–Bologna–Lake Comacchio. During planning this seems to have been lumped together with the Plain of Lombardy as good 'tank going'—an illusion which was soon to be shattered.

Only the most experienced and highly-skilled staff could have undertaken the redeployment of Eighth Army in three weeks. The whole operation had to be planned and executed in the greatest secrecy. The last paragraph of the short instruction sent by Harding on 6 August to the army commanders read:

> The scope and object of Operation Olive has been settled in discussion between the C.-in-C. and Army Commanders and will not be referred to in writing at present.

The cover-plan problem was solved by resorting to double bluff. The Germans were now to be persuaded of the spurious nature of the earlier concentrations on the Adriatic. Fifth Army would tend to show its gun areas and supply dumps, and would set up additional dummies to draw attention to the central sector; Eighth Army would do the opposite but this was not so easy because enormous quantities of ammunition had to be concealed, and large numbers of guns and tanks had to be brought into the area at the latest possible moment. The Polish Corps was to cover the concentration of V (Br) Corps and the Canadian Corps by pressing on with their advance north of Ancona. They were to try to reach the Metauro River, some 15 miles south of the Gothic positions, and to establish bridgeheads across it through which the assaulting corps would pass. If all went well the advance would be continuous with the leading divisions of V (Br) Corps and the Canadian Corps passing through the Poles without a pause, so that the Germans could be hustled back through the Gothic positions without realizing that a major Allied offensive was in progress. Provided the move over the Apennines could be made in secret, the Eighth Army would only be opposed by two infantry divisions: 278 Division, which had been withdrawing in front of the Poles for several weeks and had suffered a severe defeat very recently while defending Ancona; and the reconstituted 71 Division which had broken in front of Juin's Corps in the opening stages of Diadem. Behind these two divisions was the formidable 1 Para Division. The rest of Kesselring's mobile divisions were well to the west and out of immediate striking distance of Eighth Army's proposed breach.

Eighth Army's tactical plan was to attack initially with three corps abreast. The Poles were to take Pesaro at the eastern end of the Gothic Line and then come into Army reserve. The Canadians with 1 (Cdn) Infantry Division and 5 (Cdn) Armoured Division would attack in the centre aiming to reach the coast road north of Pesaro and then to advance along it to take Rimini. V (Br) Corps was to be the main assault corps and would have under its command five divisions—4, 46, 56 (Br) Divisions, 4 (Ind) Division and 1 (Br) Armoured Division. It would attack through the hills to the west of the Canadians and would aim to reach Route 9 in the Po Valley west of Rimini. Oliver Leese had originally planned to use V (Br) Corps in the centre, but on General Anders' advice he switched it to the inland flank because the Poles had found that left hooks through the hills were the most effective way of upsetting the Germans defending the coast road. X (Br) Corps was to continue holding the mountain sector between the two armies, and XIII (Br) Corps was to pass to the command of Fifth Army holding the sector north and north-east of Florence.

Planning was completed and orders issued by 13 August with D-day fixed for 25 August. The sappers completed their task of opening up the two routes through the Apennines on schedule by 15 August; and between that date and 22 August Eighth Army crossed the Apennines by night and with its tanks and vehicles moving without lights. During those eight days 60,000 tanks, guns and vehicles passed eastwards through Foligno into their concentration areas behind the Polish screen; and Eighth Army's logistic rail-head was shifted from Arezzo to Ancona.

On the day that Eighth Army's flank march began, Patch's Seventh Army landed on the Riviera beaches watched by Churchill and Maitland Wilson from the British destroyer, HMS *Kimberley*. Anvil had been re-christened 'Dragoon' and lived up to its new name. Meticulous staff work, the product of long experience of mounting amphibious operations in the Mediterranean, led to swift and overwhelming success. The landing, covered by the usual panoply of warships, fighters, fighter-bombers and bombers, went without a hitch. The subsequent advance up the Rhone Valley was rapid. By Olive's D-day, the Seventh Army had reached Grenoble and in northern France Eisenhower's armies had swept past Paris to Troyes. The two forces, Overlord and Dragoon, joined hands at Dijon on 11 September. By then, 50,000 Germans had been trapped in south-western France and were prisoners in Allied hands. The Americans were naturally jubilant at the success of the strategy for which they had fought so hard and their jubilation was in no way lessened by the news from the Eastern Front. The Russian summer offensive was sweeping to new successes. Roumania had been overwhelmed and declared war on Germany on 25 August; Bulgaria had withdrawn from the war on 26 August; and the Hungarians were showing fresh signs of disaffection. Churchill and Smuts, but not Roosevelt, could see the dire political consequences which would face the post-War world if the Red tide continued to flow westwards. After watching Dragoon, Churchill cabled his Majesty the King:

> Your Majesty knows my opinion of the strategy, but the perfect execution of the plan was deeply interesting. There is no doubt that Eisenhower's operations made a great diversion. The fact that this is the precise opposite of what was intended need not be stressed at the present time.

And to Smuts he telegraphed:

> My object now is to keep what we have got in Italy, which should be sufficient since the enemy has withdrawn four of his best divisions. With this I hope to turn and break the Gothic Line, break into the Po Valley, and ultimately advance by Trieste and the Ljubljana Gap to Vienna. Even if the war came to an end at an early date I have told Alexander to be ready for a dash with armoured cars.

Churchill's reference to Kesselring losing four of his best divisions was not quite correct. Since Diadem he had received five new divisions and three divisions'* worth of reinforcements. He had lost the Hermann Göring Division to the Eastern Front in July, and 3 and 15 Panzer Grenadier Divisions were ordered to the Western Front in the middle of August. He had thus lost three veteran mobile divisions and gained the equivalent of eight divisions of inferior quality. He was, however, about to occupy the Gothic Line defences, for which infantry divisions were the most suitable. He still had six mobile divisions—1 and 4 Para, 26 Panzer, 16 SS Panzer and 29 and 90 Panzer Grenadier.

With his usual lack of strategic—as opposed to tactical—sense, Kesselring misread the aim of Dragoon when it took place. He assumed that it was directed at attacking his western flank. In consequence he turned his attention away from the Adriatic just at the wrong moment and started meeting an imaginary crisis in north-western Italy. This sector of his front was now the responsibility of the Italian Marshal Graziani who commanded a mixed German and Italian force called the Army of Liguria. 90 Panzer Grenadier Division, which was poised in central reserve near Bologna, was despatched westwards to reinforce Graziani and 29 Panzer Grenadier Division was drawn back from the Florence area into reserve at Bologna. German intelligence failed to detect the massive movement of Eighth Army across the Apennines until it was too late. When Olive opened on 25 August the Germans thought, as was intended, that it was a continuation of the steady Polish advance which had been going on for several weeks. 278 Division was in the process of withdrawing through 1 Para Division in a series of routine reliefs designed to enable it to take over 5 Mountain Division's sector, so that the latter could relieve 90 Panzer Grenadier Division in the Army of Liguria. In consequence, it was some days before the Germans realized that a major offensive had opened on their Adriatic flank.

* These reinforcements arrived as newly formed divisions called *Ostpreussen*, *Wildflecken* and *Schlesien* after the areas in which they had been raised, but they were broken up and sent to the existing German divisions.

The Olive battles fall into four distinct phases: the advance to the Gothic Line; breaking the Gothic Line; the First Battle of Coriano; and the Second Battle of Coriano. During the two latter phases the Fifth Army's operations came into play, and the fortunes of both armies were then closely linked by the movements of the German mobile divisions from one front to the other, to and fro along Route 9.

In the first four days Eighth Army's plan went like clockwork. Its own traffic control problems caused more difficulty than the German opposition.

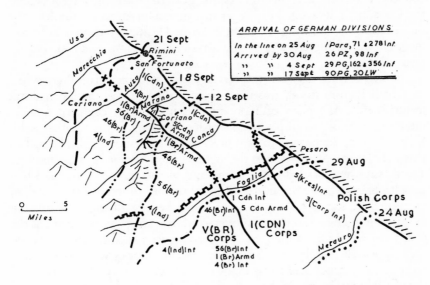

48 *Eighth Army's offensive, 25 August–20 September*

71 Division put up little resistance and fell back rapidly in front of V (Br) Corps, and the mixture of 278 Division and 1 Para Division did not do much better. The three Allied corps reached the River Foglia in front of the Gothic positions on 29 August and it was only then that the Germans began to realize what was afoot. Reinforcements were ordered up and General Herr, the commander of LXXVI Panzer Corps, issued a 'backs to the wall' order of the day but he was too late to save the Adriatic sector of the Gothic Line. On 30 August the forward positions of the line on the far side of the Foglia were overrun before they could be properly manned. Months of hard work by the German engineers and labour organizations had proved worthless. Next day German resistance began to stiffen. Elements of 26 Panzer Division had arrived from the Arno; 1 Para Division succeeded in forming a coherent front; and 98 Division from

271

Bologna started to appear. Hard fighting went on during 1 and 2 September in which the rest of the Gothic defences in front of Eighth Army were smashed, and that evening the German line gave way, reeling back in near rout to the next river line, the Conca. The Poles took Pesaro and went into Army reserve as planned. The Canadians seized a bridgehead over the Conca during the night 2–3 September. 46 (Br) Division on the right of V (Br) Corps had kept pace with the Canadians, but 56 (Br) Division and 4 (Ind) Division, operating through more difficult hilly country, could not keep up and became gradually echeloned back behind the Canadian left wing. In spite of this slower progress on the left, the impression was growing at Eighth Army Headquarters that a break-through was imminent and so the armoured divisions were moved up ready to exploit.

The key feature between the River Conca and the River Marecchia, on which Rimini stood, was the Coriano ridge. It was the last real hill feature before the plain of Romanga. If it could be captured quickly there was nothing to stop a break-through as long as the weather held. V (Br) Corps, which was to be Oliver Leese's pursuit corps, planned to pass 1 (Br) Armoured Division through 46 (Br) Division on 4 September. The division was briefed for a pursuit and was to have its armoured brigade leading with only its motor battalion and one other infantry battalion in immediate support. Fortune, which had been with Eighth Army up to this point, seemed to take this over-confident move as an affront as the plan went wrong from the start. The leading armoured regiments started their approach march on 2 September but the tracks were so bad that most of the journey had to be made in low gear. Many of the tanks fell out of the line of march with mechanical failures and others just kept going but were in no fit mechanical state to enter a battle. Constant delays had also tired the crews and left them too little time to rest before the division crossed the Conca at 10.30 a.m. on 4 September, only to find that 46 (Br) Division had not reached its objectives. The plan of attack had to be recast and it was not until 3.45 p.m. that 1 (Br) Armoured Division's attack started. By then the sun was low and shining into the British tank gunners' eyes. The Germans had the sun behind them and during the British delay, while the armoured division changed plan, they had been able to bring up tanks and self-propelled guns to defend the ridge. In the ensuing fight the strain of the approach march on the British armoured regiments began to tell. Their tank crews manoeuvred erratically, with more tanks breaking down and others becoming bogged, as they tried to overrun the German positions, which grew stronger as the evening wore on. The attack had to be stopped when dusk fell because 1 (Br) Armoured Division's infantry brigade was too far back to take over from the tanks and so the chance of a

break-through—if it had ever existed—faded as more German reinforcements moved up during the night. By next morning 29 Panzer Grenadier
and 356 Divisions had arrived from the Fifth Army front. There were
now three German mobile divisions (1 Para, 26 Panzer and 29 Panzer
Grenadier Divisions) and three infantry divisions blocking Eighth Army's
path. All except 29 Panzer Grenadier Division had suffered heavily and had
surrendered some 4,000 prisoners, but Eighth Army was beginning to
tire as well and the weather had started to break. Heavy rain fell on 6 and
7 September making manoeuvre difficult and further operations by both
attacking corps during 8 and 9 September convinced Oliver Leese that a
properly prepared Army assault would have to be delivered against the
Coriano positions before a break-through could be made. This set-piece
attack could not be mounted before 12 September.

When Kesselring had realized that the Eighth Army offensive was a
serious attempt to outflank the Gothic Line and to destroy the eastern
pivot of his line upon which his armies would have to swing if and when
they withdrew to the Po and Adige, he had ordered a general withdrawal
of the rest of the German divisions into the Gothic defences. This movement had started on 30 August and had enabled him to shorten his line,
regroup and free divisions to oppose Eighth Army. His front fell into four
distinct sectors each of which was controlled by a corps headquarters (see
fig. 48). The two most dangerous sectors were the central sector, covering
the direct route from Florence to Bologna, which was entrusted to 1
Para Corps, and the Adriatic sector, controlled by LXXVI Panzer Corps.
Between these two sectors was the difficult mountain area to the east of
Florence, around Bibbiena, controlled by LI Mountain Corps; and on the
western flank lay the cul-de-sac of the western Apennines controlled by
XIV Panzer Corps.

The Bibbiena mountain and the western Apennine sectors were clearly
the areas which would have to surrender troops as soon as it was certain
where the main Allied effort would be made. LI Mountain and XIV
Panzer Corps withdrew methodically into the Gothic positions when
Kesselring ordered them to do so on 30 August, but 1 Para Corps fell back
only about six miles north of Florence to leave itself plenty of room in
which to slow down any attempt by Fifth Army to open up the main road
to Bologna. The gaps left by the move of 26 Panzer, 29 Panzer Grenadier
and 356 Divisions when they moved eastwards to oppose Eighth Army
were soon filled by side-stepping divisions as the front contracted.

Kesselring's withdrawal in front of Fifth Army saved Mark Clark
from an opposed crossing of the Arno, and made it easier for him to
concentrate forward for Alexander's next left-handed punch. Lucca was
occupied on 6 September and Pistoia on 12 September by IV (US) Corps,

and XIII (Br) Corps followed the Germans north as they withdrew from Florence. II (US) Corps, which was to be Mark Clark's assault and pursuit corps, was brought up through Florence screened by 1 (Br) Infantry Division on XIII (Br) Corps' left flank. On 5 September Alexander had judged the moment had come to land his first left-handed punch. He had ordered Mark Clark to close up to the Gothic positions on Route 65 as soon as possible and to be ready to launch a full-scale attack on the line in conjunction with Oliver Leese's set-piece attack on the Coriano ridge.

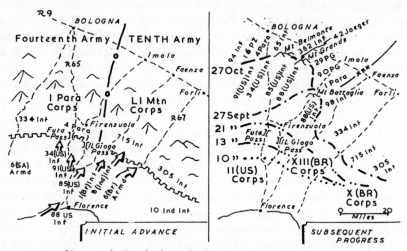

49   Fifth Army's break through the Gothic Line, 10–27 September

Fifth Army's preparations were complete by 8 September. There were two major passes on the direct roads leading to Bologna: the Futa Pass on the main road, Route 65, and the Il Giogo Pass on the secondary road to the east which ran through Firenzuola to Imola on Route 9. The Futa Pass, being on the main road, was likely to be the most heavily defended and so Mark Clark decided to make his main effort through the Il Giogo Pass. To mask his intentions, the initial advance of II (US) Corps was to be made astride Route 65 with 34 (US) Division on the western side and 91 (US) Division to the east. 85 (US) Division would move up as soon as the leading divisions were in contact with the main Gothic defences and would attack to the east of the Il Giogo Pass while 91 (US) Division swung towards it from the west. 88 (US) Division was to be held in reserve to exploit wherever success was achieved. XIII (Br) Corps would support II (US) Corps by attacking up the Faenza and Forli roads, using 1 (Br) Infantry Division on the former and 8 (Ind) Division on the latter. IV (US) Corps, which had 6 (SA) Armoured and 92 (US) Negro Divisions under command was to maintain pressure on XIV Panzer Corps in the western Apennine sector.

Fifth Army's offensive started in much the same way as Eighth Army's advance through the Polish Corps. As II (US) Corps passed through XIII (Br) Corps' left, it caught the Germans in the process of withdrawing to the Gothic Line. The American advance, like the British advance on the Adriatic, looked like the normal follow-up of a German withdrawal. There had been four German divisions in 1 Para Corps' sector, but the loss of 29 Panzer and 356 Divisions to the Adriatic had left only 4 Para Division covering both the Futa and Il Giogo Passes. 334 Division was blocking the routes further west which were not going to be attacked by II (US) Corps. 715 Division, which belonged to LI Mountain Corps, opposed XIII (Br) Corps. It is not surprising that 4 Para Division, with its three regiments in the line and with no reserve regiment, had the greatest difficulty in stopping the four divisions of II (US) Corps even with the help of the Gothic defences.

II (US) Corps' advance started on 10 September, five days after 1 (Br) Armoured Division's first abortive attempt to break through the Coriano positions covering Rimini. By 12 September, 34 and 91 (US) Divisions had forced 4 Para Division back into the Gothic positions on either side of Route 65. On 13 September, 85 (US) Division came up on the eastern flank of 91 (US) Division and Fifth Army's main offensive started. The attack went very slowly at first. The Gothic defences were quite as formidable as the Americans had expected and 4 Para Division had lost nothing of the German paratroopers' grim determination in defence. Four days' hard fighting in which some 2,000 medium and fighter-bomber sorties were flown against 4 Para Division's positions brought II (US) Corps few rewards in exchange for heavy casualties. 715 Division was not so successful in holding XIII (Br) Corps. An advance by 8 (Ind) Division over rough mountain tracks brought it through the Gothic defences and up onto the Apennine watershed. On 17 September the combined attacks of 85 (US) Division and 1 (Br) Infantry Division against the boundary between 4 Para and 715 Divisions, which was also the German inter-army boundary, proved decisive. The loss of key positions on 4 Para Division's flank and the slowness with which German reinforcements arrived led to the collapse of the Gothic defences on the Il Giogo Pass. As had happened on Eighth Army's front the coincidence of the German withdrawal and the American attack had masked the Fifth Army offensive and resulted in Kesselring reacting too slowly. It was not until 20 September that 44 and 362 Divisions were extracted from LI Mountain and XIV Panzer Corps' sectors and began to arrive opposite Fifth Army's salient. By then it was too late to save the Gothic positions. 4 Para Division was exhausted and had to pull back surrendering the Futa Pass and Firenzuola on 21 September. The moment had arrived for II (US) Corps to bring forward its reserve, 88 (US) Division, to exploit success.

The original Fifth Army plan was to exploit down Route 65 to Bologna, but the slowness of Eighth Army south of Rimini and the weakness which had appeared at the seam of the two German armies suggested that an advance down the Imola road would be the most profitable line to exploit. This would bring Fifth Army closer in behind the German forces opposing Eighth Army, and so 88 (US) Division was passed through 85 (US) Division and directed on Imola.

88 (US) Division's advance was rapid as it forced its way between 4 Para and 715 Divisions. On 27 September its leading battalion, guided by Italian partisans, seized Monte Battaglia, a key hill feature only 12 miles from Imola and Route 9. By this time German counter-measures were beginning to take effect. Desperate counter-attacks were launched against the Americans on Monte Battaglia for over a week by elements of many different divisions, some of which came from the Adriatic sector. The Germans failed to retake the feature but they stopped 88 (US) Division's dangerous thrust. The American losses were heavy, the axis of attack uninviting for a further major offensive, and the weather had deteriorated. Mark Clark decided to halt his first attempt to break through and to switch his point of attack back to Route 65. Before describing his second attempt to reach the plains we must go back to look at Eighth Army's concurrent offensive—the Second Battle of Coriano.

Oliver Leese's co-ordinated army attack on the Coriano positions opened shortly before midnight on 12 September. It had been planned with all the throughness of a typical Eighth Army battle. Heavy air and naval bombardments were used to soften up the German defending divisions during the preparatory operations. V (Br) Corps and the Canadian Corps, which was to have 4 (Br) Division and the New Zealand Division under its command, were to attack side by side in three phases: the capture of the Coriano ridge; the seizure of bridgeheads over the next small river, the Marano; and finally the clearance of the high ground overlooking the Marano and an advance or possibly a break-through past Rimini into the Plain of the Romanga. In spite of these careful preparations, the battle which followed was one of the most costly ever fought by Eighth Army in Italy. For a whole week casualties averaged not much less than 1,000 per day and in the end the weather robbed Eighth Army of its prize.

The first phase, as usual, went well. Led by their armoured divisions both corps cleared the Coriano ridge. It was soon apparent that the wet weather of 6 and 7 September had made the going difficult for tanks and

25   The reward: freedom from fear of air attack; Eighth Army reserves waiting to move forward during the advance to the Gothic Line

THE MEANING OF AIR SUPREMACY

26   The penalty: no movement in daylight; French troops passing the wreck of a German column spotted by Allied airmen and destroyed by air and artillery attack in the Esperia defile

27 Damage inflicted on the German communications by the Allied Air Forces

INTERDICTION

28 Eighth Army engineers bulldozing a route round a German demolition

this did not bode well for the future. The second phase started on 15 September and met stiffer resistance. Both corps, now using infantry divisions predominantly, crossed the Marano and gained footholds on the high ground beyond the stream. Throughout the 16 and 17 September the German positions were gradually eroded away. Both allied corps struggled for the elusive break-through, and the Germans resisted with corresponding tenacity to allow time for reinforcements to arrive. 20 Luftwaffe Division arrived from the west coast during 17 September, followed by the leading units of 90 Panzer Grenadier Division, returning from its useless move into Liguria. The elements of ten German divisions were now in the line. By the end of 18 September the British and Canadian corps had cleared their Phase II objectives and were struggling across another stream, the Ausa, covered by German positions on the last low ridge before the plains began—the Ceriano–San Fortunato spur.

The third phase began on 19 September. The Canadians made progress round the outskirts of Rimini, eventually subduing the defenders of San Fortunato, but V (Br) Corps was not so successful. It had been intended to use 1 (Br) Armoured Division to exploit a break-through, but as there was no sign of this, the armoured division was brought up to attack Ceriano (not to be confused with Coriano) with 56 (Br) Division. There was only one ford over the Ausa, which both divisions had to use, and this delayed 1 (Br) Armoured Division's forward move. In the meantime, 56 (Br) Division had managed to reach the Ceriano ridge but had been heavily counter-attacked by 90 Panzer Grenadier Division. On 20 September the armoured brigade of 1 (Br) Armoured Division attacked to help 56 (Br) Division and ran into a hail of high velocity anti-tank fire on the reverse slopes of the ridge. The armoured regiments fought on with great gallantry, losing a very large number of tanks, but were forced in the end to give up. The Canadian successes at San Fortunato now started to endanger the German divisions opposing V (Br) Corps and next day, 21 September, the Germans abandoned their positions. They blew up their installations in Rimini and as they pulled back to their next defence line on the River Uso, the Rubicon of the ancient Romans, pouring rain covered their retreat.

Olive was over: Eighth Army had reached its promised land—the Po Valley—but the cost had been high. As many as 250 tanks had been lost to enemy action and a further 230 had been bogged or suffered mechanical failure beyond the repair capabilities of divisional workshops; infantry casualties had been so severe that all the British reinforcements in the Italian theatre had been absorbed and battalions had to be reduced from four to three companies for the next six months; 1 (Br) Armoured Division had to be virtually disbanded, its headquarters remaining in being, but its units being dispersed to make up other formations; and one brigade of 56 (Br) Division was reduced to cadre and withdrawn from the line.

As the leading patrols of V (Br) Corps and the Canadian Corps felt their way forward into the plain, the promised land turned into a green nightmare of rivers, dykes and soft water meadows. The rain poured down concealing the escape of the German rearguards which withdrew in good order protected by well prepared belts of demolitions and mines.

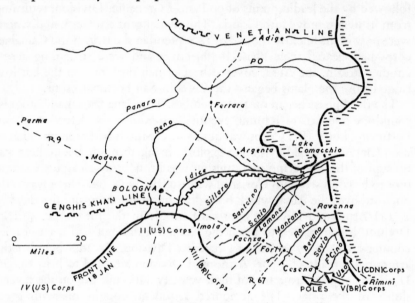

50   The German defence lines in the Po Valley

The Plain of the Romanga north of Route 9 was lush, agricultural land reclaimed over the centuries from the marshes which surround the Po Delta. Across it ran 13 major rivers which rise in the Apennines and flow north-eastwards across the plain into the River Reno or direct into the Adriatic between Rimini and Lake Comacchio. These rivers ran in dredged and embanked channels, the flood banks of which could rise as high as 40 feet above the surrounding fields. The land between the rivers was flat and drained by an intricate network of deep irrigation ditches. Few of the rivers or dykes were fordable, especially in winter, and most of them were tank obstacles. The soil was clay which baked hard in summer but becomes greasy and slippery after a shower of rain, and in winter formed a thick glutinous mud which bogged men and vehicles alike.

South of Route 9 the spurs of the Apennines ran down to the road, presenting the familiar picture which Eighth Army had become so used to in the Sangro battles of the previous autumn and in the recent Olive battles. The rivers were fordable here; the problem was how to scale the steep spurs between them from which the German defenders could cover every crossing. It was tempting to suggest wide turning movements through the hills and on the upper reaches of these rivers, but the ground rose so precipitously to the Apennine watershed and had so few good roads or tracks crossing the grain of the ridges that outflanking operations were not as easy as it might appear on the map.

Such was the land over which the Eighth Army had hoped to do great execution with its tanks. It had exchanged mountains for rivers and mud, and was to fight its coming Battle of the Rivers for six long wet months.

Kesselring realized that, if Eighth Army succeeded in forcing its way through the Romanga to link up with Fifth Army at Bologna, all German troops in north-western Italy would be endangered. The Allies might break out across the Po north of Ferrara and reach Lake Garda before the German troops to the west could be withdrawn to safety behind the Adige. He proposed to OKW that detailed withdrawal plans should be made for such an eventuality and these were codenamed 'Autumn Mist'. Appreciating that such a withdrawal was likely to be vetoed by Hitler, he set about preparing defences in depth across the Po Valley. Opposite Eighth Army, each of the many river lines was prepared for defence. The final line in this sector ran from Lake Comacchio along the Idice, covering Bologna from the east, and then into the Apennines, covering Bologna, Modena and Parma from the south. This was known as the 'Ghengis Khan' Line. The next line ran along the Po itself, but as this line would probably prove to be too long for effective resistance, a shorter and stronger position was built up on the Adige, called the 'Venetian' Line.

In Eighth Army's headquarters opinion was divided as to whether the Germans were leaving Italy or preparing to stand until the full force of the winter weather brought the Allies to a halt as it had done in front of Cassino. Agents' reports showed unusually large movements to the rear, and air reconnaissance revealed the preparations being made for the defence of the Venetian Line. Until Kesselring's intentions were clear, it was essential to keep up the pressure however unsuitable the weather and topography might be. The Canadian Corps, reinforced by 2 (NZ) Division, was to fight its way up the coast along Route 16 and V (Br) Corps was to work up Route 9 towards Bologna. The Polish Corps would be moved up if the German opposition stiffened. During the last week of September, the leading corps made steady but tedious progress. The Uso position was breached on 26 September, and by 29 September both corps were up to the Fiumicino, when four days' heavy rain brought operations to a muddy halt. Not only was it difficult to get forward against the German positions, it was impossible to move up fresh formations or supplies as many of the bridges behind Eighth Army's front had not yet been weather-proofed and were washed away by the river floods. The Polish Corps was ordered up on 29 September, but its move had to be cancelled due to loss of bridges on its route forward. The Germans took full advantage of the respite given them by the weather and withdrew a number of their divisions from the line to rest or to help 1 Para Corps defeat Fifth Army.

Mark Clark's second offensive, this time directed down Route 65, started on 2 October. XIII (Br) Corps took over the Imola axis, using 78 (Br) Division, which had just arrived back from resting and refitting in the Middle East as part of the British garrison. This enabled II (US) Corps to concentrate for the next attack which was made with all four (US) infantry divisions in line on a broad front. Each division was to hold one regiment in reserve and was to rotate regiments at five-day intervals, the roads, tracks and weather being so bad that it was impossible to pass divisions through each other. Each division had to fight its way forward from one mountain feature to the next, operating almost regardless of its neighbours, which were moving up entirely separate valleys and ridges. II (US) Corps Headquarters was only able to co-ordinate attacks at the five-day intervals when the fresh regiments were committed. The average advance per day turned out to be about a mile on the map but to the men on the ground it represented repeated climbs and descents of many hundreds of feet. The climax of the offensive came after three weeks' bitter fighting. On 20 October 88 (US) Division scaled and captured the Monte Grande Massif, only five miles from Route 9, and on 23 October 34 (US) Division took Monte Belmonte, nine miles from the centre of Bologna. By this time the Germans had reinforced 1 Para Corps and II (US) Corps was faced by 11 German divisions which stubbornly resisted its further advance on Bologna. 16 SS Panzer Division had moved across from the west coast; 29 and 90 Panzer Grenadier Divisions and 1 Para Division had arrived from Eighth Army's front, and three infantry divisions had been drawn in from elsewhere in northern Italy. Kesselring had been seriously hurt in a car accident on 25 October and had been replaced by von Vietinghoff who was determined to repeat his previous year's successful defence of the Gustav Line, this time holding Bologna instead of Cassino. General Herr of LXXVI Panzer Corps became Tenth Army Commander. II (US) Corps was by now too exhausted by its great effort to break through. On 27 October Alexander agreed with Mark Clark that the offensive should be halted until Eighth Army could draw off some of the German divisions which had packed the front against Fifth Army.

Oliver Leese had handed over command of Eighth Army to General McCreery on 1 October to take up a new appointment in Burma. McCreery had been commanding X (Br) Corps in the mountains and so felt that the best way to defeat the Germans in the Romanga was to turn their lines by a series of left hooks through the hills south of Route 9. The next Eighth Army offensive, which was to have been concurrent with Mark Clark's drive down Route 65, had been timed to open on 6/7 October, weather permitting; but weather had not permitted. Rain had been continuous and had stopped all movement in the plain. 10 (Ind) Division of X (Br) Corps, however, had made good progress through the hills, supporting McCreery's inclination to try the left flank for larger turning movements. The Polish Corps, which in the past had also found left hooks profitable, had been deployed to the south of V (Br) Corps and directed to develop a threat to the German mountain flank. This policy had soon proved effective, and between 17 and 21 October the Germans had been forced back to the River Savio, the town of Cesena on Route 9 falling on 19 October. A similar manoeuvre had started against the Savio Line, but this time the Poles had made slower progress and V (Br) Corps on Route 9 had been strongly opposed. On 24 October, however, the Germans had made one of their few voluntary withdrawals. Fifth Army's successes south of Bologna had compelled them to transfer their three mobile divisions (29, 90 and 1 Para Divisions) to meet the American threat, and to shorten their line they fell back to the Ronco.

V (Br) Corps and the Canadians reached the Ronco on 25 October and managed to seize bridgeheads over the river. During 26 October all the bridges over the Savio were swept away behind them and the Germans counter-attacked and destroyed their bridgehead over the Ronco. Eighth Army was entering one of the most discouraging periods of its existence. The whole of its sector was becoming a rain-soaked morass; its numerical strength was declining as reinforcements were not keeping up with losses, which were being increased by weather as well as by German action; and to make matters worse the withdrawal of 4 (Ind) Division for operations in Greece* was setting a new pattern which was to cost Eighth Army another two divisions before the New Year.

At the end of October Alexander's armies had shot their bolt and Bologna still lay beyond their reach. It was time to look for other ways of breaking the second winter stalemate which stared them in the face.

* The British entered Athens in the wake of the German withdrawal on 14 October and found themselves involved in the Greek civil war which broke out between the Royalist and Communist forces in the wake of the German evacuation of the Balkans.

16

The Second Winter
of Disappointment

'... it has been decided to withdraw from your theatre to the
Western Front up to five divisions ...'
Extract from Combined Chiefs of Staff Directive to Alexander,
after the 'Argonaut' conference in Malta, 3 February 1945

The second winter of the Italian campaign was one of disappointment
rather than disillusion. There was no doubt in the minds of Alexander and
his staff that another winter campaign would be as frustrating and
debilitating as the fighting around Cassino. It was essential to halt offensive
operations as soon as the Allied armies began to falter, and to use the
winter months for rest and refitting for an early spring offensive. Further
away from the front thinking was quite different: Germany seemed to be
on the brink of collapse; one more thrust might end the war. Any thought
of halting when victory seemed so near was repugnant to the planners
in far away Washington and London. Even Maitland Wilson's headquarters outside Naples—relatively near the front—was not immune from
over-optimism. Moreover, the various motives in Allied strategic
thinking about the Italian Campaign became more mixed than ever.
Churchill was no longer looking upon it as an attack on Germany through
the 'soft under-belly'; the Plain of Lombardy offered the shortest route
to forestalling the Russians in Vienna which was almost more important
to him now than crushing Hitler in Berlin. The Americans clung fiercely
to their policy of restricting the power of the diversionary theatre to sap
the main front in North-West Europe. A new threat to Eisenhower's
operations began to well up in their minds. If Alexander forced Kesselring back, or if Kesselring withdrew voluntarily to the Venetian Line,

the Germans would be able to switch up to a dozen divisions from Italy to the Western Front. It might be better to forestall this possibility by moving Allied divisions from Italy to France straight away.

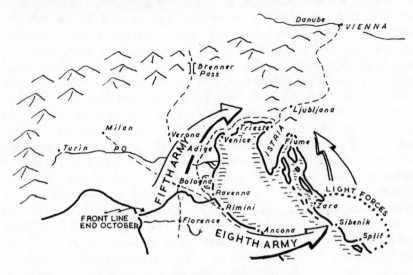

51   Alexander's trans-Adriatic plans

Alexander, quite naturally, still foresaw great possibilities for his theatre if only he could persuade his masters to let him have the necessary resources. As soon as Kesselring fell back across the Po, he would like to leave Fifth Army to pursue him over the Adige while Eighth Army crossed the Adriatic and advanced through northern Yugoslavia to meet the Fifth Army in a great pincers movement at the Ljubljana Gap for an advance on Vienna. If all went well he would destroy Kesselring's forces in the trap between his two armies and he would achieve Churchill's dearest wish of entering Vienna ahead of the Russians.

Nearer the front less optimistic views were held. Mark Clark and McCreery were struggling with the more practical problems of taking Bologna and Ravenna which they would need as supply bases for the winter and their Spring offensives. They also needed the towns and villages of Lombardy and the Romanga to shelter their men during the winter pause. The prospect of spending the months of December to March in the snow and sleet of the Apennines held few attractions for anyone. Even if the army commanders themselves hoped that the war would be over before the spring, many of their officers and men were not so optimistic. Having come this far they were determined to survive the war, but the Germans in front of them showed no signs of giving up. Losses on the Il Giogo and Futa Passes and at Coriano had been higher than at any other phase in the campaign, while the flow of reinforcements to the theatre was at its lowest. Commanders appreciated that they must use shells rather than men to drive the Germans back. In consequence, ammunition expenditure rose just at a time when a world-wide shortage of American and British gun ammunition started to make itself felt. Miscalculations months before had led to a reduction of Allied field artillery ammunition production, and the cut-back unfortunately coincided with the peak demands from Eisenhower and Alexander for their autumn and winter battles. Italy, being the lower priority theatre, was the worst hit by the shortage. Early in November Alexander's logistic staff advised him that Eighth Army could only fight at intense rates for a further 15 days and Fifth Army would only be able to manage ten days of offensive action. A further symptom of this 'end of war' psychosis appeared in the figures for desertions from Allied divisions which began to rise as the winter approached. As far as the British soldiers were concerned, the death sentence for desertion had been replaced by penal servitude. Most soldiers believed that there would be an amnesty after the war and so it was preferable to desert and survive rather than stand another winter in the mountains, taking part in hopeless attacks on strongly held German positions. They knew nothing about the impending ammunition shortage, but they could sense the uselessness of throwing away their lives when the Russians and Eisenhower's armies were doing the job for them and much more successfully. It should not be taken from this that the morale of the Fifth and Eighth Armies was low. It was not; but there were limits to what men would endure unless they could see a worthwhile prize at the end of all their efforts. The concept of crossing the Adriatic and arriving as a victorious army in Vienna would have fired their enthusiasm; slogging away through the Romanga or the hills south of Bologna had few attractions for the commanders or their soldiers.

In the middle of September, while the Gothic battles were being fought out, Churchill, Roosevelt and their Combined Chiefs of Staff met for the second time at Quebec for the 'Octagon' conference. Their primary concern was to co-ordinate plans for the quick defeat of Germany and the redeployment of resources into the Pacific and Indian Ocean areas to crush Japan. For once, the Italian theatre caused little controversy. The Americans accepted that no more troops should be taken away from Italy to reinforce North-West Europe until the Germans had been defeated south of the Po. This was not because they had begun to favour the Italian theatre; it was because Eisenhower did not need any further reinforcements until all the new US divisions earmarked in the United States had reached him.

The American Chiefs of Staff no longer objected to an advance on Ljubljana because there were now good military as well as political reasons for doing so. Dragoon had made it pointless to turn north-westwards from Italy into France. The logical direction for attack was north-eastwards into Austria. They were even prepared to leave their assault shipping in the Mediterranean for an amphibious attack on Istria to help Alexander's advance over the Adige to Ljubljana. Maitland Wilson was instructed to submit plans for such an operation by 10 October, so that a decision on how much assault shipping should be kept in the Mediterranean could be taken by 15 October.

The premise on which the Combined Chiefs of Staff took these decisions was that Alexander's armies would be on the Adige in a matter of weeks. This and subsequent planning assumptions made during the autumn were soon falsified by events. The gap between plans and reality was at its widest during Octagon. As the months went by, this gap gradually narrowed as truer assessments of German capabilities were made, or perhaps it might be more accurate to say as German capabilities shrank under constant air and land attack to the level of Allied estimates. There were four phases in this process of falsifying assumptions and of bringing plans for ending the war nearer to reality. Each stage brought another disappointment to the Italian theatre.

The first stage in the falsification of the Octagon assumptions started before September was over. In Italy 15 Army Group did not break through to the Po; in North-West Europe Montgomery was defeated at Arnhem; and on the Eastern Front the Russians suffered setbacks in East Prussia and on the Danube. It was clear that the war would not end without another major Allied offensive. When Churchill visited Alexander at the beginning of October on his way to Moscow to meet Stalin, Alexander explained to him in some detail the effects which lack of resources, caused initially by the withdrawals from Fifth Army for Dragoon and latterly by his heavy losses in the Gothic battles, was having on his operations. He also presented his ideas for a spring offensive across the Adriatic which he believed would be necessary as the war showed no signs of ending. These plans, though not their timing, appealed to the Prime Minister, who cabled to the President asking him to consider the diversion to Italy of three US divisions earmarked for Eisenhower. After Churchill left for Moscow Alexander issued his first directive to his army commanders setting out his thoughts on his trans-Adriatic operation. With greater realism than the planners had displayed at Quebec, he pointed out that, with the opposing forces in Italy being so evenly matched, the Army Group would be exhausted by the time it reached the Adige and would have to pause for some weeks to rest and refit before it could mount a new offensive to carry it into Austria. He would decide when the halt should be called, and when that moment came both armies would go over to the defensive and withdraw their divisions in turn on a timed relief programme for reorganization and retraining. He explained his idea of Fifth Army attacking over the Adige towards Ljubljana from the south-west, while Eighth Army crossed the Adriatic to advance on the same objective from the south-east. He ordered Eighth Army to be ready to withdraw three divisions for amphibious training and both armies to be ready to train their divisions in mountain warfare and river crossing operations. These plans still assumed that 15 Army Group would reach the Adige before the winter.

The second stage of disappointment now began. The President replied to the Prime Minister turning down his suggestion of diverting three new US divisions to Italy on the familiar grounds of not wasting precious resources on the secondary theatre. Hitler also stepped in by refusing Kesselring's request to implement 'Autumn Mist'—the voluntary withdrawal to the Venetian Line. Instead he issued an order of the day, which was to be read to all troops and which soon found its way into Allied hands, demanding the defence of the Apennine Line at all costs. The effect of this order had soon become apparent to Fifth Army when it had been stopped by bitter German resistance ten miles short of Bologna and to Eighth Army in the muddy battles of Romanga. The only bright spots in the dismal autumn scene were Tito's and the Russians' renewed successes in eastern Europe. Kesselring might yet be forced to withdraw to the Venetian Line by the threat to his rear.

At the end of October Alexander issued a new directive taking these new factors into account. Instead of mounting a major amphibious assault across the Adriatic, he proposed to profit by Tito's successes by landing commandos and other light forces in the Dalmatian ports of Split, Sibenik and Zara. Under the cloak of helping the partisans he would develop these ports and their communications inland, ready to receive the main body of Eighth Army which would be moved quickly and secretly across the Adriatic when the time came to open the offensive on Ljubljana. The target date for the operation was set for the beginning of February. If the armies were to be ready by this date, the present operations in Italy would have to stop by 15 November. It would be desirable to have taken Bologna and Ravenna for use as winter bases before calling a halt. The immediate problem was how to take these two objectives in the short time which was left. He proposed to do this by ordering Fifth Army to withdraw two divisions to rest and to simulate the withdrawal of a third, making it known as widely as possible that Fifth Army was too exhausted to attack again for some time. Eighth Army would continue its drive up Routes 9 and 16 hoping to take Ravenna and at the same time drawing the German mobile divisions away from Bologna. As soon as the Germans weakened their forces in front of Fifth Army and provided the weather allowed, Mark Clark was to return his divisions secretly to the line and to re-open his offensive. If this plan failed, the Allies would have to do without these towns for the winter. Eighth Army should, in any case, try to clear the lateral Route 67 from Forli to Florence to improve communications between the two armies.

Alexander discussed these plans with his army commanders on 29 October and on their advice modified the timings. Mark Clark pointed out that his army had suffered 20,000 casualties in the recent offensive and that the flow of American reinforcements would not allow him to replenish his divisions before 30 November. McCreery said that Eighth Army could keep up its pressure on the German defences until 15 December. On this advice Alexander decided that Fifth Army should be ready to attack by 30 November and that operations should stop by about 15 December. He stressed that the final Fifth Army offensive would not be launched unless the weather in the Apennines was favourable and German dispositions showed that there was a real chance of success. He hoped that Eighth Army would be on the Santerno River before Fifth Army attacked.

November brought the third stage of disappointment and reduction in the size of Alexander's plans. Churchill took exception to the suggestion that the next offensive should not open before February. This was much too late for him. 'One of the absurd things', he remarked, 'in all the plans which are submitted by [the Mediterranean Command] is the idea that if they move in February they will be in time to affect anything.' Events in eastern Europe were moving apace but the tide was running against the Western Allies. In Greece the civil war was growing worse, and by the end of the year would have drawn X (Br) Corps with 4 (Br) and 46 (Br) Divisions as well as 4 (Ind) Division away from Eighth Army. In Yugoslavia British prestige with the partisans was on the wane. The rapid Russian advances on Belgrade and Budapest made Tito turn towards his Communist allies, who had no desire to further British and American interests in their future sphere of influence. The chances of developing the Dalmatian ports and passing Eighth Army across the Adriatic with Yugoslav help were fading. Even operations in Italy were going far slower than Churchill had hoped and he began to realize that the great opportunities, which he had been sure existed in the Mediterranean, had been lost for good. The Western Allies had been too slow to seize their chances and now the Italian theatre could no longer produce decisive results. His determination to win his way in the Mediterranean gradually weakened and during the strategic debates at the turn of the year he allowed the American Chiefs of Staff to have their way by default.

In the Romanga, Eighth Army fought its way over the Roneo on 31 October; Forli fell on 9 November and in a brief period of fine weather the Germans were driven back to the Montone (*see* fig. 49). By 16 November Route 67 was clear and preparations were being made to seize the next town on Route 9, Faenza on the Lamone, and to secure a good jumping-off position on Route 16 for an attack on Ravenna. Renewed attacks between 20 and 26 November went well and the Germans were pushed back to the Lamone. On 26 November the rain began again. So far there were no signs of the Germans pulling troops out from in front of Fifth Army opposite Bologna. Unfortunately Eighth Army's advance was tending to shorten the German front, enabling them to hold their line with less troops.

On 22 November Maitland Wilson reported to the Chiefs of Staff that he believed that he would have to confine his efforts to Italy. This was already the view of Churchill and the Combined Chiefs of Staff, who issued him a new directive on 2 December, the gist of which was: the introduction of major forces into the Balkans was no longer favoured; the immediate objective should be the capture of the general line Ravenna–Bologna–Spezia; thereafter the aim should be to contain Kesselring while resting divisions in rotation. Light forces could be introduced into the Balkans to harass the German withdrawal. Any divisions which could be withdrawn from the line in Italy should be constituted as a strategic reserve ready to exploit any promising changes in the tactical situation. The directive ended by saying that the American Chiefs of Staff were sending 10 (US) Mountain Division to help Fifth Army with its relief programme.

In the meantime Maitland Wilson had been nominated to take the late Field Marshal Dill's place in Washington, and Alexander, promoted Field-Marshal, took over Supreme Command in the Mediterranean. Mark Clark took over the Army Group and Truscott came back from France to take over Fifth Army. These changes in command, however, did nothing to halt the contraction in the 15 Army Group plans.

The fourth stage in the approach to reality started with a failure to launch Fifth Army in its final autumn offensive to take Bologna. At Alexander's last conference as Army Group Commander it was agreed that Fifth Army's offensive should be delayed until 7 December. By that time Eighth Army hoped to be in a position to reach Imola and the Santerno River. Everything would depend on the weather and the movement of German reserves. Another fine spell enabled Eighth Army to attack again on 2 December. The Canadians outflanked and took

Ravenna on 4 December, while V (Br) Corps with Polish support in the hills to the south reached the outskirts of Faenza on 7 December. Von Vietinghoff decided that co-ordination of the German defence would be easier if he gave his Tenth Army sole responsibility for both active sectors now that Eighth Army was getting so near to Bologna on Route 9. He shifted the German inter-army boundary westwards giving Tenth Army command of the four corps* holding the line between the Adriatic

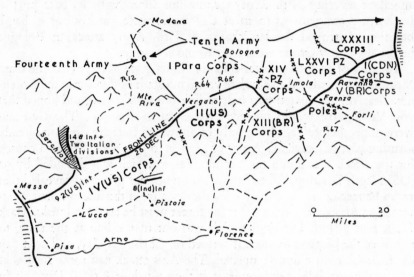

52   The German counter-attack on the Serchio

and the western side of Fifth Army's salient, pointing at Bologna. Four-teenth Army was left responsible for the quiet western Apennine sector. On 8 December the first move of a mobile division from Bologna to Eighth Army's front occurred. 90 Panzer Grenadier Division moved over to counter-attack V (Br) Corps at Faenza. It suffered severely in the action but managed to delay the British advance. It was then joined by 98 Division but neither was strong enough to stop V (Br) Corps and the Poles when they attacked again on 12 December. Faenza fell on 16 December and the Germans were forced to commit a second mobile division from Bologna. 29 Panzer Grenadier Division came over to help stabilize the next defensive line on the Senio River half-way between Faenza and Eighth Army's next objective—Imola on the Santerno. It looked as if the conditions required for Fifth Army's offensive were

* A new corps (LXXIII) was brought into the line to hold the extreme eastern flank near Lake Comacchio.

beginning to materialize although rather later than Alexander had hoped. Controlling operations from the Supreme Headquarters, he decided that Fifth Army should attack as soon as the Eighth Army crossed the Senio instead of waiting until it reached the Santerno. Fifth Army was ordered to be ready to attack at 48 hours' notice from 22 December. Soon afterwards, intelligence reports started to come in suggesting that the Germans were planning a counter-offensive in the quiet Fourteenth Army sector aimed at severing Fifth Army's communications with its base port at Leghorn. Arrangements to meet this threat were quickly put in hand, but they destroyed the last chance of Fifth Army attacking Bologna before the Army Group went over to the defensive.

The idea of an Axis counter-offensive in Italy seems to have come from Mussolini who wished to emulate von Rundstedt's offensive in the Ardennes. Graziani nominated two Italian divisions to take part and hoped that von Vietinghoff would provide two German divisions. The Germans were not so helpful, agreeing only to allow the German division already forming part of Graziani's Army of Liguria to take part. The area chosen for the attack was down the Serchio Valley which was defended by 92 (US) Negro Division. Allied interrogation of Axis prisoners revealed that 16 SS Panzer Division was being withdrawn from the line and sent westwards, so Alexander decided that the threat must be taken seriously. Mark Clark sent 8 (Ind) Division, which was out of the line at the time, to reinforce the Negro Division. It arrived on Christmas Day, and next day the Italo-German offensive opened. The Axis attack had some success at first against 92 (US) Division, but it then ran into 8 (Ind) Division in hastily dug positions. 85 (US) Division and 1 (US) Armoured Division were ordered to reinforce but these moves proved unnecessary. The Germans soon realized that the appearance of 8 (Ind) Division meant that surprise had been lost. 8 (Ind) Division counter-attacked, retaking the lost ground. Mussolini's last pathetic attempt to influence the war was over, but so was Fifth Army's last offensive of 1944. Eighth Army had reached the Senio and had used most of its meagre ammunition allotment in doing so. It could not now support a Fifth Army offensive even if one could be launched in time. Moreover, the Allies knew that the Germans had built up a central reserve of one panzer, one mountain and two infantry divisions in the Bologna area. Alexander decided the time had come to go over to the defensive and to start the winter rest and retraining programme.

Allied confidence in an early end to the war had been shaken by von Rundstedt's offensive in the Ardennes and the episode on the Serchio. The joint planners started to scrutinize the opposing orders of battle in the French and Italian theatres. By mid-April they expected 91 Allied divisions to be opposing 90 German divisions on the Western Front and

24 Allied divisions to be holding 27 German divisions in Italy. Neither theatre would have a decisive superiority, so they recommended the transfer of between six and ten divisions from the Mediterranean to France. Their first estimate of how long this would take was put at ten weeks per division. Churchill's reaction to this was that the move would deny these divisions to Alexander and would not give them to Eisenhower in time to be any use on the Western Front. However, when the Combined Chiefs of Staff met in Malta at the end of January on their way to Yalta, the planners reduced their estimate, on Eisenhower's advice, to six weeks per division. This made all the difference: six divisions could be shifted in time to take part in what was hoped would be the final offensive against Germany in North-West Europe. Churchill was running a high temperature at the time and so did not take part in the discussions about the Italian theatre, but on 31 January Alan Brooke was able to inform the meeting that the Prime Minister had agreed to the transfer of three divisions from Italy at once and two later when they could be relieved by divisions from Greece. A new directive was sent to Alexander informing him of this decision and reducing the role of his theatre to holding the front already gained, containing the Germans with limited offensive action and preparing for a more extensive advance if Kesselring withdrew. Minor operations could also be undertaken on the eastern shores of the Adriatic.

The fourth stage in the contraction of Allied operational plans thus reduced the Italian theatre to its lowest ebb. The Canadian Government had wished to concentrate all its divisions in North-West Europe for some time. The opportunity was therefore taken to meet their wishes and the Canadian Corps was secretly withdrawn from Eighth Army's front and despatched to the Canadian Army in Belgium, where it appeared in due course without the Germans being aware of its departure from Italy. With it went two fighter groups from 12 (US) Air Force. Alexander and his Army Group and Army commanders were naturally disappointed with this turn of events, but they now knew where they stood. They could start planning their final spring offensive with the same skill and efficiency which had gone into Diadem.

17

Their Just Reward

'Indeed the last battle in Italy was as hard as the first. I was not faced with a broken and disintegrated army nor was the outcome influenced in any degree by demoralization or lack of supplies on the German side. It was a straightforward military operation which, by first enveloping the enemy's left wing in a classic out-flanking manoeuvre and then breaking through with a sudden blow in his weakened centre, drove him against the Po and annihilated him there.'

Alexander's Despatches (p. 2,959)

Alexander and his senior commanders remained determined to destroy Kesselring's armies in spite of these setbacks. They had fought him too long to give up now and they were certainly not going to miss being in at the kill when Germany finally collapsed. January, February and March became months of detailed planning, reorganization and retraining. Alexander was resolved not to make the costly mistakes of the previous year by going on fighting too long. Only limited operations designed to secure suitable start-lines for the spring offensive were to be allowed. Fronts were to be held with the minimum number of troops, while divisions left the line on a phased programme to rest and retrain for what was to be their last great offensive. Every effort was made to fill the gaps amongst and within divisions by bringing in troops from elsewhere in the Mediterranean and by ruthlessly cutting down rear headquarters and administrative echelons to provide reinforcements. The Jewish brigade arrived from the Middle East; the Brazilian Expeditionary Division arrived from South America; the 10 (US) Mountain Division came from the United States; two new Polish brigades were formed; 56 (Br) Division was brought up to three brigades again; and five Italian combat groups were formed to help hold the quiet sectors of the front. In addition a num-

29 'Fantails' crossing the flooded area around Lake Comacchio

BATTLE OF THE RIVERS

30 Eighth Army tanks crossing the Savio River over assault engineer Arks;
a derelict German tank lies to the left

31 Von Senger reports, requesting instructions for the surrender of Army Group 'C', to the Allied Commanders—McCreery (left), Mark Clark (centre) and Truscott (right)

THE END

32 German prisoners from Army Group 'C'

ber of Italian partisan bands started to play an active part; the 28th
Garibaldi Brigade came into the line south of Lake Comacchio and the
36th Garibaldi Brigade helped hold part of XIII (Br) Corps' mountain
sector. Using these and many other improvisations, 15 Army Group's
strength was raised to make good part of the loss of the Canadian Corps.*

In the equipment field a great deal was done as well. The new 'Kangaroo' armoured personnel carriers were introduced. These were Sherman
tanks with the turrets removed and the crew compartment enlarged to

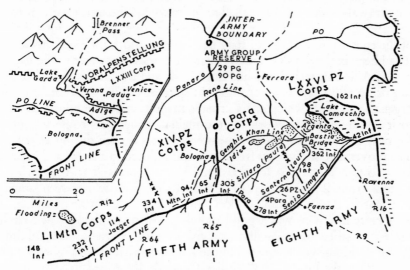

53   The German dispositions and defence lines, end of March 1945

carry infantry. Duplex Drive amphibious tanks arrived and the theatre
was offered some 400 landing vehicles, tracked, codenamed 'Fantails'.
The Duplex Drive tanks had already been used in Overlord and the LVTs
(Landing Vehicles, Tracked) had been operated successfully by the
Americans in the Pacific and by the Canadian Army in Belgium during
the autumn when they had been called 'Buffaloes'. The armoured
regiments were re-equipped with flame-thrower tanks, up-gunned
Sherman and Churchill tanks, and with tank-dozers. Some of their tanks
were fitted with widened 'platypus' tracks to enable them to move over
the soft fields of the Romanga. New armoured engineer equipment was

* Although the Chiefs of Staff originally ordered five divisions to move out of Italy
to France, only the two Canadian divisions actually did so. The others were provided
from elsewhere in the Mediterranean and Middle East from divisions destined for Italy
as part of the routine relief programme.

also produced within the theatre for rapidly bridging ditches, canals and rivers. All these new equipments and devices needed specially trained crews to man them and new tactical techniques. In the rear areas, particularly round Lake Trasimene, intensive experimental work and training went on throughout the winter.

Kesselring returned to command Army Group 'C' in the New Year, just in time to resist increasing pressure from OKW for the release of divisions to reinforce the Eastern and Western Fronts. His persuasiveness and the physical difficulty of moving divisions out of Italy reduced the withdrawals which OKW wished to make when it became clear that Fifth and Eighth Armies had gone over to the defensive. Allied air interdiction of the routes into and out of Italy had become much more effective than it had been in the days of Anzio. Allied air bases were nearer to the Alpine passes; Allied air techniques had improved; and the Luftwaffe had ceased to put up any effective opposition. In spite of the most elaborate repair organization with which the Germans made remarkable efforts to keep their communications working, the main Brenner Pass route was open for only five days and the north-easterly routes for ten during February. The movement of divisions from Italy was reduced to a crawl and became very costly. When 356 Infantry Division was ordered to move to the Eastern Front, it took 15 days to clear the Italian frontier. Between January and March, Army Group 'C' lost four divisions, only one of which, 16 SS Panzer Division, was a good mobile division. At the end of March, there were still 23 German divisions, five of which were mobile, and three Italian divisions which equated to the Italian combat groups raised by the Allies. Thus the loss of the Canadian Corps on the Allied side was amply compensated for by transfers out of Italy on the German side, but the latter were not as large as OKW would have liked or as large as the American Chiefs of Staff had feared.

Kesselring's strategic position still had many parallels with his position the previous winter. His present front line had, like the Gustav Line, survived the Allied autumn assaults, but was unlikely to withstand another offensive launched by the rested Allied armies in dry spring weather. It had none of the natural and artificial defensive strength of the Gustav Line. It was the line on which his troops happened to be clinging when Alexander decided to halt for the winter. While Alexander's troops were retraining and re-equipping, Kesselring's divisions were working hard to strengthen their defences and there was a chance that the depth of the positions which they were creating might make up for lack of fixed defences. To increase this depth he strengthened a number of the delaying positions based on the Romanga rivers and upon the ridges of hills which still lay between Fifth Army and Bologna. There was the 'Irmgard'

Line on the Senio, and 'Laura' Line on the Santerno, the 'Paula' on the Sillaro and the 'Ghengis Khan' Line covering Bologna itself. Behind these lines there was the Reno River Line which can be compared with the Hitler Line of the previous year. It ran from Lake Comacchio north-westwards and parallel to Route 9 forming an ideal backstop to interrupt any Allied penetration of the present positions. Behind the Reno came the Po, which took the place of the Caesar Line south of Rome. It was too long a line for protracted defence and so most of its defences were designed to help retreating German divisions to cross it in good order rather than to defeat Allied attempts to cross. In the Gothic Line's place came the Venetian Line on the Adige. This line was far more important to Hitler than the Gothic had been because it was destined to become the glacis protecting the southern wall of his National Redoubt. The Adige (or Venetian) Line ran from Lake Garda eastwards along the foothills of the Alps to the middle reaches of the Adige and thence along that river to the Adriatic. The line of the Alpine foothills running north-east on the inland side of the Venetian Plain had the grandiloquent but expressive title of 'Voralpenstellung'—the Forward Alpine Defences of the National Redoubt (see fig. 53). The Adige Line and the Voralpenstellung were being con- structed under the direction of a special Voralpen command headed by General Jordan; the actual defensive works being constructed by the Inspector of Land Fortifications, South-West, General Buelowius, with 5,000 German fortification specialists and many thousand impressed Italian workers under the Todt organization. The Germans went as far as removing coastal guns from the Ligurian coast to mount them in the Redoubt. All Army Group 'C's' major administrative installations were moved behind the Adige, leaving the minimum quantities of essential stocks south of the Po. The withdrawal plan Autumn Mist, which Kesselring had asked to implement in October, was revised and developed. None of the German commanders in Italy had any illusions about the prospect of holding the Allies south of the Po. Their only chance of surviving to fight for another summer was to conduct a slow and skilful withdrawal behind the Adige. All the preparations were made for such a withdrawal. The crucial question was whether Hitler would allow Kesselring to order Autumn Mist in time to withdraw his troops across the Po without losing too many from Allied air attack on this great ob- stacle, which might turn out to be a death trap rather than a shield.

A number of important changes in command and deployment occurred during the winter on the German side. Kesselring was as nervous as ever about his flanks, which could still be turned by amphibious assault. The fact that the Allies had no reasonable objectives on his western flank, and that an amphibious landing north of the Po on his eastern flank was almost a physical impossibility due to shallow water and false beaches, did little to reduce his fears of another Anzio-type operation. He decided that he must cover the Adriatic more strongly and so he moved the inter-army boundary back to the east of Bologna. Fourteenth Army was made responsible for opposing Fifth Army with LI Mountain and XIV Panzer Corps, which changed places, bringing the experienced von Senger into the important sector in front of Bologna. Tenth Army's responsibility was to oppose Eighth Army in the Romanga and to cover the Venetian shore north of the Po. The Army Group front was too long to allow Kesselring to withdraw all his mobile divisions into reserve as he had done during the previous spring. 1 and 4 Para Divisions and 26 Panzer Division remained in the line; and 29 and 90 Panzer Grenadier Divisions were held in reserve ready to move to either flank.

In the last week of March, Hitler appointed Kesselring Commander-in-Chief, West, in place of von Runstedt. Von Vietinghoff returned from commanding the German forces in Courland, where he had been sent when Kesselring had returned to Italy in January, to take over Army Group 'C'. His experience on the Baltic coast made him appreciate how lucky he was to be back in Italy. Under his command he had an unbroken and confident force which had not been engaged in major operations for three months. Its divisions were up to strength, well trained and rested. As a fighting force, Army Group 'C' was the best formation left in the German Army. His front was solidly held and his reserve defence lines well developed. He had two good panzer Grenadier divisions in reserve which was exactly equal to the reserve that Kesselring found available on the much larger Western Front. His number of serviceable tanks equated to the whole of the panzer resources of Kesselring's new command. In the line were 1 and 4 Para Divisions, by far the best divisions left in the Reich. His infantry divisions too were real divisions and not just scratch battle groups masquerading as divisions as they were on other German fronts. Logistically he was well supported also. The temporary bridges and ferries over the Po were working efficiently and Allied interdiction was in many ways helping rather than hindering him because OKW could not withdraw resources from him. He had enough ammunition, equipment and food. His Achilles' heel lay in motor fuel. Like all the other German fronts at that time, he had barely enough fuel to withdraw if he was allowed to do so.

Alexander's aim was the destruction of the German armies south of the Po. Looking at the German dispositions and the topography of the Lombard Plain, one factor stood out. The River Reno, into which all the German defence lines were keyed, rises in the Apennines south-west of Bologna and flows down the east side of Route 64 skirting west of the city to a point some 20 miles to the north where in a wide sweeping curve it turns eastward and flows into the Adriatic just south of Lake Comacchio, thus obstructing Eighth Army's path. North of the Reno there are very few obstacles between it and the Po, and the road network between the two rivers was reasonably good. Two deductions were drawn from this factor. The first was that Fifth Army should attack west of the

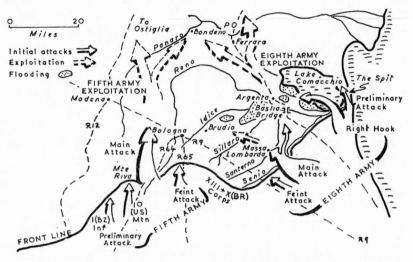

54 Plans for the last Allied offensive

Reno to avoid becoming entangled in its web. This would have the additional advantage of bringing the American thrust line to the west of the very deep German defences around Bologna. The only difficulty in doing this was the fact that the main American salient from which the attack would be launched was astride Route 65 and not on Route 64. Preliminary operations would have to be carried out to bring their positions on Route 64 further over the Apennines and level with those on Route 65. The second deduction concerned Eighth Army. Rather than continuing its attack westwards over the Reno's successive tributaries, upon each of which there was a German defence line, Eighth Army's main thrust should be directed northwards across the Reno itself as near the coast as possible. The best route for this purpose crossed the Reno at the Bastia bridge and led north-westwards to the village of Argenta and on to the Ferrara stretch of the Po in which there were a number of good crossing sites. The main attraction of this thrust line was that it would break through the hinge upon which the German armies would have to pivot as they withdrew to the Adige, and it would enable Eighth Army to cut off all German divisions south of the Po by an advance along its south bank to Bondeno. Again there was a snag as there was with the Fifth Army's proposed axis. The route lay through the very narrow gap between Lake Comacchio and extensive flooding which had been deliberately carried out by the Germans south-west of Bastia. The gap had been further reduced by flooding the fields on the southern shore of Lake Comacchio as well. This gap, which became known as the Argenta Gap, was sure to be mined and would be easily blocked if the Germans appreciated that this was to be Eighth Army's line of attack.

Fifth Army's problem was solved by the arrival of 10 (US) Mountain Division. In order to give it battle experience, an operation was mounted in the middle of February to bring the Fifth Army front forward west of and astride Route 64. 10 (US) Mountain Division supported by 1 Brazilian Division executed a brilliant operation, clearing several very high peaks including roping a whole battalion up the precipitous 3,000-foot Riva Ridge (see fig. 54). So successful were they that the Germans hastily committed 29 Panzer Grenadier Division to stabilize this part of their front. By that time, however, Fifth Army had secured the start-line which it needed for its main offensive west of Bologna.

Eighth Army's problem was not so easily solved. Not only was it difficult to reach the Argenta Gap across the Reno and the floods, it was also essential not to draw the Germans' attention to the area. A parachute operation was one possible answer, but the air forces considered that the anti-aircraft defences around Bastia were too strong. They suggested that it might be possible to destroy these guns by fighter-bomber attack just before the parachute drop but Alexander considered this too great a risk. The Fantails offered another solution. The difficulty with them was that their capabilities were not fully known in the theatre and their arrival might be too late for the operation. It was therefore decided that, although plans should be made to force the Argenta Gap using Fantails across Lake Comacchio and the floods, an alternative plan should be worked out.

The whole of Eighth Army could not possibly advance through the Argenta Gap, so another thrust line would be needed in any case. There were three possibilities: an advance from the XIII (Br) Corps sector in the Apennines to turn the Romanga river lines from the south; an advance up Route 9; or an advance between Route 9 and the Reno on a secondary road through Massa Lombarda to Brudio north-east of Bologna. The first was impracticable because there were not enough roads to allow a major force to operate. The second was blocked by two of the best divisions in the German Army—4 Para and 26 Panzer Divisions—and was the most obvious and most heavily defended axis. The third possibility had several advantages. It was not so heavily defended. The Senio River's course curved into Eighth Army's positions offering a suitable salient for a river crossing operation. A successful crossing here, followed by a crossing of the next river—the Santerno—in the same sector, would enable Eighth Army to turn north to Bastia and the Argenta Gap, or to continue westward to Brudio to arrive behind the Bologna defenders. Which axis Eighth Army would take after crossing the Santerno—north to Bastia or west to Brudio—would depend on the tactical situation at the time. McCreery decided that his plan would consist of a right hook across the Lake to Argenta and a main assault across the Senio opposite Massa Lombarda. If the right hook went well he could turn his main thrust northwards to break through the Gap; if, on the other hand, the Fantails proved a failure or something else went wrong with the right hook, he would drive westwards to cut in behind the Bologna defences to help Fifth Army's attack west of Bologna.

The next problem to be solved was how to deceive the Germans on the strategic and tactical level. It was not certain until quite a late stage in planning which army's attack was to be considered the primary thrust. If, as Eighth Army Headquarters assumed, they were to deliver the decisive attack, then Fifth Army should attack first to draw the German reserves westwards. If, as Mark Clark assumed, his old army should be given the honour, then Eighth Army should open the offensive. The difficulties of the Eighth Army front, the uncertainties about the Fantails, and the problem of creating a realistic deception plan all pointed to Eighth Army attacking first. The deception plan would inevitably involve some variation on the theme of amphibious threats to Kesselring's flanks. A threat to Genoa would hardly be plausible; a threat to Istria or Venice would possibly be more credible, but it would bring German reserves nearer to the Adriatic coast than Eighth Army, with the problem of the Argenta Gap on its mind, would have liked. If Alexander had been Army Group Commander instead of Mark Clark, McCreery might have won the day. All the cards, however, were stacked in favour of Fifth Army and so the decision was made by Mark Clark, with Alexander's concurrence, that Eighth Army should attack first about four days before Fifth Army to draw the German reserves eastwards. The deception plan would be to magnify Eighth Army's strength by including an American force in its notional order of battle. It would also include suggestions of an amphibious landing north of the Po by showing landing craft at Ravenna and increased assault shipping at Ancona. These measures should ensure the move of German reserves eastwards away from Fifth Army's point of attack.

At the tactical level, Eighth Army problem was to disguise its right hook across Lake Comacchio by the Fantails and to draw the Germans' attention away from the Massa Lombarda axis of attack. The right hook was to be concealed by taking the 'Spit' which cuts Lake Comacchio off from the sea. An attack here would look like an attempt to reach the Po along the coast in conjunction with amphibious forces. The Massa Lombarda attack was to be disguised by suggesting the main Eighth Army attack was coming down Route 9 as it had done so often during the autumn battles of the river lines. On Fifth Army's front, all the fighting, except for 10 (US) Mountain Division's preliminary attack, had been astride Route 65 directed towards Bologna. It would be relatively simple to suggest that the thrust would come this way again. In any case, by the time Fifth Army attacked, there should be very few German reserves left on the Bologna front.

The last major problem to be solved was that of timing. Rainfall charts, river-flow graphs, mist and visibility records, and agricultural practice in the area, were all studied in detail and the best advice was obtained to decide the optimum time at which to launch the offensive. All factors and views seemed to conflict. When the Romanga rivers were likely to be low, the Po would probably be in flood due to snow melting in the Alps; when the Romanga rivers and the Po were right, river mists would obscure the air forces' visibility; and so on. In general, however, May or June looked the best months from the point of view of the 'going'. The two key factors were soon seen to be the readiness of the Allied divisions, including the availability of Fantails for the right hook, and the timing of the major spring offensives on the Eastern and Western Fronts. The latter were not likely to be mounted before May. If the Italian front was to have a decisive effect on the war, as Alexander and Mark Clark hoped it would, then the Italian offensive would have to be started in April. On the other hand, an attack in April would mean less troops rested and reorganized, fewer Fantails, and perhaps worse conditions in the battle area. After a long debate, 10 April was set as the target date.

The final Army Group Plan was for Eighth Army to open the offensive with a series of minor preliminary operations on Lake Comacchio in preparation for its right hook. Its main attack would then be launched across the Senio and would either turn north through the Argenta Gap or continue in a north-westerly direction to cut in behind Bologna. Fifth Army would attack northwards well to the west of Bologna some four days later. Once the German front had been broken, both armies would co-operate in encircling as many Germans as possible south of the Po, while sending armoured forces northwards across the river to disrupt the manning of the Adige Line. Eighth Army would cross the Po north of Ferrara, aiming for Padua and Istria; and Fifth Army would cross at Ostiglia, aiming for Verona, Lake Garda and the Brenner Pass.

Eighth Army's plan for its last great offensive was appropriately in keeping with the pattern of its traditional set-piece battle. It included, as it had usually done in the desert days, a hook round the exposed German flank, this time a right instead of a left hook. The main attack and right hook were to be undertaken by V (Br) Corps supported by the Polish Corps. XIII (Br) Corps and X (Br) Corps* were to cover the long mountain sector on the southern side of the battlefield.

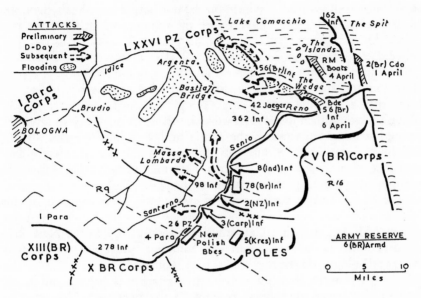

55 Eighth Army's plan for its last offensive

V (Br) Corps entrusted the right hook to 56 (Br) Division with Royal Marine commandos and 2 (Br) Para Brigade in support. On 1 April, 2 (Br) Commando Brigade would capture the Spit and would try to exploit round the north-east side of Lake Comacchio. On 4 April a Royal Marine special boat squadron would seize the islands in the centre of the lake to cover preparations on the south-east corner. On 6 April a brigade of 56 (Br) Division, using storm boats, would capture an area on the southern shore called the 'Wedge' and would gain access to the flooded areas. The Fantails had proved disappointing in the lake itself where the water was too shallow and the bottom too muddy. However, they proved ideal in the flooded areas where the bottom was firmer.

* XIII (Br) Corps reverted to Eighth Army's command during the winter reorganization, and X (Br) Corps returned from Greece in time to take part in the last offensive.

They were, therefore, reserved for the main right hook which was to be launched when V (Br) Corps crossed the Santerno. The right hook was to consist of a drive by a second brigade of 56 (Br) Division across the flooded area in Fantails to attack the Bastia bridge in conjunction with the first brigade advancing from the Wedge. Two or three days later a third brigade would make a wider hook across the lake to attack Argenta in conjunction with a parachute landing by 2 (Br) Para Brigade.

V (Br) Corps' main attack across the Senio would start from a three-divisional front—8 (Ind) Division on the northern flank, 78 (Br) Division in the centre and 2 (NZ) Division on the southern flank. Only the two flank divisions would attack on the first day and would cross the river on either side of the Senio salient. 78 (Br) Division would demonstrate but would not try to force a crossing. On the second day, 8 (Ind) Division and the New Zealanders would advance side by side to the Santerno and would seize a large bridgehead over the river. 78 (Br) Division would then move forward and, passing through 8 (Ind) Division, would strike north towards the Bastia bridge to link up with 56 (Br) Division's right hook. 8 (Ind) Division and the New Zealanders' subsequent action would depend on events. They might cover 78 (Br) Division's flank or they might push westwards to Brudio.

The Polish Corps was to place its two newly-raised brigades astride Route 9 in a holding role and was to attack across the Senio well to the north of Route 9 with 3 Carpathian Division alongside the New Zealanders. Once across the Senio and Santerno, the Poles would drive towards Bologna on the northern side of Route 9.

The fire plan for the main Eighth Army attack was original and ingenious, and dictated the actual timings of the operation. The strategic bombers were to arrive early in the afternoon of D-day and drop some 175,000 20-pound fragmentation bombs in a 'carpet', covering the German gun areas and the areas thought to contain their immediate tactical reserves. The strategic bombers were to be followed by about 200 medium bombers attacking individual gun areas with precision bombing. Next 500 fighter-bombers would attack smaller tactical targets closer to the forward troops. The artillery programme would then start. This consisted of five false-alarm bombardments, each lasting 42 minutes with ten-minute intervals. In the intervals the fighter-bombers would attack the enemy positions in and around the western flood banks of the Senio almost under the noses of the attacking divisions. As the fifth barrage ended, the fighter-bombers would swoop again but this time without firing. This was the signal for the infantry to advance. Supported by flame-thrower tanks, assault engineer vehicles to make crossings and their own close support weapons, they were to cross the river just as it was getting dark while the roar of the fighters kept the Germans in their shelters. During the night 100 heavy night-bombers would pound targets on the Santerno marked for them by the artillery firing special marker shells. At the same time 100 light night-bombers would add to the weight of counter-battery fire put down by the army artillery. V (Br) Corps and the Polish Corps would be supported by a total of 1,020 field guns

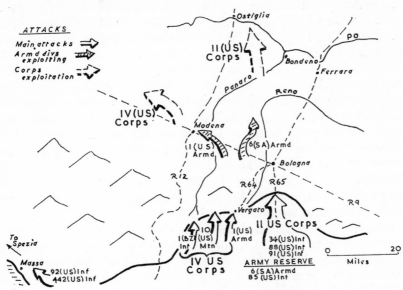

56 Fifth Army's plan for the final offensive

with an allotment of just under 2,000,000 rounds of artillery ammunition.

If a break-through occurred, Eighth Army planned to fight two separate battles; the destruction of the German forces south of the Po and the pursuit across the Po to the Adige (*see* fig. 54). V (Br) Corps would concentrate on the battle of annihilation. If the Argenta Gap was pierced, it would exploit to Ferrara and turn westwards along the south bank of the Po to encircle the German divisions trying to reach the river. If it had difficulty in getting through the gap, XIII (Br) Corps Headquarters would come round and take charge of those divisions which were advancing on Brudio to attack the rear of the Germans opposing Fifth Army, leaving V (Br) Corps free to concentrate on the Argenta area. X (Br) Corps Headquarters was to be responsible for the crossing of the Po and would take charge of the Special Po Task Force of engineers with their bridging equipment. X (Br) Corps with the Special Task Force would pass through the Argenta Gap and come up on the right flank of V (Br)

Corps, taking under its command whatever division was detailed to make the Po crossing. Plans were also made to drop small parties of Italian volunteers behind the retreating German columns to increase confusion and to spread alarm. Large numbers of volunteers came forward from the Italian Combat groups, but there was only time to train about 250 for the operation which was codenamed 'Herring'.

Fifth Army's plan was to advance astride and to the west of Route 64 and the Reno with IV and II (US) Corps. IV (US) Corps' front was still some way back behind II (US) Corps' salient on Route 65, so it was to attack first with three divisions, from left to right 1 Brazilian, 10 (US) Mountain and 1 (US) Armoured Divisions. When IV (US) Corps drew level with II (US) Corps, both corps would continue the attack until they had punched a hole through the German defences west of Bologna wide enough for the two armoured divisions—1 (US) Armoured and 6 (SA) Armoured—to pass through and to fan out into the Po Valley. 1 (US) Armoured Division would turn west for Modena, and 6 (SA) Armoured Division would turn east to encircle Bologna, joining hands with V (Br) Corps on the Po at Bondeno. II (US) Corps would follow, making for the Po at Ostiglia, while IV (US) Corps wheeled west to protect the left flank of Fifth Army from the attentions of Graziani's Army of Liguria.

Fifth Army's plan included elaborate deception arrangements. The aim was to suggest to von Vietinghoff that the whole Allied effort would be made against the hinge of his line through the Eighth Army sector. The illusion was to be created of II (US) Corps moving secretly into reserve behind Eighth Army, leaving IV (US) Corps to cover the whole of the existing Fifth Army front. To heighten the illusion, a preliminary attack was to be made up the west coast towards La Spezia to suggest to the Germans that this was the Allies' diversionary attack to draw their reserves westward away from Eighth Army. This attack was to be carried out about the same time as Eighth Army's Commandos attacked the Spit. 92 (US) Negro Division was in charge of the operation and was reinforced for it by the 442 (Japanese-American) Regiment from France and an *ad hoc* force called 473 Regiment made up of disbanded anti-aircraft units.

While Fifth and Eighth Armies were making their final preparations, Eisenhower's armies were crossing the Rhine and a Russian army under Tolbukin entered Austria. The Russians were now nearer to Vienna than Alexander's forces. Churchill had definitely lost the race which he had, in fact, already conceded when he allowed the Combined Chiefs of Staff to kill Alexander's proposals for an Adriatic crossing. More significantly from the Italian theatre's point of view were the secret peace feelers, known only to Alexander and his most senior staff officers, from SS

General Wolff through intermediaries in Switzerland for the surrender of Army Group 'C'. Wolff was the Wehrmacht Plenipotentiary-General in Italy responsible for liaison with Mussolini's Republican Government and for the internal security of German-occupied northern Italy. His first approaches were made in early February and at that time it looked as if Kesselring, with his acute political instincts, would support Wolff in secret negotiations with the Allies. Kesselring's elevation to the thankless task of C.-in-C. West, delayed Wolff's plans because von Vietinghoff, a simpler soldier, was unlikely to break his soldier's oath to Hitler and might well look upon such approaches as treason. The clandestine meetings between Allied and German representatives went on fitfully throughout March, but, as Alexander could place no reliance upon them, he pushed forward his preparations for the last offensive, hoping that its success would make Wolff's task of winning von Vietinghoff over much easier.

Von Vietinghoff was under no illusions about the seriousness of the position of Army Group 'C'. He had tried to persuade Hitler to allow him to adopt a mobile defence. General Herr, commanding Tenth Army, proposed to emulate Ludendorff's withdrawal to the Hindenburg Line which had been so successful in throwing the Allies off-balance in 1918. He believed the Eighth Army would attack astride Route 9 and he had his best troops covering that road. He suggested that, as soon as he judged the Allied attack to be imminent, he should pull back under a heavy artillery barrage so that the Allies would have to reshape all their carefully laid plans before they could attack again. There was enough room and enough prepared river lines to play variations on this theme for weeks. Von Vietinghoff put the idea to OKW and received a brusque refusal. If OKW was not prepared to allow him to carry out a tactical withdrawal of the type which Herr suggested, what hope had he of persuading Hitler to let him implement Autumn Mist? The answer was clearly none; and, as Alexander puts it in his official account of the last offensive, the German generals could only accept the inevitable results of OKW's rigid defence, like Napoleon's generals before Waterloo, 'without fear and without hope'.

The first moves of the spring offensive started on the German side. Von Vietinghoff and his staff fell for the Allied cover plan suggesting an amphibious attack north of the Po. At the end of March he despatched 29 Panzer Grenadier Division from reserve near Bologna north-eastwards to the Venetian coast. This left only 90 Panzer Grenadier Division in reserve south of the Po near Modena. Worse was to come. Eighth Army's preliminary attack on the Spit was completely successful. The 162 (Turkoman) Division, holding the area, lost 900 prisoners and 42 Infantry

Division lost its reconnaissance battalion. 29 Panzer Grenadier Division, which was still moving towards Venice, sent its own reconnaissance battalion south to help stabilize the position and lost a number of minor units when the Commandos seized the islands in Lake Comacchio. All this fighting east of the lake confirmed von Vietinghoff in his view that a major parachute and amphibious assault was imminent north of the Po.

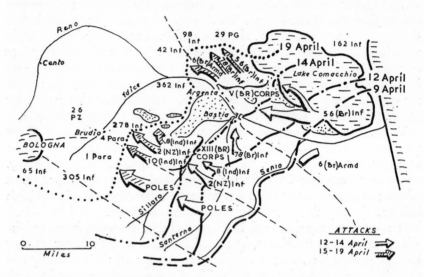

57   Eighth Army's final offensive, 9–19 April

29 Panzer Grenadier Division continued its move away from the battle-field. On the other coast 92 (US) Negro Division's diversion opened on 5 April. 142 Infantry Division fought well but was forced to surrender the last remaining stretches of the Gothic Line and fell back, leaving 500 prisoners in American hands. General Lemelsen, commanding Fourteenth Army, felt obliged to retrieve the situation on his western flank and committed a regimental group of 90 Panzer Grenadier Division. There was thus no complete mobile division in central reserve when Eighth Army opened its main attack on 9 April.

The Germans were not surprised by the Eighth Army attack. They had been alerted several times since the last week of March. What did surprise them was the weight of attack and the fact that it came well to the north of Route 9 in the 98 and 362 Infantry Division's sectors. They were further disconcerted by the ingenuity and weight of attack against the Argenta Gap. They were under no illusions about the importance of the Bastia Bridge area, but they felt it could only be attacked from the south. 56 (Br)

Division's amphibious operations across the lake and through the floods were quite unexpected. As it happened the Luftwaffe did manage to take a photo of the lake area which showed a concentration of Fantails, but it reached Tenth Army Headquarters too late for its significance to be realized and acted upon.

Fine weather on 9 April allowed Eighth Army's air and artillery programme, which started a day earlier than the agreed target date of 10 April, to succeed beyond its planners' wildest dreams. The timings and accuracy were excellent though the fighter-bomber pilots found difficulty in locating their targets in the huge dust clouds which billowed up from previous bombing and shelling. The infantry attack, when it went in under the dummy fighter-bomber attacks, was immediately successful unlike the attacks across the Rapido the year before. The intense flaming of the far bank by the flame-thrower tanks reduced opposition and added to the lurid horror of the scene. By the following evening 8 (Ind) Division and the New Zealanders were nearing the Santerno with 1,300 prisoners in their hands. The Poles, as was inevitable, met stiffer resistance from the higher class German divisions facing them. Although their progress was slower and more costly they were up to their objectives by nightfall on 10 April.

The intensive combined training carried out between the Allied armies and air forces during the winter began to pay dividends. The heavy and medium bombers again attacked during 10 April, and the fighter-bombers, directed on their targets by controllers on the ground, did great execution. The Germans complained later that even lone despatch riders were attacked by swarms of fighters. By 12 April both corps had shallow bridgeheads over the Santerno and that afternoon the New Zealanders, fighting against increasing resistance, took Massa Lombarda, bringing the first phase of Eighth Army's offensive to a successful conclusion.

Meanwhile 56 (Br) Division's right hook had been meeting similar success. The Wedge was taken as planned on 6 April, 42 Infantry Division surrendering a further 700 prisoners. The British sappers worked fast to establish launching points for the Fantails and to bridge gaps in the approach routes. The second phase of 56 (Br) Division's operation went in as V (Br) Corps reached the Santerno and again took the Germans by surprise. The Fantails landed the second brigade behind the Reno Line and by 12 April the two brigades of 56 (Br) Division had linked up but were being fiercely opposed and were not strong enough to break through to Bastia.

Mark Clark had intended that Fifth Army should attack on 12 April, but bad flying weather caused postponement until 14 April. There was, as yet, no clear indication as to whether Eighth Army should concentrate on its Argenta or Brudio thrust lines, so McCreery decided to continue to develop both. For the northern thrust 78 (Br) Division was ordered to pass through 8 (Ind) Division and to attack northwards towards Bastia. 56 (Br) Division was to despatch its third brigade across the floods towards Argenta. Unfortunately the strength of the German anti-aircraft defences in the area was clearly too great to risk dropping 2 (Br) Para Brigade so the Commandos were ordered to help 56 (Br) Division with whatever storm boats and other craft they could muster. For the westward thrust XIII (Br) Corps was ordered to move round with 10 (Ind) Division into the New Zealand sector, where it would co-ordinate the drive of the New Zealanders and 10 (Ind) Division on the northern flank of the Polish Corps, which was meeting determined resistance from the para and panzer divisions on Route 9.

Von Vietinghoff had by this time appreciated that there would be no landing north of the Po. He also realized the danger of 56 (Br) Division's operations towards Bastia. He ordered 29 Panzer Grenadier Division to move at best speed to the Gap. 78 (Br) Division's advance northwards went well and it managed to seize the Bastia bridge on 14 April before it was completely destroyed. 56 (Br) Division's second amphibious hook was a failure because it landed too near the previous landings and ran into the first of 29 Panzer Grenadier Division's regimental battle groups to arrive on the scene. 78 (Br) Division was similarly checked in front of the village of Bastia and V (Br) Corps was forced to pause to lay on a co-ordinated attack to clear the stiffening German resistance in the Gap. Some fears were expressed in Eighth Army Headquarters that the Argenta Gap was now too strongly held and another route to the Po would have to be found.

V (Br) Corps' co-ordinated attack resulted in three days of prolonged and bitter fighting. 362 and 42 Infantry Divisions fought back gamely and a second regiment of 29 Panzer Grenadier Division was committed. The village of Bastia did not fall until 16 April and it was only after a heavy air attack on Argenta that the Tenth German Army Commander was persuaded to pull back his troops to the northern half of the Gap during 17 April. V (Br) Corps maintained its pressure the following day and by evening 78 (Br) Division emerged beyond the last of the German prepared positions. 6 (Br) Armoured Division was placed under V (Br) Corps on that day and passed through Argenta coming up on the western flank of 78 (Br) Division. By the evening of 20 April V (Br) Corps had its three divisions pressing outward in a fan on the northern side of the Gap. All three were still meeting determined resistance.

XIII (Br) Corps and the Polish Corps pressed on with their westerly advance using a great weight of artillery and air bombardment to crush resistance on each successive delaying line. The Paula Line on the Sillaro went on 15 April, and by 17 April both corps were fighting their way towards the Ghengis Khan Line on the Idice, the last river covering the eastern face of Bologna. The two German parachute divisions had now joined hands and were getting ready to put up a determined defence of Bologna with 26 Panzer Division in reserve behind them. The German infantry divisions, on the other hand, were beginning to disintegrate and von Vietinghoff was being forced to depend, as usual, on the great

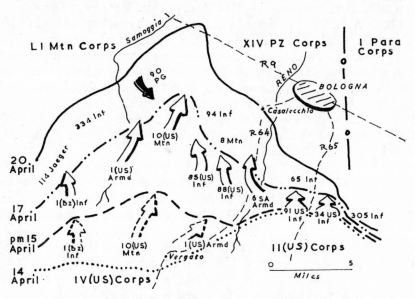

58 Fifth Army's final offensive, 14–20 April

fighting qualities of his mobile divisions. The climax of the battle was near. To the west of Bologna, Fifth Army's offensive had started on 14 April and was now gathering such momentum that it would soon have its effect on the German divisions opposing Eighth Army.

One aspect of the Allied plan had been disappointing. Von Vietinghoff did not fall for the suggestion that II (US) Corps had moved into reserve behind Eighth Army. The only diversion of German strength that occurred from Fifth Army's front was the move of part of 90 Panzer Grenadier Division to the west coast. In an appeal to Hitler dated 14 April, von Vietinghoff gives his appreciation of the situation. He explains that the Allied aim is to destroy the German Tenth and Fourteenth Armies with a crushing weight of shells and bombs, and suggests that the way to defeat these tactics is to adopt a mobile defence. He points out that only Eighth Army has attacked so far; II (US) Corps is poised ready to attack any day now south of Bologna. It would take two weeks to withdraw the Army of Liguria and Fourteenth Army back behind the Po. Unless the withdrawal is ordered soon Tenth Army will be unable to hold the hinge long enough to allow the more westerly units to escape. He ends by saying, 'This is considered the only way in which the Northern Italian areas, so important to our war industry, can be preserved for the German Army until the day of our decisive battle'. Naive though these last sentiments may be, he was quite correct in expecting Fifth Army to attack at any moment.

On 14 April the skies cleared and Fifth Army's attack could begin with the whole weight of the Allied air effort concentrated on its front. The battle which followed was reminiscent of Fifth Army's battle the previous year when it broke through the Gustav Line in the Garigliano sector. On that occasion the break-through occurred in an unexpected sector and was made by the French Mountain Corps. This time the break came in IV (US) Corps' sector instead of, as expected, in the more powerful II (US) Corps' area; and the break was made by mountain troops again—this time by 10 (US) Mountain Division.

Progress was slow at first. IV (US) Corps opened its attack before II (US) Corps and had to fight hard for its first successes. On 15 April the air forces dropped a record load of some 1,500 tons of bombs on Fifth Army's front and 800 tons on the German rear areas. By the end of 15 April IV (US) Corps was level with II (US) Corps, which opened its offensive that night. Attacking nearer to the Bologna defences, II (US) Corps made slower progress than its sister corps to the west. IV (US) Corps, spearheaded by 10 (US) Mountain Division, had already taken the German winter positions on its front and was now pushing through the dwindling hills towards Route 9 in the Po Valley. The German divisions of Lemelsen's Fourteenth Army fought back with staunch determination which was just as fierce as the opposition met by Eighth Army's troops. By 16 April the weight of the American attack was starting to tell. 8 Mountain and 94 Infantry Divisions blocking IV (US) Corps' path began to show signs of fatigue and on 17 April 94 Infantry Division, which had been severely mauled by II (US) Corps during the Diadem offensive a year before, broke and allowed 10 (US) Mountain Division to advance swiftly towards Route 9. Lemelsen committed his only reserve, 90 Panzer Grenadier Division, to check IV (US) Corps' advance; while Truscott committed his Fifth Army reserve, 85 (US) Division, in IV (US) Corps' sector instead of through II (US) Corps as he had originally intended. 90 Panzer Grenadier Division lost most of its tanks in a tank versus tank action with 1 (US) Armoured Division and failed to re-establish the German line. During the afternoon of 20 April 10 (US) Mountain Division broke through into the plain and cut Route 9 halfway between Modena and Bologna. That evening 88 (US) Division and 6 (SA) Armoured Division of II (US) Corps took Casalecchio, a suburb on the western outskirts of Bologna. The first and hardest part of Fifth Army's offensive was accomplished.

Von Vietinghoff's request to withdraw had been turned down by Hitler on 14 April who demanded:

> All further proposals for a change in the present war strategy will be discontinued. . . . under no circumstances must troops or commanders be allowed to waver or adopt a defeatist attitude as a result of such ideas apparently held in your headquarters. . . . The Führer expects now as before the utmost steadfastness in the fulfilment of your present mission, to defend every inch of the north Italian areas entrusted to your command. . . .*

On 20 April von Vietinghoff realized that he had no alternative but to order a withdrawal to the Po whatever Hitler might say. He knew it was too late, but he was determined to do the best he could to save as much of his Army Group as possible. In a final signal to Hitler reporting his decision, he says:

> My Führer!
> Resolved by my unshakeable will to hold the Italian front under all circumstances and to carry out your orders to the last, I report to you, my Führer, that as a result of heavy battle losses our forces in the Italian theatre are strained to such an extent that, if we persist in our policy of static defence, an enemy break-through at Lake Comacchio, Bologna and La Spezia can in all probability not be prevented despite the heroic resistance and determination of our officers and men. All available forces have been concentrated in the focal points of the battle, and other sectors of the front, not under direct heavy attack, have consequently been denuded to provide reinforcements. Mobile reserves are no longer available. Thus, the enemy threatens to achieve his object, i.e. to split and subsequently crush the German front. In a mobile strategy, however, I still see a possibility of preventing this threat from being carried out and of continuing our resistance with a chance of success. Difficult as it is for me, I consider it my duty, my Führer, to send you this report at this hour and to await your orders.
>
> von Vietinghoff
>
> 20 April 1945   C.-in-C., South West.

When von Vietinghoff ordered his army commanders to start the withdrawal to the Po, the tactical situation was still manageable and no worse than some of the other crises which the German armies in Italy had survived. Tenth Army's front was unbroken. LXXVI Panzer Corps was successfully containing V (Br) Corps' attempts to burst out of the Argenta

* Jodl to von Vietinghoff, 14 April 1945.

Gap. I Para Corps was firm on the Idice and ready to resist XIII (Br) Corps
and the Poles. Fourteenth Army was less well placed. Its LI Mountain
Corps was still intact and was not under pressure, but XIV Panzer Corps'
front had broken. 90 Panzer Grenadier Division had been unable to restore
the situation and there were no other mobile reserves available. Attempts
were made to withdraw 305 Infantry Division from south-east of Bologna

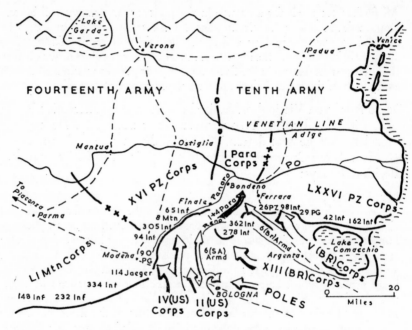

59   *The destruction of Army Group 'C', 20 April–2 May*

and to move it round to help close the gap. The American advance was
too quick and the gap remained open. There was, however, still no need
to despair. Behind the Ghengis Khan Line there was the Reno Line and
behind that the Po. Under ordinary circumstances a rapid withdrawal to
the Reno behind the usual belts of demolitions, covered by rearguards,
should suffice to halt the American drive. The circumstances, however,
were not ordinary.

In the previous German disengagements the front had been narrow and
confined between the Apennine range and the coast. The Allies had been
forced to pursue up restricting valleys with only one good road per corps.
In the Po Valley the front widened, the roads multiplied and the bridges
over the many water obstacles multiplied as well, becoming too numerous
for the German sappers to destroy with that methodical efficiency which

they had perfected south of the Gothic Line. The greater number of roads enabled the Allies to deploy more divisions, and conversely the Germans had to commit more troops and had fewer reserves. The reserves they did manage to muster had to move further to counter-attack; these moves took longer and used more petrol; and they were also vulnerable for longer to the Allied air forces. Great changes had occurred as far as the Allied airmen were concerned as well. Instead of having to bomb and strafe twisting mountain roads and rocky hillsides on which targets were difficult to find, they could now attack all movement on the highly developed road network of the Po Valley beyond the 'bomb line', and they had the prominent bridge sites on the wide River Po to keep closed to German traffic. The air forces, moreover, dislocated the German communications network: bombing destroyed the telephone lines and cables; and the strafing of command vehicles and headquarters by marauding fighter-bombers decimated their radio network. Within the German divisions casualties from ground and air attack were far higher than they had been in previous battles and it is surprising that there were not more failures in morale than there were. Right up to the last days of the battle the German officers and men fought on with extraordinary gallantry. Their undoing was the refusal of OKW to allow a withdrawal in time and von Vietinghoff's loyal obedience to Hitler until too late. Faced with the changed circumstances, more and not less time was needed to put withdrawal plans into operation. The Reno Line had to be manned and through this the divisions in contact would fall back to cross the Po while their rearguards clung to the Reno. Such a plan would have been possible if it had been ordered on 15 April when the weight of Fifth Army's attack became apparent and when Eighth Army's progress through the Argenta Gap was obvious. Even then LI Mountain Corps would have had to march very fast to get back over the Po before the centre of the line was forced back. 20 April was much too late.

The two German army commanders had to improvise as best they could when the order to withdraw was given. LXXVI Panzer Corps was ordered to hold the Argenta area as long as possible to stop British troops attacking the flank of 1 Para Corps as it withdrew to the Reno, and to block the crossings over the Po north of Ferrara. 1 Para Corps was to pull back from the Idice, east of Bologna, to the Reno covered by 362 and 278 Infantry Divisions which would then fall back through the paratroopers to make their escape over the Po. XIV Panzer Corps was to withdraw to the westward extension of the Reno Line based on the Panaro. It would then make for the Mantua area. LI Mountain Corps would have to pull out north-westwards towards Piacenza, covered by 90 Panzer Grenadier Division blocking Route 9 to hold the Allies in check while the extreme westerly divisions made good their escape. Graziani's Army of Liguria was directed to fall back on Milan.

The rupture of XIV Panzer Corps' front had been serious but not irreparable. Disaster struck von Vietinghoff's armies from another direction. 6 (Br) Armoured Division had been placed under V (Br) Corps on 18 April. It broke out of the Argenta Gap and advanced north-westward along the north bank of the Reno aiming for V (Br) Corps' objective, Bondeno on the Po. It struck the flank and rear of the 362 and 278 Infantry Divisions, which were covering the withdrawal of 1 Para Corps, and broke through across the paratroopers' line of withdrawal, taking Bondeno late on 22 April. It then swept on to join hands, on 23 April, with 6 (SA) Armoured Division, which had broken through round the western side of Bologna, at a village appropriately named Finale. The armoured columns were not strong enough to bar all escape, but many men from 1 and 4 Para Divisions were forced to surrender—a far cry from the Cassino days—while others, including Heidrich, swam the Po to escape. The centre of the German line was now wide open. Only LXXVI Panzer Corps, struggling to hold Ferrara, and LI Mountain Corps, making a hasty retreat to the west, were unbroken.

The Allies do not seem to have been aware of their overwhelming success at this stage and made their plans as if there would still be many hard battles ahead. The Poles had entered Bologna from the east and the Americans had come in from the west on 21 April. Eighth Army pulled the Poles back into reserve and sent XIII (Br) Corps northwards chasing the withdrawing 1 Para Corps. XIII (Br) Corps took 6 (Br) Armoured Division under command and closed up to the Po to force a crossing. V (Br) Corps brought up its reserve division, 8 Indian, which advanced past the western outskirts of Ferrara and reached the Po due north of the town late on 23 April. LXXVI Panzer Corps, which now included 26 Panzer and 29 Panzer Grenadier Divisions, was hemmed in between the Po and the Po delta. Ammunition shortage was beginning to worry the Eighth Army Staff, but the air forces made up for any deficiencies in fire power. Bridging equipment was running short as well. For instance, in one day 29 separate bridges were built by Eighth Army sappers using over 1,500 tons of equipment. The Special Po Task Force was still intact and was moving up behind V (Br) Corps. Unfortunately, the Commander X (Br) Corps' health broke down* and so McCreery did not use its head-quarters for the Po crossing. He divided the Special Task Force between XIII and V (Br) Corps and ordered both corps to cross the river as soon as their sappers could establish ferries and bridges for them. They were

---

* General Hawksworth died not long afterwards.

then to advance on parallel axes northwards to break the Venetian Line before the Germans could man it.

Meanwhile in LXXVI Panzer Corps' bridgehead 26 Panzer and 29 Panzer Grenadier Divisions continued to fight with their customary bravery. By the evening of 24 April the Corps Commander, General von Schwerin, who succeeded Herr when he was promoted to Tenth Army, realized there was nothing more he could do to save his corps. Tanks, guns and vehicles were abandoned and those men who could swim escaped across the river. Von Schwerin himself surrendered to V (Br) Corps the following morning. Three of the four German corps which had started the battle on 9 April had now been destroyed and four out of the five remaining veteran mobile divisions had been reduced to unequipped cadres.

For the first time Eighth Army began to realize that the war was almost over. Operation Herring (see p. 304) was mounted with some success, the Italian parachute troops causing considerable additional confusion in the German rear. The two leading British corps crossed the Po on 24 April against no opposition. By 27 April they had both established bridgeheads over the Adige and were advancing rapidly towards Venice and Trieste, which they were destined to reach on 29 April and 2 May.

During the same period Fifth Army had made even swifter progress. IV and II (US) Corps had fought their way through and widened the gap left by the collapse of XIV Panzer Corps. IV (US) Corps had swung three divisions north-westwards to cut off LI Mountain Corps and had sent the ubiquitous 10 (US) Mountain Division and 85 (US) Division due north aiming at Verona. II (US) Corps blasted due north as well with everything it had. By 25 April Fifth Army had five divisions over the Po on a wide front astride Ostiglia. On 26 April 10 (US) Mountain Division entered Verona. II (US) Corps then wheeled eastwards to advance parallel to Eighth Army across the Adige which it reached at the same time as the British corps. IV (US) Corps crossed Lake Garda using Fantails and Duplex Drive tanks to cut the Brenner Pass road and pushed out westwards to clear Milan and the other great cities of north-west Italy. The Italian Committee of Liberation had ordered a general insurrection on 25 April, making further German withdrawals almost impossible. By 28 April all escape routes into the Alpine passes had been closed. Graziani surrendered the Army of Liguria. 90 Panzer Grenadier Division, the last of the veteran mobile divisions, made a last great effort to hold the escape route open for the divisions in the west but was forced to surrender after its divisional commander and his staff had been captured.

General Wolff's attempts to negotiate the surrender of all German forces in Italy bore fruit later than he had hoped. Von Vietinghoff did not agree to negotiate until after he had sent his signal to Hitler reporting his withdrawal to the Po. He then gave Colonel von Schweinitz authority to accompany Wolff to Alexander's headquarters at Caserta. The German delegates arrived on 28 April and finally agreed to a cease-fire timed for noon on 2 May. After a number of last-minute difficulties caused by the arrest and subsequent release of von Vietinghoff, the surrender became effective at 6 p.m. on 2 May.

On 4 May, General von Senger und Etterlin, who had fought from Sicily to Bologna, arrived at General Mark Clark's headquarters as German Liaison Officer charged with ensuring the terms of capitulation. The Battle for Italy was over. The problems of occupation and of return to the ways of peace had taken its place.

Conclusion

Alexander summed up the Battle for Italy in the following words:

Any estimate of the value of the campaign must be expressed, not in terms of the ground gained, for the ground was not vital, in the strict sense, either to us or to the enemy, but in terms of its effect on the war as a whole. The Allied Armies in Italy were not engaged with the enemy's main armies and their attacks were not directed, as were those of the Allies in the west or the Russians in the east, against the heart of the German Fatherland and the nerve-centres of Germany's national existence. Our role was subordinate and preparatory. Ten months before the great assault in the west our invasion of Italy, at first in very moderate strength, drew off to that remote quarter forces that might have turned the scale in France. As the campaign progressed more and more German troops were drawn in to oppose us. The supreme directors of Allied strategy were always careful to see that our strength was never allowed to grow above the minimum necessary for our tasks; at one time and another during those 20 months no less than 21 divisions in all were removed from my command for the benefit of other theatres. The Germans made no comparable detachments. Except for a short period in the spring of 1944 they had always more formations in Italy than we had, and we made such good use of that brief exceptional period that in the summer of 1944, the crisis of the war, they found themselves forced to divert eight divisions to this secondary theatre. At that time, when the value of our strategic contribution was at its greatest, 55 German divisions were tied down in the Mediterranean by the threat, actual or potential, presented by our armies in Italy. The record of the comparative casualties tells us the same story. On the German side they amounted to 536,000. Allied casualties were 312,000. The difference is the more remarkable in that we were always the attackers. Four times we carried out that most difficult operation of war, an amphibious landing. Three times we launched a prepared offensive with the full strength of an army group. Nowhere in Europe did soldiers face more difficult terrain or more determined adversaries.

The conclusion is that the campaign in Italy fulfilled its strategic mission.

The summary of the Allied and German orders of battle given at Appendix E bear out Alexander's contention that he fulfilled his strategic mission. At the critical points of the campaign the relative divisional strengths were:

	Allied	German
Advance to the Volturno	19	19
Autumn battles of the Bernhardt Line	11	18
Winter battles of the Gustav Line	21	23
Diadem offensive	25	24
Fall of Rome and Normandy landings	25	26
Autumn battles of the Gothic Line	20	26
Final offensive	17	21

At the moment when Eisenhower's landings began in Normandy, the number of German divisions drawn into Italy reached the peak figure of 26 divisions and was held at that figure throughout the summer months of 1944 when stalemate could so easily have engulfed the Allied main effort in North-West Europe.

But, although there is little doubt that Alexander fulfilled his strategic mission, there is less certainty about the correctness of that mission. Which of the two competing schools of strategic thought—British or American—will history favour? Both sides can look back upon the events of the campaign and claim that they prove its case. Let us look briefly at each in turn.

The British case is that great opportunities for far-reaching military and political successes in the Mediterranean were sacrificed through American strategic inflexibility and political myopia. If Churchill had been allowed to pursue his own strategy, unfettered by American restraints, the Iron Curtain would not have descended as far west as it did and many of the agonies of the post-War world would have been lessened by the arrival of Allied troops on the Danube ahead of the Russians. The Americans' case is that these opportunities did not exist and are mere figments of British imagination. More whole-hearted British support for the Overlord concept in 1943 would have shortened the war and brought the Allies into the heart of Germany before the Russians could advance so far westwards.

The argument is best illustrated by looking at the three critical phases of the campaign when the Americans insisted upon making the planned withdrawals of veteran divisions from Italy in spite of the opportunities which seemed to beckon to the Allies in the Mediterranean. If we take the number of German divisions actually available to Kesselring for operations (i.e. by subtracting from the total number of German divisions those which were needed in northern Italy for internal security and for the protection of his lines of communication from partisan attack), the figures are revealing.

	Allied divisions	German divisions	Percentage of Allied operational superiority	
	in the operational areas			
Advance to the Volturno	19	12	58	
Autumn battle of the Bernhardt Line	13	11	18	7 Allied divisions withdrawn for Overlord
Winter battles of the Gustav Line	18	15	20	
Diadem offensive	25	18	40	
Autumn battles of the Gothic Line	20	22	− 10	6 Allied divisions withdrawn for Dragoon
Final offensive	17	19	− 12	Canadian Corps withdrawn.

Progress was rapid after Salerno when the Allies enjoyed nearly a 60 per cent superiority, but the autumn rains and the withdrawal of the seven veteran divisions for Overlord slowed their advance to a crawl. An 18 per cent superiority in bad weather was not enough to enable them to break through the Gustav Line and to seize Rome. The British can claim that, if the withdrawal of these seven divisions with their associated landing ships and supporting aircraft had not taken place, the Allies would probably have wintered in front of the Gothic instead of the Gustav Line with Rome in their hands. The Allied air forces would have been closer to the Reich, making the combined bomber offensive more effective. The German Army would have been forced to deploy more divisions to hold the longer Gothic defences thus weakening the Eastern and Western fronts still further. And Hitler would have been forced to react more strenuously to prevent the Allies breaking into the Balkans and central Europe to rob him of resources which his economists believed were vital to Germany's continued war effort. The strength of the British case at this juncture lies in the knowledge we now have of the struggle between the Rommel and Kesselring schools of thought. The Rommel school would have won if Kesselring had failed to hold the Gustav positions, and the Germans would have withdrawn to the northern Apennines leaving Rome and its airfields in Allied hands. The weakness of the British case lies in the logistic field. It is very doubtful whether the

Allies could have supplied the extra seven divisions advancing in winter over the logistic desert which the Germans would have left behind them as they withdrew. As it was, shortage of shipping crippled the Allied build-up throughout the winter and would have made it very difficult to support larger forces than in fact advanced on the Gustav Line.

The second withdrawal of troops occurred after Diadem. Summer weather and 40 per cent superiority led to Alexander's victory and the fall of Rome. The British can argue that, if the Dragoon attack on southern France had been cancelled, Alexander's troops would have reached Ljubljana before autumn. As it was they fought the Gothic battles with an operational inferiority and without the French mountain troops and, in consequence, failed to reach even the Po. The British can also claim that Dragoon did not help Eisenhower, decisively, whereas it crippled Alexander. The American counter-argument is that the country gets no easier as the Alps and Ljubljana Gap are approached. In fact, it gets far more difficult to advance through and is much easier to defend. Moreover, the German lines of communication would be shortening all the time and becoming less vulnerable. In their view there was no easy path to Germany's back door as the British always claim.

The third withdrawal of troops (the Canadian Corps to Eisenhower's armies in January 1945) took place when the chances of reaching Vienna ahead of the Russians had faded and even Churchill had given up the pursuit of a Mediterranean strategy. The final battle in Italy, however, tends to confirm the British in their view that more could have been achieved if only Alexander had been left with his armies intact after Diadem. Attacking with a nominal 12 per cent inferiority, Alexander smashed von Vietinghoff's Army Group 'C' in the spring of 1945 on the very ground upon which he had intended to fight his decisive battle at the end of the previous summer if his army had not been weakened and disorganized by the Dragoon decision. Fought eight months earlier, as it might have been, the Battle of the Po Valley would have drawn more German troops southwards into Italy and might have enabled Eisenhower to break through on the Western Front before winter. Arnhem might have been a decisive victory instead of a defeat. The American counter to such arguments is, quite rightly, that this is mere speculation. Why continue to attack through such easily defended country when the whole of the north German plain lies open for the main effort? Unless there was a real chance of achieving strategic surprise by advancing through such a difficult country as Italy, operations should have been confined to holding attacks as soon as the Allied air forces were secure on the Rome airfields from which they could extend the combined bomber offensive to its optimum level of intensity.

CONCLUSION

In weighing these arguments it seems clear that Churchill under-estimated the military difficulties of operations in Italy and the Balkans, while Roosevelt belittled the political dangers of a Russian advance into central Europe. The 'soft under-belly' of Europe was far from soft, and the 'Iron Curtain', when it descended, was thicker and longer-lasting than even Churchill would have predicted in 1944. Both sides were at fault in their strategic thinking; the Americans were too rigid and the British too pragmatic. Alexander's favourite two-handed strategy might have offered the best solution. If it had been agreed that the two western theatres (Normandy and Italy) were to be co-equal, then resources could have been switched between fronts to keep the German reserves on the move and to profit by successes wherever they occurred. This would not have meant moving divisions between theatres because there was the large pool of undeployed American divisions in the United States waiting shipment to Europe. These could have been sent to Alexander or Eisen-hower as the situation demanded. The argument that it was necessary to move experienced divisions from the Mediterranean to Europe was disproved by events. It is generally accepted that the new divisions trained in the United States and United Kingdom fought better in Normandy than the veteran divisions from the Mediterranean whose battle experience tended to make them over-cautious. It would have been better to transfer experienced commanders, staff officers and training cadres from the Mediterranean to leaven the new divisions rather than returning whole divisions which contained a high proportion of men who believed that they had taken the risks for long enough and that it was the turn of the untried divisions to bear the brunt of the fighting in Normandy.

What of the rest of the campaign? Five factors stand out. First, there are the lessons of amphibious operations. They are not as easy to mount as Continental nations believe. They need careful planning, extensive train-ing and preparation, and very expensive equipment which few nations can afford. They will only succeed under effective air cover. The attacker can often gain strategic surprise but the defender will usually be able to concentrate his troops quicker in the early stages of the operation and will try to counter-attack the beachhead before it becomes too strong. Well-controlled naval gunfire, close air support and carefully chosen defensive perimeters are the key factors in repelling these attacks. In the Battle for Italy the Allies always gained strategic surprise and succeeded in holding their beachheads but there were several desperate moments when it looked as if they might be driven back into the sea.

Secondly, there are the lessons of air warfare. The Allies achieved air supremacy, but this did not give them immediate victory on the ground. Techniques of ground-air co-operation improved steadily and were at their best in the last offensive, but there were many disappointments before really close co-operation was achieved. The bombing of the Monastery before 4 (Ind) Division was ready to attack and the destruction of Cassino without creating conditions for a break-through were outstanding examples of misappreciation in the use of air power. On the other hand, the rare appearances of the Luftwaffe over the battlefield was conclusive proof of the effectiveness of the Allied air policy of winning the air battle first before turning to the close air support of the soldiers in the field.

The third lesson is the successful use of artillery to save soldiers' lives. The casualty figures given by Alexander in the quotation at the beginning of this chapter show that for once in war the attacker lost less than the defender, even though the defender had the advantage of ideally defensible country. This reversal of the usual trend was almost entirely due to the Allied techniques of concentrating artillery fire, which were superior to those of the Germans. The ammunition expenditure rates were very high but casualty lists were correspondingly reduced. The lessons of the Battle of the Somme were deeply engrained in British tactical methods and were copied and improved upon by the Americans.

Then, fourthly, there is the skill with which Alexander outwitted Kesselring before each major Allied offensive, and there is Kesselring's corresponding ability to recover and assemble sufficient forces at the decisive point to prevent a break-through and the possible collapse of his Army Group. Both commanders owe much to their Chiefs of Staff—General Harding and General Westphal—whose well directed headquarter staffs helped to achieve these successes.

And, finally, tribute must be paid to the men of so many different nations who fought side by side in the Allied armies in Italy, sharing the risks, the failures and the victories. And let us also remember the handful of German mobile divisions which fought through every phase of the campaign, saving the day time after time by swift moves, hastily mounted counter-attacks and stubborn defensive actions when the rest of the German line was in disarray. In the end they received no reward—only the ignominy of unconditional surrender at the end of their long hard road. The 3, 15, 29 and 90 Panzer Grenadier Divisions, 16 and 26 Panzer Divisions, the Hermann Göring Division and 1 and 4 Parachute Divisions were worthy opponents.

APPENDIX A

List of Abbreviations and Codewords used in the text and on sketches

1 *Formation Titles*

AB Div Airborne Division
Armd Div Armoured Division
Bde Brigade
FEC French Expeditionary Corps
Inf Div Infantry Division
Jaeger Div Jaeger Division

Mtn Div Mountain Division
Para Div Parachute Division
PG Div Panzer Grenadier Division
PZ Div Panzer Division
Regt Regiment

Divisional Titles use Arabic numerals, e.g. 5 (Br) Div.
Corps Headquarters use Roman numerals, e.g. XIV PZ Corps.
Army Headquarters are spelt out in full, e.g. Eighth Army.

2 *National Suffixes*

Br British
Bz Brazilian
Cdn Canadian
Fr French—**Mot** Motorized
  Moroc Moroccan
  Alg Algerian
Ind Indian

It Italian
NZ New Zealand
Pol Polish—**Carp** Carpathian
  Kres Kresowan
SA South Africa
US United States

No suffix is included in the German Formation Titles, e.g. 362 Inf = 362nd
German Infantry Division.

3 *Codenames, Codewords and abbreviations*

Achse Final German plans for dealing with Italian defection.
Alarich First German Plan for dealing with Italian defection.
Anvil Allied attack on southern France (renamed DRAGOON).
Argonaut Allied conferences at Malta in Jan 45 as a preliminary to Yalta.

Autumn Mist German plans for withdrawal to the Po and the Venetian Line.

Avalanche Fifth Army landing at Salerno.

Barbara Line German delaying position between Volturno and Garigliano rivers.

Barracuda Direct attack on Naples (cancelled).

Baytown Eighth Army's crossing of the Straits of Messina.

Bernhardt Line German defensive position in front of Gustav Line based on the Mignano defile.

Bradman Bombing of Cassino Town.

Brimstone Fifth Army invasion of Sardinia.

Buccaneer British return to Andaman Islands (cancelled).

Buffalo Canadian name for landing vehicle, tracked.

Buttress X (Br) Corps landing on 'Toe' of Italy in the Gulf of Gioia (cancelled).

Caesar Line German defensive line covering Rome (also known as Line 'C.')

Crabs German two-man steel shelters.

Diadem Alexander's spring offensive in 1944 leading to the capture of Rome.

Dragoon Seventh Army's landing in southern France (previously called ANVIL).

DUKW American 2½-ton amphibious truck.

Ernte einbringe German codeword for disarming the Italians.

Eureka Allied conference in Teheran in December 1944.

Factory Name given to Fascist Community Centre at Aprilia in Anzio beach-head.

Fantail Codename for landing vehicle, tracked when used in Italy.

Firebrand French invasion of Corsica.

G Day Date on which Italian surrender would be announced.

Gangway Direct attack on Naples (cancelled).

Genghis Khan Line German final defence line covering Bologna.

Giant I 82 (US) Airborne Division's drop on Volturno River Bridges (cancelled).

Giant II 82 (US) Airborne Division's drop on Rome airfields (cancelled).

Goblet V (Br) Corps landing at Crotone (cancelled).

Goliath German remote-controlled and explosive-filled miniature tank used at Anzio.

Gothic Line Main German defence line across northern Apennines between Pisa and Rimini (also called the Green Line).

Green Line German defence line covering the Po valley (also called the Gothic Line).

Gustav Line Main German defence line for the winter of 1943–44 based on Cassino.

Herring Drop of Italian parachutists north of the Po during the final offensive in Italy, 1945.

Hercules Attack on Rhodes (cancelled).

Husky Invasion of Sicily.

HG Abbreviation for Hermann Göring Division.

HQ Force 141 Planning staff for invasion of Sicily.

Influx 1940 Plan for invasion of Sicily.

Innocuous Codeword to stop 82 (US) Airborne Division dropping on the Rome airfields.

Irmgard Line German defence line on River Senio.

Kangaroo Codename for Sherman Tank modified to act as an armoured infantry carrier.

Laura Line German defence line on River Santerno.

Lehrgang German evacuation of Sicily.

Line 'C' German defence line covering Rome; also called Green Line and Caesar Line.

LST Landing ship, Tank.

Musket Fifth Army landing at Taranto (cancelled).

Mustang Direct assault on Naples (cancelled).

Mulberry Artificial harbour used in Normandy.

Nebelwerfer German multi-barrelled rocket launcher.

Octagon Second Allied conference at Quebec in September, 1944.

OKW Ober Kommando Der Wehrmacht; the German Supreme Command.

Olive Eighth Army's Plan for breaching the Gothic Line.

Overlord The Invasion of Normandy.

Panther German medium tank.

Paula Line German defence line of the Sillaro River.

Quadrant First Allied conference at Quebec in August, 1943.

Rain Coat X (Br) Corps and II (US) Corps attack on Monte Camino.

Rheinhardt Line German defence line based on Mignano defile; also called Bernhardt Line.

Richard German alarm scheme covering the Anzio area.

Sextant Allied conference at Cairo; November and December, 1943.

Shingle Allied landings at Anzio.

Slapstick Allied *ad hoc* landing at Taranto.

Spit Isthmus between Lake Comacchio and the sea.

Strangle Allied air interdiction plan before DIADEM offensive in spring of 1944.

Symbol Allied conference at Casablanca in January 1943.

Tiger German heavy tank.

Trident Allied conference in Washington in May 1943.

Venetian Line German defence line based on the Adige River.

Wedge Triangle of ground in the floods on the south-west edge of Lake Comacchio.

Whipcord 1941 Plan for invasion of Sicily.

Zitadelle Hitler's main summer offensive in Russia in 1943; stopped due to the invasion of Sicily.

APPENDIX B

Notes on German and Allied
Divisional Organisations

1 Most German and Allied divisions were made up of three regiments or three brigades. The title of regiment used by the Germans, Americans and French approximates to the British use of the word brigade. A regiment or brigade consisted of three infantry battalions and was normally supported by its own artillery, engineer and logistic units. The method of providing tank support varied and was one of the two principal differences between the various divisional organizations. The other difference was the degree of mechanization. In the German Army, only the *panzer* (armoured) and *panzer grenadier* (armoured infantry) divisions were fully mechanized; the bulk of the German Army consisted of infantry divisions which still depended largely on horses for towing guns and supply vehicles. The British and American Armies rarely used horses and then only in special pack transport units to supply their divisions in mountain country.

2 The Germans had three types of mobile division and three types of the slower moving horse-drawn division:

MOBILE DIVISIONS

a *The Panzer Division* in which the tank was the principal weapon and which contained a higher proportion of tanks than any other German division. It normally contained one panzer regiment and two panzer grenadier regiments.
b *The Panzer Grenadier Division* which was essentially a motorized infantry division with three panzer grenadier regiments and one tank battalion.
c *The Parachute Division*, the élite of the German Army, which had three parachute regiments and was usually given motor transport when fighting as an infantry division. It had no tanks of its own.

d *The Infantry Divisions* which comprised the bulk of the German Army and in which the infantry marched or were lifted by pools of transport, or, more often, by rail. The standard infantry division had three infantry regiments and no tanks of its own.

e *The Jaeger Division* which was a light division used on the flanks or in difficult country and possessed only two lightly equipped infantry regiments and no tanks.

f *The Mountain Division* which was specially trained and equipped for mountain operations and had only two mountain regiments and no tanks.

3   The main difference between the British and American divisions was the British system of concentrating their tanks in Independent Armoured Brigades which supported infantry divisions as required. The Americans allotted individual tank battalions to their infantry divisions on an as required basis. Otherwise their three types of division were very similar. These were:

a *The Infantry Division* of three infantry regiments or brigades in which only the infantry marched and then only in the battle area; otherwise they were lifted by pools of transport.

b *The Armoured Division* which had tanks and infantry permanently grouped together and which was fully mechanized.

c *The Airborne Division* consisting of three parachute regiments or brigades, and, in the case of the British only, one glider-borne air-landing brigade instead of the third parachute brigade.

4   Comparative strengths of divisions are misleading because the different logistic system caused varying numbers of logistic personnel to be included in the totals. Even a rough cross-check of the number of battalions is difficult to make because the British, for instance, had four rifle companies to all other nations' three. It is simplest in a strategic study to equate all divisions, i.e., Major-Generals' commands.

APPENDIX C   Allied and Axis Orders of Battle of Divisions during the Campaign in Sicily

1 As at Husky D-day 10 July 1943

SEVENTH ARMY	EIGHTH ARMY	GERMAN	ITALIANS
II (US) Corps 1 (US) Inf 45 (US) Inf	**XIII (Br) Corps** 5 (Br) Inf 50 (Br) Inf	**XIV PZ Corps** (in Italy) 15 PG (West Sicily) HG PZ (East Sicily) 3 PG (In Italy) 16 PZ (in Italy)	**Sixth (It) Army** **XII (It) Corps** (West) 26 (Assietta) Inf 28 (Aosta) Inf Three and one third Coastal Divisions Two Naval Base Garrisons
Army Troops 3 (US) Inf	**XXX (Br) Corps** 1 (Cdn) Inf 51 (Highland) Inf	**Moving into Italy** 26 PZ 29 PG	**XVI (It) Corps** (East) 4 (Livorno) Inf★ 54 (Napoli) Inf Two and two thirds Coastal Divisions Three Naval Base Garrisons
Floating Reserve 2 (US) Armd	**In Reserve in North Africa** 1 (Br) Airborne 78 (Br) Inf	**Sardinia** 90 PG	
In Reserve in North Africa 9 (US) Inf 82 (US) Airborne		**Totals** 6 German and Italian Mobile Divisions in Sicily 6 Italian Coastal Divisions in Sicily 5 German Divisions in Italy and Sardinia.	
Totals 8 Divisions afloat 4 Divisions in North Africa			

★ Held in Sixth (It) Army Reserve.

328

2 As at 'Lehrgang' D-Day 11 August 1943

SEVENTH ARMY	EIGHTH ARMY	GERMANS	ITALIANS
II (US) Corps	**XXX (Br) Corps**	**XIV PZ Corps**	**Sixth (It) Army**
3 (US) Inf } Messina	(Messina Peninsula)	15 PG	26 (Assietta) }
9 (US) Inf } Peninsula	50 (Br) Inf	HG PZ	28 (Aosta) } Remnants
1 (US) Inf } Reserve	51 (Highland) Inf	1 Para (Elements only)	4 (Livorno) only }
45 (US) Inf }	78 (Br) Inf	29 PG	54 (Napoli) }
Provisional Corps	**XIII (Br) Corps**	**Southern Italy**	
2 (US) Armd	(Preparing to cross Straits of Messina)	**LXXVI PZ Corps**	
82 (US) Airborne	1 (Cdn) Inf	3 PG	
	5 (Br) Inf	26 PG	
	In North Africa	**Sardinia**	
	1 (Br) Airborne	90 PG	
Totals		**Totals**	
11 Divisions in Sicily		3½ German Divisions in Sicily	
1 Division in North Africa		3 German Divisions in Southern Italy and Sardinia	

APPENDIX D

Orders of Battle of Allied Divisions in Post-Husky Contingency Plans

FIFTH ARMY

1 **Sardinia** (Brimstone)
(cancelled 20 July 1943)

VI (US) Corps
  1 (US) Armd
  34 (US) Inf
  36 (US) Inf

V (Br) Corps
  1 (Br) Inf
  4 or 56 (Br) Inf

Army Troops
82 (US) Airborne

2 **Taranto** (Musket)
(cancelled 27 July 1943)

VI (US) Corps
  1 (US) Armd
  34 (US) Inf
  36 (US) Inf
  82 (US) Airborne

One US or French Division to be nominated as follow-up.

3 **Naples** (Gangway and Barracuda)
(cancelled 27 July 1943)

Direct attacks on Naples in event of an Italian collapse. No orders of battle worked out.

4 **Salerno** (Avalanche)
(executed 9 September 1943)

VI (US) Corps
  36 (US) Inf
  45 (US) Inf
  1 or 2 (US) Armd

X (Br) Corps★
  46 (Br) Inf
  56 (Br) Inf
  7 (Br) Armd

Army Troops
  1 (Br) Airborne
  34 (US) Inf
  82 (US) Airborne

★ Loaded for either Avalanche or Buttress.

APPENDIX D

BRITISH FORCES

1 **Gulf of Gioia** (Buttress)
(cancelled 4 September 1943)

X (Br) Corps

46 (Br) Inf
56 (Br) Inf
7 (Br) Armd

2 **Crotone** (Goblet)
(cancelled 4 September 1943)

V (Br) Corps

1 (Br) Inf
4 (Br) Inf
78 (Br) Inf
82 (US) Airborne

3 **Crossing the Straits of Messina**
(Baytown)
(executed 3 September 1943)

XIII (Br) Corps

1 (Cdn) Inf
5 (Br) Inf

4 **Taranto** (Slapstick)
(executed 9 September 1943)

1 (Br) Airborne

APPENDIX E   Summary of Allied and German Divisions in 15 Army Group and German Army Group 'C'

Period	Dates	Allied Divisions British Sponsored — Br	Com-w'lth	Pol	US Sponsored — US	Fr	Bz	Total
1 Salerno to Volturno	October 1943	8	2	—	9	—	—	19
2 Bernhardt Line	December 1943	4	3	—	5	1	—	13
3 Gustav Line/Anzio Landing	22 January 1944	5	5	1	5	2	—	18
4 End of Winter Offensives	March 1944	5	5	2	6	3	—	21
5 **Diadem**	May 1944	5	7	2	7	4	—	25
6 Fall of Rome and the Beginning of **Overlord**	June 1944	5	7	2	7	4	—	25
7 Gothic Battles	August 1944	6	7	2	5	—	—	20
8 End of Autumn Offensives	December 1944	4 (d)	6 (e)	2	6 (f)	—	1	19
9 Final Offensive	April 1945	3 (g)	4	2	7 (h)	—	1	17

Notes (a) Five German mobile divisions replaced by four infantry divisions.
   (b) Four German divisions arrived from other fronts; one disbanded and five withdrawn to rear areas to reform in Italy.
   (c) Strength of all non-mobile divisions reduced by 1,700 men each.
   (d) 4 (Br) Inf to Greece and 1 (Br) Armd disbanded.

German Divisions			Operational Zone Divisions only			Allied withdrawals ordered by combined chiefs of staff
mobile	non-mobile					
PZ, PG or Para	Inf, Mtn or Jaeger	Total	Allied	German	Allied Superiority	
12	7	19	19	12	+7	
7 (a)	11	18	13	11	+2	Seven Allied divisions withdrawn for **Overlord**
9	14	23	18	15	+3	
9	15	24	21	17	+4	
8	15	23	25	18	+7	
9	17	26 (b)	25	19	+6	
8	18	26	20	22	−2	Six Allied divisions including all four French divisions withdrawn for **Dragoon**
6	21 (c)	27	19	20	−1	
5	18	23 (j)	17	19	−2	1 (Cdn) Corps and 1 (Br) Division withdrawn to North-West Europe

(e) 4 (Ind) Inf to Greece.
(f) 92 (Negro) Inf arrived from U.S.A.
(g) 46 (Br) Inf left for Greece.
(h) 10 (US) Mtn arrived from U.S.A.
(j) Four German divisions sent to Eastern and Western Fronts.

APPENDIX F Orders of Battle of Allied and German Divisions in Italy

1 From Salerno to the Volturno October 1943

ALLIES

GERMAN

FIFTH ARMY
(West Coast)

VI (US) Corps
1 (US) Armd
3 (US) Inf
34 (US) Inf
45 (US) Inf

X (Br) Corps
7 (Br) Armd*
46 (Br) Inf
56 (Br) Inf

Army Troops
36 (US) Inf
82 (US) Airborne*

EIGHTH ARMY
(Adriatic)

V (Br) Corps
1 (Br) Airborne
8 (Ind) Inf
78 (Br) Inf

XIII (Br) Corps
1 (Cdn) Inf
5 (Br) Inf

XXX (Br) Corps
50 (Br) Inf*
51 (Br) Inf*

SEVENTH ARMY (Sicily)
2 (US) Armd*

II (US) Corps
1 (US) Inf*
9 (US) Inf*

Total: 19 Divisions

*Earmarked for Overlord

C.-IN-C. SOUTH
(Kesselring)

LXXVI PZ Corps
(Adriatic)
16 PZ
1 Para
29 PG

XIV PZ Corps
(West-Coast)
26 PZ
3 PG
HG
15 PG

1 Para Corps
(Rome)
2 Para

ARMY GROUP 'C'
(Rommel)

Adriatic Command
162 (Turco) Inf†
18 PZ†
71 Inf

LI Mtn Corps
65 Inf
Adolf Hitler PZ
44 Inf

LXXXVII Corps
24 PZ
90 PG
305 Inf
94 Inf
76 Inf

Total: 19 Divisions

†Arrived after the Salerno Landings

Note *German Corps and Divisions are listed in sequence from east to west across the front.*

2 Gustav Line in early December 1943

ALLIES

GERMAN

FIFTH ARMY (West)

VI (US) Corps
34 (US) Inf
45 (US) Inf
2 (Moroc) Inf

II (US) Corps
36 (US) Inf

X (Br) Corps
46 (Br) Inf
56 (Br) Inf

Army Troops
3 (US) Inf
1 (US) Armd

EIGHTH ARMY (East)

V (Br) Corps
2 (NZ) Inf
8 (Ind) Inf
78 (Br) Inf

XIII (Br) Corps
1 (Cdn) Inf
5 (Br) Inf

Total: 13 Divisions

TENTH ARMY (Main Front)

LXXVI PZ Corps
65 Inf
26 PZ
1 Para
90 PG (arriving)

XIV PZ Corps
305 Inf
44 Inf
29 PG
15 PG
94 Inf

XI Para Corps
HG
3 PG

FOURTEENTH ARMY (Northern Italy)

Adriatic Command
162 (Turco) Inf
71 Inf
371 Inf

LI Mtn Corps
278 Inf
188 Mtn

LXXXVII Corps
356 Inf
334 Inf

In process of Forming
4 Para
16 SS PG
362 Inf

Total: 18 Divisions + 3 Forming

3 Anzio Landing 22 January 1944

ALLIES

FIFTH ARMY
Anzio Force

VI (US) Corps
1 (Br) Inf
3 (US) Inf

Reserve
1 (US) Armd
45 (US) Inf

Main Front

FEC
2 (Moroc) Inf
3 (Alg) Inf

II (US) Corps
34 (US) Inf
36 (US) Inf

X (Br) Corps
5 (Br) Inf
46 (Br) Inf
56 (Br) Inf

EIGHTH ARMY

V (Br) Corps
1 (Cdn) Inf
8 (Ind) Inf

XIII (Br) Corps
4 (Ind) Inf
78 (Br) Inf

Arriving in Army Area
3 (Carp) Inf
5 (Cdn) Armd

ARMY GROUP RESERVE
2 (NZ) Inf

Total: 18 Divisions

GERMAN

TENTH ARMY
(Main Front)

LXXVI PZ Corps
1 Para
26 PZ
334 Inf
305 Inf
3 PG

XIV PZ Corps
5 Mtn
44 Inf
71 Inf
15 PG
HG†
29 PG†
94 Inf

I Para Corps
90 PG†
4 Para *
92 Inf *

FOURTEENTH ARMY
(Northern Italy)

Adriatic Command
162 (Turco) Inf
16 SS PG

LI Mtn Corps
362 Inf
278 Inf

LXXXVII Corps
356 Inf
65 Inf

Army Troops
114 Jaeger
188 Mtn

Total: 23 Divisions

*Still Forming   †Earmarked as Army Group Mobile Reserve

4 The End of the Winter Offensive March 1944

ALLIES | GERMAN

ALLIES

FIFTH ARMY
Anzio Beachhead

VI (US) Corps
1 (Br) Inf
1 (US) Armd
3 (US) Inf
5 (Br) Inf
45 (US) Inf

Main Front

II (US) Corps
34 (US) Inf
36 (US) Inf

FEC
2 (Moroc) Inf
3 (Alg) Inf

X (Br) Corps
4 (Moroc) Mtn
88 (US) Inf

NZ Corps
2 (NZ) Inf
4 (Ind) Inf
78 (Br) Inf

EIGHTH ARMY

XIII (Br) Corps
6 (Br) Armd

I (Cdn) Corps
5 (Cdn) Armd

II (Pol) Corps
3 (Carp) Inf
5 (Kres) Inf

V (Br) Corps
1 (Cdn) Inf
8 (Ind) Inf

Army Troops
4 (Br) Inf

Total: 21 Divisions

GERMAN

TENTH ARMY
(Main Front)

LI Mtn Corps
305 Inf
334 Inf
114 Jaeger

XIV PZ Corps
5 Mtn
44 Inf
1 Para
15 PG
71 Inf
94 Inf

FOURTEENTH ARMY
(Anzio)

LXXVI PZ Corps
715 Inf
362 Inf

I Para Corps
3 PG
65 Inf
4 Para

Army Reserve
26 PZ
92 Inf (forming)

Army Group Reserve
90 PG
29 PG

ARMY GROUP VON ZANGEN
(Northern Italy)

Adriatic Command
16 SS PG
278 Inf
188 Mtn

LXXV Corps
(Liguria)
HG
162 Inf
356 Inf

Total: 24 Divisions

5 The 'Diadem' Orders of Battle 11 May 1944

ALLIES		GERMAN	
FIFTH ARMY *Anzio Beachhead*	EIGHTH ARMY	FOURTEENTH ARMY (Anzio)	TENTH ARMY (Main Front)
VI (US) Corps 1 (Br) Inf 1 (US) Armd 3 (US) Inf 5 (Br) Inf 34 (US) Inf 45 (US) Inf	**X (Br) Corps** 2 (NZ) Inf **XIII (Br) Corps** 4 (Br) Inf 6 (Br) Armd 8 (Ind) Inf 78 (Br) Inf	**LXXVI PZ Corps** 715 Inf 362 Inf 26 PZ **I Para Corps** 3 PG 65 Inf 4 Para	**Gruppe 'Hauck'** 305 Inf 334 Inf 114 Jaeger **LI Mtn Corps** 5 Mtn 44 Inf 1 Para
Main Front **FEC** 1 (Fr) Motor Inf 2 (Moroc) Inf 3 (Alg) Inf 4 (Moroc) Mtn **II (US) Corps** 85 (US) Inf 88 (US) Inf	**I (Cdn) Corps** 1 (Cdn) Inf 5 (Cdn) Armd **II (Pol) Corps** 3 (Carp) Inf 5 (Kres) Inf **Army Troops** 6 (SA) Armd	**Army Reserve** 29 PG 92 Inf	**XIV PZ Corps** 71 Inf 94 Inf 15 PG **Army Reserve** 90 PG

FIFTH ARMY (Main Front)	EIGHTH ARMY	FOURTEENTH ARMY (Anzio)	TENTH ARMY (Main Front)
Army Troops 36 (US) Inf	ARMY GROUP TROOPS (Adriatic) **V (Br) Corps** 4 (Ind) Inf 10 (Ind) Inf	ARMY GROUP VON ZANGEN HG 162 (Turco) Inf 356 Inf 278 Inf 188 Mtn	
	Total: 25 Divisions	**Total: 23 Divisions**	

6 Changes in the German Order of Battle Caused by 'Diadem'

1 The following additional divisions were sent to reinforce Army Group 'C' just as **Overlord** was launched:

> 16 SS PG from Hungary
> 19 Luftwaffe from Holland
> 20 Luftwaffe from Denmark
> 42 Jaeger from the Balkans

2 As a result of the heavy losses sustained during **Diadem** the following divisions were withdrawn from the front to reform in Northern Italy:

> 65, 71, 94, 362 and 715 Inf

3 92 Inf was disbanded.

4 Army Group Von Zangen was reduced to 2 divisions.

5 Thus by the beginning of June when **Overlord** began the Allied Armies in Italy were containing 26 German Divisions of which 5 were by then too weak and disorganized to stay in the line.

7 The Gothic Line Battles end of August 1944

ALLIES

FIFTH ARMY
(West of Apennines)

XIII (Br) Corps
1 (Br) Inf
6 (Br) Armd
8 (Ind) Inf

II (US) Corps
34 (US) Inf
88 (US) Inf
91 (US) Inf

IV (US) Corps
1 (US) Armd
6 (SA) Armd
85 (US) Inf

EIGHTH ARMY
(Adriatic)

I (Cdn) Corps
1 (Cdn) Inf
5 (Cdn) Armd

II (Pol) Corps
3 (Carp) Inf
5 (Kres) Inf

V (Br) Corps
1 (Br) Armd
4 (Br) Inf
4 (Ind) Inf
46 (Br) Inf
56 (Br) Inf

X (Br) Corps
10 (Ind) Inf

Army Troops
2 (NZ) Inf

Total: 20 Divisions

GERMAN

FOURTEENTH ARMY
(West)

I Para Corps
356 Inf
4 Para
362 Inf

XIV PZ Corps
3 PG
26 PZ
65 Inf
16 SS PG

Army Reserve
29 PG
90 PG
20 Luftwaffe*

TENTH ARMY
(East)

LXXVI PZ Corps
278 Inf
71 Inf
5 Mtn
1 Para
162 (Turco) Inf

LI Mtn Corps
114 Jaeger
44 Inf
305 Inf
334 Inf
715 Inf

Army Reserve
15 PG
98 Inf

ARMY OF LIGURIA AND ADRIATIC COMMAND

LXXV Corps
42 Jaeger
34 Inf

Adriatic Command
188 Mtn
94 Inf

Total: 26 Divisions

*Absorbed 19 Luftwaffe Division

8 The End of the Allied Autumn Offensive 30 December 1944

ALLIES

FIFTH ARMY
(West)

XIII (Br) Corps
1 (Br) Inf
6 (Br) Armd
8 (Ind) Inf
78 (Br) Inf

II (US) Corps
1 (US) Armd
34 (US) Inf
85 (US) Inf
88 (US) Inf
91 (US) Inf

IV (US) Corps
1 (Bz) Inf
6 (SA) Armd

Army Troops
92 (US) Negro Inf

EIGHTH ARMY
(East)

I (Cdn) Corps
1 (Cdn) Inf
5 (Cdn) Armd

II (Pol) Corps
3 (Carp) Inf
5 (Kres) Inf

V (Br) Corps
2 (NZ) Inf
10 (Ind) Inf
56 (Br) Inf

X (Br) Corps
Independent
Brigades only

Total: 19 Divisions

GERMAN

FOURTEENTH ARMY
(Inactive Western Front only)

LI Mtn Corps
232 Inf
145 Inf

ARMY OF LIGURIA

LXXV Corps
34 Inf
5 Mtn

ADRIATIC

XCVII Corps
257 Inf
188 Mtn
710 Inf
155 Reserve

Army Group Troops
162 (Turco) Inf

TENTH ARMY
(Active Bologna and Adriatic Fronts)

LXXIII Corps
114 Jaeger
16 SS PG
356 Inf

LXXVI PZ Corps
278 Inf
29 PG
90 PG

XIV PZ Corps
715 Inf
334 Inf

I Para Corps
1 Para	65 Inf
42 Jaeger	4 Para
362 Inf	94 Inf

Army Reserve
26 PZ	305 Inf
98 Inf	157 Mtn

Total: 27 Divisions

Note   *The establishment of German Infantry, Jaeger and Mountain Divisions were each reduced by 1,700 men from this period onwards.*

9 The Final Allied Offensive April 1945

ALLIES

FIFTH ARMY
(West)

II (US) Corps
6 (SA) Armd
34 (US) Inf
88 (US) Inf
91 (US) Inf

IV (US) Corps
1 (US) Armd
1 (Bz) Inf
10 (US) Mtn

Army Troops
85 (US) Inf
92 (US) Negro Inf

EIGHTH ARMY
(East)

V (Br) Corps
2 (NZ) Inf
8 (Ind) Inf
56 (Br) Inf
78 (Br) Inf

II (Pol) Corps
3 (Carp) Inf
5 (Kres) Inf

X (Br) Corps
Independent
Brigades
only

XIII (Br) Corps
10 (Ind) Inf

Army Troops
6 (Br) Armd

Total: 17 Divisions

GERMAN

TENTH ARMY
(East)

LXXIII Corps
155 Inf
29 PG

XXVI PZ Corps
42 Jaeger
362 Inf
98 Inf
162 (Turco) Inf

I Para Corps
26 PZ
4 Para
278 Inf
1 Para
305 Inf

FOURTEENTH ARMY
(West)

XIV PZ Corps
65 Inf
94 Inf
8 Mtn

LI Mtn Corps
334 Inf
114 Jaeger
232 Inf
148 Inf

Army Group Reserve
90 PG

ARMY OF LIGURIA

LXXV Corps
34 Inf
5 Mtn

ADRIATIC

XCVII Corps
237 Inf
188 Mtn

Total: 23 Divisions

APPENDIX G A Chronology of the Battle for Italy

Month	Strategic events		Tactical events		
	ALLIES	AXIS	SEVENTH US ARMY	EIGHTH BR ARMY	AXIS FORCES
January 1943	Casablanca Conference				
February 1943	Husky Planning starts	Ambrosio replaces Cavallero as Italian Chief of Staff			Guzzoni becomes C.-in-C. Sicily
March 1943	First Husky Plan approved by Combined Chiefs of Staff	Hitler and Mussolini meet at Klesheim			
April 1943	Husky Plan revised to meet Montgomery's objections				
May 1943	12 Final Husky Plan approved Trident Conference starts in Washington 29 Churchill visits Eisenhower with Marshall to discuss post-Husky Plans	10 Ambrosio accepts three German divisions 19 Hitler orders preparation of Plan Alarich 22 Ambrosio accepts fourth German division	8 Preparations for Husky start	7 Fall of Tunis	During May 15 PG Div forms in Sicily 90 PG Div forms in Sardinia Hermann Göring Div reforms near Naples

	Allied Command / Strategy	Sicily Operations	**Husky**	Axis / German Moves
June 1943	**14** Ambrosio accepts a total of six German divisions and two Corps HQs		**7** Intense bombing of Pantelleria starts **11 Pantelleria falls**	**15** 3 PG, 16 PZ, 26 PZ and 29 PG Divs and XIV and LXXVI PZ Corps warned for Italy **20** HG Div moves to Sicily and 15 PG Div moves to Palermo **26** Kesselring's last conference with Guzzoni before **Husky**
July 1943	**5** Operation **Zitadelle** starts in Russia **13** Operation **Zita-delle** stopped by Hitler **16** Alexander issues directions for development of operations **17** Eisenhower advises attack on Italy, not Sardinia **19** Bombing of Rome marshalling yards **19 Hitler and Musso-lini meet at Feltre**	**11** HG Div's counter-attacks driven off **16** Agrigento falls **16** Prima Sole Bridge taken **18** Patton starts drive for Palermo **19** Canadians reach Leonforte	**3** Second Phase of **Husky** Air Plan **10 Husky** Landings **11** Syracuse falls **12** Augusta falls **13** Advance on Catania starts	**13** XIV PZ Corps, I Para and 29 PG Divs ordered to Sicily **15** Guzzoni orders withdrawal to San Stefano Line

	Strategic events		Tactical events		
Month	ALLIES	AXIS	SEVENTH US ARMY	EIGHTH BR ARMY	AXIS FORCES
July 1943 *(cont)*				21 Leonforte falls; Montgomery decides to change plan	
			22 Palermo falls		
			23 North coast road cut		
		24 Fascist Grand Council meets			
		26 Fall of Mussolini			
	27 Planning of **Avalanche** starts	27 Planning evacuation of Sicily ordered by OKW			27 Withdrawal to San Fratello Line authorized
					28 Evacuation planning starts
			28 Nicosia falls	28 Agira falls	
				29 78 (Br) Div committed at Catenanuova	
		31 Italian Crown Council decides to seek peace. **Achse Plan** ready	31 San Stefano falls		
August 1943		1 Ambrosio authorizes entry of German 44 Div into Italy 2 Army Group 'B' starts to enter Italy in strength 3 First Italian emissary arrives in Lisbon			
	3 Alexander asks Navy and Air Forces to seal Straits of Messina			3 Centuripe falls	3 Withdrawal to Tortorice Line authorized
			5 Troina falls 7/8 Amphibious landing at San Fratello	5 Catania falls	

August 1943
(cont)

14 Quadrant Conference starts in Quebec

15 Castellano arrives in Madrid

17 'Short Terms' agreed as basis for surrender negotiations

8 Kesselring orders evacuation of Sicily

11/12 Landing at Brolo

15/16 Abortive landing at Barcelona
16 **Fall of Messina**

8 Bronte falls

15 Taormina falls

15/16 Landing at Scarletta

17 Commandos reach Messina

8 Bronte falls

11 Hube starts evacuation of Sicily

17 Hube reports evacuation of Sicily complete

The Conquest of Sicily complete—The Invasion of Italy starts

	FIFTH ARMY	EIGHTH ARMY	GERMAN FORCES
August 1943	Preparation for Avalanche	Preparation for **Baytown**	Preparation for defence of Italian mainland and Sardinia

18 Post-**Husky** Plans approved
19 Bedell Smith and Strong arrive in Lisbon to meet Castellano

25 Zanussi arrives in Lisbon
27 Castellano returns to Rome with 'Short Terms'
30 Final revision of Plan **Achse**
31 Castellano arrives for final negotiations at Alexander's HQ

1 Badoglio accepts terms
3 Castellano signs instruments of surrender

End of August
16 PZ Div moves to Salerno

September 1943

3 XIII (Br) Corps cross Straits of Messina (Operation **Baytown**)

Month	Strategic events		Tactical events		
	ALLIES	AXIS	SEVENTH US ARMY	EIGHTH BR ARMY	AXIS FORCES
September 1943 (*cont*)		**8 Announcement of Italian Surrender**			
		9 Achse ordered King and Badoglio escape	**9 Salerno Landing** (Operation **Avalanche**)	**9** Taranto occupied by I (Br) Airborne Div (Operation **Slapstick**)	**9 Achse** implemented
	10 Measures taken to reinforce Salerno				**10** Evacuation of Sardinia and Corsica started
					11 Rome in German hands
					11 onwards Concentration of XIV and LXXVI PZ Corps at Salerno
			Battle of Salerno		
				16 Patrols reach Fifth Army	**16** Von Vietinghoff accepts defeat at Salerno and advises disengagement
		17 Kesselring orders withdrawal to Volturno	**17**		
	21 Alexander's First Plans for winter in Italy				
				22 Bari occupied	
			23 Advance from Salerno begins		
				24 Ofanto River crossed	
				27 Foggia falls	
			28 Avellino falls		
				29 Fortore River reached	

October 1943

1 Alexander starts major review of strategy

4 Hitler orders Kesselring to hold South of Rome

November 1943

21 Kesselring confirmed by Hitler as C.-in-C. South-West

22 Sextant Conference starts in Cairo

---

5 Volturno River reached

12 ⎫ **Crossing of**
15 ⎭ **Volturno River**

2 Garigliano River reached

First Battle of Camino
5
15
16 Preparations start for attack on Bernhardt Line

---

1 Naples falls

3 ⎫
6 ⎭ **Battle of Termoli**

15 Vinchiaturo reached

2 Crossing of Trigno River

8 Sangro River reached

19 Preliminary operations over Sangro
20
28 Rain stops operations

---

3 16 PZ Div sent to Termoli

6 16 PZ Div withdraws to Trigno River

Mid-October
Inf Divs start moving south to relieve mobile divisions in the line

4 Withdrawal to Gustav Line starts on Adriatic Coast

10 26 PZ Div switched to Fifth Army Front

Mid-November
29 PG Div reinforces front opposite Fifth Army

25 26 PZ Div returns to Adriatic with 90 PG Div

	Strategic events		Tactical events		
Month	ALLIES	AXIS	SEVENTH US ARMY	EIGHTH BR ARMY	AXIS FORCES
November 1943 (*cont*)	28 Eureka Conference starts in Tehran			29 ⎱ Battle of 1 ⎰ Sangro	
December 1943	3 Final Cairo Conference		2 ⎱ **Second Battle of Camino** (Operation **Rain Coat**) 10 ⎰	4 ⎱ **First Battle of Orsogna** 7 ⎰	
	11 Churchill ill at Carthage		17 Monte Samoucro falls 18 Mark Clark advises cancellation of **Shingle**	18 Second Battle of Orsogna 23 Third Battle of Orsogna 20 ⎱ **Battle of Ortona** 28 ⎰ 30 Montgomery hands over to Oliver Leese	
	25 Churchill confers with commanders on future operations 28 Roosevelt agrees to retention of shipping in Mediterranean until 5 February				
January 1944	2 Alexander orders **Shingle** for 21 January 8 Maitland Wilson assumes supreme command of the Mediterranean Theatre				

January 1944
(cont)

12 Directive for winter offensive issued

9 VI (US) Corps leaves line to prepare for **Shingle**

15 Gustav Line reached before Cassino

17 X (Br) Corps' crossing of Garigliano River

20 36 (US) Div's abortive attack over Rapido River at St Angelo

22 **Anzio Landing (Operation Shingle)**

20 29, 90 and HG Divs counter-attack X (Br) Corps on Garigliano

22 Alarm Scheme **'Richard'** implemented —Garigliano counter-attacks stopped

23 Fourteenth Army and LXXVI PZ Corps move to Anzio Beachhead

MAIN FRONT

ANZIO BEACHHEAD

24 II (US) Corps starts 1st Battle of Cassino

First Battle of Cassino

24 Hitler orders destruction of 'Anzio Abcess'

25 First break-out stopped at Campoleone and Cisterna

30 Second break-out fails

3 Von Mackensen starts first preliminary attack at Anzio

7 Second preliminary attack

11 NZ Corps takes over at Cassino

15 Bombing of Monastery

February 1944

4 British Salient destroyed

7 'Factory' lost

351

	Strategic events		Tactical events		
Month	ALLIES	AXIS	SEVENTH US ARMY	EIGHTH BR ARMY	AXIS FORCES
February 1944 (*cont*)			19 First German counter-offensive defeated	16 Second Battle of 18 Cassino	16 First German 19 counter-offensive at Anzio
	22 Wilson asks for cancellation of **Anvil**. Harding's appreciation for Spring offensive completed				
	25 Eisenhower's compromise on **Anvil** accepted			24 NZ Corps ready to attack Cassino again when weather is suitable	
March 1944			3 Second German counter-offensive defeated		28 Second German 3 counter-offensive at Anzio
		4 Kesselring orders withdrawal of mobile divisions into reserve			4 Von Mackensen orders Fourteenth Army onto defensive
	20 Alexander decides to halt operations and to prepare for **Diadem** 24 Postponement of **Anvil**			15 Bombing of Cassino Town 15 Third Battle of Cassino 25	19 Heidrich's counter-attack at Cassino

March 1944 (*cont*)

26 XIII (Br) Corps relieves NZ Corps at Cassino

April 1944

17 Directive issued by British Chiefs of Staff to Alexander to carry out **Diadem**

Rest and preparation for Spring Offensives

May 1944

19 Alexander authorizes move of 36 (US) Div to Anzio

DIADEM OFFENSIVE

13 90 PG Div committed
17 26 PZ Div committed; 305 and 334 Divs ordered over from Adriatic
19 29 PG Div committed

18 Cassino falls
19 Gaeta falls

23 Withdrawal to Caesar Line ordered. Hitler orders four extra divisions to be sent to Kesselring

23 Hitler Line broken

23 Breakout starts at Anzio

25 HG Div committed

26 Mark Clark changes direction and advances on Rome

28 Arce falls

30 Monte Artemisio found unoccupied
1 Final Drive for Rome

11 ⎱ DIADEM ⎰ 4

June 1944

4 Von Mackensen replaced by Lemelsen

Rome Falls

2/3 HG Div breaks off engagement; Caesar Line collapses.

6 Overlord Landings

353

	Strategic events		Tactical events		
Month	ALLIES	AXIS	SEVENTH US ARMY	EIGHTH BR ARMY	AXIS FORCES
June 1944 *(cont)*	7 Alexander submits appreciation of future operations 8 ⎫ **Last Anvil Debate** 29 ⎭ 30 Churchill's last effort to stop **Anvil**		7 Civitavecchia falls		
July 1944	2 Directive issued to mount **Anvil**		9 Viterbo falls 19 Elba falls 20 ⎫ 30 ⎭ 5 ⎫ 15 ⎭ 19 Leghorn falls	**Transimene Line Battles** **Arrezo Line Battles** 18 Ancona falls	
August 1944	4 Change of Plan for breaching Gothic Line; **Olive** plan accepted by Alexander at Orvicto 15 **Dragoon** (Anvil) launched on French Riviera 19 **Paris** entered by Eisenhower's Armies 24 **Grenoble** reached by **Dragoon** Forces		4 Arno River reached	4 Florence entered 13 Plan **Olive** issued 22 Eighth Army crosses Apennines	4 Withdrawal to north bank of Arno River

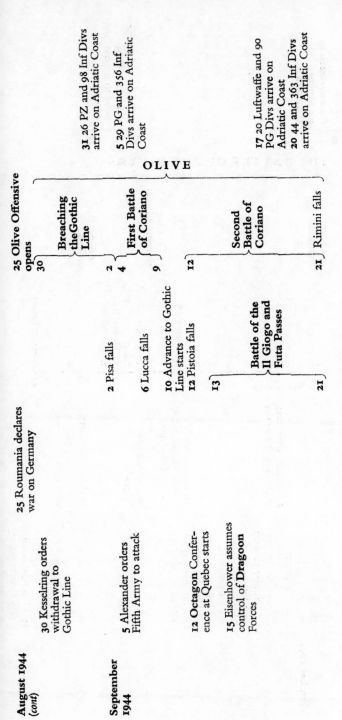

August 1944
(cont)

25 Roumania declares war on Germany

30 Kesselring orders withdrawal to Gothic Line

31 26 PZ and 98 Inf Divs arrive on Adriatic Coast

September 1944

5 Alexander orders Fifth Army to attack

5 29 PG and 356 Inf Divs arrive on Adriatic Coast

2 Pisa falls

25 Olive Offensive opens

OLIVE

30 Breaching the Gothic Line

6 Lucca falls

2

4 First Battle of Coriano

9

10 Advance to Gothic Line starts

12 Pistoia falls

12 Octagon Conference at Quebec starts

13 Battle of the Il Giogo and Futa Passes

12 Second Battle of Coriano

15 Eisenhower assumes control of Dragoon Forces

17 20 Luftwaffe and 90 PG Divs arrive on Adriatic Coast

20 44 and 363 Inf Divs arrive on Adriatic Coast

21

21 Rimini falls

	Strategic events		Tactical events		
Month	ALLIES	AXIS	SEVENTH US ARMY	EIGHTH BR ARMY	AXIS FORCES
September 1944 (cont)	26 Defeat at Arnhem		**22** **Advance on Imola Road** / **27** Monte Battaglia falls	**22** On the Uso River / **25** Crossing the Uso River	**28** } **Counter-attacks on Monte Battaglia** **4**
October 1944	7 Alexander presents plans for trans-Adriatic operations to Churchill asks Roosevelt for three US Divs for Italy / 15 4 (Ind) Div starts moving to Greece / 29 Alexander briefs Army Commanders on winter plan	5 Germans withdraw to Hungarian frontier / **Mid-October** Russians on Danube, South of Budapest / 20 Russians enter Belgrade / 25 Kesselring hurt; Von Vietinghoff takes over	**2** } **Advance on Route 56** / **20** Monte Grande taken / **23** Monte Belmonte taken / **26** **27** Offensive halted	**29** On the Fiumicino River / **17** Crossing of Fiumicino River / **24** Savio River crossed	**20** } 16 PZ, 29 and 90 PG and 1 Para Divs move to oppose Fifth Army **24**

THE BATTLE OF THE RIVERS

November 1944

Mid-November Russians stopped near Budapest

22 Maitland Wilson advises against trans-Adriatic operations
25 Alexander assumes Supreme Command in Mediterranean

31 Ronco River crossed
9 Forli taken
16 Route 67 cleared

26 Lamone River reached

December 1944

1 Von Vietinghoff changes Army boundary to give both active fronts to Tenth Army

2 Chiefs of Staff direct Alexander to confine operations to Italy

THE BATTLE OF THE RIVERS

8 90 PG Div moves to Adriatic
12 98 Inf Div moves to Adriatic

4 Ravenna falls
7 Faenza approached

7 Fifth Army ready to resume offensive

16 Alexander orders Fifth Army to be ready to attack

16 Ardennes counter-offensive launched

16 Faenza falls

17 29 PG Div moves to Adriatic

26 ⎫ Mussolini's
28 ⎭ Serchio offensive

26 ⎫ Serchio Offensive stopped by 92 (US)
28 ⎭ and 8 (Ind) Divs

29 End of the Battle of the Rivers

357

Month	Strategic events		Tactical events		
	ALLIES	AXIS	SEVENTH US ARMY	EIGHTH BR ARMY	AXIS FORCES
December 1944 (*cont*)	**30** Alexander orders defensive and start of preparations for Spring Offensive		**30 Both Allied Armies go over to the Defensive**		
January 1945	**8** Alexander submits plans for Spring Offensive	**1** Kesselring returns to command in Italy			
		20 Hungarians sign Armistice		Rest and Retraining	
	30 Argonaut Conference in Malta **31** Five Divisions ordered from Mediterranean to North-West Europe				
February 1945		**Mid-February** Tentative peace feelers from SS General Wolff **13** Russians enter Budapest		Rest and Retraining	
March 1945	**7** Third US Army crosses Rhine at Remagen	**8** SS General Wolff starts negotiations for surrender of Army Group 'C'. Kesselring promoted C.-in-C. South-West. Von Vietinghoff takes over in Italy		Rest and Retraining	
				Rest and Retraining	

March 1945 (*cont*)	**23** Montgomery crosses Rhine			
	29 Russians enter Austria			**29** PG Div moves towards Venice
April 1945			**1** 'Spit' taken	
			4 Islands taken	
			6 Landing on 'Wedge'	
			9 Final Offensive Opens	
				7 90 PG Div sends one regiment to West Coast
	13 Vienna falls to Russians			
	14 Hitler turns down Von Vietinghoff's request to withdraw to Po River	**14 Final Offensive Opens**		
	20 Von Vietinghoff orders withdrawal to Po River			
		21 Bologna entered		
			22 Breakout from Argenta Gap	
		23	Armoured Divisions meet at Finali	
		25	Crossing the Po River	
		26 Verona entered		
		27	Adige River crossed	
	28 German delegates at Caserta			
May 1945		**2 Army Group 'C' surrenders to 15 Army Group**		

359

SHORT BIBLIOGRAPHY

This account of the Battle for Italy is based on three groups of sources:

1 The Official Reports and Despatches of the Allied Commanders

The Report by the Supreme Allied Commander Mediterranean, Field-Marshal The Lord Wilson of Libya, to the Combined Chiefs of Staff: Parts I, II and III, HMSO, 1948

The Report by the Supreme Allied Commander Mediterranean, Field-Marshal The Earl Alexander of Tunis, to the Combined Chiefs of Staff, HMSO, 1951

The Despatches of Field-Marshal The Earl Alexander of Tunis to the Secretary of State for War.

The Conquest of Sicily, London Gazette, 12 Feb 1948

The Allied Armies in Italy, London Gazette, 12 June 1950

2 Official Histories So Far Published

The History of the Second World War (HMSO)
Grand Strategy, vol. V
Grand Strategy, vol. VI
The War at Sea, vol. III
The Strategic Air Offensive, vols. I to IV

The US Army in World War II (Department of the Army, Washington)
Strategic Planning for Coalition Warfare 1943–1944
Mediterranean Theatre of Operations (Sicily to the Surrender of Italy)
The Official History of the Canadian Army in the Second World War: *The Canadians in Italy*, 1956

The Official History of New Zealand in the Second World War: *The Campaign in Italy*, 1960

The Royal Air Force 1939–45, vols. II and III, HMSO, 1954

The US Army Air Forces in World War II, vol. II, 1949

The Rise and Fall of the German Air Force (Air Ministry), 1948

The History of United States Naval Operations in World War II vol. IX, 1957

3 **Memoirs and Biographies of Senior Commanders**

The Alexander Memoirs, ed. John North, 1962

Anders, General, *An Army in Exile*, 1949

Badoglio, Marshal, *Italy in the Second World War*, 1948

Bradley, General Omar, *A Soldier's Story*, 1951

Churchill, Sir Winston, *The Second World War*, vols. IV, V, VI, 1954

Count Ciano's Diaries, ed. Andreas Major, 1952

Clark, General Mark, *Calculated Risk*, 1950

Cunningham of Hyndhope, Admiral of the Fleet the Viscount, *A Sailor's Odyssey*

Eisenhower, General, *Crusade in Europe*, 1948

Farago, Ladislas, *Patton*, 1963

Guingand, General de, *Operation Victory*, 1947

The Memoirs of Field-Marshal Kesselring, 1953

Montgomery of Alamein, Field-Marshal the Viscount, *El Alamein to the Sangro*, 1948

Von Senger und Etterlin, General, *Neither Fear nor Hope*, 1963.

Additional background information has been culled from:

Böhmler, Colonel R., *Monte Cassino*, 1964

Buckley, Christopher, *Road to Rome*, 1945

Kippenberger, General, *Infantry Brigadier*, 1949

Linklater, Eric, *The Campaign in Italy*, 1945

Majdalany, Fred, *The Monastery*, 1945 and *Cassino; Portrait of a Battle*, 1957

Pond, Hugh, *Sicily*, 1962 and *Salerno*, 1961

Starr, Colonel C. G., *Salerno to the Alps: A History of Fifth Army*, 1948

Warlimont, General Walter, *Inside Hitler's Headquarters*, 1964

Index

INDEX

Barbara Line, 131, 135, 140
Barcellona, Sicily, 76
Bari, 85, 96, 98, 99, 123, 125
Barletta, 125, 147
Barracuda, Plan, 84
Bastia:
    Bridge, 297, 302, 306, 308
    Corsica, 119
    Romanga, 298, 299, 307, 308
Battaglia, Monte, 276
Battapaglia, 112, 114–17, 125
Baytown, Plan, 85–7, 94, 118
BBC, 94
Belgium, 291, 293
Belgrade, 287
Belmonte, Monte, 280
Belvedere, Colli, 188
Benevento, 125, 127
Bergamini, C., Italian Admiral, 106
Berio, Alberto, 88
Berlin, 282
Bernhardt Line, 131, 132, 141–4, 154, 172, 180, 318, 319
Bessel, German Gen., 117
Bibbiena, 250, 274
Biferno, River, 127, 128
Big Red One, 52
Bizerta, 103, 116
Bode:
    Blocking Group, 227, 232
    German Col., 228
Bologna, 253, 254, 267, 270–6, 279–90, 294–300, 304, 305, 309–14
Bolshevik East, 23
Bon, Cap, 33
Bondeno, 298, 304, 314
Bordeaux, 207
Boundaries, 57, 60, 65
Bradley, O., US Gen., 45, 47, 53, 59, 60, 63–65, 73, 265
Bradman, Codeword, 210
Brazilian Expeditionary Division, 258, 292, 298, 304
Brenner Pass, 70, 71, 89, 97, 98, 254, 294, 300
Brimstone, Plan, 83, 85
Brindisi, 96, 98
British Army:
    15 Army Group, 53, 58, 60, 65, 78, 136, 178, 234, 258, 264, 265, 285, 286, 290–4
    First Army, 19, 122
    Eighth Army, 19, 30, 36–9, 45, 50–4, 60–7, 73, 76, 85, 87, 94, 96, 99–102, 107, 112, 113, 117–27, 135–49, 152, 156, 161, 166, 172, 176, 181, 184, 185, 188, 189, 204, 210, 211, 222–7, 238–51, 255, 259, 264–90, 294–315
    Twelfth Army, 30
    Corps:
        V, 83–5, 96, 125–8, 142, 143, 147–52, 224, 250, 251, 266, 268, 271, 272, 276–81, 289, 301–7, 311, 314, 315
        X, 83–5, 88, 108–10, 114–17, 124–40, 154, 156, 171–83, 189, 204, 224, 244, 250, 251, 259, 266, 269, 281, 301–3, 314

        XIII, 37, 45, 50, 52, 56, 59–63, 66, 67, 73, 76, 101, 102, 125–8, 143, 147, 151–3, 223, 224, 232–8, 244, 250, 259, 266, 269, 274, 275, 280, 293, 301, 303, 308, 312, 314
        XXX, 38, 45, 50, 58–63, 66, 67, 73, 76
    Divisions:
        1 (Br) Inf, 40, 167–73, 183–90, 198, 200, 207, 225, 242, 274
        1 (Br) Airborne, 49, 61, 62, 96, 118, 124, 125, 127, 147
        1 (Br) Armd, 268, 272, 275, 277
        4 (Br) Inf, 224, 232–5, 250, 268, 276, 287
        5 (Br) Inf, 45, 61, 63, 67, 73, 76, 101, 102, 118, 127, 128, 147, 153, 172, 176, 208, 225, 242
        6 (Br) Armd, 215, 224, 235, 243, 250, 308, 314
        7 (Br) Armd, 108, 116, 119, 126, 127, 133–5, 140, 141, 154, 172
        46 (Br) Inf, 108, 111–15, 126, 127, 133–5, 140, 141, 155, 181, 268, 272, 287
        50 (Br) Inf, 45, 61–3, 67, 73, 76, 140
        51 (Highland) Inf, 45, 58, 60–3, 66, 67, 73, 76, 140
        56 (Br) Inf, 108, 111–14, 127, 133–5, 140, 141, 155, 156, 176, 177, 190, 198, 199, 207, 208, 268, 272, 278, 292, 301, 302, 306–8
        78 (Br) Inf, 67, 73, 125–8, 135, 142, 143, 147–53, 166, 189, 209, 210, 215, 224, 235, 280, 302, 308
    Brigades:
        1 (Br) Airlanding, 49
        1 (Br) Guards, 215
        2 (Br) Para, 301, 302, 308
        4 (Br) Armd, 147, 150
British Chief of Combined Operations, 21
British Chiefs of Staff, 12, 20, 21, 36, 85–7, 119, 137, 163, 168, 206, 219–22, 251, 252, 257, 264
British Colonialism, 12
British Fleet, 48, 106
    12 Cruiser Squadron, 96, 109, 118
    15 Cruiser Squadron, 109
British Imperialism, 12
British Joint Planners, 21, 31, 33, 121, 290
Brolo, Sicily, 76
Brooke, The Viscount Alan, British Field Marshal, 20, 21, 255, 257, 291
Brudio, 298, 299, 302, 303, 308
Buccaneer, Plan, 163, 165, 168
Budapest, 287
Buelowis, German Gen., 295
Buffalo, Codename, 293
Bulgaria, 269
Burma, 163, 281
Buttress, Plan, 83–8

Caen, 40
Caesar Line, 223, 241–5, 249, 295
Cairo:
    Egypt, 30, 37, 161, 164, 165
    Monte, 188, 192, 209, 236–8, 244
    Village, 188

INDEX

INDEX

INDEX

C02022496

RENEWALS 458-4574

DATE DUE

MAY - 7			

D
763
.I8
J25
1967b

B5136387

Library
University of Texas
at San Antonio

SWITZERLAND

Brenner
Pass

• Feltre

ALPS

ALPS

L. Garda

Adige

MILAN

VERONA

PADUA

VENETIAN LINE

Ve

MANTUA

Adige

Turin

Po

ALESSANDRIA

PIACENZA

Po

Ostiglia

Bondeno

FERRARA

L. Comacchio

PARMA

R9

MODENA

R12

Panaro

Reno

R9

Argenta

LIGURIA

APENNINES

Serchio

Vergato

R64

Bologna

R16

RAV

R9

Imola

Genoa

Firenzuola

Faenza

LA SPEZIA

R1

Futa

R67

Forli

GULF OF GENOA

PISTOIA

R65

Cesena

RIMINI

GOTHIC LINE

LUCCA

Florence

PISA

Arno

Bibbiena

APEN

Leghorn

Cecina

Volterra

AREZZO

R69

Cecina

R1

SIENA

PERUGIA

R2

L. Trasimene

Chiusi

Orcia

GROSSETO

Ombrone

BASTIA

ORVIETO

R2

ELBA

R3
TE
R

Corsica

VITERBO

R1

R2

CIVITAVECCHIA

ROME

Ostia

CAESAR LINE

ANZI